Praise for *Girt*

"Hilarious and insightful – Hunt has found
the deep wells of humour in Australia's history."
CHRIS TAYLOR, THE CHASER

"A sneaky, sometimes shocking peek under
the dirty rug of Australian history."
JOHN BIRMINGHAM

"There is barely a page in *Girt* that won't inspire a chortle. It's our early
history told by a writer with a wit sharp enough to slice tomatoes."
THE HERALD SUN

"*Girt* ... cuts an irreverent swathe through the facts, fools,
fantasies and frauds that made this country what it is today,
hoisting sacred cows on their own petards and otherwise sawing
the legs off Lady Macquarie's chair. I was transported."
SHANE MALONEY, THE AGE

"Historiography as practised by Mr Hunt is an exceedingly clever way to
skewer the rapier of truth through the carcass of officious mendacity ...
Hunt quickly had his wicked way with me."
BARRY GITTENS, EUREKA STREET

"Australian history never looked like this! Beneath the humour
is an interesting analysis backed by extensive research,
which has uprooted some little-known historical gems."
BOOKS+PUBLISHING

"This book taught me that our history is full of dodgy,
booze-peddling charlatans. Somehow I found this reassuring."
DOMINIC KNIGHT

By David Hunt

The Unauthorised History of Australia

GIRT

TRUE GIRT

For children and the young at heart

THE NOSE PIXIES

TRUE GIRT

The Unauthorised History of Australia • Volume 2

DAVID HUNT

ILLUSTRATIONS BY AD LONG

Black Inc.

Published by Black Inc.,
an imprint of Schwartz Publishing Pty Ltd
Level 1, 221 Drummond Street
Carlton VIC 3053, Australia
enquiries@blackincbooks.com
www.blackincbooks.com

National Library of Australia Cataloguing-in-Publication entry
Hunt, David, 1971– author.
True girt: the unauthorised history of Australia / David Hunt.
9781863958844 (paperback)
9781925435320 (ebook)
Frontier and pioneer life–Australia.
Australia–History.
994

Book design by Peter Long
Typeset by Duncan Blachford & Tristan Main
Cover: image of Andrew George Scott ('Captain Moonlite') from the
Victoria Police Historical Collection, National Portrait Gallery of Australia;
image of cockatoo © Isselee, Dreamstime.
Image p.116 courtesy of the National Portrait Gallery of Australia.

Printed in Australia by McPherson's Printing Group.

For X. & V.B.

Truth is stranger than Fiction, but it is because
Fiction is obliged to stick to possibilities; Truth isn't.

MARK TWAIN, *FOLLOWING THE EQUATOR*, 1897

Farewell, Australia! You are a rising child,
and doubtless some day will reign a great princess
in the South: but you are too great and ambitious
for affection, yet not great enough for respect.
I leave your shores without sorrow or regret.

CHARLES DARWIN, *NARRATIVE OF THE VOYAGES*
OF H.M. SHIPS ADVENTURE AND BEAGLE, 1839

Australia seems all right. There is an awful lot of it.
Every city seems to despise every other city.

IRIS MURDOCH, LETTER TO BRIGID BROPHY, 1967

PREVIOUSLY IN *GIRT* ...

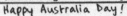

Contents

Introduction

Looking back is a bad habit.

Reuben J. "Rooster" Cogburn, *True Grit*

THIS WAS THE WILD SOUTH, THE FURTHEST FRONTIER OF
Empire, an unforgiving land for Britain's unforgiven. The pickpockets, prostitutes and handkerchief thieves who unwillingly
called Australia home, and those who guarded them, had no interest
in the vast alien landscape that pressed upon their tiny settlements.

Australia was a sentence and its reluctant inhabitants were waiting
for the full stop. And so they desperately clung to the coast, hoping
for a ship to take them ... anywhere.

The point of a prison is to keep people confined, yet the convict
colony had no walls. Its genius was not confinement of the body, but
confinement of the mind. Those who ventured into the bush, untrained
in the arts of hunter-gathering, were confronted by a lack of food and
water and a surplus of hostile natives keen to debate the fine points
of British colonial policy with the fine points of their spears.

And the animals! When God was handing out venom, He started
with Australia and then got bored. There were poisonous snakes,
spiders, ants, wasps, bees, ticks and centipedes – even the cute little river beaver with the duck's bill had venomous spurs on its hind
legs. And you wouldn't think about swimming in the sea, which was
a playground for fish, rays, stingers, shells and octopi equipped with
enough nerve toxin to take out half of Yorkshire – and Yorkshire
folk are tough. Then there were the sharks ...

The children of the first colonists did not share these fears. For them, the rolling green pastures and ordered hedgerows of England were as foreign as Gulliver's Lilliput. This was the only land they knew and they wanted to know it better, as did the growing number of free settlers. Australia was more than a prison – it was a land of untapped opportunity. Some of the convicts and their guards also began to see Australia in this light.

Freed convicts were granted land and opened businesses, competing with the soldiers and officials who'd once dominated farming and trade. Some of the unshackled became fabulously wealthy and, under the patronage of Governor Lachlan Macquarie, were appointed to high office. Many of those untainted by the convict stain were unhappy with these arrangements and spent decades pointedly not inviting former convicts around to dinner and demanding their exclusion from public life.

Britain reluctantly approved the spread of settlement, partly because of its growing addiction to the fine wool produced by southern sheep and partly because the French were once more sniffing around the continent and giving bits of its coast ridiculous French names. But expansion would be strictly controlled to balance the objectives of:

1. Keeping the convicts in; and
2. Keeping the French out.

The only problem with this policy was that an increasing number of people cared nothing for the edicts of Whitehall. It was sealers and whalers who first pushed the boundaries of the frontier. These were men with long hair and wild beards, who spurned society's expectations and sought a life of freedom from government control. These champions of the Georgian counterculture were the hippies of their era – albeit hard-drinking, sexist, violent, whale-spearing, seal-clubbing hippies whom you really wouldn't want to drop a tab of acid with.

The hard men of the sea were joined by escaped convicts who

preferred the discomforts of the bush to the leg-iron's chafe. These bolters, a danger to settlers and Aboriginal people alike, became the first bushrangers. Bushrangers robbed people, assaulted people, shot people and sometimes ate people. Yet they were loved by the people because they thumbed their noses at authority and chose "Death or Liberty" over a life of bondage. Teenage boys put "WANTED" posters on their bedroom walls, with Bold Jack Donohoe the Shane Warne of his generation (minus the sex scandals and bad hair).

Sheep farmers moved their flocks beyond the borders that had been set to contain them, illegally occupying tracts of land larger than some European states. These were men with money and influence, and the government, rather than challenging the self-crowned Squatter Kings, abandoned the attempt to limit settlement. The floodgates had opened.

Loggers logged. Miners mined. Drovers droved. Explorers ventured further into the blank spaces of the Australian atlas, drawing the lines for settlers to follow. Some of them even made it back alive.

This was the Age of the Beard, where men were men and so were some of the women. Rugged frontiersmen cultivated vast bushy brushes that you could hide a penguin in, rejecting effete British clean-shaven fashion. They wore patched, homespun clothes, supplemented by furs stripped from the nearest seal or marsupial. They didn't bathe regularly, but you wouldn't point that out to them because they carried guns and bad attitudes. They lived on a diet of damper, dried meat, moonshine and, unable to break entirely with British ways, tea. They smoked tobacco, snorted tobacco, chewed tobacco and spat tobacco. And when they visited town, they stopped in at brothels like the one run by Hobart Town Poll, who employed girls called Bones, the Bull Pup and Cross-Eyed Luke, names befitting the Wild South.

The convict colony of New South Wales fractured under the weight of the expanding frontier, with Van Diemen's Land (Tasmania),

Victoria, New Zealand and Queensland forging their own destinies.[1]
Land speculators, entrepreneurs and other members of Britain's
white-shoe brigade settled Western Australia, while honest yeo-
men, industrious German peasants and creepy weirdos settled South
Australia. The citizens of these colonies did not yet see themselves
as a single people and, rather than being bound by common ties,
competed for control of the continent's resources and called each
other nasty names.

The Evangelical Christians who now ruled Britain were going
off the whole convict business, which they believed was nothing
more than slavery in whiteface. Even worse, cooping up lots of men
together resulted in unacceptable levels of gayness.[2]

Britain would replace Australia's gay slaves with heterosexual
free settlers, with women a priority. The short history of Australia's
European settlement had well and truly lived up to Jane Austen's
assessment of history generally – "the men all so good for nothing,
and hardly any women at all". That would have to change and the
colonies looked for someone to make them more female-friendly.
Caroline Chisholm was just the man for the job.

Religious and racial tensions increased, as Protestants and Catholics engaged in an alms race to sponsor migrants of their own faith,
and squatters imported Indian and Chinese labourers who could be
exploited for a pittance, a business model later perfected by 7-Eleven.[3]

There was also political unrest. Britain had long exported its
machine breakers, haystack burners, cow killers, trade unionists,
Irish republicans and other social malcontents to Australia. They

---

1   Kiwis should not be offended that they were briefly part of Australia, as it is
     inevitable they will be so again. Australia already claims Phar Lap, Russell Crowe,
     Fred Hollows and the good Finn brother – it's only a matter of time until it claims
     the rest of New Zealand.

2   Acceptable levels of gayness were set by British public schools and the Royal Navy.

3   DISCLAIMER: This is a reference to 7-Eleven Australia and some of its franchisees.
     I am sure 7-Elevens in other countries exploit their workers far more sensitively.

were now joined by refugees from the failed European revolutions of 1848, pro-democracy activists and, alarmingly, women who wanted the same rights as men.

And then gold was discovered in the Bathurst hinterlands. Everything exploded. A human tidal wave washed over Australia, spilling into the untouched interior.

Every good frontier story has conflict with simple native folk who don't understand or appreciate the gift of civilisation. Australia would not disappoint. The settlers swarmed onto Aboriginal land like flies to roadkill. And while there was resistance, there was only ever going to be one result. Hunter-gathering is incompatible with protracted conflict – you can't ask your enemy to stop chasing you while you pick berries. Spears, clubs and knowledge of country were ultimately no match for influenza, guns and poisoned Christmas puddings. As Charles Darwin mused during his 1836 visit to Australia, "wherever the European has trod, death seems to pursue the Aboriginal."

Who would shape the history of the Wild South? Would the new Australians prevail over the First Australians, or share the continent's bounty with them?[4] Would freed convicts or their exclusivist enemies triumph? Would Catholics or Protestants win the battle for Australia's souls? Would men rule unchallenged or would women get a fair shake of the sauce bottle? Would the native born or immigrants fashion the Aussie character? Would Australians tug the forelock to the British monarchy or pander to republican America?[5] And would Australia's destiny be forged by the state or by its people?

Where to begin this tale of the wild frontier? Let's start with the wildest frontier of all.

Tasmania.

---

4   See above.

5   Australians impressively managed to do both.

I

Notes from a small island

Two heads are better than one.

John Heywood, *The Proverbs of John Heywood*, 1546

THE APPLE DOESN'T FALL FAR FROM THE TREE

THE APPLE DOESN'T FALL FAR FROM THE TREE IN THE
Apple Isle, an isolated speck in our southmost seas where
the genetic distance between any two people is relative.
Inbreeding is a popular island pastime and Tasmania, to this day,
remains a popular island.

Tasmania, or Van Diemen's Land as it was officially known until
1856, was certainly popular with Charles Darwin.[1] When the HMS
Beagle docked at Hobart in 1836, the aspiring young naturalist-cum-
geologist happily collected 133 different kinds of insect and an unknown
number of boring rocks. He enjoyed the climate, which reminded
him of Britain's (i.e. cold, wet and miserable), and the society of the
island's gentry, marvelling that Hobart was sophisticated enough
to host "a Fancy Dress Ball at which 113 were present in costumes".
He would also, no doubt, have admired the Vandemonians' famed
enthusiasm for cousindry.[2]

---

1   Darwin was not a fan of Australia more generally, writing, "My opinion is such
    that nothing but rather sharp necessity should compel me to emigrate."

2   Darwin sexually selected his first cousin, Emma Wedgwood, after writing up a list
    of pros and cons under the headings "Marry" and "Not Marry". Prominent among
    the cons were "less money for books" and "terrible loss of time", while the principal

Darwin's study of island life during the *Beagle*'s five-year voyage led him to write in his notebook, "animals on separate islands ought to become different if kept long enough apart with slightly differing circumstances". When he was not busy riding or eating the giant tortoises of the Galápagos Islands, he noticed that tortoises on one arid outcrop had longer necks and limbs than those on more fertile isles. He later concluded they had incrementally changed over time to better access the island's sparse vegetation.[3]

Darwin's musings on islands and tortoises eventually gave rise to the Theory of Evolution, set out in his 1859 blockbuster, *On the Origin of Species by Means of Natural Selection, or the Preservation of Favoured Races in the Struggle for Life*. *On the Origin of Species*, as it was known after Darwin hired a decent editor, popularised the idea that species evolved over time through a process of natural selection – that is, individuals better suited to the environment were more likely to survive and to pass on their beneficial traits to future generations.

Inbreeding is more prevalent on islands, and genetic diversity accordingly lower, as descent from a small founding population and isolation from the wider world reduces the likelihood of hooking up with someone who isn't a relative. Iceland, for example, is full of tall, blond, sexy people because most Icelanders are descended from

---

advantage was "constant companion and a friend in old age ... better than a dog anyhow".

3 Darwin wrote of the tortoises, "I frequently got on their backs, and then giving a few raps on the hinder part of their shells, they would rise up and walk away; – but I found it very difficult to keep my balance." After an invigorating ride, he would eat his mount. Darwin was a founding member of Cambridge University's Glutton Club, a group dedicated to eating "birds and beasts which were before unknown to the human palate". The *Beagle* voyage allowed Darwin to compare the taste of several subspecies of tortoise, armadillos and a puma. Darwin, however, had nothing on William Buckland, the man who first scientifically described a dinosaur, when it came to zoöphagy, the eating of unusual animals. Buckland, committed to tasting every animal in existence, devoured flies, mice (on toast), a mole, a panther, a porpoise, bat urine and, for its sheer novelty value, the preserved heart of King Louis XIV of France.

a small group of migratory tall, blond, sexy people.[4] There has been little further immigration to Iceland over the centuries because most people don't want to freeze on an isolated volcanic rock while being made to feel short, swarthy and unattractive.

Island life is also more likely to experience population bottle-necks – sharp population declines caused by environmental events or human activity. Island-dwellers simply have nowhere else to go when a fire rages across their island or bad men with guns chase them. Population bottlenecks further reduce genetic diversity.

As diversity reduces, risk of disease increases. The Tasmanian devil, one of the world's most bad-tempered, foul-smelling and inbred animals, is a case in point. Devils are so genetically similar that, since 1996, a transmissible cancer called devil facial tumour disease (DFTD) has more than halved their population. When a devil is bitten by one of its carcinogenic brethren, its immune system doesn't identify the cancer as coming from a foreign body. Inbreeding-acquired DFTD threatens to make devils extinct in the wild by 2024.[5]

Island life, with all of its quirks and anachronisms, also fascinated Alfred Russel Wallace. Wallace developed a theory of evolution based on natural selection before Darwin published his, but the fact that he was not an independently wealthy gentleman who owned a country house with a swan-encrusted ornamental lake and hedge maze meant Darwin got all the glory. Wallace's *Island Life* considered how isolation could preserve animals such as Mauritius's dodo and New Zealand's moa, but left them totally unprepared for contact with dogs, pigs and hungry sailors and/or Māori, which rapidly population-bottlenecked them into extinction.

---

4   Björk is a genetic aberration. Biotechnology companies have flocked to Iceland to conduct experiments on the genetically homogenous non-Björk population, with Iceland now the world leader in human genomic research.

5   There are only two other known transmissible cancers in the world. One attacks dogs, as pedigree breeding has resulted in the rapid loss of canine genetic material. The other afflicts the notoriously incestuous Syrian hamster.

The Tasmanian tiger, or thylacine, shows the susceptibility of island life to outside invaders. The thylacine was out-competed on mainland Australia by the dingo, but clung on in the southern isle until the white man brought guns, dogs and an intense dislike of all things that ate his sheep to Tasmania, with the last known thylacine checking out in 1936. The Tasmanian emu didn't eat sheep but lasted only until the 1850s because the white man and his dogs liked supersized drumsticks.[6]

Darwin moved on from islands and tortoises in 1871, with the publication of *The Descent of Man, and Selection in Relation to Sex*. In this work, Darwin stated his long-held belief that man and ape shared a common ancestor, which pissed off the churches and honest God-fearing folk. He also argued that the male desire to excel was driven by female choosiness in selecting a mate (sexual selection) and that men choosing bigger and better weapons and tools over the years had caused them to "become superior to woman", which, unsurprisingly, pissed off a lot of women. Darwin also challenged the dominant view of the time that the human races were separate species, which pissed off the Confederate Americans, who argued that it was their inalienable right to own black folk who picked cotton for free.[7]

Darwin's view that all men were of the same species didn't mean he believed all men were equal. He wrote of an evolutionary break "between the negro or Australian and the gorilla" and, applying

---

6   Tasmanian emu fat was also a popular ingredient in deep-fried dishes. Slippery Bob, a hillbilly delicacy of kangaroo brains battered in emu lard, was described as an early-nineteenth-century Vandemonian dish by Edward Abbott, a Tasmanian MP, who in 1864 penned Australia's first published cookbook, *The English and Australian Cookery Book: Cookery for the Many, as Well as for the "Upper Ten Thousand"*.

7   Fans of slavery cited *Crania Americana*, written in 1839 by phrenologist Dr Samuel Morton. Morton had the world's largest collection of human skulls, which he insisted proved that God had separately created the races of man and that Adam and Eve were a beautiful pink colour, while the later-created races came in a variety of inferior shades. Morton, who regarded cotton plantations as an early form of national park, argued that enslaving black people was both a kindness and a moral responsibility, as freeing slave races would lead to their extinction.

natural selection to whole societies, concluded, "At some future point, not distant as measured by centuries, the civilised races of man will almost certainly exterminate and replace the savage races throughout the world."

While Darwin was saddened by the thought of the inevitable extinction of "the savage races", the same cannot be said of one of his cousins whom he didn't marry, Francis Galton.

Galton made Darwin look like an intellectual tortoise, and not one of the fun-to-ride-and-eat ones. A genius of the first order, Galton was the father of historiometry, conceived the statistical concepts of correlation and standard deviation, pioneered the use of scientific questionnaires and surveys, devised the first weather map, invented the composite photograph and ultrasonic dog whistle, and developed the fingerprint classification system still used by hot American actresses whom we are expected to believe have nothing better to do than hang around crime scenes and conduct ballistic experiments on pig carcasses in basement laboratories.

Galton, when not making the world a better place, used his spare time to invent eugenics, which he regarded as the natural extension of evolutionary theory. He believed that the government should give gentlemen of high rank money to marry women of high rank in order to produce children who would inherit their high rank, money, clearly superior genes and, ultimately, the earth. "Inferior" people and their unwanted genes should be bred out of existence by confining them to monasteries or other places where heterosexual sex was at worst discouraged and at best impossible. As there were not enough monasteries to store the world's black people in, Galton proposed immigration to displace them.

Nineteenth-century Australian politicians and pastoralists seized on the writings of Darwin, Wallace and Galton to mount the case that the Tasmanian Aborigines were a small population of inbred, savage, maladapted, disease-prone, uncompetitive, simple island folk who got what was coming to them, evolutionarily and eugenically speaking.

In recent years, Keith Windschuttle has given this argument a new twist – the Tasmanian Aborigines were a small population of inbred, savage, maladapted, disease-prone, uncompetitive, simple island folk who got what was coming to them, without us giving it to them.[8]

Hang on a minute ... who were these Tasmanian Aborigines? Hadn't Charles Darwin written in 1836, just thirty-three years after white settlement of the island, "Van Diemen's Land enjoys the great advantage of being free from a native population"?

FIG. 1: THE DESCENT OF WINDSCHUTTLE

THE NATIVE POPULATION

The native population would have been taken aback by Darwin's conclusions as to their non-existence, as they'd been happily natively populating Tasmania for at least 34,000 years before Darwin mounted his first tortoise.

The Tasmanian Aborigines were rudely cut off from their mainland cousins about 10,000 years ago, when rising sea levels left Tasmania well and truly girt. Millennia of forced separation produced noticeable

---

8   Keith Windschuttle is the world expert on the denial of Tasmanian massacres. The author is looking forward to the release of Windschuttle's rumoured next work, *Martin Bryant Just Slipped*.

differences between the new islanders and their northern kin, with
the former being generally shorter, rounder-faced and ruddier in hue.
The Tasmanian men, some of whom were redheads, sported afros,
which they conditioned into dreadlocks with grease and ochre, while
the women shaved or cropped their hair.

François Péron, a one-eyed French trainee zoologist who had
joined the 1801–02 Nicolas Baudin v Matthew Flinders Race Around
New Holland after a failed affair, reported that the bodies of native
Tasmanian women were disfigured by incisions and raised scars. He
attributed this to domestic violence, although he never witnessed
physical conflict between the sexes during his Vandemonian sojourn.
Windschuttle, in his book *The Fabrication of Aboriginal History: Volume One: Van Diemen's Land 1803–1847*, cites Péron when arguing
that the Tasmanian Aborigines were world champion wife-beaters
whose savage treatment of their women hastened their inevitable
extinction. In contrast, Captain Cook and other early observers of
traditional Tasmanian life noted that the bodies of the men bore
similar markings, concluding that the scars on both men and women
were ritualistic in nature.

Admittedly, Germaine Greer would have something to say about
traditional Tasmanian gender relations.[9] Early French visitors to
the island's shores reported that the men occasionally stirred to
hunt kangaroos and wallabies, and sometimes each other, but otherwise spent their days playing with their kids, eating and taking long
afternoon naps. The women caught possums and shellfish, hunted
muttonbirds and seals, gathered plants, constructed huts and canoes,
wove baskets, carried their children and possessions when moving
to new hunting grounds, and slaved over a hot campfire every day,
feeding the menfolk before themselves.[10]

---

9   This is not a particularly high threshold, as Germaine Greer has something to say
about everything.

10 Like *Desperate Housewives* without the houses. *Desperate Housewives* star Teri
Hatcher is also noted for her ritualistic incisions.

The Tasmanian Aborigines, like their continental counterparts, lived in small family groups. There were several such groups to a tribe, sharing a language, cultural practices, spiritual beliefs and seasonal patterns of migration to gather food and resources. Unlike the mainlanders, some southern Tasmanian Aborigines lived for much of the year in well-constructed permanent huts. They had even got around to inventing the door, which would have thrown a serious spike into the wheels of *terra nullius* had the British taken any interest in Tasmanian architecture before the southern Tasmanian Aborigines ceased living in such dwellings or, indeed, anywhere else.[11]

Like on the mainland, significant places were often named for human body parts, as the Tasmanians saw themselves and their land as integrated parts of creation.[12] The Tasmanians believed that friendly spirits walked the earth by day, while malevolent spirits owned the night; the resulting fear of the dark was a significant impediment to their later campaigns against the pale demons from beyond the big water. Little is known of Tasmanian creation myths, although the Bruny Island people told missionaries that their world had been made by Laller, a small ant, rather than a bearded white guy who let his only kid get nailed to two pieces of wood.

---

11 The legal doctrine of *terra nullius* (Latin for "land belonging to no one") enabled European powers to claim sovereignty over land that barbarous locals had not bothered to occupy, without going to all the effort of declaring war on them. A sturdy hut, complete with the latest in bark-door technology, was a lay-down misère in the occupation game.

12 For example, Canberra is sometimes reported to mean "meeting place" in the Ngunnawal language, although local elders insist that *nganbra*, from which Canberra allegedly derives, is Ngunnawal for "breasts". Australians are the only people in the world who would name their national capital "Tits". This is symptomatic of the Australian tendency to appropriate Aboriginal words without understanding their meaning. Melbourne's Moomba Festival provides another example. Melbourne City Council was mischievously advised that *Moomba* meant "Let's get together and have fun" in a local Aboriginal dialect, while it actually derives from the words *moom* (bottom) and *ba* (up), and more correctly translates as "Shove it up your arse". Festival organisers and other luvvies are quick to point out that the two meanings are not mutually exclusive.

Windschuttle argues that the Tasmanians were "the most primitive society ever discovered" and, "lacking any outside source of competition or innovation", "experienced a technological regression". Archaeologists dispute his claim that Tasmanian Aborigines lost the use of barbed spears, boomerangs, hafted stone implements and edge-ground axes, pointing out that they never had them to lose in the first place. While Windschuttle accurately notes that Tasmanians ceased making fish hooks and eating fish (a well-known brain food) about 4,000 years ago, others counter that fishing stopped when the island's grasslands expanded, as it became far easier to spear a fat grass-loving wallaby than to hook a wallaby-weight of whiting.

Windschuttle correctly points out that Tasmania is cold and miserable, while incorrectly stating that the Tasmanian Aborigines "went around completely naked" because they were too technologically regressed to invent clothes to be warm and happy in. In fact, when chilly, the first Tasmanians would slip into an uncured kangaroo skin, smear themselves with animal fat and sit around the fire.

Windschuttle concedes the Tasmanians knew how to sit around a fire, but insists they didn't know how to make one, "a skill that even Neanderthal Man had mastered". Accusing an Aborigine of not being able to light a fire is like accusing a Boy Scout of not being able to tie up a tent flap, or a scoutmaster of not being able to tie up a Boy Scout.

There is no doubt that Tasmanian Aborigines carried fire from place to place and were protective of it, as were many European arrivals until the advent of mass-produced friction matches in the 1830s – not because they didn't know how to light one, but because Tasmania is damper than a diabetic's armpit and getting a good fire going from scratch was a pain in the *moom*. Numerous French and English explorers reported Tasmanian Aborigines keeping flint and tinder, while other sources describe them enthusiastically rubbing two sticks together.

While fire and fish are two battlegrounds of the History Wars between Windschuttle and "orthodox historians",[13] some of the fiercest fighting rages over how many Tasmanian Aborigines there were pre-contact, and how many were killed post-contact. When you wipe out an entire people in the span of a single human life – or, as Windschuttle contends, when people kick a spectacularly large number of own goals – it's important to keep score.

Most estimates of Tasmania's pre-contact population fall between 3,000 and 8,000, but range as high as 22,000 and as low as 1,500. Windschuttle's estimate is about 2,000, a figure that would have placed the Tasmanians on the precipice of gradual extinction without the additional strains imposed by European contact.

Recent genetic studies suggest that something or someone population-bottlenecked the hell out of the Tasmanian Aborigines shortly before European settlement, with the smart money being on French explorers, who were carriers of exotic disease, and hard-living sealers, who were carriers of big spiked clubs.[14]

The truth is that nobody really knows how many Tasmanian Aborigines there once were. We just know how many there soon weren't.

CLOSE ENCOUNTERS OF THE FRENCH KIND

We also don't know how many Tasmanian Aboriginal people died in frontier conflict or as a result of colonisation.[15] What we do know is,

---

13   "Orthodox historians", according to Windschuttle, are the "arrogant" and "self-indulgent" historians who disagree with him (i.e. 99 per cent of historians). Orthodox historians are a Marxist collective who hate Australia, Australians and all that is good and pure in this world. They tell lies about the past in order to pursue a political agenda of unnecessary apologies, Aboriginal "rights" to land they haven't paid for, and government handouts for fair-skinned bludgers who masquerade as blackfellas.

14   And exotic disease – with sealers you get the population-bottleneck quinella.

15   Windschuttle points out, "colonization offered the indigenous people the gift of civilization, bringing them all the techniques for living developed by the Old World". The fact that "pure-blooded" Tasmanian Aborigines rejected the techniques for

disease aside, we can't blame the French, even though they were the first outsiders to encounter the native Tasmanians. This is a shame, as the French can be blamed for Marcel Marceau, unpasteurised cheese, blowing up small Pacific islands and those who object to same, and many of the other ills of Western civilisation.[16]

The French, while the first to make contact with the Tasmanians, were not the first Europeans to visit their island. Abel Tasman, of the Dutch East India Company, dropped by in 1642 to name the new land after his boss, Anthony van Diemen. He stayed long enough to plant the flag of the Prince of Orange, claim possession of the territory and, to the delight of generations of Australian schoolboys, draw the first map of Tasmania.

The Dutch didn't meet any Tasmanians, but the widely spaced notches they found carved into tree trunks (and perhaps some of the spices they'd been smoking) led them to speculate that Van Diemen's Land was inhabited by a race of tree-dwelling giants.

Unlike the Dutch, who were only interested in meeting new people with empty spice racks and full wallets, the French explored the globe in the hope of encountering exotic foreigners who would help them advance human knowledge and, if they were lucky, sleep with them.[17]

Binot Paulmier de Gonneville took a wrong turn near the Cape of Good Hope in 1503 and claimed to have discovered the "great Austral Land", a utopia where nobody had to work. This appealed to the French, who interrupt their long holidays to strike against the draconian labour laws that interfere with a Frenchman's inalienable right not to work between holidays and the foreigners who exploit this by selling things that are not made in France.

---

living by dying within decades of colonisation is seized upon by orthodox historians and other socialist agitators to falsely claim that the colonists, rather than the Tasmanian Aborigines themselves, were responsible for this extinction.

16 There are no French stereotypes, just clichés.

17 François Péron was not lucky – Tasmania's young women rebuffed his repeated attempts to expand their sexual horizons.

When James Cook returned from the *Endeavour* voyage without discovering *Terra Australis*, Louis XV dispatched two ships to search for Gonneville Land, as the French now referred to the mysterious southern continent, despite de Gonneville's shirker's paradise actually being located in southern Brazil.

The French landed on Western Australia's Dirk Hartog Island on 30 March 1772 and were so moved by its Dutch plate that they left a French bottle behind.[18] Inside was a message that, if read by any passing Hollander or Englander, would make it clear that Louis XV and any little Louis that might succeed him now owned this territory.[19]

In the same month, Marc-Joseph Marion du Fresne made first contact with the Tasmanians. Du Fresne was a man's man, despite the girly middle name and people inexplicably calling him Marie-Joseph. Only a man's man could have assisted in the daring rescue of Bonnie Prince Charlie from the storm-wracked coast of western Scotland, as the Protestant English dogs nipped at his heels and urinated on the legs of the throne that was rightfully his.[20] Only a man's man would have spent months imprisoned by the degenerate Englanders and then have returned to gloriously surrender to them yet again. And only a man's man would tell his sailors to take off all their clothes before stepping onto a Tasmanian beach in the middle of autumn.

---

18 Readers who want to know more about the Dutch fetish for nailing kitchenware to posts should read "New Holland Welcomes Careful Sailors", at page 20 of *Girt*.

19 There are more effective ways of claiming possession of a territory than leaving a plate or bottle lying around (a well-equipped army normally helps). Bottles are particularly unreliable. Sting did not sing, "I know you'll get my message in a bottle." Someone must not only find your bottle, but also open it, read its contents and take them seriously. Queen Elizabeth I further reduced the likelihood of unwelcome bottle messages getting through (any French message, by definition, would be unwelcome) by appointing a royal Uncorker of Ocean Bottles and making it a capital offence for any other person to open such bottles and read their contents.

20 Perhaps du Fresne felt an affinity for Charlie, whose second-last name was Maria and who, after his defeat at the Battle of Culloden in 1746, was picked up by French sailors while disguised as Betty Burke, a winsome Irish serving maid.

Du Fresne was a naturist in both the philosophical and practical sense. His penchant for nuding up when encountering "savages" in their native state was inspired by the teachings of the French philosopher Jean-Jacques Rousseau, the world's first hippy.

Rousseau, in his 1750 *Discourse on Arts and Sciences*, argued that savagery was man's ideal state and that "all the subsequent progress has been in appearance so many steps towards the perfection of the individual, and in fact towards the decay of the species". Western civilisation and culture, he said, corrupted man's natural morals. Rousseau's message, when stripped of the flowery language, boiled down to, "We've got to get back to nature, dude." Rousseau's writings contributed to the development of the idea of the "noble savage", a being of uncorrupted virtue, physical strength and chiselled good looks.

When du Fresne first spied the Tasmanians on a beach, he ordered two of his sailors to strip and swim ashore with gifts. An Aboriginal man gave a firebrand to the sailors, who provided the traditional mirror in return. Du Fresne and two boatloads of sailors then came ashore, gifting knives, handkerchiefs and a duck to the surprised Tasmanians. Surprise turned to hostility when a third boat approached, with the Aborigines pelting the Frenchmen with spears and stones, wounding du Fresne and several of his party.

After du Fresne was again attacked upon attempting to land a short distance away, the French opened fire, killing at least one Tasmanian and wounding several. The template for relations between Tasmanians and Europeans had been set.

Du Fresne decided to head for New Zealand, where he and twenty-four of his crew got their just deserts – or rather, they were just desserts for the warrior Māori, who killed and ate them.[21] After a pitched battle with over 1,500 Māori, some wearing the clothes of du Fresne and his companions, the surviving Frenchmen left behind another message in a

---

21   The Gallic explorer La Pérouse may have suffered a similar fate in the Solomon
      Islands sixteen years later. Pacific cannibals like French food.

bottle, this time proclaiming that New Zealand was now to be known as *France Australe*, the latest province of the glorious French empire.

The later expeditions of Bruni d'Entrecasteaux and Nicolas Baudin to Van Diemen's Land were friendly and respectful. The French artists on d'Entrecasteaux's 1793 expedition painted portraits of Tasmanians in heroic Greek poses, while Baudin's men danced and wrestled with the natives, who painted the faces of the French with charcoal.[22]

But du Fresne's assault by the Tasmanians and his subsequent firsthand experience of the inside of a Māori pit oven had horrified Rousseau and put a serious dent in the duco of the noble savage. By the time the British settled Tasmania in 1803, romantic racism had lost its romance.

THE SAGA OF JØRGEN JØRGENSEN

> *Lo! Jørgen, Jørgen's son, yclept he*
> *Dire Dane, sayled swyfte yn boat Britaine*
> *Fore first thrust he thro' Strayte Bass blacke*
> *Fell Phillip's Port fall fast uponne*
> *Flinders' friend, convycte carryed he*
> *Dark Diemen woke from slumber-sleepe*
> *Sure struck hys speare the river wayle*
> *& clubbed cubbe seale's sypt bloode wassail*

Jørgen Jørgensen was born in 1780, the son of Jørgen Jørgensen, royal watchmaker to the Danish court. Fluent in Danish, English, French, German and Latin, the little smartarse left school at the age of fourteen for a life of adventure. Fast-talking, self-promoting, addicted to risk, opportunistic and notoriously amoral, Jørgen Jnr would today have found work as a subprime mortgage broker. But in 1795, the future pirates of Wall Street sought their fortunes at sea.

---

22 It is not politically incorrect to wear blackface applied by a black person.

Jørgensen left the pickled herring of his homeland for the smoked kipper of an English collier, before being press-ganged into the Royal Navy and sailing to New South Wales. He made the second-ever passage to Sydney through Bass Strait and, after arriving in 1801, reinvented himself as John Johnson and joined the mostly convict crew of the HMS *Lady Nelson*.

The Admiralty had commissioned the *Lady Nelson* in response to British concerns about the whole French bottle business. The ship was tasked with claiming sovereignty over strategic parts of New Holland before the French moved in with their croutons, onion dip and hunchbacks.

The *Lady Nelson* explored the bay of Western Port, finding Phillip Island and lots of fairy penguins, and surveyed the Hunter River, where Governor King established the convict camp of King's Town, later renamed Newcastle. King's Town was the first settlement outside the Sydney Basin and Norfolk Island, and its coal became one of the colony's earliest exports.[23]

Jørgensen and his buddies sailed south again and discovered Port Phillip, just around the corner from Western Port, which they claimed for Great Britain on 8 March 1802 without any loss of tableware.

Anglo–Franco tensions intensified a month after the British claimed Port Phillip. The Baudin expedition visited Western Port and named its large island *Ile des Français* (Isle of the French), which sent Governor King's blood pressure through the roof.

Baudin, when he visited Sydney shortly afterwards, was careful to emphasise that his was a voyage of discovery, not acquisition. To reinforce this, he ventured inland to collect natural history specimens, guided by one Jørgen Jørgensen. That the job went to the newly arrived Dane, who knew nothing about the inland and even less about its flora and fauna, proved his credentials as a champion bullshitter.

---

23   Exporting coal is patriotic. You can pick up a lump of coal, admire its wonderful Australianness and then flog it to China. You can't do that with wind or sunshine.

Baudin maintained the good-natured French naturalist facade until the farewell party that Governor King held for him in November 1802. Baudin, who was recovering from the death of his pet monkey, got drunk with Lieutenant-Colonel William Paterson, who was recovering from being shot by John Macarthur, and confided that he was thinking of colonising Van Diemen's Land.

When Paterson dobbed on Baudin to King, the governor ordered Charles Robbins to sail after the Frenchman in the *Cumberland* to persuade him to abandon his territorial ambitions. Robbins caught up with the French on King Island in Bass Strait, where he staged the first performance of *Carry on Back to France*.

The French were minding their own business when Robbins rushed into their camp and hung the Union Jack from a gum tree. Discovering that he had no gunpowder to stage the military salute that Britain used in place of kitchenware, he asked to borrow some from the nonplussed French, who acquiesced with admirable *sangfroid*. Robbins then fired his gun three times and made a garbled proclamation of possession of Van Diemen's Land, a completely separate island. It was then he realised he'd hung the Union Jack upside down.

Baudin tersely informed Robbins that he had "no intention of annexing a country already inhabited by savages".[24] He sent King a letter that made it clear he thought the British approach to possession lacked *élan*:

> I was well convinced that the arrival of the Cumberland had another motive than merely to bring your letter, but I did not think it was for the purpose of hoisting the British flag precisely on the spot where our tents had been pitched for a long time previous to her arrival. I frankly confess that I am displeased this has taken place.

---

24 While historians debate Baudin's territorial ambitions, Péron kept notes on British military deployments in New South Wales and drafted a secret *Mémoire sur les Établissements Anglais à la Nouvelle Hollande*, which advocated a French conquest of Sydney with the aid of rebellious Irish convicts.

> The childish ceremony was ridiculous and has become more so from
> the manner in which the flag was placed, the head being downwards,
> and the attitude not very majestic ... I thought at first it may have
> been a flag which had served to strain water and then hung out to dry.

While Robbins was perfecting his slapstick routine, Jørgensen and
the *Lady Nelson* escorted Matthew Flinders in his attempted cir-
cumnavigation of New Holland. Upon the *Lady Nelson*'s return to
Sydney, the increasingly Francophobic Governor King commissioned
her to make good Robbins' claim by transporting forty-nine hardy
souls, under the command of Lieutenant John Bowen, to establish a
settlement at Risdon Cove on Van Diemen's Land's Derwent River.

Jørgensen was present when the island was first settled by Britain
in September 1803, and he returned in February 1804, transporting
Lieutenant-Governor David Collins and other evacuees from the
failed settlement at Port Phillip.

Jørgensen, looking for new challenges, left the *Lady Nelson* and
embraced the ancient Scandinavian tradition of murdering whales,
boasting that he was the first man to harpoon a cetacean on the Derwent. When Australia's new Ahab needed a break from whaling, he
relaxed by beating baby seals to death. His Viking bloodlust finally
sated, he set sail for Copenhagen in 1805.

But the restless adventurer, whom the nineteenth-century Australian author Marcus Clarke described as "a human comet", would
one day return to the new society he had helped birth.

Just not in the manner he would have planned ...

A SEAL WALKED INTO A CLUB

It was whalers and sealers like Jørgensen, not governors or pastoralists, who drove the early spread of Europeans in Australia.

Governor Phillip, who started his career as a whaler, welcomed
the whaleboat captains Thomas Melvill and Eber Bunker to New

South Wales in 1791.[25] Melvill and Bunker came out from England with holds full of convicts and returned with holds full of blubber. Phillip awarded Melvill an inscribed silver cup "for killing a Spermaceti Whale on the 26th October 1791. Being the first of its kind taken on this coast since the Colony was established."

Whaling stations sprang up on the isolated shores of Van Diemen's Land and the southern mainland. Whaling would be a major Australian industry until the mass-production of petroleum in the 1850s crippled the whale oil industry, and the mass-production of food that didn't taste awful confined whale meat to the Eskimos, Scandinavians and scientifically certified Japanese school lunch boxes.[26]

Charles Bishop became the father of the Australian sealing industry when his trading vessel accompanied Bass and Flinders to Bass Strait in 1798 and returned with 5,000 sealskins.[27] And so the seal rush was born.

Surly sailors, antisocial psychopaths and escaped convicts made for Bass Strait to murder every fur seal, hair seal and elephant seal they could find. Elephant seals were stabbed in the heart so blood would not contaminate their blubber, their tongues sold to European gourmands. Adult fur and hair seals were lanced, their babies clubbed and their pelts sold in China, America and Britain. Sealers would approach

---

25 Thomas Melvill is not to be confused with *Moby-Dick* author Herman Melville, who believed in killing whales for vengeance rather than money.

26 Scandinavians love awful-tasting seafood. Icelanders eat *kæstur hákarl*, a dish made from a poisonous shark that is buried in a hole to rot for up to three months, before being dug up to hang outdoors for a few months more. World food expert Anthony Bourdain described *kæstur hákarl* as "the single worst, most disgusting and terrible tasting thing I have ever eaten". The Swedes get off on *surströmming*, fermented herring in a can that consumers are advised to open underwater and eat outdoors to minimise the stench. *Surströmming* has failed European Union food safety standards and been banned from many commercial airlines as an explosive risk. German Wolfgang Fassbender wrote, "the biggest challenge when eating *surströmming* is to vomit only after the first bite, as opposed to before."

27 Bishop, less fortunately, was also the father of the Australian mental health industry, being the first person declared insane by a New South Wales jury (1805) and involuntarily committed to a room with lovely soft walls.

the largest sleeping bulls, hold a musket to their heads and pull the trigger. Seals, which can sleep through anything, would continue to doze as their neighbours were shot, stabbed and bludgeoned.[28]

Sealers were originally sail-in sail-out (SISO) workers. They would be left on islands or isolated stretches of coast for months before the sealing ships returned to collect them and bits of dead seal. They ate dead seal, they wore dead seal, and their work tanning sealskin and boiling blubber meant everything stank of dead seal. When not making more dead seals, they killed the islands' other edible wildlife, wiping out entire species of emu and wombat.

Sealers got lonely on cold winter nights, and seals, contrary to popular belief, will not always do tricks for a small fish. During the sealing season, the sealers would trade dogs, simple tools and food with the Tasmanian Aborigines in exchange for their women. Mannalargenna, chief of the Plangermaireener, came up with the bright idea of kidnapping the women of other tribes to sell to the sealers.

Sealers and whalers may have passed on influenza, pneumonia and tuberculosis through encounters with women, which may explain the genetic evidence of rapid Tasmanian population decline before formal settlement. The nineteenth-century Tasmanian historian James Bonwick wrote of a strong Aboriginal oral tradition of an epidemic before 1803:

> Mr Robert Clark, in a letter to me, said: "I have gleaned from some of the aborigines, now in their graves, that they were more numerous than the white people were aware of, but their numbers were very much thinned by a sudden attack of disease which was general among the entire population previous to the arrival of the English, entire tribes of natives having been swept off in the course of one or two days' illness."

---

28 Southern seal species are divided into two families: earless seals (*Phocidae*) and eared seals (*Otariidae*). You'd think that at least the eared seals would hear their friends being turned into hats and lubricant, but no.

The sealers and whalers also exposed Tasmanian women to syphilis and gonorrhoea, as did later settlers on the Tasmanian mainland. These diseases not only killed, but left many survivors infertile.

Sealing was bad work but good business, with ex-convict entrepreneurs like Simeon Lord and Mary Reibey making a fortune from the trade. In 1804 alone, 107,591 seals (give or take a few) were killed in Australia, with seal skin and oil the continent's principal exports, valued at many times the budget and total agricultural output of the colony. Wool exports did not reach similar levels until the late 1820s, so for a quarter of a century Australians did not so much ride on the sheep's back as balance on the seal's nose.

But sealing on this scale was unsustainable. François Péron noted the "mercantile greed" of the sealers had caused "a noticeable and irreparable reduction in the population of these animals". By 1810, declining seal numbers meant the SISO model was no longer viable and the sealers became permanent residents of the Bass Strait islands and Kangaroo Island, off the coast of present-day South Australia.

For the Tasmanian Aborigines, this would be a very bad thing. But it would also prove to be their only hope for survival.

2
Down and out in Hobart and Risdon

If its safety, like Sodom and Gomorrah,
depended on finding six honest men ...
it would be swallowed up in all its iniquity.

William Broughton, Van Diemen's Land Acting
Commissary, on Van Diemen's Land, 1817

MISERABLE MELBOURNE

D AVID COLLINS WAS HAVING WOMAN PROBLEMS. HE'D had two kids and several hats with the young convict milliner Ann Yeates and he wasn't sure how his wife, Maria, would take this. So, despite losing his job as deputy judge-advocate in New South Wales, he declined Maria's increasingly frantic requests that he return home.

Still clueless as to how he should solve a problem like Maria, Collins finally arrived back in London in 1797. His long-suffering wife, who'd written the bonnet version of *Fifty Shades of Grey*, became the editor of Collins' book, the not nearly as racy *An Account of the English Colony in New South Wales*. The book was so thorough and humourless that it was translated into German.

Collins' writings on New South Wales, as well as favourable reports from governors Phillip and Hunter, led to his appointment as lieutenant-governor of the planned colony at Port Phillip Bay in 1803. He left Maria behind and never saw her again.

The 308 male convicts who sailed with Collins aboard the HMS *Calcutta* and HMS *Ocean* were a diverse lot. There were Dutch, Polish, German, Portuguese, Jewish and African-American convicts, as well as a gypsy who had conformed to stereotype by stealing nine donkeys.[1] But one convict stood out from all the rest. William Buckley was a 1.98 metre colossus who'd served as a pivot man against Napoleon in the Netherlands before being cut down to size for receiving a bolt of stolen cloth.[2] There was also a scattering of free settlers, some the wives and children of convicts, including ten-year-old Johnny Fawkner, son of a Cripplegate metal refiner transported for receiving stolen goods.[3]

Collins was a compassionate man of the Enlightenment who cared deeply for his charges – in particular Hannah Power, the wife of the banknote forger Matthew Power. Hannah caught Collins' attention when she asked him to send a boat ashore to fetch her pet poodle.[4] Johnny Fawkner later wrote that Collins installed Hannah as his mistress before the *Calcutta* was out of sight of England. Mr Power was rewarded for his blind eye by having his leg-irons removed and being allowed to freely roam those parts of the ship not presently occupied by Mr Collins and Mrs Power.

---

1   This was problematic, as being in the company of gypsies for a month was a capital offence, and the voyage to Port Phillip took six months, exposing the convicts to the risk of execution and making Collins an accessory to aggravated gypsy accompaniment.

2   A pivot man was an unusually tall and therefore highly visible soldier whom other soldiers would pivot around when receiving orders to change direction on the battlefield. This was not a good job, as pivot men were also highly visible to the enemy, who would take pot shots at them. Pivot men would have come under additional fire from the French, as Napoleon hated tall people.

3   Metal refiners were part recycler, part Arthur Daley, and would literally fence fences. Many convicts were sent to Australia for stealing lead from church roofs, a crime that remains popular to this day. Metal theft is Britain's fastest-growing crime in the twenty-first century, driven by China's demand for scrap.

4   This was not a euphemism.

While Collins enjoyed the next few months at sea, Port Phillip failed to fulfil his expectations. There was more sand than soil, the waterways were salty and the limited timber of poor quality. Collins sent his surveyor, George Prideaux Harris, and Lieutenant James Tuckey to explore the bay, including the current site of Melbourne.

Melbourne was a very different place in 1803. Harris and Tuckey couldn't find a decent soy latte, second-hand fixed-gear bike shop, feminist percussion collective or beard-grooming salon anywhere. All they found was a band of Aborigines who were not happy that the *Ocean*'s landing party had, before Collins' arrival, shot them, burned down their huts and stolen their goods. The two explorers were lucky to make it back to camp alive.

The Boonwurrung people were perplexed by the inconsistent behaviour of these new white demons. Two years earlier, Jørgensen and co. had fired on them with muskets and the *Lady Nelson*'s cannon. A month later, French officer Pierre Milius materialised on a beach, performed a solo dance routine for them and disappeared without killing anyone. And now it was back to bang-bang again.

Collins' attempts to mollify the Boonwurrung with biscuits and blankets were unsuccessful and the colonists fought 200 warriors at Corio Bay, shooting dead two, including their chief. At night, the colonists were kept awake by the fires and war cries of the natives. Collins had had enough and, with Governor King's approval, decided to relocate to Van Diemen's Land.

William Buckley knew he'd be unlikely to escape from the southern island and, determined to reach Sydney, absconded with five accomplices and a kettle. One of his companions was shot by sentries, another was speared by Aborigines, three returned to camp, and the kettle was discarded as both heavy and unnecessary. But Buckley toughed it out, although he soon realised he'd never be able to walk the 600 miles to Sydney alone. Instead, he'd collect driftwood, eat periwinkles, grow a beard and start talking to seagulls. What were the chances of his survival?

Buckley's.[5]

As Jørgensen and the crew of the *Lady Nelson* transported Port Phillip's refugees to Van Diemen's Land, little Johnny Fawkner would have looked at the receding shoreline, never imagining that he would return thirty-two years later to help build one of the largest and richest cities on earth.[6]

Or that William Buckley would be waiting for him.

THUS IN STRENGTH DID HOBART GROW

Collins was unimpressed by John Bowen's tiny settlement at Risdon Cove, which he believed lacked sufficient harbourage and fresh water. But he would have approved of Bowen's domestic arrangements, which resembled his own.

Bowen met Martha Hayes on the ship out from England and, while her convict mother remained in Sydney, Martha accompanied Bowen to Van Diemen's Land. Reverend Henry Knopwood, Van Diemen's Land's only churchman for the first fifteen years of settlement and its most prolific diarist,[7] tactfully referred to Martha as "Gov Bowen's young friend", as she was only fourteen or fifteen years of age when she gave birth to the island's first European child.

---

5   The Australian slang term *Buckley's* is short for *Buckley's chance*, meaning "bugger-all chance", which was the considered likelihood of anyone, other than angry Aborigines or seagulls, ever seeing William Buckley again. The term *Buckley's and none*, meaning "two apparent chances with zero probability" (i.e. no chance at all), is most likely a later adaption that plays on the name of the Melbourne store Buckley and Nunn.

6   Lieutenant Tuckey, while under the influence of both alcohol and irony, had prophesised of the Port Phillip settlement, "I beheld a second Rome, rising from a coalition of banditti. I beheld it giving laws to the world and, superlative in arms and in arts, looking down with proud superiority upon the barbarous nations of the northern hemisphere."

7   For younger readers, the diary was the nineteenth century's Instagram. Knopwood's self-absorbed postings informed his followers what he'd had for breakfast, what the weather was like and what he was doing in his garden. Knopwood was also an early adopter of txt-speak – on several occasions his diary records his interest in "pot8os".

Collins settled at Sullivan's Cove, across the Derwent from Risdon. He named the settlement Hobart Town after Robert Hobart, Britain's secretary of state for war and the colonies. He built a house for the Powers near his own and, according to the ancient legal principle of *quid pro quo*, appointed Matthew Power Van Diemen's Land's printer, removed his name from the list of convicts, gave him some land and ignored his grog running.

But the erotic adventures of David Collins were always more Benny Hill than Fanny Hill. When the Powers returned to England in 1808, Collins returned to chasing young girls, the time-proven balm for his loneliness. He hooked up with the fifteen-year-old convict Margaret Eddington who, like Ann Yeates, bore him two sons, but was sadly deficient in the hat department.

Collins took command of Bowen's settlement three months after arriving. Bowen returned to England while Martha was pregnant with his second child. He never saw her or his children again.

Yet there was so much more to Tasmania than paedophiles and teenage pregnancies. There was also malnutrition and illiteracy.[8]

Several of Collins' charges died of scurvy before George Phipps, his convict gardener, produced a crop of greens. Little Johnny Fawkner went all Tiny Tim, losing the use of his right leg to malnutrition.[9] As the settlement's food supplies dwindled, Collins resorted to rationing. He wrote mournfully to his father:

---

8   New South Wales and Queensland both named their Styx Rivers after the mythological Greek river that separates the worlds of the living and the dead. Tasmania named its Styx River because there were lots of sticks around and the people responsible for naming things in Tasmania couldn't spell. To cover up their embarrassment, they later named one of the Styx's tributaries the Charon, after the skeletal boatman who ferries spirits to the Greek underworld, but they weren't fooling anyone.

9   This is a reference to Tiny Tim, the crippled son of Bob Cratchit in Charles Dickens' *A Christmas Carol*, not the crazy-haired ukulele player with the nails-down-a-blackboard falsetto. It is not possible to tiptoe through the tulips without a right leg.

> I find that I am spending the prime of my life at the farthest part of the world, without credit, secluded from my family, my connexions, from the world, under constant apprehensions of being starved.

But the settlers soon realised that Van Diemen's Land had one critical advantage over Sydney. Lots of lovely edible animals.

While the island's thick woods rendered guns largely ineffective, there was richer hunting in Van Diemen's Land than anywhere else in the British Empire. The animals had never encountered dogs before, and the settlers' vicious wolfhound/greyhound crosses (and Mrs Power's poodle) caught game at will.

While whales and seals were being slaughtered in the island's seas and rivers, the settlers were butchering tens of thousands of kangaroos, wallabies, emus and swans. Aspiring chefs created fantastic new dishes, with nouveau-Tasmanian food critics commending roast echidna, stuffed with sage and onion, for its similarity to goose.[10] The Devil, as the Tasmanian devil was first known, was just about the only animal that wasn't eaten, as its rancid scent and love of carrion was a turn-off for Tasmania's foodies.

The reliance on hunting, rather than on agriculture, meant the colonists embraced, rather than feared, the bush. They pushed into the wilderness, giving landmarks names with a creepy Appalachian vibe – Murderer's Plains, Killman Point, Hell Corner and Four Square Gallows. When Lachlan Macquarie toured in 1811 and renamed everything Macquarie, Lachlan or something Scottish, the Vandemonians tore down his signboards. Tasmania was a local place for local people, and foreigners, with their fancy placenames, were not welcome.

The convicts' love of the great outdoors was a challenge to Collins and his successors. While in Sydney the bush was a natural barrier to escape, in Van Diemen's Land it gave both food and freedom. Collins

---

10   The echidna is an ideal bush tucker *hors-d'oeuvre* as it comes with its own toothpicks.

responded by bringing in laws to restrict convicts hunting. Native
animals and game birds were reserved for military and civil officers
and the hunters who worked for them.[11] This not only ensured there
were more animals for gentlemen to kill, but also made convicts
dependent on the officers for food. Without this dependency, it was
feared the convicts would not work.

The game restrictions allowed the military and civil officers to
become rich. They sold meat to whalers and the government store, with
fur and feathers hawked to passing traders. Edward Lord, a marine
officer, made a motza in meat, and Reverend Knopwood's profits
from kangarooing dwarfed his clergyman's salary. Knopwood was a
"sporting parson" who'd blown an £18,000 pound inheritance trying
to keep up with the hunting and shooting set of Viscount Clermont.
Hunting had destroyed his fortune and hunting would restore it.

When Knopwood tallied the number of animals he'd killed in
the first year of settlement, he penned the motto that now adorns
Hobart's coat of arms: *Sic Fortis Hobartia Crevit* – "Thus in strength
did Hobart grow."[12]

STRAIGHT OUTTA RISDON

Henry Hacking, who'd shot Pemulwuy, the Eora resistance leader, so
that Sir Joseph Banks might keep his head in a pickle jar, had fallen
on hard times. He'd served with Jørgensen on the *Lady Nelson*, been

---

11   Convicts were also appointed to hunt leeches, which thrived in Tasmania's
     miserable dampness. Up to 300 leeches were needed each month for hirudo-
     therapy, the topical application of leeches to drain the "bad blood" of people with
     fever, headaches, insomnia, gout, cancer, general listlessness and just about every
     other conceivable ailment. Convict leech hunters were live bait, being forced to
     stand in the nearest bog to be eaten by hungry bloodsuckers. On the plus side, the
     job came with free healthcare.

12   The two animals on the coat of arms are exemplars of this meat-lover's motto.
     The Tasmanian emu has been eaten into extinction and the Forester kangaroo
     out of 90 per cent of its territory.

pardoned by Governor King for shooting and wounding a Sydney woman, and then transported to Van Diemen's Land for stealing from Matthew Flinders' *Investigator*, a crime King believed had been committed to support Hacking's alcohol addiction.

Having proved he could shoot Aborigines and women, Hacking was appointed Collins' gamekeeper and told to try his hand at kangaroos. While returning from a hunt, he was surrounded by Aborigines who gave him the choice of his kangaroo or his life. He handed over the roo and lived to drink another day.

The decimation of kangaroo stocks around Hobart Town was depriving the Aborigines of their major food source, and disputes over game grew more frequent. Knopwood mourned the death of his unimaginatively named but creatively spelled dog, Spott,[13] one of many hounds speared by Aborigines in their campaign to protect their roos from the white hunters.

Skirmishes over kangaroos presented a challenge to Collins, who'd received the War and Colonial Office's now-standard instructions "to endeavour by every means in your power to open an intercourse with the natives, and to conciliate their goodwill, enjoining all persons under your Government to live in amity and kindness with them".

Concerned about the survival of Britain's most distant and lightly populated settlement, Collins had chosen not to communicate his orders that violence against the natives would be punished. It was therefore inevitable that some of the settlers would test the practical limits of amity.

The eighty people at Risdon Cove felt particularly vulnerable, as they lived in the middle of grasslands that the Oyster Bay Aborigines loved setting alight. Although the Aborigines did this to drive out game and regenerate forage, setting fire to farmland was all the rage in Irish republican and land-enclosure protest circles back in Britain.

13   See what I mean about Tasmanian literacy?

As land-burning was often a prelude to being skewered with a pike or a pitchfork, it understandably set British teeth on edge.

On 3 May 1804, according to Lieutenant William Moore, several hundred Aborigines approached the Risdon settlement, took a kangaroo from one of his servants, used violence upon a settler's wife and beat a man, whose house they planned to burn down. Moore reported that his men opened fire on the natives in self-defence, that his shooting at them with a cannon ended the three-hour skirmish, and that only two Aborigines were killed that day.

Jacob Mountgarrett, a surgeon who'd settled at Risdon, wrote to Knopwood that 500 to 600 Aborigines had made a premeditated attack on the settlement. He asked the cleric to christen a two-year-old boy whose parents were killed in the conflict, and said Lieutenant Bowen should pop around to his place tomorrow if he wanted to watch him dissect a dead native.

By contrast, the convict Edward White testified to a later inquiry that the natives were nowhere near the settler they'd allegedly beaten, hadn't come to attack the settlement (as shown by the lack of spears and the presence of women and children in their party), that the soldiers came down from their camp to attack and "there were a great many of the Natives slaughtered and wounded".

We'll never know exactly how the day unfolded or whether there were three or fifty Aboriginal deaths. Whatever the body count, Risdon Cove was a turning point in Tasmanian race relations, with Lieutenant-Governor George Arthur later attributing the outbreak of native violence to the actions of Moore and his men.

Risdon certainly shaped Collins' policies towards the Tasmanian Aborigines. He believed that, as a result of Risdon, "these undiscriminating savages will consider every white man as their enemy, and will if they have the opportunity, revenge the death of their companions upon those who had no share in the attack."

Collins also disapproved of the christening of the boy whose parents had been killed in the conflict, ordering that the recently dubbed Robert Hobart May be returned to his people. This direction was never followed, as the Oyster Bay tribe was now making itself scarce. Robert disappeared from the historical record after receiving a smallpox inoculation in 1805.

Collins had been a champion of closer ties between the colonists and the Eora of Sydney. Now, disillusioned by the failure of his one-time friend Bennelong to integrate into British society, and by the conflict at Risdon, he no longer encouraged contact with Aborigines or invited them into town. The old and new Vandemonians, Collins believed, should leave each other alone to live their separate lives. This would prove an impossible dream.

TWO-TOWN TASSIE

Britain was not satisfied that a scattering of hovels on the Derwent would be sufficient to deter Napoleon's territorial ambitions. And so, in October 1804, William Paterson settled the island's northern shores to keep the strategically important Bass Strait free of unwanted Frenchmen.[14]

The following year, Paterson went all Colonel Kurtz and took his people up a river into the island's dark heart. There he established Patersonia, which was renamed Launceston in 1807, as Paterson lacked Macquarie's knack for self-memorialisation.[15]

Between 1808 and 1810, the hunters of Launceston and Hobart Town moved ever outwards to occupy the 200 kilometres of grassland that separated the settlements. It was now impossible to find a kangaroo within a day's travel of the two towns, and the convict hunters spent long periods away from the comforts of civilisation. These were

---

14   Editor's note: tautology.

15   Launceston was built to house the refugees of Norfolk Island, which was being abandoned. Norfolk Island was resettled by convicts in 1825, by the descendants of the *Bounty* mutineers in 1856 and by Colleen McCullough in 1980.

wild frontiersmen, Tasmanian Daniel Boones in possum-skin hats
who sported beards that would make a barista blush and who lived
on a heady mix of testosterone, adrenalin and rum.[16]

These hardy pioneers expanded British settlement far more rapidly than had occurred in New South Wales. Yet conflict with the
tribes quietened, as the trade in dogs transformed Aboriginal society.
Aboriginal men now hunted more game for less effort, enabling them
to spend most of the day with their feet up, waiting for the missus
to serve them the evening roast. And if they needed to trade their
women – or, even better, women kidnapped from another tribe – for
these wonderful new four-legged labour-saving devices, well, that
was a price some of them were willing to pay.

Farmers and shepherds followed in the hunters' wake, as grass
that was good for kangaroos was also good for cattle and sheep. The
meat magnate Edward Lord was now the island's largest stock-owner
and had also got into the retail game, selling goods through the store
run by his convict housekeeper turned wife, Maria.

Things were also looking up for John Pascoe Fawkner, as little Johnny
Fawkner was now known. He'd regained the use of his leg and was working as a shepherd on his father's fifty-acre farm, where he lived alone
(except for the sheep) for weeks at a time in a windowless sod hut. Still,
it wouldn't be long until the ambitious and morally agnostic Fawkner
would thrust himself up into the windowed classes. When Governor
Macquarie visited in 1811, he granted John fifty acres of his own. The
malnourished cripple from Cripplegate was now a man of property.

Yet Van Diemen's Land's growth was stunted by the indifference of
Britain and New South Wales. Once Napoleon's southern ambitions

---

16 Tasmanian Daniel Boones are not to be confused with Tasmanian David Boons.
    In the words of the renowned historians of 20th Century Fox, "Daniel Boone was
    a man. Yes, a big man!", while David Boon is 5'3" on a good day. David Boon's hat
    was made of flannel, not skinned animal; he had a moustache that only a walrus
    could love, in place of a proper beard; and he lived on a heady mix of Four'N
    Twenty pies, Benson & Hedges and Victoria Bitter (allegedly up to fifty-two cans
    in a single session).

were thwarted, Britain promptly lost interest in its remotest outpost. It treated Collins like Collins treated his wife, never responding to his plaintive letters. New South Wales saw the island as London's project and largely left the Vandemonians to their own devices.

Collins died suddenly on 24 March 1810. He'd been a popular figure among his convict charges – he'd fed them, slept with them and, in the words of the *Derwent Star and Van Diemen's Land Intelligencer*'s obituarist, had been "ever more ready to pardon than punish the offender". He received a less charitable obituary from his wife, who complained that he had left her a measly £36, and from many of his peers, who complained he was a lecher and poor administrator.

Collins' government papers disappeared with him. Some historians believe they were burned by Edward Lord on the day of Collins' death, lest they reveal the murky intermingling of Lord's public and private interests. Others believed Collins had instructed that they be buried in his coffin, and, being both inquisitive and macabre, dug him up in 1925. They found no records of Collins' rule, just the withered husk of a lonely and compassionate man who had done his best for the people of Van Diemen's Land.

FRIVOLITY AND LOW BUFFOONERY

Military commandants ruled Hobart Town in the three years after Collins' death. Edward Lord moved into Government House before Governor Macquarie, who regarded him as "a dangerous and troublesome man", relieved him of his duties. Captain John Murray, who is hated by sensationalist historians for his unassuming rule and unblemished character, spent two years ably administering the settlement. He was briefly succeeded by Lieutenant-Colonel Andrew Geils, who stole large quantities of spirits, grain, sugar and hardware from the government store, and was condemned by Macquarie as "a Man of weak judgment, extremely venal and rapacious, and always inclined to sacrifice the interests of the Public to his own sordid and selfish views".

These were words of praise, compared with those Macquarie reserved for Collins' eventual successor, Lieutenant-Colonel Thomas Davey, whom he denounced as "so dissipated in his Manners and Morals, so expensive in his habits, so very thoughtless and volatile, and so very easily imposed upon by designing plausible Characters".

Davey would drink anything, as long as it had been brewed, distilled, fermented or drained from the bladder of a hobo sleeping rough outside an unguarded methylated spirits factory. He is credited in Australia's first published cookbook for creating the Blow My Skull cocktail, a Tasmanian moonshine mix of two pints boiling water, one pint rum and half a pint of brandy.[17] The twin gods of inebriation and irony had smiled on Thomas his entire life, as he was born to a woman named Temperance Wynes.

Davey was also unlucky with money. He'd racked up debts through the poor investment of his men's wages while a paymaster in the marines and the British Treasury garnished his salary to recover what it was owed. Macquarie ensured Davey could not piss away Van Diemen's Land's money by forbidding him to make contracts without Macquarie's authority, draw bills on the British Treasury, charter ships or grant land. He was, in almost every sense, a Claytons lieutenant-governor.[18]

Davey was strangely reluctant to travel to Van Diemen's Land, even though he would be the first man to preside over a unified settlement,

---

17   The word *cocktail* most likely derives from *cock ale*, an English drink of ale, spices and mutilated chicken. A recipe for cock ale can be found in the 1739 edition of Eliza Smith's *The Compleat Housewife*: "Take ten gallons of ale, and a large cock, the older the better; parboil the cock, flay him, and stamp him in a stone mortar till his bones are broken (you must craw and gut him when you flay him); then put the cock into two quarts of sack, and put it to three pounds of raisins of the sun stoned, some blades of mace, and a few cloves; put all these into a canvas bag, and a little before you find the ale has done working, put the ale and bag together into a vessel; in a week or nine days time bottle it up; fill the bottle but just above the neck, and give the same time to ripen as other ale."

18   "The lieutenant-governor you have when you're not having a lieutenant-governor." Davey was not a Claytons lieutenant-governor in the sense that Claytons is a non-alcoholic drink.

with Hobart Town and Launceston to be joined under his rule. He spent four months in Sydney waiting for his luggage to turn up, only to discover that it had been stolen by an American privateer.[19] Davey's extended stay gave Macquarie the opportunity to assess him as being "in a constant state of intemperance" and having an "extraordinary degree of frivolity and low buffoonery".

When Davey was finally poured out onto Hobart Town's dock on 20 February 1813, he delayed his arrival at Government House by stopping off at the first pub. He then outraged Macquarie by shortening his capital's name to Hobart – if a name change was required, what was wrong with Macquarieton, Macquarieville or Macquarieopolis?

Davey's "conviviality and earthy good nature" (love of a drink and a dirty joke) made him well liked in his new home, but he was not entirely respected. His graceless eccentricities, particularly when under the influence (which was often), led his subjects to name him Mad Tom.

THE HORNS OF MAD TOM'S DILEMMA

Mad Tom had two immediate problems. The first was Aboriginal children. The taking of Robert Hobart May in 1804 started a trend, and by 1813 an Aboriginal baby was a must-have accessory in the world of free-settler fashion. When it came to having children who would not only clean their own room, but also every room in the house, black was the new black.

The child abduction craze had two main causes. First, some well-intentioned Christian families took in Aboriginal infants so that they might be baptised out of barbarism. Second, as only two convict ships arrived between 1804 and 1816, and many of the convicts' sentences had expired, the settlers needed to find some new people to do all

---

19 New arrivals to Sydney will have some sympathy for Davey, as it can take up to four months to pass through customs and retrieve one's luggage at the city's international airport. And don't even get me started on its parking fees. American pirates have got nothing on the Sydney Airport Corporation.

the shit jobs. These factors were not mutually exclusive, as concerned Christians also had dirty floors.

Some children were "lent" to the settlers, while others were orphaned in armed conflict or kidnapped by raiding parties. These children were never really accepted into Vandemonian society. One of them, George Van Diemen, was taken to England at the age of nine. He returned six years later, well educated and literate, but his dreams of a junior government position came to nought. Yet members of Tasmania's stolen generation were subject to the white man's law. In 1818, a youth who left the settled districts was sentenced to twelve months' hard labour on a chain gang for "wandering in the woods without any visible means of obtaining a livelihood" (i.e. for being Aboriginal).

The abduction of Aboriginal children sometimes resulted in their tribes launching payback attacks. Davey believed "the resentment of these poor uncultivated beings has been justly excited by ... the robbery of their children". In 1813, he issued a proclamation to "express his utter indignation and abhorrence" of the abductions, and ordered them to cease. This was treated with the same casual disregard as Mad Tom's other deluded ravings.

The kidnappings didn't stop until the early 1820s, when the Colonial Times reported, "many of the native tribes were suffering from the most loathsome coetaneous disease ... [which] prevents many of the Settlers in the interior from taking into their service infant natives, as has been the case, for the purpose of bringing them up in a civilised manner". It was impossible to have a clean floor when your domestic dropped large flakes of infected skin on it as soon as he'd swept it.

Mad Tom's second problem was the two boatloads of convicts who'd arrived in 1812. New South Wales had decided Van Diemen's Land would be a place of secondary punishment for the colony's finest hard men, deviants and toothless nut-jobs – the supermax of the south seas.

A shipload of scum scraped from Sydney's underbelly was joined by the inmates of the *Indefatigable*, the first ship to bring convicts direct to Van Diemen's Land from England. Among them were Charles Routley, a sadist who was missing part of his jaw, had a wooden arm and iron hook for a hand and who sewed a fellow *Indefatigable* prisoner into a bullock skin before roasting him alive, and who shot, bludgeoned, poisoned, strangled and beheaded six other men.[20] The *Indefatigable* convicts also included a Scottish wife-murderer, assorted highwaymen and common thugs, sixteen military deserters and five participants in the first Luddite riots.

The Luddites were textile workers who raged against the machines of the Industrial Revolution. Textile mills, with their new-fangled stocking frames, spinning frames and power looms, were replacing skilled weavers with low-paid labourers. The skilled weavers responded by gathering on the Nottinghamshire moors at night, where they practised smashing machines and machine owners while screaming "Ludd!"[21]

The machine breakers' attacks on textile factories, merchants and local magistrates resulted in the British Army being deployed in the northern counties, with more soldiers fighting the Luddites at one stage than were fighting Napoleon on the Iberian Peninsula. The British government ended the Luddite uprising by passing the *Destruction of Stocking Frames, etc. Act 1812*, which enabled the execution of machine breakers, and staging a mass show trial of any northerner who knew one end of a loom from the other.

Lord Byron's defence of the Luddites in parliament and his subsequent "Song for the Luddites", the first unionist/anarchist/republican

---

20   Being able to thread a needle with a hook hand is a most impressive feat. Some suggested that Routley sewed John "Pretty Jack" Butler into a cow skin so that he might eat him while maintaining the illusion that he was consuming beef.

21   The Luddites took their name from Ned Ludd, a youth who was said to have smashed two stocking frames in 1779. The Luddite leaders recognised that invoking the uncharismatic-sounding name of a pimply small-time vandal might affect their membership drive, so they created the mythical King Ludd, who, like Robin Hood, lived in Sherwood Forest, from which he would periodically emerge to smash the machines of the rich mill-owners and give jobs to the poor weavers.

FIG. 2: "I BET YOU CAN MOO LIKE A COW. LET'S MOO. MOO NOW. MOOOOOO!"

anthem, were not enough to save the machine breakers.[22] Luddites and those vaguely suspected of Luddism were hanged or transported to New South Wales or Van Diemen's Land, which, on the bright side, was an anti-technologist's paradise.

The 1812 arrivals, with their reputation for recreational ultra-violence, changed the complexion of Vandemonian society. The only reason it remained safe to drop the soap in the world's newest prison state was that most of the 1812 inmates didn't know what soap was.[23]

---

22   Byron's only legitimate child, Ada Lovelace, dashed her father's poetic Luddite vision. Ada's mother, who resented Byron for leaving her when Ada was a month old, insisted that her daughter study mathematics to prevent her from inheriting her father's Romantic insanity. In 1842, Ada wrote the first algorithm to make mathematical calculations for Charles Babbage's Analytical Engine. Although the Analytical Engine was never built, Ada is credited as the world's first computer programmer and the mother of the modern computer, a machine that has put more people out of jobs than all the mill machinery of the Industrial Revolution.

23   And if they had known, they wouldn't have had a bar of it.

Davey would have been able to control the expanded convict population if his criminals had stayed in the settled districts. But freedom's call echoed out from the island's dripping forests and rugged hills. And so Australia experienced its first and greatest bushranger plague.

BANDITTI, BEARDS AND BOUNTIES

Bushrangers were highwaymen in search of a highway, although most lacked the chivalry of the romantic rakes of the road. There was nothing romantic about your average bushranger, unless your idea of romance involved a bit of rough play and a lot of beard. Violence came easily to the men who'd adapted the dandy highwayman's catchphrase to "Your money and your life."[24]

There was no single reason that men (and a couple of women) signed up as bushrangers. Some loved the freedom of the bush, some were running away from their troubles, some preferred theft to labour, some were just vicious psychopathic bastards, and some ticked all these boxes.

Australia's first bushranger was the giant African First Fleet convict Black Caesar, who escaped into the bush in 1789 and survived by robbing settlers' gardens.[25] He was shot dead two weeks after Governor Hunter placed a bounty of five gallons of spirits on his head.

Caesar's fate was typical of those who followed him. Bushrangers were shot, speared, bludgeoned, burned, strangled, poisoned, savaged by dogs and hanged with monotonous regularity. Life insurance salesmen avoided them like the plague, with Charles Darwin writing in 1836 that the bushranger "will sooner be killed than taken alive". Tasmania's Martin Cash was notorious for being "the only bushranger to die in his own bed".

---

24 Adam Ant would never have played a bushranger because any bushranger caught wearing makeup or braids would have been shot by his peers.

25 "Your cabbage or your life" just doesn't have the same ring to it.

John Wilson, a paedophile bushranger with a kangaroo-skin loincloth, and his three only slightly less unsavoury companions were, in 1797, the first Australians to be declared "outlaw". Outlaws were literally outside the protection of the law and could be taken "dead or alive" by any British subject, without worrying about irritating things like the presumption of innocence or the right to a trial.[26]

Bushrangers were originally known as banditti, but the *Sydney Gazette* was determined to come up with a less woggy name. *Bushranger* first appeared in a 17 February 1805 article about three men who held up a cart, instead of the traditional stagecoach, and proceeded to not assault anyone or steal anything. Clearly they were still getting the hang of the whole bushranging thing.

The *Gazette*'s journalist had obviously spent too much time reading the new Romantic poets. Instead of condemning the men as common criminals who deserved to hang, he wrote a sympathetic piece about the loneliness and remorse of a life lived in the bush, robbing and killing people:

> How deplorable must be the prospect of terminating an existence under all the accumulated horrors of such an exile! without a friend at hand to administer the last kind offices, or to alleviate affliction by human condolence! parching with thirst, perhaps, but deprived by famine of the power to quench it! Instead of the delightful confidence which Christian resignation can alone inspire, each succeeding pang embittered with self-accusation and remorse, heightened by the surrounding gloom to all the agonies of deep despair.

Governor Macquarie also lamented the bushranger's plight:

---

26 New South Wales repealed its outlaw legislation in 1976, although it was not used during the twentieth century. The United Kingdom's House of Commons introduces the *Outlawries Bill* after the Queen's speech at the beginning of each parliamentary session because it has done so since 1727 and the British see no need to stand in the way of mindless tradition. The United States of America retains outlaw arrangements so it can drone strike, disappear and torture un-Americans.

I have no doubt that many convicts who might have been rendered useful and good men, had they been treated with humane and reasonable control, have sunk into despondency by the unfeeling treatment of such masters; and that many of those wretched men, driven to acts of violence by harsh usage, and who, by a contrary treatment, might have been reformed, have taken themselves to the woods, where they can only subsist by plunder, and have terminated their lives at the gallows.

These writings reflected the bushranger myth that had taken root in the Australian consciousness since the colony's earliest days. These were good men turned just bad enough to be sexy. These were underdogs deserving of sympathy. These were kids who just needed to be given a bit more time to grow up. After all, boys will be wild colonial boys.

OH, GIVE ME A HOME WHERE THE BUSHRANGERS ROAM

Nowhere did bushrangers like Van Diemen's Land did. The island's banditti were the ISIS of the nineteenth century. OK, they didn't have the black flags and whack-job interpretation of the Koran, but they had the beards, beheadings, terror and violence, an effective propaganda machine, not many women, and the will and means to bring a government to its knees.

Most of Van Diemen's Land's early bushrangers were bolters (escaped convicts) who stole dogs to help them survive in the bush. Reverend Knopwood, who had lost Spott to the Aborigines, lost Miss to bushrangers. The £10 reward for Miss's return, a year's income for some labourers, was claimed by William Williams, the suspected dognapper.

Paying up in this way encouraged theft for ransom, but some of the island's more sophisticated bushrangers considered stealing things a mug's game. Instead they charged settlers for not having things stolen, and Van Diemen's Land became the protection-racket capital of the world.

Sydney was bordered by the sea, mountains and wide rivers, which meant New South Wales' early bushrangers didn't have much bush to range in. Van Diemen's Land's banditti were not similarly constrained and roamed far and wide. They were among the island's earliest explorers; John Brown and Richard Lemon were the first Europeans to make the overland crossing from Launceston to Hobart Town. The intrepid duo also held the more dubious distinction of being Australia's first serial killers.[27]

Women found it difficult to break through the eucalypt ceiling and were under-represented in the bushranging workplace. Bush-rangers therefore traded goods for access to Aboriginal women or took them by force. James Carrett shot an Oyster Bay man who was attempting to protect his wife, then cut off his head, attached it to a string and made his widow wear it as a necklace, before forcing her into sex slavery. It was easy for pastoralists and others who came into later conflict with Aboriginal people to blame the Carretts of this world for Tasmania's fractured race relations.

The two convict transports that arrived in Van Diemen's Land in 1812 incubated the bushranger epidemic that ravaged the island during Davey's rule. The most notorious of the 1812 arrivals was Michael Howe, a Yorkshire sailor turned soldier turned deserter turned highwayman turned convict turned bushranger.

Howe, "a stout wicked looking man" with "long and bushy black ringlets", was assigned as a servant to John Ingle, a Hobart merchant

---

27 Australia's first serial killers were Tasmanian because South Australia had not
     yet been settled. Brown and Lemon shot dead Corporal John Curry, lay in wait
     for two other soldiers, trussed them up and marched them 30 kilometres into the
     bush before shooting them. They were later joined by Richard Scanlan, who, like
     Brown, was Irish. Lemon shot Scanlan through the head while he was making
     breakfast and then hung him by his heels from a tree because he was irritated that
     Scanlan and Brown spent their time nattering away to each other in Gaelic. When
     Brown returned to camp, Lemon led him to Scanlan's corpse and said, "Now,
     Brown, as there are only two of us, we shall understand one another better for
     the future." Tasmanians, who love this sort of gruesome story, named the area of
     Scanlan's death Murderer's Plains.

who'd made his fortune staging the Liberace-esque extravagance that was David Collins' funeral. Howe promptly absconded, declaring, "I have served the King, and will be no meaner man's slave!", conveniently ignoring that he had also run away from the king's service.

Howe joined the island's largest bushranging gang, led by John Whitehead, a gardener transported in 1801 for stealing two pairs of pants. Howe's great strength, intelligence and casually cheerful approach to violence led to his rapid promotion as Whitehead's deputy.

Howe and Whitehead were inventive when it came to murder. They made a pair of giant moccasins for John "Looney" Hopkins, a dim-witted gang member and suspected informer, then filled them with bull ants before filling them with John Hopkins' feet. Looney's agonising death served as a deterrent to others thinking of ratting out the gang. Howe shot another colleague, Edwards, for giving a shawl to Howe's partner, Mary Cockerill (a.k.a. Black Mary), one of two Aboriginal girls who had joined the Whitehead gang. This served as a deterrent to others thinking of cutting Howe's grass.

Whitehead's men stole all the arms, ammunition and portable property from the settlers at New Norfolk and terrorised the settled districts. They allied themselves with convict hunters and shepherds who warned them when the law was approaching and tipped them off when there were vacant houses or coaches full of rich nobs to be robbed. They also took up stock theft and formed alliances with some of the island's less scrupulous landowners. Edward Lord's stock was never targeted and he was suspected of buying kangaroo skins from the bushrangers, as well as animals stolen from his rivals.

Everyone who was anyone was in on the bushranger act. Surgeon Mountgarrett and Reverend Knopwood were accused of aiding and harbouring bushrangers. The deputy-commissary, George Williams, and the former deputy surveyor, Peter Mills, grew beards and took to the woods in the hope that shooting people for money would

be more enjoyable than working in the public service.[28] Captain
McKenzie, the commandant at Launceston, wrote to Davey in 1814,
"almost everyone here is, I firmly believe, more or less, a villain."

John Pascoe Fawkner certainly dabbled in villainy, supplementing
his income as a farmer and baker with people smuggling and theft.
He was sentenced to 500 lashes and three years' labour for outfitting
a boat to help seven convicts escape to South America, then transported to Newcastle for "committing some atrocious Robberies and
Depredations".

Macquarie sent the 46th Regiment to deal with Tasmania's rampant banditti, who now controlled everything outside Hobart and
Launceston and quite a bit within. The men of the 46th spent weeks
beating around the bush, with nary a ranger to be found. Their red
coats were completely impractical bushwear, and many took to wearing kangaroo and possum skins – the same attire worn by the men
they were hunting. Marsupial-clad groups of soldiers, unable to tell
friend from foe, spent their time shooting each other.

On 14 May 1814, Macquarie ordered an amnesty for the twenty-
nine members of the Whitehead gang if they handed themselves in by
the beginning of December. This was a six-month licence to commit
crime, and bushranging rates skyrocketed. Howe and several other
gang members surrendered, claimed immunity for past misdeeds,
then returned straight to the bush to commit fresh ones. Macquarie
really hadn't thought this through ...

The increasingly desperate and isolated Davey was unable to deal
with those charged with bushranging offences, as the nearest court for
capital crimes was in Sydney and witnesses were generally unwilling
to travel 650 miles to testify while vengeful bushrangers ransacked
their uninhabited homesteads. So Davey declared martial law on
25 April 1815, proclaiming, "Any person now caught committing acts

---

28 It was, but then so is watching mould grow on cheese and removing your own ears
    with a blunt hacksaw.

of murder, robbery, rape or other capital offences will be the subject of a speedy court-martial and summary execution."

Macquarie considered this "not only illegal and irregular, but also highly derogatory of my authority as Governor". But it was effective. A number of the Whitehead gang were captured and summarily hanged. Whitehead himself died during a gunfight in the hallway of a house he was robbing a month after martial law had been declared. After being shot, he staggered towards Howe, crying, "Take my watch! Take my watch!", some of history's most unusual but thoughtful last words.

Posterity does not record whether Howe took Whitehead's watch, but he did take his head, hacking it off with a penknife to prevent it from being handed in to Davey for a reward. Whitehead's headless corpse, along with that of a fellow gang member, was hung in chains in an iron cage for a year to welcome new arrivals to Van Diemen's Land, Australia's most ill-conceived tourism campaign until the advent of Lara Bingle.[29]

THE LIEUTENANT-GOVERNOR OF THE WOODS

Howe led the gang after Whitehead's death. The Lieutenant-Governor of the Woods or the Governor of the Ranges, as Howe now styled himself, engaged in increasingly audacious attacks. He even raided Davey's mansion, demanding that Davey's steward fry up some ham for his men. The bushrangers then sat down for breakfast at Davey's table, enjoying the ham and a mixture of eggs, cream and spirits that they'd liberated from Davey's coldroom. Howe ransacked the house after the meal and politely asked Davey's steward for a dictionary, which was given to him on the proviso that it be returned after he'd finished with it. Howe agreed.

Howe was a literary bushranger. He kept a kangaroo-skin journal in which he recorded, in kangaroo blood, his dreams and nightmares

---

29   Van Diemen's Land was the last place in the British Empire to stop displaying hanged corpses in gibbets (1837), enhancing its backwoods reputation.

and a list of seeds he wished to collect so that he might create an idyl-
lic garden in the woods. He established a bushrangers union, with
the members signing a petition to Davey (again in kangaroo blood)
demanding that he be "either for us or against us", and wrote regular
letters to Davey and his successor, in which he mused on current
events and the meaning of life.

Macquarie wanted Davey removed on the grounds that he had
failed to deal with the bushranger crisis, was "dissipated and profligate",
condoned the smuggling of spirits and had given preferential trading
concessions to Edward Lord. Earl Bathurst, secretary of state for war
and the colonies, offered Davey 2,000 acres to go quietly, rather than
face dismissal. Davey accepted in 1816 and then lobbied for further
land grants and £4,500 in compensation for his lost luggage. Despite
being granted 8,000 acres, he failed as a settler and died in 1823, leaving his wife an estate valued at less than £20.[30]

Davey's successor, William Sorell, was far more effective in addressing the bushranger problem. The Old Man, as he was known for his
shock of white hair, increased the number of police, arrested the
bushrangers' supporters, upped rewards for informants, restricted
the sale of arms, introduced compulsory identity passes and used
convict guides and native trackers to hunt the bushrangers down.

When armed soldiers surrounded Howe and Black Mary, the
bushranger shot his girlfriend as he fled, probably in an attempt to
prevent her from being captured and informing on him. Hell hath no
fury like a woman gunned down by her lover; Mary, after her wound
was patched up, guided the soldiers to the gang's huts, which were
then burned to the ground.

---

30 Davey, like Collins, left few official records of his rule, but nobody dug him up
    to see if he'd stashed them in his coffin. Davey claimed that he had entrusted
    his government's documents to the Earl of Harrowby, and the Earl of Harrowby
    claimed that Davey was a drunken liar. A senior public servant later confessed that
    the government had simply run out of paper – and nobody had thought to record
    government business on dead kangaroo.

Howe, now seriously unnerved, wrote a letter "From the Governor of the Ranges to the Governor of the Town", offering to surrender in return for a pardon. Sorell agreed to seek Macquarie's approval for such a deal and Howe returned to Hobart. While Howe lodged at the gaol, he walked the streets of the capital during the day, where he was greeted like a celebrity. After three months, the pardon had still not materialised and Howe returned to the bush.

But the Lieutenant-Governor of the Woods had lost his aura of invincibility. He was now a common fugitive and Mary and Mosquito, an Eora tracker, were hunting him down.

Mosquito finally located his quarry on 21 October 1818. Howe was cornered by convict Thomas Worrall, before Private William Pugh "battered his brains out" with the butt of his firearm.

Pugh got the money, Worrall got a pardon and Mosquito, who'd been promised a return passage to Sydney, got nothing because promises made to black people didn't count.

The reign of the banditti was over, although Sorell's secretary, Thomas Wells, fuelled the bushranger myth with his 1818 book, *Michael Howe: The Last and Worst of the Bushrangers of Van Diemen's Land*, the first general work of literature published in Australia.[31] This meant nothing to the Lieutenant-Governor of the Woods, whose body was buried in an unmarked grave and whose head stared at the citizens of Hobart with sightless eyes from the display stand on which it was mounted.

THE OLD MAN AND MRS KENT

William Sorell, Van Diemen's Land's most enlightened and competent ruler, transformed Vandemonian society during his 1817–24 rule.

---

31   *The Bushrangers*, penned by Henry Melville in 1834, was the first full play to be written, published and performed in Australia. *The Story of the Kelly Gang*, released in 1906, was Australia's and the world's first full-length feature film. Australia's love of bushrangers was the major impetus in the development of an Australian arts culture.

The Old Man spent a little time each day standing at the gates of Government House, talking to passers-by so as to better understand the concerns of his constituents. He opened up the island to free settlers, with the European population swelling from 2,000 to 12,600 in just seven years. Van Diemen's Land, which had greeted the colonists with famine, now exported grain to Sydney and Asia and had six times the per-capita agricultural productivity of New South Wales. Sorell imported sheep from John Macarthur's famous flock and 182,000 sheep grazed in Van Diemen's Land's grassy woodlands by 1820, more than twice the ovine population of New South Wales.

The new free settlers called for Van Diemen's Land to be renamed Tasmania, and their campaign got a kick along with the 1823 publication of *Godwin's Emigrant's Guide to Van Diemen's Land More Properly Called Tasmania*. This was a rebranding exercise, as the name Van Diemen's Land was indelibly associated with depraved illiterate convicts, violent bearded bandits and drunken fornicating lieutenant-governors. Although the island's name was not officially changed until 1856, Tasmania was in common use by the mid-1820s.

Tasmania was the fastest-growing part of the British Empire and a land of opportunity for those on the make. John Pascoe Fawkner was one of those. He'd returned to Hobart after a stint as a convict timber cutter, thrown himself into the illegal liquor trade, been fined for short-changing his bakery customers with underweight loaves and placed on probation for robbing the government store. Moving to Launceston, he married a convicted baby stealer and became a successful builder, sawyer, newspaper proprietor and publican. His many run-ins with the law had honed his bush-lawyer skills and he regularly represented others in the courts – for a fee, of course.

Lieutenant-Governor Sorell, like Fawkner, had his vices – or, rather, vice – "the very pretty and interesting" Mrs Kent. Sorell had met Mrs Kent, the wife of a junior officer, while serving at the Cape of Good Hope. Mrs Sorell and her seven children moved out, Mrs

Kent moved in and the aggrieved Lieutenant Kent successfully sued Sorell for £3,000 for having "criminal conversation" with his wife.

Sorell continued that conversation in Van Diemen's Land, with Mrs Kent producing several little Sorells while residing at Government House. These domestic arrangements meant ladies felt unable to attend social functions with the governor and eventually resulted in his sacking. Knocking up teenage convict girls was one thing, but openly living with a separated woman was quite another. This was the start of the creeping puritanism in Australian social life that burst into a full sprint during the Victorian era.[32]

Sorell and Mrs Kent lived happily ever after. Alas, the same cannot be said for the Tasmanian Aborigines.

LITTLE GIRL LOST

Truganini, daughter of Mangerner, leader of the Nuenonne of Lunawanna-Alonnah, was born into an age of change. While the Nuenonne clung to their tribal ways at the time of Truganini's birth in 1812, they had known the Europeans for decades – their island off the south-east coast of Van Diemen's Land was a popular supply stop for ships venturing into the Pacific.

The Nuenonne had seen the giant cloud-rafts of Tasman and du Fresne track the coast that marked the boundary between the world of men and the endless water. They had fled into the woods when Tobias Furneaux appeared in 1773 to leave furs without skin and shiny see-me stones[33] in their hurriedly vacated huts. They first spoke to the pale ghosts in 1777, when the one called Cook gifted them with

---

32   Queen Victoria, with her dowdy black dresses and face that had just sucked a lemon, is unfairly blamed for Victorian morality. Victoria was actually a bit of a goer, as evidenced by her love of drawing and collecting male nudes, her breathless wedding night diary entry, and the nine children she had with her first cousin, Prince Albert of Saxe-Coburg and Gotha (who, contrary to popular opinion, did not sport the genital piercing named after him, as Victoria was not *quite* that racy).

33   The usual blankets and mirrors.

a bronze medal before returning to the spirit world.[34] The loud and angry shade of William Bligh haunted them in 1788 and 1792, planting strange fruit and felling trees to feed his cloud-raft.[35]

The ghost who wore the head-decoration of a different spirit-tribe, Bruni d'Entrecasteaux, visited the Nuenonne in 1792 and 1793 and told them that they lived on an island, which they already knew. Mr Bass and Mr Flinders, a spectral double act, camped with them in 1798, and Baudin materialised in 1802 to tell them that they no longer lived on Lunawanna-Alonnah, but on Ile de Bruni, named to honour the "discovery" of the apparition of forty seasons past.[36] The lesser spirits who accompanied Baudin tried to lie with Truganini's aunts and cousins, who rebuffed their otherworldly advances. The Nuenonne might see dead people, but there was no way they would sleep with them.

As Truganini's childhood passed, so did her people's traditional way of life. In 1818, Captain James Kelly, "the father of whaling" in Tasmania, received the first land grant on Bruni Island. American whalers, who had sheltered in the island's northern bay for decades, set up new stations along the coast. Loggers moved in to harvest Bruni's rich forests.

Bruni Island was no longer a place of safety. Truganini's uncle was shot by a soldier, her mother was stabbed to death by sailors during a raid on her family's camp and her sister, Moorina, was abducted by sealers. But Truganini was a survivor.

---

34 Cook, who made first contact with the Nuenonne during his third voyage of discovery, belonged to an era in which most men of science and religion believed that the white man was superior to the yellow man and the yellow man was superior to the black man. A bronze medal was awarded for coming third in the human race.

35 It wasn't only Bligh's language that was fruity. While it took Bligh two attempts to introduce breadfruit to Jamaica, the potty-mouthed greengrocer of the high seas planted Tasmania's earliest apple tree and grape vines on his first go.

36 The British, who later built their stone humpies on Lunawanna-Alonnah and stripped her of her forests, called the land Bruni Island but renamed it Bruny Island in 1918 to downplay the French connection.

Truganini was only 129 centimetres tall but, according to a lady of Hobart, "exquisitely formed, with small and beautifully rounded breasts. The little dress she wore was loosely thrown around her person, but always with grace and a coquettish love of display." This description reads like an advert in the adult services section of the *Hobart Classifieds*, which is not all that surprising, as Truganini had fallen into a life of prostitution.

Truganini exchanged sex for food and protection in the whaling, logging and convict camps of Bruni Island and the adjoining mainland. When Paraweena, who was to be her husband, and another Nuenonne youth came to take her back to Bruni from a mainland camp, the trio accepted the offer of two timber-getters to row them across the D'Entrecasteaux Channel. During the short trip, the two young men were thrown overboard and, when they tried to hold onto the boat's gunwale, had their hands hacked off with a hatchet. The timber-getters left the young men to drown and forced Truganini to return to their camp.

Truganini experienced all of this before she had turned eighteen – her childhood a microcosm of what was occurring across Van Diemen's Land.

3
The Man in Black

Theirs not to make a reply,
Theirs not to reason why,
Theirs but to do and die.

Alfred Lord Tennyson, "The Charge of the Light Brigade", 1854

GOD'S SOLDIER

SORELL'S SUCCESSOR, GEORGE ARTHUR, WAS THE LAST man you'd expect to preside over the destruction of Truganini's race. He was an Evangelical Christian, a fierce opponent of slavery, a protector of native peoples, and a hardworking and able administrator.

Arthur fought in the Napoleonic Wars, where he developed an admiring distrust of the French. He was shot by them in Egypt and fought them in Britain's then-largest military campaign, when 37,481 British soldiers played hide-and-seek with Napoleon in Flanders. The French cut Flanders' dykes, leaving the British up to their knees in sea water. While only 107 British men were killed in action, 3,960 died of disease from flooded canals, with a further 11,500 ill at the time the sodden army waded back to its transports. Arthur, who knew what the dastardly French were capable of, was the perfect choice to keep them out of Van Diemen's Land.

Arthur was a workaholic careerist who admitted to "promotion being my idol". He toiled up to eighteen hours a day and kept meticulous records of all his decisions and instructions, with Van Diemen's Land's assistant surveyor, James Erskine Calder, later complaining he was "the most indefatigable quill-driver of his own or any other age".[1]

Arthur, who expected others to share his work ethic, abhorred the "natural indolence" of his son Leonard and regarded another son, Edward, as an idler who "trusted to chance and good luck", neither of which Arthur believed in. A further son, Sigismund, pulled a knife on his headmaster when about to be caned for idleness, but Arthur was more concerned by his son's sloth than his attempt to shiv the principal.[2]

Arthur valued mathematics for its certainty and believed that poetry should be "read with the greatest caution". He distrusted philosophers, particularly those who asked questions about free will, labelling David Hume "a wretched infidel". Questions about free will inevitably led to questions about God, and God was not to be questioned.

Arthur found God in Jersey,[3] becoming a tedious born-again Christian[4] while posted to the Channel Isles in 1811. He would have been first in line to bang a tambourine and sing uplifting songs about Christ, except that tambourine playing and singing were sinful. Arthur briefly flirted with Methodism before rejecting it as too touchy-feely – he wanted a religion that allowed him to wear black and frown upon the miserable sinners of the world (i.e. everyone). Calvinism was the perfect fit.

1　The recipients of his endless memoranda often had no idea what he was on about, as his writing was lengthy, convoluted and peppered with words like "importunate" (annoyingly persistent) and "promptitude" (the habit of being prompt, of which Arthur very much approved except in his own writing).

2　Sigismund "just escaped from being expelled". What did you have to do to be sent down from a nineteenth-century British public school – burn the head boy's crumpets or bugger the rowing team's badger mascot?

3　Which was lucky, because you can't find anything else there.

4　Editor's note: another tautology.

Arthur's Calvinism led him to embrace the doctrine of total depravity, which is not nearly as much fun as it sounds. The doctrine asserts that man is a worthless slave to sin and inherently rejects God, with salvation entirely dependent upon God's will. Arthur wrote, presumably after indulging in a little morning flagellation:

> I now know that the heart of every man is desperately wicked, and at enmity with God, and the absolute abhorrence I feel in contemplating my sad mis-spent life makes me stand self-accused and self-condemned before my perfect Judge, whose laws I have violated.

One of the good things about Calvinism is that all men, whether black or white, are equally wicked in the eyes of the Lord. As the white man is not morally superior to the black man, it is therefore unfair for him to make the black man his slave. Arthur became an acolyte of William Wilberforce, the Evangelical politician who'd championed the *Abolition of the Slave Trade Act 1807*, which made it an offence to buy or sell slaves in the British Empire, but still allowed for their possession. Wilberforce, Arthur and other abolitionists continued to campaign for an end to slave ownership.[5]

One of the bad things about Calvinism is that a person's thoughts and deeds are immaterial to his or her salvation. Arthur wrote, "I place no reliance on good works, for Faith is the Rock." People who don't believe in good acts also don't believe in bad ones. When in positions of power, these people can be very, very dangerous.

The ambitious young officer commanded a corps of black soldiers in Jamaica, where his dour competence saw him promoted to superintendent of Belize in Honduras. Honduras was a Spanish

---

5   Wilberforce never got to see the realisation of his lifelong dream, as he dropped dead just three days after the *Slavery Abolition Act* passed the House of Commons in 1833. It took a further decade for all British slavery to cease, with slaves over the age of six reclassified as unpaid apprentices (i.e. slaves) until 1838 and slavery continuing in Ceylon, Saint Helena and East India Company territories until 1843. You can't rush principle.

territory and its British settlers were only permitted to live there if they were not directly ruled by Britain. They therefore established a citizen democracy where public assemblies, rather than Whitehall, approved significant decisions. The superintendent was little more than a glorified lunch monitor, answerable to both the assemblies and the governor of Jamaica. Arthur did not like this at all.

The superintendent set to work subverting Britain's only real representative democracy, acting beyond his powers in introducing religious regulations that he conceded were "the source of much dissatisfaction". He banned "noisy amusements" and dancing on Sundays, punished drunkenness as "the Parent of almost every crime" and decreed that "no kept mistress" was to sit in his church pew. On the plus side, he initiated a successful street-cleaning program to address the number of turtles lying about town "in a dreadful state".

Arthur was interested in the welfare of the local Mosquito Indians, believing that they should cease wandering for game and take up "Agriculture and Fishing". He was also intrigued by the new concept of Indian reserves. Arthur would later have the opportunity to apply these ideas in Van Diemen's Land.

Arthur declared that owning Mosquito Indians was unlawful and freed the slaves who worked Belize's mahogany plantations. Although he acknowledged that their masters had enslaved them in good faith, he recommended that they be prosecuted and fined. Arthur was recalled in response to complaints that he'd exceeded his authority.

None of this deterred Earl Bathurst, a fellow abolitionist, from appointing Arthur lieutenant-governor of Van Diemen's Land. Commissioner Bigge had just tabled his reports into Lachlan Macquarie's administration, which concluded that transportation was not serving as an effective criminal deterrent. Bathurst wanted an autocratic hardman who would give the convicts hell. George Arthur was just the man for the job.

YOU ARE NOT HERE TO HAVE FUN

Arthur took office on 12 May 1824. His authoritarian nature, fuelled by the frustrations of Belize, led to his lobbying for independence from Sydney. Edward Lord, while visiting Britain, also campaigned to cut Van Diemen's Land loose from the apron strings of New South Wales, arguing that successful businessmen (i.e. himself) shouldn't have to travel to Sydney to sue people and that Vandemonians should be able to hang their own without the need for a trial on the mainland. Their efforts bore fruit on 3 December 1825. Van Diemen's Land was now a British colony in its own right.

Arthur was a very different man to his predecessors. There were no teenage convict girls or married women (other than Mrs Arthur). There was no heavy drinking, with Arthur's dinner guests complaining about the lack of good wine at his table. Indeed, there were very few dinners, as Arthur considered entertaining to be a wasteful frivolity.

Arthur detested the bread and circuses rule of Lachlan Macquarie. He refused to enter the Turf Club and banned competitive walking, as racing and gambling were sinful. "Public Dances, Concerts and Cards" were dangerous "Pomps and Vanities of this wicked world".[6] Smoking was discouraged, as it "tended to other bad habits from which few men eventually escaped", with Arthur convinced that tobacco had inflamed the passions of his eldest son, Frederick (another disappointment), leading to his shipboard affair with Maria Rasmus, a promiscuous and degenerate actress.[7]

Arthur also rejected Macquarie's distressingly liberal approach to emancipated convicts, refusing to engage with them socially. He was horrified that serving convicts mingled with free settlers and roamed the countryside with little or no supervision. He particularly disliked

---

6   Calvinists abstained from dancing as it led to extra-marital sex, while Methodists
      abstained from extra-marital sex as it led to dancing (rhythm Methodism).

7   Arthur believed all actresses to be promiscuous and degenerate.

convict clerks, who avoided hard labour and, he believed, were lazy, dishonest and "usually confirmed drunkards".

The new lieutenant-governor believed convicts had it too easy. He introduced longer convict work hours to instil industry and encourage reformation. He adopted a broken-windows approach to law enforcement 165 years before New York did, with minor crimes attracting harsh punishment. Arthur explained, "if the minutest Regulation be not observed, the most extensive mischief must follow to a measure of great national importance."

The naughtiest convicts were sent to Macquarie Harbour, Van Diemen's Land's first and, at the time of Arthur's arrival, only penal station. Australia's answer to Alcatraz operated between 1822 and 1834 on Macquarie Harbour's Sarah Island, off Tasmania's uninhabited (except by Aborigines) west coast. The 300 kilometre sea voyage from Hobart took an average of twenty-seven days and up to three months when the weather was particularly foul (it rained on Sarah Island ten months a year). Ships travelling there had to sail through Hell's Gates, a name hinting that those who dared this treacherous channel risked more than just seasickness.

Sorell, who established the penal station, reported, "Prisoners upon trial declared that they would rather suffer death than be sent back alive to Macquarie Harbour. It is the feeling that I am most anxious to be kept alive." Arthur, nothing if not a traditionalist, was determined to uphold Sorell's vision.

The station was so crowded that inmates were unable to sleep on their backs. Malnutrition, dysentery and scurvy were constant companions. Inmates' bodies were broken with a cat-o'-nine-tails three times heavier than the one employed in Hobart, with leather cords that were dipped in salt water and dragged through sand every five strokes.[8]

---

8 Flogging victims were commonly rubbed with salt and lemon to protect them from infection. Anybody who has ever made salad dressing while suffering a paper cut will appreciate this was more painful than the flogging itself. The term *flogged*

Their spirits were broken with solitary confinement on nearby Grummet Island, backbreaking work and sheer, bloody monotony.

Of the eighty-eight convicts who met their end on Sarah Island, only thirty-five died of natural causes. Twenty-seven drowned, eight were killed accidentally and eighteen were killed deliberately (three were shot by guards, three were executed and twelve were murdered by their fellow inmates). The dead were buried on a nearby cemetery isle that a wag named Holiday Island.

The surveyor who mapped Sarah Island concluded that the chances of escape were "next to impossible". This did not stop the inmates from trying. George Clay, Steven Toole and William Humpage made a boat out of a toilet and a couple of water casks, escaping about four miles before drowning. Of the 116 prisoners who absconded from Sarah Island between 3 January 1822 and 16 May 1827, only fifteen survived. Some of those who, against the odds, succeeded took to the high seas.[9]

Others reignited the bushranger flame that had all but sputtered out following the execution of Michael Howe. As there were no nearby farmsteads or shepherds' huts to raid, this second generation of bushrangers grew hungry ...

---

with a wet lettuce, used to describe a soft punishment, is grossly misleading if the lettuce is wet with lemon dressing.

9   Sarah Island, using convict labour, was for a time the largest shipyard in the Australian colonies. The authorities did not appear to consider the impact that training convicts to build boats would have on Sarah Island's inescapability. The last ten convicts at Sarah Island commandeered the ship they had been building, the *Frederick*, after John Barker, a convict blacksmith, manufactured a tomahawk and two pistols, which were considerably more effective than the usual sharpened toothbrush. The *Frederick* escapees, led by James Porter, sailed to Chile. After Arthur arranged the extradition of four convicts residing there, Porter ran an effective public sympathy campaign, largely built around the escapees' kind treatment of Tom, the *Frederick*'s cat. Porter successfully appealed a piracy conviction on the grounds that: (a) the *Frederick* was seized in a harbour and piracy could only be committed on the high seas; and (b) the *Frederick* had not been registered and therefore was not legally a ship, just some nailed together bits of wood that floated and housed a not-ship's cat. Porter later escaped to New Zealand and was never seen again, his story appropriated by Marcus Clarke in *For the Term of His Natural Life*.

I EAT CANNIBALS

Alexander Pearce was a twinkle-eyed Irishman of twenty-eight summers when transported to Van Diemen's Land for stealing twelve shoes. At a leprechaunish 160 centimetres, with a slight build, Alexander's peers would have laughed if told he would gain notoriety as Tasmania's most infamous killer.[10]

Pearce had the instincts of Houdini and the enthusiastic incompetence of the guy played by Steve McQueen in *The Great Escape*. While he could be relied upon to undo his shackles and leg it while no one was looking, his escape skills were counterbalanced by a remarkable talent for recapture. His early efforts at absconding earned him a ticket through Hell's Gates.

Pearce and seven accomplices escaped from Sarah Island in 1822, picking up an axe and cook pot on the way. Five of the escapees would come to regret their choice of baggage. Alexander Dalton, the first of the escapees to be eaten, was axed in his sleep and cook-potted by the escapees' self-appointed leader, Robert Greenhill. Edward Brown and William Kennerly, worried that they'd been cast to play main and dessert to Dalton's entrée, escaped the next morning with the pot. The loss did not deter their erstwhile companions from dreaming up exciting new recipes for each other.

When the escapees ran out of Dalton, they agreed to choose their next meal by lot. Thomas Bodenham drew the short straw and was permitted to pray before he was eaten, allowing his companions to skip straight to the meal without saying grace. John Mather and Matthew Travers were the next courses in this Tasmanian degustation.[11] Pearce and Greenhill, who now had only the axe for company,

---

10   Martin Bryant took Pearce's title in 1996. At the age Pearce was misappropriating footwear, Bryant shot dead thirty-five and wounded twenty-three visitors to Port Arthur, the penal station that replaced Macquarie Harbour.

11   Both courses would have been perfectly complemented by a nice chianti.

spent their remaining time together eyeing each other suspiciously, licking their lips and trying very, very hard not to fall asleep. When Greenhill finally closed his eyes for a moment, Pearce had enough food to complete the long walk back to the settled districts.

Pearce was found in the company of two sheep thieves 113 days after his escape. The thieves were hanged but Reverend Knopwood, the local magistrate, told Pearce to pull the other one when he confessed to eating his fellow escapees. Pearce was sent back to Sarah Island and told to go easy on the escaping for a while.

Pearce did not heed this advice. On his final escape, he was joined by the young Thomas Cox, who served as both companion and takeaway. Pearce again thoughtfully packed an axe, but this time also managed to make off with some biscuits. This didn't stop him from cooking and consuming Cox, bits of whom were found in Pearce's pockets after he handed himself in to the authorities. The other bits of Cox, minus his hands, head, and the slices of buttock, thigh and calf that Pearce had already devoured, were found hanging upside down from a tree.

Alexander Pearce was hanged in Hobart Town Gaol at 9 a.m. on 19 July 1824, his body given to anatomists to dissect and his skull given to phrenologists to fondle.[12] His last reported words were, "Man's flesh is delicious. It tastes far better than fish or pork."[13]

---

12 Phrenology was a popular "science" developed in 1796 by the eminent German skull-fondler Franz Joseph Gall. Phrenologists, who believed that a skull's bumps and indentations determined personality type, intellect and behaviour, collected the skulls of many bushrangers and other condemned criminals to study the links between skull shape and types of criminal behaviour. They would embarrass themselves at parties by saying things to the host like, "You have the occipital ridge of a rapist," or "Your prominent jaw suggests you would enjoy the taste of human flesh. I'll pass on the *hors-d'oeuvre*."

13 This is at odds with the earlier account of Robert Greenhill, who encouraged his fellow escapees to expand their culinary horizons by advising them, "It tastes very like pork." This may be the reason that the second man to successfully escape Sarah Island, Mordecai Cohen, did not try the other white meat.

The Alexander diet was adopted by other Tasmanian escapees.[14] Messrs Broughton and Macavoy were hanged in 1829 for eating Patrick Fagan, Mr Coventry and the evocatively named Richard "Up and Down Dick" Hutchinson. Thomas Jeffries cut an accomplice into steaks, which he fried up with mutton, during a three-week sex-offending, baby-murdering, cop-killing, man-eating spree.

The sensationalist British press feasted upon the cannibal capers of Pearce and co. Charles Dickens included cannibal convicts in *Bleak House*, while the escaped prisoner in *Great Expectations*, Abel Magwitch, threatened to roast and eat the heart and liver of young Pip.[15] None of this did anything to enhance Van Diemen's Land's reputation.

RABBIT AND MOSQUITO

The Tasmanian Aborigines had been shot, kidnapped, raped, enslaved and infected with new diseases. Their children had been stolen and their kangaroos smothered with gravy and turned into hats. And now they were being moved off their traditional lands.

Although only 3 per cent of Van Diemen's Land was subject to land grants in 1823, other areas were inhabited by frontiersmen who cared little for city folk and their fancy title deeds. Arthur assigned more than a million acres of prime Aboriginal hunting ground over the next eight years as the European population doubled, believing that the natives could continue to do whatever natives do in the island's "wild, unproductive, impervious ringed mountains and dense forest".

---

14   The Alexander diet is not to be confused with the Atkins Diet, although both are low in carbohydrates and high in protein. Alexander's recipes should also not be confused with those of Stephanie Alexander, who uses more crème fraîche.

15   Dickens took a great interest in the Australian colonies. *Great Expectations'* Miss Havisham, who wore her bridal dress for life and left her wedding cake to rot on the table after being jilted at the altar, was inspired by Sydney's Eliza Emily Donnithorne, who did likewise. You can visit Eliza's grave at Camperdown Cemetery. It's a fun day out.

The new settlers, unlike the convict backwoodsmen who pre-
ceded them, built permanent homes, planted crops, erected fences
and imported vast herds and flocks. They considered the migratory
Aborigines who crossed their lands a threat to property and safety
and were grateful that the law allowed such threats to be terminated
with extreme prejudice.

The settlers also brought new pests. A rat plague was reported in
1816, and in the same year Reverend Knopwood sighted rabbits, which
soon became "troublesome and mischievous" and went lippity-lippity
all over the island's burgeoning farmlands.[16] But the rabbit was only
a minor inconvenience. The real pest was Mosquito.

The Aboriginal tracker, furious that his promised return to Sydney
after the capture of Michael Howe had not eventuated, joined forces
with Black Jack, a native Tasmanian, and members of the Oyster Bay
tribe. This group was blamed for attacks on settlers during 1823 and 1824.

Mosquito, dubbed The Black Napoleon, is said to have taught
tribal Aborigines tactics for fighting men with firearms (i.e. wait for
them to shoot at you and then spear them before they can reload).
For some he was an Aboriginal resistance leader and for others, like
Windschuttle, he was just another bushranger.

Mosquito was eventually shot and captured by another Aboriginal youth, Tegg, who was promised a pine boat for his efforts but, in
true promise-made-to-black-man style, received a sad affair made

---

16   As Mr McGregor would testify, rabbits are a bloody pest and the guy who wrote
     Watership Down needs his head checked. Mainland Australia remained free of wild
     rabbits until 1859, when Thomas Austin decided he needed something small and
     furry to shoot on his Victorian estate. The next decade saw the fastest-recorded
     spread of a mammal anywhere in the world, with bunny plagues wreaking
     havoc on the Australian environment for the next century. In 1907, Western
     Australia built the world's longest fence (1,833 kilometres) to keep rabbits out of
     its farmlands. The fence was originally three feet high and six inches deep, with
     the designers apparently unaware that rabbits can burrow and jump. Although
     myxomatosis and rabbit haemorrhagic disease have reduced Australian rabbit
     populations, there are still hundreds of millions of the little buggers and not nearly
     enough pies to put them all in.

of stringybark. The disgusted Tegg turned bushranger and swore to kill any white man who came near him.

Mosquito and Black Jack were the first Aborigines to be tried and executed in Van Diemen's Land. Until their 1825 conviction, Aborigines had been excluded from the courts on the grounds that they were incapable of distinguishing good from evil. While the justice system now permitted them to be tried and hanged, their unchristianity precluded them from swearing to tell the truth, thus preventing them from briefing counsel, calling witnesses or speaking in their own defence.[17]

When sentenced to hang, Mosquito said, "Hanging no bloody good for a blackfellow." After his gaoler inquired, "Why not good for blackfellow as for whitefellow?" Mosquito quipped, "Oh, very good for whitefellow, he used to it."

When two other Aboriginal men, Jack and Dick, were hanged for murder in 1826, Arthur announced that the executions were intended "not only to Prevent the Commission of similar Atrocities by the Aborigines, but to induce towards them the Observance of a conciliatory line of Conduct".

Hanging Aborigines, surprisingly, did not have the desired conciliatory effect. Henry Melville, in his 1836 *History of Van Diemen's Land*, suggested it might be more conciliatory to prosecute and hang a few white settlers who had murdered Aborigines, lamenting, "not one single individual was ever brought to a Court of Justice for offences against these harmless creatures".

---

17   Daniel Moowattin, in 1816, was the first Aboriginal man to be tried and hanged in Australia. Daniel had been adopted by New South Wales' hangman, Richard Partridge (a.k.a. The Left Handed Flogger), and helped botanists to collect seeds and flowers before he himself was collected by the greatest botanist of them all, Sir Joseph Banks, who paid for Moowattin's upkeep in London and showed him off to all his posh chums. Moowattin returned to New South Wales and was charged with the rape and robbery of Hannah Russell. Samuel Marsden testified that his hanging around hangmen, botanists and chinless wonders meant that he could distinguish good from evil and therefore die at the end of a rope as a civilised man.

Mosquito is regarded by many as the harbinger of, in the words of historian Henry Reynolds, "the biggest internal threat that Australia has ever had" – the Black War.

But that's another story ...

BATMAN AND THE JOKER

Arthur had few concerns about the restive natives. He had a far bigger problem. The bushrangers were back.

Matthew Brady was, according to historian James Bonwick in one of his Mills & Boon moments, "tall, robust and handsome, capable of the most withering sneer, or winning smile" and "formed by nature for the control of man and the conquest of woman".

The Prince of Bushrangers, as Brady was known by his many admirers, was a far more dangerous proposition than his cannibal peers, who spent most of their time eating each other, rather than terrorising the general populace.

Brady and fourteen other Macquarie Harbour convicts escaped in a whaleboat in June 1824 and embarked on a two-year rampage through the settled districts. Brady's unfailingly polite manner and his habit of forcing wealthy settlers to wait on their servants while he was raiding their houses endeared him to the masses. His activities depressed Vandemonian immigration and seriously worried Arthur, who had a second bushranger emergency on his hands.

Arthur, like Grace Kelly, believed that "it takes a thief to catch a thief". He appointed "the best conducted prisoners" to his new police force, offering a pardon for continued good service. The felon police were designed to destroy convict unity, with Arthur reporting, "the employment of these convicts had a most powerful effect on suppressing bushranging by creating distrust and division."

Arthur also encouraged private citizens to turn vigilante in the vendetta versus the vile villains who vainly envisioned Vandemonian vanquishment. When good Tasmanians huddled together in fear; when danger stalked the streets of Launceston; when there was trouble in Hobart City – Arthur called Batman.

John Batman didn't live in a stately manor, employ a superannuated butler or play dress-ups with wards of the state in a secret cave, but this didn't prevent him from becoming Tasmania's leading vigilante. The Sydney-born Batman started his crusade against crime when he reported a blacksmith – his boss – for burglary. The blacksmith was hanged and Batman was out of a job, proving that crime fighting doesn't pay.

Batman moved to Van Diemen's Land, fell in love with a distributor of dodgy banknotes[18] and became a successful farmer who hunted bushrangers in his spare time. Putting bushrangers away didn't just leave Batman with the quiet satisfaction of bringing evildoers to justice, it also left him with a healthy bank balance, thanks to the contracts Arthur took out on enemies of the state.[19]

When Arthur offered £25, twenty gallons of rum and a conditional pardon for Brady's death or capture, the Prince of Bushrangers responded with his own bounty notice:

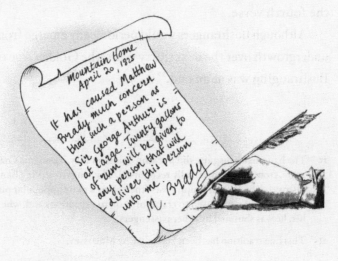

---

18   Vigilantes are allowed a female criminal love interest. Just look at Catwoman.

19   OK, crime fighting does pay sometimes.

But the felon police and Batman were whittling down the joker's gang. After Brady was shot in the leg, Batman hunted down the wounded outlaw and called on him to surrender. Brady handed himself in, but was furious to be placed in a cell with the despicable Thomas Jeffries. His anger grew when he and three of his men mounted the gallows to be hanged with the man-eating baby-killer. Why couldn't he be hanged with a sensitive poet, a fallen clergyman, or one of the promiscuous young actresses Arthur so despised?

Tasmanian hangings had a pantomime air about them. It was traditional for the hangman to wear a false beard, blackened face and/or hood, while wags in the crowd shouted amusing things like "Behind you!"[20] The audience would break into song if they liked the condemned. Sometimes those on the scaffold would join in, although not for long. In Britain, professional balladeers would sell individually tailored dirges to the crowd.[21] Tasmania, though, had a dearth of professional lyricists, so the mobs of Hobart and Launceston made do with "The Song of Death", a cheery standard. Matthew Brady and his accomplices were dangling by the end of the fourth verse.

Although bushrangers would periodically emerge from the island's undergrowth over the next thirty years, the Golden Age of Tasmanian Bushranging was at an end.[22]

---

20   The hangman's disguise did not stop Solomon Blay, Tasmania's hangman for fifty years, from being universally recognised. The longest-serving hangman in the history of the British Empire was "the colony's most unpopular public servant". Coachmen often refused to transport him to executions and, when he obtained a lift, he was shunned by other passengers.

21   This fine tradition has been kept alive by Morrissey.

22   Later Tasmanian bushrangers were generally an insipid lot. William Westwood was so respectful to his victims that he was known as the Gentleman Bushranger, while Daniel Priest was known as the Friendly Bushranger on account of his "almost unparalleled mildness and kindness towards persons with whom he came into collision in pursuit of his lawless career".

MY SEALSKIN BRINGS ALL THE BOYS TO THE YARD

Arthur, while hunting bushrangers on land, also turned his attention to the "aquatic bushrangers", as Sydney businessman W. Stewart called the sealers.[23] In 1826, the Balfour Commission into Bass Strait's fisheries reported that the strait's many small islands:

> ... provide constant Shelter and secure retreat for runaways, and villains of the worst description. Almost every Rock throughout the Straits has become the habitation of some one or more accurately the most desperate and lawless of mankind ... The whole of the Straits seem to present one continued scene of Violence, Plunder, and the commission of every species of Crime.

The life of Moorina, Truganini's sister, was a case in point. She was abducted by sealers and sold to an American, John Anderson (a.k.a. Abyssinia Jack), and lived with him, and later James Everett (a.k.a. Hepthernet), on Kangaroo Island.[24] The Kaurna people of nearby South Australia know Kangaroo Island as Karta, the same word they use for female genitalia, which gives you a pretty good idea of what happened to many of the kidnapped women taken there. Moorina was later shipped out to an island in Bass Strait, where she was shot by the sealer Robert Gamble (a.k.a. Bob).[25]

Moorina's story was by no means unique. Abduction, known as "gin-raiding", became the norm after the sealers in Bass Strait confirmed that their abductees' angry husbands and fathers hadn't yet got around to inventing rafts or canoes capable of following them.

---

23 While Arthur had Batman to help him deal with terrestrial bushrangers, there was no Tasmanian Aquaman to help him crack down on their maritime counterparts.

24 Aspiring DJs could do worse than borrow the stage name of a nineteenth-century Bass Strait or Kangaroo Island sealer. Other sealers went by Longtom, Little West, Big Mouth, Piebald and Fireball.

25 OK, his pseudonym needed some work.

The sealers had cut out the middleman, shooting and wounding Mannalargenna, who'd once kidnapped women for them, abducting his sister and three of his daughters.

Several hundred Tasmanian Aborigines were abducted or killed between 1810 and 1832, with girls as young as eight stolen. Captain James Kelly testified to the Balfour Commission that "every man has from two to five of these women for his own use". And useful they were. The sealer James Munro recalled:

> When the black women were first brought over from the main, they were intended principally to gratify the sealers, but ... on one occasion the sealers ... found on their return a quantity of kangaroo which the black women had caught, at sight of which the sealers resolved to make them hunt in the future.

The women did more than just hunt. They cured sealskins, crewed boats, dived for shellfish, dug muttonbirds from their burrows, grew and harvested crops, cooked, cleaned, and mended clothes. In 1832, the Quaker missionaries James Backhouse and George Washington Walker inquired into the lives of Aboriginal women living with sealers, concluding that most were slaves.[26]

Most of the women were stripped of their very names.[27] Moorina was dubbed Kit, but many women were given seriously ghetto

---

26 The Quakers, unlike Arthur and his fellow Calvinists, were driven by the belief that "faith by itself, if it is not accompanied by action, is dead" (*James 2:17*). They testified their faith by actively opposing slavery, capital punishment, participation in war, the consumption of alcohol, and gambling. Their belief that all people were equal meant they opposed the use of titles, the payment of tithes, bowing and hat honour (the doffing of one's hat as a sign of deference). They rejected priests for the same reason, believing that all people experienced a direct and personal relationship with God. Quakers also believed in money and chocolate, founding Barclays and Lloyds banks and Britain's three largest confectioners, Cadbury, Rowntree and Fry's.

27 Although, in fairness to the sealers, if you can say Nickerumpowwerrerter, Pollerwotteltelterrunner, Toogernuppertootenner, Woreterleepoodyenniner or Woreterneemmerunnertatteyanne without drinking at least ten beers, you're doing a bloody good job.

monikers – Mother Brown, Black Judy, Little Buck, Blind Poll, New
Maria, Peacock, Jumbo, Cush and Smoker.[28]

These women were all too often the victims of violence. James
Everett murdered Worethmaleyerpodeyer because she did not clean
muttonbirds to his satisfaction. Henry Walter Parker wrote in *The
Rise, Progress, and Present State of Van Diemen's Land*, an 1833 publication
designed to encourage Tasmanian immigration:

> Harrington, a sealer, procured ten or fifteen native women, and
> placed them on different islands in Bass's Straits, where he left
> them to procure skins; if, however, when he returned, they had not
> obtained enough, he punished them by tying them up to trees for
> twenty-four to thirty-six hours together, flogging them at intervals,
> and he killed them not infrequently if they proved stubborn.[29]

Yet genuine partnerships between sealers and Aboriginal women also
formed amid the carnage, with James Bonwick recounting that some
women "proved faithful and affectionate to their new husbands" and
did not wish to return to their "native tribe".

Whatever the origins and eventual nature of the relationships
between the sealers and the Tasmanian Aboriginal women who lived
with them, history would prove these women to be more fortunate
than those left behind on the Tasmanian mainland.

THE CORRECTIONS

With Brady dead and bushranging quelled, Arthur was determined
to crack down on anyone from the lower classes who'd supported
the bushrangers. And so began a two-year hanging spree, with 123

---

28 God knows what the sealers who renamed their women Duncan and Towser
    were into.

29 This and the "Come See a Headless Bushranger Rotting in a Cage" campaign for
    newly arrived immigrants confirm that marketing was not a Tasmanian strong suit.

Vandemonians left dangling in 1826–27, a rate of execution never
seen before or since in Australia. The bodies of the condemned were
left to dangle for a month, to rot and be eaten by Tasmanian wildlife
pleasantly surprised to find the boot on the other foot for once.

The mass hangings were not so much designed to punish offenders
as to shock and awe the Tasmanian people into submission.

Arthur was drawn to the thinking of Elizabeth Fry, England's
favourite Quaker and most famous prison reformer, who preached
criminal reformation through industry, education, Bible study and
humility. But Arthur's approach had a sterner tone. He wrote to
Macquarie Harbour's commandant:

> Unceasing labour, total deprivation of Spirits, Tobacco and Com-
> forts of any kind, the sameness of occupation, the dreariness of
> situation must, if anything will, reform the vicious characters who
> are sent to you.

Arthur introduced chain gangs, increased the weight and shortened
the length of leg-irons to punish bad behaviour, and brought in convict
clothing designed to humiliate and inflict pain, from trousers that
buttoned up the inside of the leg, reducing the wearer to an infant-
like state, to punishment shoes with nails on the inside and holes at
the ankle to encourage the leg-iron's chafe.

Arthur advised the War and Colonial Office that convicts "should
be kept rigidly at the spade and pick-axe and wheel-barrow ... from
morning till night, although the immediate toil of the convicts be
the only beneficial result of their labour".

The Bridgewater Causeway was the zenith of Arthur's Sisyphean
punishment regime. Over 200 chain gangers laboured to build a bridge
across the Derwent, hand quarrying over two million tonnes of stone and
fill. However, the stones placed in the deepest part of the river sank in
the mud or were washed away, leaving each day's work no further along
than the last. The unfinished bridge was abandoned after seven years.

The man in black developed a carefully graded system of punishments: reprimand, the treadwheel, hard labour by day and solitary confinement by night, solitary confinement on bread and water, hard labour on the roads, flogging, labouring in a chain gang, confinement at a penal station, and execution.

While very much a stick man, Arthur occasionally brandished the carrot, particularly for convicts who informed on their peers. Good behaviour might be rewarded with a ticket-of-leave, allowing convicts who continued to play nice to live independently and earn wages.

Arthur established the British Empire's first juvenile prison at Point Puer (*puer* being Latin for "boy"). Housing more than 3,000 boys between 1834 and 1849, Point Puer focused on education, religious instruction, trade skills and casual brutality, the latter administered by the Port Arthur convicts who guarded the boys.[30]

Placing boys in the care of these inmates, the British Empire's most hardened criminals, was perhaps not Arthur's smartest move. Port Arthur, which succeeded Macquarie Harbour as Van Diemen's Land's leading penal station in 1833, was noted for its cruelty and violence.

Arthur located Port Arthur on the Tasman Peninsula because it was close to Hobart yet considered inescapable, being connected to the Tasmanian mainland by the 46-metre-wide Eaglehawk Neck.

The Neck's defences were worthy of a James Bond supervillain. The narrow isthmus was covered in mantraps and guarded by soldiers and half-starved giant hounds known as the Lions, which had macho names like Caesar, Ajax, Pompey and Achilles. It was lit by whale-oil lamps at night, its paths covered with seashells that made crunchy sounds when trodden on by escaping convicts. Offal was hurled into the Neck's waters to attract sharks and repel convicts. Dogs stationed on floating platforms would bark if they sighted a swimmer.

---

30 Well-behaved convicts were appointed as prison guards in Tasmania. They were known as "javelin men" for their long poles, each fitted with an axe blade, spike or hook for catching, impaling or hacking to death unruly prisoners. The Tasmanian javelin man Isaac Solomon inspired the character of Fagan in Dickens' *Oliver Twist*.

George "Billy" Hunt attempted to hop across the Neck disguised as a kangaroo. His marsupial impersonation was so convincing that he was targeted by hungry guards, but he surrendered when the warders lined him up in their sights. William Westwood's two partners in escape were eaten by sharks. John Mortlock, attempting to swim past the dogs disguised as floating kelp, was detected when a wave dislodged his seaweed. Martin Cash successfully swam the Neck, carrying his clothes on his head – his garments were washed away and he began his bushranging career naked.

Convict shipbuilders secretly worked on escape craft, which were collected by Commandant Booth, who proudly displayed them on his verandah. A recaptured escapee claimed to have escaped in a canoe that he'd built in an hour. Booth refused to believe this and offered the convict a discount to his sentence if he could replicate the feat. The convict whipped up a kayak and paddled it around the Isle of the Dead, as Port Arthur's cemetery island was known. He got his discount and Booth got a boat for his collection.

Arthur applied the same harsh physical punishments he'd applied at Macquarie Harbour, but Port Arthur later became infamous for being Australia's first Model Prison, the logical endpoint of the reformation through psychological punishment philosophy of Elizabeth Fry. Convicts in Port Arthur's Separate Prison, built in 1850, were under almost constant surveillance and put in solitary confinement. They were not allowed to talk, were hooded when taken from their cells and were placed in individual stalls when they attended chapel so they couldn't see other prisoners. This was an Australian Abu Ghraib.

Arthur would have approved.

FRY, FACTORIES & THE FLASH MOB

Arthur, being a gentleman, treated lady convicts differently – and he had a lot of them; from the mid-1820s, more female criminals were sent to Van Diemen's Land than to New South Wales.

In 1823, Elizabeth Fry provided plans for a female factory in Hobart, to replace the makeshift one built by Sorell. Arthur built the Cascades Female Factory on the site of an old rum distillery in 1828 and used Sorell's stopgap women's prison to store rum – alcohol and women being inextricably linked in Arthur's mind as agents of sin.

The female factories served as holding depots for recently arrived female convicts, those too unruly to be assigned as servants, and those between assignments. They were also places of punishment for women who committed offences within the colonies. The inmates were instructed in religion, did the settlers' laundry, spun wool, sewed, and made shoes.

For women who could not be assigned, escape was an attractive option. Catherine Henrys, an Irish lifer, escaped from Cascades in 1841 dressed in men's clothing and continued to conceal her gender, finding work as a timber splitter. After she was recaptured, she again escaped, this time using a sharpened spoon to cut through her cell's bars and a rope made from blankets to scale the factory's wall. Other women escaped the factories through marriage.

The factories were the nineteenth-century equivalent of RSVP, with eager male settlers and convicts attending to inspect women who would "rank up" in the hope of being chosen as a bride.

James Mudie, a slightly unhinged Scotsman who'd served as a magistrate, explained how the arranged marriages came about:

> The convict goes and looks at the women, and if he sees a lady that takes his fancy, he makes a motion to her, and she steps on one side; some will not, but stand still, and have no wish to be married, but this is rare.

The New South Wales barrister Roger Therry described how an aspiring groom would travel to the factory and choose his bride in a day, court and marry her the next, and take her home on the third. Some of these unconventional marriages were politely ignored by

FIG. 3: THE FARMER WANTS A WIFE.

government. Others were state-sanctioned, with the Reverend Samuel
Marsden advertising in the 1832 *New South Wales Government Gazette*
for applications to marry Parramatta Female Factory convicts.

Other arrangements were more Tinder than RSVP, with inmates
hooking up for alcohol, tobacco and other goods not permitted in
the factory. It also took a surprisingly long time for some convicted
women to reach their factories, with the *Independent* reporting:

> The disgraceful scenes which have been carried on by the parties con-
> ducting the females to and from George Town ... numbers of females
> sent for punishment to the factory at that place who have been weeks
> and weeks on the way, stopping at almost every hut and cabin of the
> government sawyers, and remaining till satisfied with debauchery ...

Fry proposed a system where a woman's deportment in the factory
determined her privileges and recommended that poorly behaved

convicts have their heads shaved to humiliate them into reformation. Other recommended punishments included reduced rations,
solitary confinement, hard labour and labelling (e.g. wearing a sign
that read "Blasphemer").

Arthur enthusiastically embraced the concepts of head shaving
and solitary confinement, with 100 solo cells completed in 1832. Quite
naughty women were placed in light cells, small solitary rooms with
enough natural light for them to unpick ships' ropes, which was
finger-splitting labour. Very naughty women were locked up alone
in completely dark cells.

Arthur incarcerated unmarried pregnant convicts, believing
this would discourage single women from having sex. He effectively
criminalised childbirth out of wedlock for convict women, leading
to an increase in abortions and infanticide.[31]

Arthur was concerned for the future of bastard babies, writing
that "the colony is overrun with illegitimate children ... born to no
certain provision of inheritance but the vices of their parents and
consequent misery." His solution was to separate these children from
their mothers, creating a white Stolen Generation.

The children were removed at about nine months of age and
cared for in female factory nurseries, where their mothers might visit
them once a month. When old enough, they were sent to the Orphan
School, where their mothers were permitted to visit four times a year
for three hours at a stretch.

Arthur visited Cascades in 1832 and found the children's bedding
"quite black with fleas". Poor nutrition, overcrowding, damp and

---

31   Mary McLauchlan left her five- and three-year-old daughters in Scotland after
      confessing to a theft that was probably committed by her husband. She was
      assigned as a servant and soon fell pregnant, resulting in her incarceration in a
      female factory. She was convicted of infanticide after her newborn baby was found
      dead in a factory toilet and, despite protesting that the baby had died in childbirth,
      was sentenced to hang. Arthur refused Mary clemency because she refused to
      admit her guilt. Mary was the first woman hanged in Tasmania, her corpse given
      to the Colonial Hospital and dissected in front of an invited audience.

neglect meant Tasmania's female factories had a much higher infant mortality rate than the general population, with 40 of 103 factory infants dying in 1833.

Adult mortality rates were also high. Cascades was set in a cold, wet valley that didn't see the sun in winter, cells were damp, bedding soaked, and increasing numbers of female convicts meant it was constantly overcrowded.

A group of unruly and sometimes violent women called the Flash Mob preferred to stay with each other in the factory, rather than work towards assignment. They wore fancy dresses, smuggled contraband goods, bullied other inmates, swore, sung bawdy songs and had lots of lesbian sex – all very *Prisoner: Cell Block H*.[32]

The Flash Mob were suspected of instigating riots.[33] Riots were triggered by head shavings, inadequate rations, the confiscation of contraband, and other slights and niggles common to prison life. The Reverend William Bedford, known to the Cascades inmates as "Hollie Willie" on account of his interminable moralising, was the victim of one such riot:

> As he was crossing the courtyard of the Female House of Correction, some dozen or twenty women seized upon him, took off his trousers and deliberately endeavoured to deprive him of his manhood. They were, however, unable to effect their purpose in consequence of the opportune arrival of a few constables who seized the fair ladies and placed them in durance vile.

The most Australian of protests took place in 1838, when Arthur's successor, Lieutenant-Governor Sir John Franklin, visited Cascades.

---

32 Robert Hughes, who liked his history hot and steamy, wrote in *The Fatal Shore* that Cascades "swarmed with lesbians". Australia has suffered from swarms of locusts, rabbits, mice and cane toads, as well as lesbians.

33 Today, flash mobs assemble in public places to perform wacky dance routines or engage in other pointless activities before dispersing, rather than rioting or making you their prison bitch. Life is safer today, but a lot less interesting.

Franklin, Matthew Flinders' nephew by marriage and Britain's leading Arctic explorer, was known as "the man who ate his boots" for
gnawing on his own shoes during his ill-fated 1819–22 attempt to
find the fabled Northwest Passage connecting the northern Pacific
and Atlantic oceans. He is also believed to have eaten a murdered
member of his exploration party, after being assured he was dining
on hare, partridge and wolf. Franklin's familiarity with freezing at
the arse end of the world and eating people made him ideal for the
Tasmanian posting.

Franklin was accompanied by his high-spirited and broad-minded
wife during his visit to Cascades.[34] The lieutenant-governor was
used to being treated with respect, but at Cascades he was treated to
Australia's first and greatest mass mooning. The event was described
in the only surviving browneyewitness account:

> The three hundred women turned right around and at one impulse
> pulled up their clothes showing their naked posteriors which they
> simultaneously smacked with their hands making a loud and not
> very musical noise.

You could lock the sisters up, but it was hard to keep them down.

---

34 Lady Jane Franklin was an enthusiastic tramper, being the first woman to climb
    Mount Wellington and to travel overland from Melbourne to Sydney and from
    Hobart to Macquarie Harbour. She attempted to rid Tasmania of snakes by
    offering a one-shilling bounty for every snake head delivered to her, which
    cost her £600 one year and 14,000 snakes their lives. She was instrumental in
    establishing Van Diemen's Land's Royal Society, the first such scientific body
    outside Britain, and funded a botanical garden and a natural history museum in a
    replica Greek temple, which was used to store apples after her departure. Sir John
    disappeared while again looking for the elusive Northwest Passage in 1847, and
    Lady Jane privately funded a seven-year search for him, which greatly advanced
    Arctic exploration. The search party established that Franklin had discovered the
    passage and frozen to death in it after his ship was locked in ice. Some of Franklin's
    crew lasted years before dying of botulism from eating seals, lead poisoning from
    eating food from lead tins, or cannibalism from being eaten by sailors who'd run
    out of seals and lead tins.

BIG BROTHER IS WATCHING YOU

Arthur's achievements in transforming convict life were unequal to his ambition. If he could not change the world, he would at least change Tasmania. And he would brook no interference from the island's growing middle class, who clamoured for freedom of the press, trial by jury, responsible government and other namby-pamby liberal reforms.

Arthur demanded that the free settlers stop whingeing about their rights and submit to his draconian rule. Those who had chosen to live in "an immense Gaol or Penitentiary" should "abide cheerfully by the rules and customs of the Prison", endure "the temporary sacrifice of many principles of law", and show Arthur "unquestioning obedience". Arthur was determined to turn Van Diemen's Land into the world's largest British public school – and those who dawdled on the way to class, wore their boaters at an inappropriately jaunty angle or showed their thingies to matron would feel the headmaster's wrath.

The lieutenant-governor sought to restrict access to the bush, as those on the frontier could not be effectively controlled. He required stock to be fenced, not only to preserve the purity of the new bloodlines of sheep that had made Tasmania a wool superpower, but also to limit the movements of stockmen and shepherds who would otherwise roam the wilds. He introduced the 1830 *Dog Act*, extending his influence over the hunters who relied on dogs for their survival. He imposed Van Diemen's Land's first domestic tax, the Dog Tax, to restrict dog ownership to the more respectable members of Vandemonian society. He required bush workers, like those who gathered wattlebark for Hobart's tanneries, to be licensed. Only the sealers, in the distant islands, escaped the creep of Arthurian regulation.

Arthur exerted an iron grip over his subjects by establishing the most policed state in the history of the world. Tasmania had one policeman for every eighty-eight people within a decade of Arthur's arrival, more than two-thirds of whom were serving convicts whose continuing freedom was Arthur's gift.

While most of the world's police forces were subject to local control, Arthur established a centralised system, where local police magistrates sent weekly reports to the chief police magistrate, who reported weekly to Arthur. Arthur sent orders down through this chain of command, directing which crimes should be targeted, what sentences should be imposed and which police should be hired or fired.

Police were originally paid in liquor, and later received wages that could generously be described as minimum. The *Launceston Advertiser* reported that no "honest" man could live on a constable's salary, which is why the average Hobart copper had a bigger brown paper bag collection than Terry Lewis.[35] Tasmanian police were also notorious for arresting people for trivial offences and launching false prosecutions, as prosecuting officers were entitled to a portion of the fines imposed by the courts.

The *Dog Act* allowed for fines of up to £25 for unsecured dogs, a sum far in excess of a constable's annual salary. Enterprising police officers like Constable Endger, known as "the dog-seizing constable", entrapped dogs by walking bitches down the street. This encouraged amorous male hounds to break their leads or escape from their masters' properties, with their masters given the option of prosecution or the payment of a £2 bribe. Constables also received a five-shilling bounty for killing dogs that savaged sheep, encouraging them to frame and then execute placid family pets.

Arthur outlawed selling spirits on Sundays, which encouraged undercover police to hang around hotels after church in the hope of entrapping the local publican. Pragmatic publicans simply put "traps", as police were colloquially known, on their payroll.

---

35   The disgraced former Queensland police commissioner collected $700,000 worth of brown paper bags and a fourteen-year prison term in 1991, becoming just the fourteenth person since the fourteenth century to be stripped of a British knighthood.

The free settlers came to adopt many of Arthur's social attitudes. The colony of swingers was now full of respectable prudes. Churches, once emptier than a lawyer's soul, now needed extra pews. And, while emancipated convicts held positions of influence in government and business in New South Wales, Tasmania's free settlers adopted the prejudices of their ruler.

Ex-convicts were excluded from Vandemonian society. The convict stain was not washed out by death, with Chaplain Philip Conolly, the first free Catholic priest in Van Diemen's Land, refusing a former convict's request to be buried in a vault above his free wife's grave. Convictism, like original sin and ginger hair, was passed down through the generations, with John Montagu, an Arthur favourite, expressing his disgust that Mrs Pedder, the wife of the chief justice, would lower herself to write to a woman whose grandfather was a convict.

Tasmania was the first Australian colony where people were encouraged to keep granny's convict skeleton in the closet, with its anti-convict prejudices slowly infecting the other colonies as transportation declined and immigration increased. Australians invented wonderful new family histories for themselves, claiming descent from French nobles, decorated war heroes, runaway actresses, or tiger-taming refugees of the Raj. Anyone but a convict.[36]

But if you think Arthur was hard on convicts, bushrangers, women, bastard children, slavers, poets, David Hume, lazy people, street-turtles, competitive walkers, actresses, smokers, dog owners and other degenerates, spare a thought for the Tasmanian Aborigines.

---

36 Convict ancestors, like flared trousers and handlebar moustaches, became fashionable in the 1970s.

4

Genocide is painless

*This is the first major nation in the history
of the world to have secured full independence
and sovereignty without killing anyone.*

Emeritus Professor Claudio Véliz, 9 December 2002

THE NUN'S PICNIC

EMERITUS PROFESSOR CLAUDIO VÉLIZ DROPPED THE above bombshell when launching Keith Windschuttle's *The Fabrication of Aboriginal History: Volume One: Van Diemen's Land 1803–1847*. As the assembled conservaratti harrumphed approvingly into their cognac balloons, Véliz followed up by likening the colonisation of Australia to "a nun's picnic".[1]

This is a perfectly reasonable comparison, at least for those picnics where Reverend Mother has filled the hamper with AK-47s, dropped a

---

1   The conservaratti flocked to Windschuttle because he helped them to feel "comfortable and relaxed" about their history, which is what the Australian prime minister, John Howard, told them they should feel in a 1996 speech that helped ignite the History Wars. Howard declared, "the balance sheet of our history is one of heroic achievement", urging those who nursed any qualms about the manner in which our nation's founders dealt with Indigenous Australians to have a Bex and a good lie-down. The prime minister accused those who refused this prescription of wearing "black armbands", a term he borrowed from historian Geoffrey Blainey, who was happy to loan it out indefinitely. It's always dangerous when politicians insist that a particular group of people wear armbands. It's only a matter of time until they start decorating them with yellow stars or pink triangles.

few roofies in the novices' thermos of sacramental wine and extended invitations to Attila the Hun, Ivan the Terrible and Rolf Harris.

Windschuttle, to his credit, acknowledges that someone might have been killed in the British settlement of Australia, but this would have been a vile aberration, at odds with the enlightened Christian policy of the British and colonial governments. He writes:

> In all colonial encounters with the New Worlds of the Americas and the Pacific, the colony of Van Diemen's Land ... was probably the site where the least indigenous blood of all was deliberately shed.

Windschuttle describes the "so-called 'Black War'" of 1824–31, in which at least 219 settlers and a disputed number of Aborigines were killed, as "a minor crime wave by two Europeanised black bushrangers [Mosquito and Black Jack] followed by an outbreak of robbery, assault and murder by tribal Aborigines".[2]

The Aborigines, according to Windschuttle, welcomed British occupation:

> Far from generating black resentment, the expansion of settlement instead gave the Aborigines more opportunity and more temptation to engage in robbery and murder, two customs they had come to relish.

The Tasmanian Aborigines did not want their land back, or people to stop abducting their women and children – "their principal objective was to acquire flour, tea, sugar and bedding, objects that to them were European luxury goods", giving a whole new meaning to the phrase,

---

2   Windschuttle suggests there were seventy-two Tasmanian Aboriginal deaths at the hands of the colonists between 1824 and 1831 "for which there is a plausible record of some kind", considerably fewer than the number of settlers killed during the non-conflict. Other historians, who recognise that Aborigines often refused to die in front of plausible record keepers and that plausible record keeping was, in any event, not always a priority (and indeed was an impediment to plausible deniability), estimate that up to 900 Aboriginal people (i.e. most of the remaining population) were killed.

"I'd murder for a cuppa and a good lie-down." The Aborigines should not be compared with the warrior Zulu, Māori or Cherokee, but to the crazed shopaholics who queue overnight for the Kmart mid-year sale.

As the Aborigines were not fighting for anything except cheap consumer goods, and tried to avoid fighting soldiers and other groups of large men who could shoot them, Windschuttle concludes they were not at war with the settlers – Arthur and many of his contemporaries had it wrong. The colonists were, however, at war with the Aborigines, as they were defending their lives, homes and Christian values, and didn't avoid fighting anyone. This was a one-sided war.[3]

THE OTHER VERSION ...

The other version is that the Tasmanian Aborigines had had enough, and bands of warriors, driven from their lands and near starvation, attacked homesteads, burned farms and crops, destroyed stock and killed (and occasionally tortured) settlers and their families.

The *Hobart Town Courier* reported in 1828 that the natives "have formed a systematic organised plan of carrying out a war of extermination against the white inhabitants of the colony". When many of your own people are agitating for genocide, it's a smart move to tar your enemy with the same brush first.[4]

Arthur's soldiers had little success in combatting the Aborigines,

---

3   One-sided wars, like the War on Terror, are fun because any enemy who engages you in combat is a non-combatant. Enemy non-combatants may safely be disappeared, kept in black hoods and have electrodes applied to their genitals, without your having to worry about the conventions of war or human decency. Those who engage in one-sided wars are the same sort of people who engage in one-sided sex acts.

4   Genocide requires the commission of certain acts "with intent to destroy, in whole or in part, a national, ethnical, racial or religious group". There is no doubt that relevant acts were intentionally committed against the Tasmanian Aborigines, but there is debate as to whether they were committed with an intent to destroy. Raphael Lemkin, the guy who coined the term in 1944, maintained that the Tasmanian Aborigines were victims of genocide. Was he right? Read on.

who launched their attacks from hilly and forested terrain. The Aborigines moved quickly and silently and were adept at covering their tracks and leaving false trails. Firearms were of limited effect in the forests and Tasmania's perpetual damp meant gunpowder often failed to fire. Still, guns were a damn sight more effective than the Aborigines' pointy sticks and wooden clubs.[5]

Convict and ex-convict trappers, hunters, shepherds and stock-men – men who were familiar with hardship and the bush – inflicted most of the Aboriginal casualties. These intrepid hunters of human game sometimes took Aboriginal body parts as trophies. Hugh Hull, a commissariat officer during the Black War, recalled that "one European had a pickle tub in which he put the ears of all the blacks he shot".

The brutal ear-pickling men of the frontier were the perfect scapegoats for Arthur's administration. Arthur wrote in 1830:

> That the lawless convicts who have, from time to time, absconded, together with the distant stock-keepers in the interior, and the sealers employed in remote parts of the coast, have from the earliest period, acted with great inhumanity towards the black Natives, particularly in seizing their women, there can be no doubt, and these outrages have, it is evident, first excited, what they were naturally calculated to produce in the minds of savages, the strongest feelings of hatred and revenge.

Forget the wealthy landowners who tolerated, and sometimes directed, attacks on Aborigines, or the colonial pen-pushers responsible for setting native policy – it was poor, violent, criminal scum who were to blame.

At first, Arthur was reluctant to pursue aggressive policies towards the first people of Van Diemen's Land. He wrote to Lord Goderich, secretary of state for war and the colonies, on 10 January 1828:

---

5   The unlucky (or lucky, depending on your perspective) James Cupid survived nine pointy stickings between 1826 and 1831. In Tasmania, Cupid was famous for his spears, not his arrows.

I cannot divest myself of the consideration that all aggression origi-
nated with the white inhabitants, and that therefore much ought to
be endured in return before the blacks are treated as an open and
accredited enemy by the government.[6]

But two of Arthur's policies later that year helped seal the Aborigines' fate. His April 1828 *Proclamation of Demarcation* stated that "the
coloured population should be induced by peaceful means to depart,
or should otherwise be expelled by force from the settled districts
therein", unless their leaders obtained passports. Magistrates were
ordered to "resort to whatever means a severe and inevitable necessity
may dictate and require" in enforcing this.

There were four main problems with the proclamation. First, the
use of the word *or* suggested that forceful expulsion was a perfectly
acceptable alternative to peaceful inducement. Second, neither the
colonists nor the Aborigines really knew where the settled districts
began and ended. Third, there was no plan to inform the Aborigines
of the proclamation. And fourth, nobody knew where a passport
could be obtained – Aborigines would presumably need to wander
deep into the settled territories without a passport in search of a clerk
capable of issuing one. The effect of the proclamation was to make
traditional migration a capital offence.

Six months later, Arthur proclaimed martial law on the basis
that "the outrages of the Aboriginal natives amount to a complete

---

6   Lord Goderich was actually prime minister at the time Arthur penned the letter,
     but resigned eleven days later, with his successor as colonial secretary, William
     Huskisson, reporting during Goderich's flailing premiership: "Poor Goderich is
     quite unnerved, and in a most pitiful state. Much of this misfortune is perhaps the
     natural effect of his character, but it is, in the present instance, greatly aggravated
     by the constant worry in which he has been kept by his all but crazy wife, and by
     the entire ascendancy which his good nature (not to say his weakness) has allowed
     her to assume." Goderich lost the confidence of King George IV, who described
     him as "a damned, sniveling, blubbering blockhead", which was quite a put-down
     from a monarch best known for low buffoonery. Goderich's 144-day premiership
     was the second shortest in British history.

declaration of hostilities against the settlers" and "Terror may have the effect which no proffered measures of conciliation have been capable of inducing." While the proclamation was meant to exclude many unsettled regions and stated that "bloodshed be checked as much as possible", the popular view was that it provided immunity for the killing of Aborigines.

The attorney-general advised Arthur not to prosecute Alfred Goldie, a Van Diemen's Land Company employee who'd shot an Aboriginal woman in the back and then hacked her to death with an axe in front of a six-year-old girl, as the natives were "open enemies to the King, in a state of actual warfare against him", which carried greater legal weight than the martial law provision that "defenceless women and children be invariably spared".

In 1829, George Frankland, the colony's surveyor-general, came up with the bright idea of publishing a proclamation that the Aborigines could understand. Frankland was described by an acquaintance as "a gentleman of the highest talents but without one atom of common sense", an assessment borne out by the comic-strip signboards he tied to trees during his survey expeditions. James Bonwick described this wonderfully misguided PR campaign as "the expedition against the Aborigines on the principle of the Fine Arts".

Frankland's proclamation boards had four panels. The first depicted an Aboriginal man and white man embracing in easy camaraderie; an Aboriginal child and white child holding hands; and an Aboriginal woman and white woman nursing each other's babies. The second depicted a family of Aborigines meeting the governor, soldiers and a settler, with the governor and Aboriginal leader shaking hands. The third showed an Aboriginal man spearing a settler and then being strung from a tree by a soldier, with the governor looking on appreciatively. The final panel depicts a settler shooting an Aborigine and then being strung from a tree by a soldier (over the Aborigine's still-bleeding corpse – a nice artistic touch), with the governor looking on appreciatively.

As Henry Melville noted in his 1836 *History of Van Diemen's Land*, the fourth panel was pure fantasy. The other three panels, apart from the picture of the white woman holding a nice black baby, also bore little relationship to Aboriginal reality.

Arthur, who believed every problem could be solved by the stroke of his pen, issued dozens of directives on the treatment of Aborigines. Some rebuked settlers for not suppressing Aboriginal violence more "vigorously", while simultaneously demanding they show greater kindness to the natives. Some played to the town liberals and British Evangelicals who clamoured for peaceful coexistence, while others pandered to the frontiersmen who sought government sanction for their attacks.

A correspondent to the *Launceston Advertiser* highlighted Arthur's mixed messaging, writing, "which of the 999 orders relative to them is it intended should be obeyed?" The genocidal settler George Hobler hit the nail on the head when he noted that Arthur's directions were of little concern to the men waging war on the frontier. He wrote, "our canting Gov^t contents itself with issuing proclamations which might as well be directed to the shark in Bass's Strait."

THE SAGA OF JØRGEN JØRGENSEN CØNTINUED

> Lo! Jørgen, Jørgen's son, yclept he
> Fought felle foe yn fjords of flaym
> Kyng-crowned he of darke dogge days
> Spyed Waterloo yr caught yn chayns
> Death cheated, Diemen bounde
> Shorne sheepe frend & savyge foe
> Blacke skynne roved & Blacke Lyne strode
> A Quynne tooke he yn Tasman's dawne
> & scrybed hys tayle 'fore death maske worne

With martial law in effect, six roving parties were formed to hunt and capture Aborigines venturing into the settled areas. Jørgen Jørgensen, who'd renamed himself Jorgen Jorgenson in an attempt to sound less Danish, was back in Van Diemen's Land and took command of one of them.

To say that Jørgensen had led a busy life since returning to Copenhagen in 1805 would be a gross understatement ...

In 1807, Britain was concerned that neutral Denmark-Norway was preparing to throw in its løt with the French. The Royal Navy bombarded Copenhagen with its new rockets, razed the city and seized the Scandinavian fleet.[7]

The Danes, who'd just got a hearty dose of what their ancestors had dished out to everyone else during the Viking Age, joined Team Napoleon. Jørgensen, who was a patriot when it suited him, took command of a privateer, the *Admiral Juul*, and set about hunting British ships.

The Danish livewire, with his usual hyperbole, claimed to have taken out "eight or nine" British vessels, although everyone else credited him with three. But then the *Admiral Juul* was captured by the HMS *Sappho*, the only ship in the history of the Royal Navy to be named after a Greek lesbian poet.[8] Jørgensen was taken to England as a prisoner of war.

The following year, while on parole, Jørgensen won £1,000 in a lottery and invested his winnings in a failed smuggling operation. In serious debt, he talked himself into an interpreter's job on a British trade expedition to the Danish protectorate of Iceland. Jørgensen, who was not a patriot when it suited him, convinced the British sailors to arrest the Danish governor, declared Iceland independent and

---

7   This was the first time in history that a state had stolen, rather than destroyed, the fleet of a defeated enemy. Confiscating the ships of a foe, as Russia did with Ukraine's Crimean fleet in 2014, is now known as *Copenhagenisation*, making Copenhagen famous for something other than pensive metal mermaids and 1970s porn.

8   The *Sappho* was named early in the Romantic era, in which melodramatic poetry, swooning, consumption, frilly shirts and unnatural love were in vogue among Britain's bohemian elite. The Royal Navy had been doing the frilly shirts and unnatural love thing for three centuries, so it's surprising that there were not actually more ships of the Classical Dyke class.

designed an Icelandic national flag (three codfish rampant on a blue background).[9] Jørgensen then installed himself as "His Excellency, the Protector of Iceland and the Commander of Sea and Land".

Backed up by a bodyguard of five Reykjavík heavies, Jørgensen travelled the island and issued orders to the confused populace that commenced with the regal words, "We, Jørgen Jørgensen". The Icelanders, excited by this injection of seemingly blue blood into their stagnant gene pool, renamed Jørgensen *Jörundur hundadagakonungur* (Jörundur the Dog Days King).[10]

Jørgensen's two-month reign ended when the Royal Navy turned up to see what had happened to the trade expedition and discovered, to its considerable surprise, that the expedition's convict interpreter was now king of an independent Iceland. The Royal Navy took Jørgensen back to Britain under armed guard and apologised to the Danes for any misunderstanding. The codfish flag was taken down and Iceland returned to Denmark-Norway's rule, but Jørgensen is still hailed as a hero of Icelandic independence.[11]

---

9   The Prime Minister's Office of Iceland speculates that Jørgensen's ensign may have been inspired by the flag designed by Eggert Ólafsson in 1752–54 (it takes a long time to design a flag in Iceland). Ólafsson's flag, commissioned by Sheriff Skúli Magnússon, was the symbol of Reykjavík's first industrial workshop and the ships *Friðriksósk* and *Friðriksgæfa* (i.e. most of the gross domestic product of eighteenth-century Iceland). It showed a split salted cod with the letters *PII*, which stood for Privileged Icelandic Interests. This sort of thing is always useful to know at dinner parties.

10   The Dog Days are the hottest and driest days of the Icelandic summer, the period of Jørgensen's short 1809 rule. The Dog Days coincide with Sirius, the Dog Star, rising in the northern hemisphere at the same time as the sun, as noted by the Greek poets Hesiod, Aratus and Homer. The Icelanders adapted the name to their local circumstances, explaining that this was the period during which local dogs ate grass ("possibly because they were in need of additional nutrients after the hard work of early summer, when dogs played an important role in herding sheep to their upland pastures") or which, in the west of the island, dolphins (known locally as fish-dogs) "had grown so fat ... that they could hardly see, and were easy to catch".

11   Full independence was finally achieved on 17 June 1944. Jørgensen's liberation of Iceland is celebrated in the popular Icelandic musical *Þið munið hann Jörund* (Remember Old Jörundur?).

On the voyage back to London, one of the ships in the naval convoy caught fire. Jørgensen, though a prisoner, directed the sailors on his ship to pull alongside the burning vessel, went aboard and rescued the passengers, including William Hooker, a famous botanical buddy of Sir Joseph Banks.

Upon his return to Britain, Jørgensen was imprisoned in a hulk full of Danish prisoners. These were dangerous years for Jørgensen, as Denmark-Norway, unimpressed with his conquest of Iceland, had declared him a traitor and put a price on his head. He went on a boozing and betting spree after his 1811 release, ending up in debtor's prison. Freed in 1815, his chutzpah, linguistic skills and capacity for double-dealing led to his recruitment as a British spy. He observed Napoleon's defeat at the Battle of Waterloo and spent two years playing baccarat and drinking martinis on the continent.

After leaving the secret service, Jørgensen embarked on a career as a writer and returned to alcoholism and gambling with Hemingwayesque enthusiasm. As writing, drinking and gambling are all notoriously unprofitable pursuits, the hard-up Dane pawned the sheets from a hotel bed in an effort to pay a gaming debt and was again gaoled, with orders to leave Britain upon his release.

Jørgensen was sentenced to death for staying in London after he was freed, but William Hooker's intervention saw that commuted to transportation to Van Diemen's Land for life.[12] While waiting for the boat, Jørgensen worked as a prison doctor, became a lay preacher and wrote the hippy-happy-clappy *The Religion of Christ is the Religion of Nature*.

In April 1826, the one-time King of Iceland arrived as a prisoner to the island he had transported the first convicts to some twenty-three years earlier. He worked as a clerk, identified a forgery scam, was rewarded with a ticket-of-leave and assigned to the Van Diemen's

---

12   Hooker said of Jørgensen, "His talents were of the *highest order*; but for his character, moral and religious, it was always of the lowest order."

Land Company, which set him to work exploring northern Tasmania for good places to keep its sheep. In 1828, he wrote PR pieces on the company for the Hobart and London press and was appointed a convict-constable in Arthur's felon police. It was in this role that he took the leadership of a Black War roving party.

Other notable roving parties were led by Gilbert Robertson (a.k.a. Black Robertson), the illegitimate son of a Scottish plantation owner and his Jamaican mistress, and Batman, who, having run out of bushrangers, now protected fair Hobart City from the Aboriginal supervillains who assailed her.

The roving parties had orders to capture natives but could shoot if the Aborigines ran or fought back. As the Aborigines inevitably ran or fought back, the roving parties effectively had a licence to kill. Batman injured two warriors when firing on a fleeing band and, unable to get the wounded men to walk back to captivity, reported, "I was obliged therefore to shoot them."[13]

Yet the roving parties were largely ineffective, mostly capturing women and children. Ad hoc vigilante groups (i.e. lynch mobs) were far more effective in thinning the enemy's numbers. Jørgensen attributed his failures to his native guides guiding him away from other natives. He marched for thirty or forty miles a day, for two or three weeks on end, and the exhausted Jørgensen's frustrations were obvious. A police magistrate reported, "Jorgenson was really insane many days last week. Mr Robertson too, is evidently mad."

Jørgensen hunted Aborigines on Van Diemen's Land's infamous Black Line, but was forced to look for another job when the roving parties were abandoned in 1831 as "worse than useless". He enjoyed a brief and inglorious career as a farmer, returned to the police, and married Norah Corbett, an illiterate, alcoholic, suicidal Irish convict. Jørgen and Norah's regular domestics degenerated into public

---

13   Arthur wrote admiringly of Batman's sympathy for the Aborigines, while
      acknowledging he "had much slaughter to account for".

street brawls and the drunken Dane was cast aside by his friends.[14]

Jørgensen worked as a scribe for the illiterate during his declining years and published works on politics, the need for trial by jury and other democratic reforms, and *Aboriginal Languages in Tasmania*, a scholarly treatise. His *A Shred of Autobiography, Containing Various Anecdotes, Personal and Historical, Connected with these Colonies* was a startling mix of one part memoir and three parts bullshit.

Sailor, explorer, natural historian, whaler, sealer, privateer, prisoner of war, smuggler, vexillologist, king, rescuer, traitor, spy, drunkard, gambler, writer, thief, doctor, preacher, convict, copper, rover, farmer, scribe, political commentator, democratic reformer, linguist, memoirist and career counsellor's nightmare – Jørgensen's restless lust for adventure placed him front and centre at defining moments of Australian and world history. When Jørgensen died in Hobart's Colonial Hospital in 1841, Australia lost its very own Forrest Gump.

I WALK THE LINE

At the beginning of the Black War, Aboriginal groups included children and the elderly. By 1830, there were no such groups outside the west coast. Only fit adults could travel the forty to fifty miles per day necessary to evade pursuers. The elderly were left behind and reports of Aboriginal infanticide reached Hobart.

The war was not going well for the Aborigines. The tribes occasionally cooperated, but never united. Their fear of night spirits meant they never attacked after dark and their campfires pinpointed their locations for the enemy, forcing them to move constantly.

Traditional society was breaking down, with the customs of millennia abandoned or adapted for a life of skirmishes on the run. In

---

14 The gargoyles of Ross Bridge, built in 1836, can still be viewed today. They include a mocking likeness of Jørgen, complete with crown, and a harpy-like Norah as his queen.

the west, Tarenorerer, known as Walyer by the sealers with whom she'd been living, returned to the Tasmanian mainland and gathered followers from the western tribes. A woman leading warriors was unheard of. The Amazon, as she was known, trained her men in the use of muskets, the first Aborigines to use firearms against the invaders.

In February 1830, Arthur approved a £5 bounty for the capture of each Aboriginal adult and a £2 bounty per child. While the bounty was meant to exclude "inoffensive Natives of the remote and unsettled parts of the territory" and those who had assimilated into Vandemonian society, frontiersmen moved further into the wilderness in search of black gold. Aborigines who had spent their lives cleaning floors were now handed in for quick, easy cash.

Arthur rejected the suggestion of his colonial secretary, John Burnett, that the bounty should only be paid for uninjured Aborigines, arguing, "it would scarcely be possible to capture any of the blacks without in some way wounding them".

The government placed convicts in remote huts and promised tickets-of-leave to those who "rendered effective service" in "defensive" operations. If offensive operations were conducted, well, that would be the work of proven criminals.

Arthur wrote to Sir George Murray, secretary of state for war and the colonies:

> The Aboriginal natives of this colony are, and ever have been, a most treacherous race; and the kindness and humanity which they have always experienced from the free settlers has not tended to civilize them in any degree.

Alfred Stephen, the colony's solicitor-general, emphasised the government's duty to protect settlers and convicts, concluding, "And if you cannot do so without extermination, then I say boldly and broadly, exterminate!"

Stephen's Dalek rhetoric was mirrored in the press. The *Tasmanian* reported, "Extermination seems to be the only remedy. It is a dreadful one." The *Colonial Times*, which had misplaced the capslock key on its printing press, thundered:

SELF DEFENCE IS THE FIRST LAW OF NATURE. THE
GOVERNMENT MUST REMOVE THE NATIVES. IF NOT
THEY WILL BE HUNTED DOWN LIKE WILD BEASTS
AND DESTROYED!

The removal option had been put on the table by Arthur in 1828, when he wrote to Lord Goderich:

The measure which I rather incline to attempt, is to settle the
Aborigines in some remote quarter of the island, which should be
strictly reserved for them, and to supply them with fresh food and
clothing, and afford them protection.

Arthur dusted off this idea, modelled on Indian reservations, after receiving a most disturbing order from Murray in August 1830. Murray had instructed Arthur to prosecute and hang colonists who killed Aborigines, writing, "nothing, I am certain, will tend more effectually to check the evil than to bring before a court of justice any person who may have been instrumental to the death of a native."

Arthur's Executive Council advised him that informing people of this order would be "exceedingly impolitic and would lead to the most unhappy results". The order had arrived only four months after being dispatched from London, rather than the usual six, so Arthur decided to go all out against the Aborigines before he was forced to respond to Murray.

On 9 September 1830, Arthur called on every settler and ticket-of-leave holder capable of bearing arms to form a militia. The 2,200 men of the Black Line, supported by a few Aboriginal guides, formed a human chain more than 300 kilometres long to drive the central

and south-eastern tribes across Eaglehawk Neck onto the Tasman
Peninsula. The Neck would be guarded to prevent any natives from
escaping their new 660 square kilometre prison. Or, at least, that
was the plan.

The enthusiasm of the ethnic cleansers soon turned to despair,
with torrential rain, hail and snow leaving them freezing in their
cotton clothing. One starving participant "was obliged to eat the
sheep skin straps of his knapsack". Footwear failed and shoeless men
deserted. One night, "one of the soldiers not being accustomed to the
nocturnal ramblings of the Opossums" set off a one-sided firefight
that wasted 200 rounds. Men shot at their own sentries in the belief
that they were Aborigines trying to break the Line and, when news
filtered through that the Aborigines had indeed broken through and
were setting fire to unguarded homes, morale hit a new low.

The Black Line remains the largest domestic military offensive in
Australian history. It lasted seven weeks and cost over £30,000, half
the colony's annual budget. The result? Three Aborigines killed, a man
and boy captured, and no Aborigines driven onto their new reservation.
Arthur acknowledged, with some understatement, that the Black Line
"had not been attended with the full success which was anticipated".

Three weeks before the operation ended, Arthur received a letter
from Murray:

> The great decrease which has of late years taken place in the amount
> of the Aboriginal population, render it not unreasonable to appre-
> hend that the whole race of these people may, at no distant period,
> become extinct ... and the adoption of any line of conduct, having
> for its avowed, or for its secret object, the extinction of the Native
> race, could not fail to leave an indelible stain upon the character of
> the British Government.

Arthur was not looking forward to Murray's response when informed
of the Black Line snafu. But he needn't have worried. George IV had

done him a favour by eating one too many pies and dying.[15] The
subsequent change of government restoring Lord Goderich as secretary of state for war and the colonies. Goderich, when confronted
with a carpet, looked for something to sweep under it. When the
parliament requested correspondence between Arthur and the War
and Colonial Office on military operations against the Aborigines,
Goderich provided censored copies and removed all references to
Murray's earlier orders.

Arthur was off the hook. He adroitly switched to a policy of
conciliation, placing his faith in the missionary efforts of George
Augustus Robinson.

THE BIBLE IS MIGHTIER THAN THE BULLET

George Augustus Robinson was a human toby jug – thickset, with
a florid face topped by a luxuriant auburn wig and black puffy hat
that made him look like Snap, Crackle and Pop's sinister older
brother.

Robinson had been born into poverty in England and started
work as a bricklayer at the age of eleven. He found God through an
Evangelical outreach program for child labourers and started hanging
around missionaries.[16] Robinson fled to Van Diemen's Land in 1823,
after being implicated in a financial scandal involving the Church
Missionary Society. He found work as a brickie and builder and

---

15 In mid-1829, the royal portrait painter Sir David Wilkie reported that George had
    become so obese that he looked "like a great sausage stuffed into the covering".
    After George's death, the *Times* opined that the king would always prefer "a girl
    and a bottle to politics and a sermon" and "There never was an individual less
    regretted by his fellow-creatures than this deceased king. What eye has wept for
    him? What heart has heaved one throb of unmercenary sorrow? ... If he ever had
    a friend – a devoted friend in any rank of life – we protest that the name of him or
    her never reached us."

16 In these more innocent times, men of the cloth could befriend poor young boys
    without suspicion.

joined the Seamen's Friend and Bethel Union Society and numerous other Bible groups.[17]

Robinson's wife and five children joined him in 1826. Bricklaying and Bible studies no longer paid the bills, so Robinson responded to Arthur's 1829 job ad for a storekeeper to provision the Aborigines of Bruni Island, who had so far refrained from setting fire to farms and inserting pointy sticks into farmers. Arthur, impressed with Robinson's pledge to "instruct the natives in the acts of civilisation" and "teach them Xian religion", gave him the £50 a year job and 500 acres of land.

But Robinson had a problem. The fifty Aborigines present at his arrival became seventeen in six months, as respiratory and venereal disease swept across Bruni. No Aborigines meant no £50 job.

Robinson needed to find some new natives and convinced Arthur that he and some of Bruni's survivors should form "a conciliatory mission" that would travel the west coast delivering "a message of peace". The pacified Aborigines, he suggested, would all move to Bruni Island and live with Robinson and Christ. In the meantime, Arthur would appreciate the need to move those surviving Bruni Islanders not chosen for the mission into Robinson's outhouse, which would cost Arthur a mere £12 more a year to rent.

The only surviving adult male islander, Woorraddy, wanted some company on the mission and asked Robinson if he could procure him Truganini, who was turning tricks at a nearby whaling camp. Robinson obliged.

In 1830, Robinson set off on a nine-month coastal trek to Launceston, accompanied by his teenage son, Charles, fifteen convict porters and thirteen Aborigines, including Truganini, Woorraddy, Kickertepoller (who'd fought alongside Mosquito under the nom de guerre of

---

17   The Seamen's Friend and Bethel Union Society encouraged sailors to trade in their rum, tattoos and prostitutes for lively discussions about the Bible. Strangely, it never really took off.

Black Tom) and Umarrah (who'd led attacks against the settlers before his capture). Including these former belligerents in the group was a propaganda coup – the white man, like his God, would welcome the penitent sinner into his kingdom.

Robinson showed genuine interest in Aboriginal culture during his first mission. He ate his guides' traditional food and shared blankets and skin diseases with them. He attempted to learn their language and played his flute when they sang and danced. He approached the tribes with respect and provided them with gifts and provisions. The missionary formed a close bond with Truganini, although there is little evidence it was sexual, as some suggest.[18] She saved Robinson's life when he attempted to escape hostile warriors by rafting across a river on two bits of wood lashed together with his garters (he couldn't swim). When the garters snapped, Robinson held the raft together with his cravat, and Truganini pushed the makeshift vessel across the river as spears fell around her.

Robinson's first mission was an abject failure. While the tribal Aborigines thanked him for the food and trinkets, they showed no inclination to leave their ancestral lands for his outhouse. He had more luck with Aborigines who worked with sealers on Robbins Island, convincing an Aboriginal youth, Tunnerminnerwait, and two others to join his party as guides.

But Robinson's compassion was ultimately no match for his greed. As soon as he learned of Arthur's bounty, he returned to Robbins Island to round up Aborigines who were neither aggressive nor "trespassing" in the settled districts. He offered to take an Aboriginal worker back to the Van Diemen's Land Company's settlement and bribed a tribal Aborigine into his boat with promises of trousers and a blanket. He then promptly shipped them, along with two of his Aboriginal guides,

---

18   In his diary, Robinson noted Truganini's "loathsome disease" (VD) and condemned the sexual exploitation of Aboriginal women. The missionary's position on sexual matters was conservative, although he later fell into sin on Flinders Island when he embarked on an affair with Mrs Dickerson, an employee's wife.

off to Hobart with an invoice for £20, rationalising that it was for their own protection.

The bricklaying Bible-thumper was also a victim of his own vanity. It was not long before he boasted, "The government have engaged me to enquire into the state of the aboriginal population of this country ... I ... am the only person that can judge of what is best to be done," before dismissing the opinions of "those wiseacres at their parlour fireside at Hobart Town".

He then informed the chief wiseacre that there were 700 Aborigines in the island's north-east whom he could "capture" – a marked change in his rhetoric. This figure of 700 did not violate the Ninth Commandment because Robinson had no idea whether it was true or not. In reality, there were probably fewer than eighty Aborigines left in the area, of whom only three were women, the sealers having taken the rest.

Arthur permitted Robinson to try to round them up, urging him to use "gentle means", if possible. Robinson found seven Aborigines on 1 November 1830 and told them all about the Black Line, which was then in full swing.

Although the Black Line netted only two captives, Jørgensen and others thought it laid the groundwork for Robinson's subsequent success. The Black Line may not have shown the colonists to be competent, but it sure as hell convinced the Aborigines they were serious.

Robinson offered the seven his protection from the Line. They agreed and he took them to Swan Island, a tiny lump of granite in Bass Strait, telling them he was taking them on a muttonbirding trip and promising he'd be back for them after liberating their women from the sealers. Instead, he returned to the mainland, where he found another six Aborigines waiting to surrender. The Swan Island seven became thirteen, which is not a lucky number – Robinson had no intention of taking them back to the mainland.

On the day Arthur ended the Black Line, he praised Robinson's success and announced that the government would consider:

... whether it is not proper to place those who are now secured ...
together with any others who may be captured, upon an island from
whence they cannot escape, but where they will be gradually induced
to adopt the habits and feelings of civilized life.

In the following weeks, Robinson convinced fourteen Aboriginal
women living with Bass Strait sealers to join his new Swan Island
community, where he planned to marry them off to the Aboriginal
men he'd stranded there – a cross between *Blind Date* and *Survivor*,
but without any prospect of being voted off the island.

One of the fourteen, Mary Anne, had recently been captured by the
sealers and had attempted to murder one of them. After disembarking
at Swan Island, Mary Anne was revealed to be Tarenorerer when her
dog, Whiskey, who had been taken to the island earlier, greeted her
with enthusiasm. Robinson regarded it a "most fortunate thing that
this woman is apprehended and stopped in her murderous career".
He ordered that the Amazon be placed in solitary confinement to
prevent her inciting rebellion. She died of influenza six months later.

Many more would follow.

ETHNIC CLEANLINESS IS NEXT TO GODLINESS

The Great Conciliator returned to Hobart in triumph in January
1831. He claimed to have voluntarily settled thirty-three Aborigines
on Swan Island, singlehandedly outdoing the 2,200 men of the Black
Line by a factor of 16.5.[19] Arthur granted the hero 2,560 acres (the
largest land grant possible), quintupled his salary, backdated the
increase and gave him an additional £100 for good measure.

Although Norfolk Island and Van Diemen's Land were Australia's
first offshore detention centres, Robinson's Bass Strait Solution proved

---

19   While Robinson voluntarily settled the Aborigines on Swan Island, the
      Aborigines did not voluntarily settle there. One man's free choice is another
      man's determinism. Discuss.

that there was money to be made in imprisoning vulnerable people on godforsaken islands.[20]

Many Vandemonians rejected the Bass Strait Solution and continued to agitate for a Final Solution. They railed against Black Robinson, as he was now derisively known, with the surveyor James Erskine Calder writing:

> The current of popular dislike ran so strongly against him, on both sides of the island, that he was almost universally denounced as an impostor, and no terms, however vulgar, were too vulgar if only applied to him.

Robinson was unperturbed by the vulgarities of the hoi polloi. He now not only had land and money, but also the respect of the colony's movers and shakers.[21] If he played his cards right, fortune and reputation were his for the taking. Unfortunately for the Aborigines, the only card in Robinson's deck was the race card.

The Swan Island Aborigines requested to meet Arthur but Robinson refused, as he did not want their opinions getting in the way of what

---

20 Transfield Services has since perfected Robinson's business model, but has applied it to IMAs (illegal maritime arrivals) rather than NTIs (native terrestrial inhabitants), which is much fairer. IMAs deserve to be locked up indefinitely because they travel by boat, while NTIs travelled by a much less offensive raft-canoe that would sink if taken more than six kilometres offshore. IMA boats can travel at least 22.2 kilometres offshore, at which time they leave the territorial waters of Indonesia or other evil people-smuggling states and can be "turned back". Whether they are or aren't turned back is of no interest to the Australian people, as on-water matters don't.

21 shakers are not to be confused with Shakers, a communal Quaker sect led by women. Shakers made beautifully crafted chairs, believed God was a hermaphrodite and expressed their religious visions through ecstatic dance, all of which proper Evangelicals like Robinson frowned upon (except for the chair bit). Shaker dancing, however, did not lead to Shaker sex, as Shakers blamed all the world's evils on Eve putting out and were therefore sworn to celibacy. The Shakers had not really thought this through, as their commitment to shaking only on the vertical axis deprived the world of new generations of little Shakers. Shaker numbers peaked at about 6,000 in the mid-nineteenth century, but today the world's only Shaker community is Sabbathday Lake Shaker Village in Maine (pop. 4).

was good for them. They might ask embarrassing questions like, "Can we go home now?" Robinson's continued influence relied on him being the sole contact point between the Aboriginal and colonial leaders.

Robinson told Arthur's Executive Council that he believed the entire Aboriginal population of Van Diemen's Land would voluntarily migrate to a Bass Strait island and that he did not think they would "feel themselves imprisoned there, or pine away in consequence of the restraint, nor would they wish to return to the mainland or regret their inability to hunt or roam about in the manner they had previously".

The Executive Council endorsed the Bass Strait Solution, with only Chief Justice Pedder dissenting. Pedder argued that the Aborigines "would soon begin to pine away when they found their situation one of hopeless imprisonment" and that offshore detention should be reserved for Aborigines captured in hostilities, pending the negotiation of a treaty.

Arthur would later concede that a treaty at first settlement "would have avoided injurious consequences which have followed our occupation, and which must forever remain a stain upon the colonisation of Van Diemen's Land", but he believed that the time for negotiation had passed. He made sure that future council meetings on Aboriginal policy would be held on days when Pedder was unavailable, as his objections would not look good in the minutes provided to London.[22]

Arthur's official policy was that hostile natives could surrender and consent to relocate to Bass Strait in return for food, clothing and protection from aggression, although his instructions to Robinson emphasised the importance of keeping them in captivity. The duplicitous missionary spent the next four years playing Bass Strait travel agent, with little regard to issues of hostility or consent. He lured

---

22   Arthur wrote of Pedder, "Though a man of great talents and unbending integrity, of the purest intentions and a very safe adviser, he is so tedious and so minute that life is much too short to wait for his opinions and decision." And when Pedder expressed opinions that were contrary to Arthur's, life was much too short to give him a forum to express them in.

Aborigines to various islands in the strait with promises to reunite them with their women and later return them to hunt in their own lands. One group was dumped on an island after being offered a day trip on a boat. Robinson justified his deceit of the Aborigines "as being the only way to save their lives".

Robinson was greatly assisted by Mannalargenna, who had joined his mission as a guide and envoy. The chieftain had fallen on hard times. He'd led ten men during the Black Line, all that was left of his people and the Tamar River tribe. He'd surrendered to Batman, but deserted ten days later with the kangaroo-caped crusader's dogs and provisions. He was an immediate asset to Robinson – if the great warrior and wise man submitted, then resistance was clearly futile.

The Black War ended on New Year's Eve in 1831, when the twenty-six surviving members of the Oyster Bay and Big River tribes surrendered to Robinson. Seven days later, the victorious missionary triumphantly led the sixteen men, nine women and a child to Government House, where they were greeted by a brass band and given trousers. The Aborigines, on Robinson's advice, believed they were meeting Arthur to settle Aboriginal grievances, but ten days later they were loaded onto a boat bound for Bass Strait and Robinson was £400 richer.

Although this signalled the end of conflict in the settled districts, Robinson continued his island package-tour business. From 1833, he removed most Aborigines by force, brandishing muskets to encourage the volunteering spirit. Robinson secured his captives with gifts of trousers – one of his diary entries stated, "Trousers is excellent things and confines their legs so they cannot run."

Why did Robinson's Aboriginal guides assist him? Many didn't consider members of other tribes their kin and were happy to sell them out for bread and blankets. Some, like Umarrah, were prisoners who saw Robinson as their ticket to freedom. Mannalargenna saw the opportunity to continue traditional hunting and practices without getting shot. Truganini, in later life, said she saw Robinson's mission as the last chance to save her people.

Robinson had a George W. Bush moment on 3 February 1835, when he declared, "The work here is done." His claim to have processed all the natives offshore earned him £900, plus a £200 annual pension for life, with the grateful public passing the hat around for a further £8,000.[23] He wrote, "By taking the whole I gain not only the reward but celebrity."

But the latest darling of Hobart's only red carpet had missed a few pesky stragglers. Robinson sent one of his sons to round up six of them in November 1836, providing nice new names for their nice new life, including Albert, William and Frank, with one later named Barnaby Rudge.[24] Van Diemen's Land's last Aborigines – a warrior, his wife and their three sons, the youngest of whom was renamed William Lanne – were captured by sealers and transported to Bass Strait in December 1842.

Robinson, who'd removed over 220 Tasmanian Aborigines to Bass Strait in one of history's most efficient ethnic cleansing programs, expressed hope that the "time is not far distant when the same humane policy will be adopted towards the aboriginal inhabitants of every colony throughout the British Empire".

MY ISLAND HOME

On 28 September 1831, the government decided it would be easier to keep an eye on the Tasmanian Aborigines if they were all in one place. The Aborigines were picked up from their various rocks and

23 It was a big hat.

24 This could have started a craze of naming Tasmanian Aborigines after Dickens' characters, but by this stage there weren't enough Tasmanian Aborigines to put a dent in Dickens' back catalogue. Robinson enjoyed giving natives proper names. He renamed Tunnerminnerwait Jack Napoleon and Tranlebunna Achilles, while Maulboyheener was known as Robert Timmy Jimmy Small-boy. Robinson called Truganini Lalla Rookh, after the dusky heroine of Thomas Moore's 1817 novel of the same name, while Woorraddy was dubbed Count Alpha and The Doctor (a TARDIS would have been handy on a Bass Strait island).

relocated to Flinders Island, the prototype Aboriginal reserve that informed the separatist policies of colonial and Australian governments for well over a century.

The Tasmanian Aborigines traditionally believed that after death they would awaken as white spirit-men on an island. The first fifty-one Aborigines brought to Flinders Island by Robinson in late 1831 must have asked themselves if they had died during the Black War and arrived in paradise.

The answer was no. First, they were still black. Second, the island was damp and windswept and they had nothing to eat but rice and potatoes, supplemented by the occasional unlucky muttonbird, which was not what the afterlife was cracked up to be.[25] Third, dead people don't die again – the fact that thirty-one of them expired from respiratory disease within a few months was the clincher.

In October 1832, the Aboriginal camp was relocated to a better part of the island, called Wybalenna ("black man's houses" in the Plangermaireener language), where an Aboriginal village administered by white military and civilian officers was established. A further 198 inmates arrived over the next ten years. The adults were to be instructed in agriculture, and their children were to be taken away and raised by the storekeeper and a lay preacher, who would instruct them in literacy, numeracy and Christianity.

Robinson was appointed commandant of Flinders Island in October 1835. By this time, his predecessor in the post, Henry Nickolls, had reported that the Aborigines "evinced a determined hostility to anything like work" and the settlement relied almost entirely on convict labour imported from the Tasmanian mainland. There was conflict between traditional tribal enemies who were now forced to live with each other. Birth rates were at near Shaker levels, with Fanny

---

25 Windschuttle, in contrast, insists that "Flinders Island enjoys a temperate, maritime climate, much like that of a southern Mediterranean port", a Tasmanian Aboriginal Ibiza.

Cochrane, born in 1834, one of the few Aboriginal children of Flinders Island. Respiratory disease claimed many, including Mannalargenna, who'd failed to reclaim a favoured daughter from the sealers, shaved off his ochred hair and beard in despair and succumbed to pneumonia within two months of his island arrival.

Robinson wrote in December 1835:

> The sad mortality which has happened among them since their removal is a cause for regret but after all it is the will of providence, and better they died here where they are kindly treated than shot at and inhumanly destroyed by the depraved portion of the white community.

Robinson believed that it was better to fade away than to burn out. But the slow decline of the Aborigines distressed him, so he recommended that they be relocated to mainland Australia where he could not see them dying and their "inevitable extinction" would cause less "excitement". New South Wales refused as it had too many Aborigines of its own.

Robinson, unhinged by the ever-expanding gap between reality and expectation, took to referring to himself in the third person, with his journal now cataloguing the activities, musings and delusions of "the Commandant". The Commandant wrote report after report on how wonderfully happy and civilised the natives now were, embedding the reservation model in the British colonial consciousness.

Robinson claimed to have introduced a wage economy, where Aboriginal workers used their wages to purchase goods from the island's store. He created false ledger books to support this, which officers on the island refused to sign. He also created fake school reports for Aboriginal children, for example, "Cleopatra: Perfect in the alphabet; repeats the Lord's Prayer", which officers on the island also refused to endorse.

It was time for Robinson to move on. He took up the lucrative post of chief protector of Aborigines at the new Port Phillip settlement in February 1839, taking Truganini, Woorraddy and fourteen other members of his early missions with him.

Arthur had been recalled in 1836. His successor, John Franklin, ordered an inquiry into the Flinders Island settlement. The inquiry contradicted Robinson's reports, finding no evidence of education, religious knowledge, a wage economy or progress towards civilisation. It found fraud in the island's store, Aboriginal rations missing, and funded public works unbuilt. The inquiry concluded, "The preservation of these people as a race appears altogether hopeless."

The inquiry's findings were sent to Robinson for comment. Robinson claimed there was no documentary evidence against his administration, which was true, as he had taken all the documents to Port Phillip. Franklin was so embarrassed by the inquiry's report that he blocked its release. As far as the rest of the world knew, Flinders Island remained a model settlement of happy, thriving, Christian, almost civilised natives.

THE DOWNWARD SPIRAL

Truganini and her people built a new house for Robinson at Port Phillip, laboured in his fields and accompanied him on tours of the countryside. Robinson's interest in his Tasmanian charges waned as he focused on protecting the not nearly as depressing Aborigines of Australia the Happy.[26]

Truganini absconded in August 1841. Accompanied by Tunnerminnerwait, Maulboyheener and two kinswomen, she became one of Australia's few female bushrangers. The Flinders Five stockpiled guns, stole from settlers, burned huts, assaulted stock-keepers and

---

26 New South Wales surveyor-general Major Thomas Mitchell named the rich pasturelands of south-west Victoria *Australia Felix*, Latin for "Australia the Happy" or "Australia the Lucky", during his 1836 expedition from Sydney to the southern coast. Donald Horne riffed off this theme by ironically referring to Australia as the Lucky Country in his 1964 book of that name.

murdered two whalers, one of whom Truganini clubbed to death after he'd been shot in the chest.

Charles La Trobe, the superintendent of Port Phillip, organised a police party, guided by Kulin trackers, to hunt down the "black marauders". Truganini was found hiding under a blanket during a police raid. A pistol was held to her head and she was ordered to call on her companions to surrender (which they did).

The Kulin trackers were subsequently appointed to form the nucleus of Australia's first native police force, a policy development that would have dire consequences for Aborigines on the ever-expanding Australian frontier. Truganini and co., charged with murder, were defended by the dashing Irish lawyer Redmond Barry, whose open affair with a married woman during his voyage to Australia ensured he would find no employment in stuffy Sydney, forcing him to defend savages and other riffraff in the southern badlands.

Robinson sought mercy for Truganini during the trial, testifying that she had saved his life in Van Diemen's Land and that the Aboriginal women in the band were completely ruled by their menfolk.

Maulboyheener and Tunnerminnerwait were awarded the unhappy honour of being the first people hanged in Australia the Happy, ascending the gallows on 20 January 1842. Tunnerminnerwait welcomed his death with the cryptic claim that he had "three heads, one for the scaffold, one for the grave, and one for Van Diemen's Land".[27]

Truganini and her female companions were acquitted and sent back to Flinders Island with Woorraddy, who died of senility a few months later. Flinders was now a near ghost town. Its dwindling survivors shuffled the island's trails; infertile, ill and aging.

In 1846, eight Aboriginal leaders of Flinders Island signed the first petition to a reigning monarch from any Aboriginal group in Australia. The petition to Queen Victoria, arguing their right to return to the Tasmanian mainland, stated:

---

27   This is one more head than most Tasmanians have.

... that we are your free children that we were not taken prisoners but freely gave our country to Colonel Arthur then the Governor after defending ourselves ... Mr Robinson made for us and with Colonel Arthur an agreement which we have not lost from our minds since and we have made our part of it good.[28]

The petition was "received graciously" by Queen Victoria. Despite counter-petitions from outraged Vandemonians, Lieutenant-Governor Denison relocated the ten surviving children to Hobart's orphan school and Truganini and the other thirty-three adult survivors to a former convict settlement at Oyster Cove, opposite Bruni Island. Truganini had come full circle.

Most of the new Oyster Cove tribe suffered from chronic chest complaints, four were morbidly obese, one was blind, one was senile and one suffered acute arthritis. The Aborigines were treated as pensioners of the state, which meant they were supported in the most inexpensive manner possible.[29] The men drank and the women prostituted themselves for alcohol.

Truganini refused to acknowledge Robinson when he visited Oyster Cove in 1851. The man who'd made his name (and a very comfortable living) out of Aboriginal exile returned to Britain and married a woman thirty-eight years his junior. Tasmania's Geoffrey Edelsten toured Italy, Germany, Switzerland, Holland, Belgium and Spain with his youthful bride and took an apartment on the Champs-Élysées before retiring to Bath. Life had worked out surprisingly well.

---

28   Robinson had promised the Aborigines they might return to Van Diemen's Land after the cessation of violence. Henry Reynolds characterises this as the first treaty between the British and Aboriginal Australians, although there is no evidence that Robinson advised Arthur of this arrangement or that Arthur agreed to it – indeed, Arthur had advised Britain that a treaty was impossible. The Aborigines would have to wait a few more years until Batman made the first and only treaty with Aboriginal people.

29   This is in stark contrast to pensioners today, who are generously compensated by the government every time the price of tinned asparagus goes up.

TO YOUR SCATTERED BODIES GO

There was no opera, champagne, can-can performances or relaxing spas for the Tasmanian Aborigines. By 1859, only fourteen remained on the Tasmanian mainland.

As Darwin's writings gained popularity in the 1860s, it was speculated that the native Tasmanians were the missing link between ape and man. Photographers came to photograph them. Phrenologists came to fondle their skulls while they were alive and anthropologists came to steal their skulls when they were dead. Tasmanian body parts soared in value as the number of bodies to which they were attached dwindled.

William Lanne, the last Aborigine removed from Van Diemen's Land, died in Hobart's Dog and Partridge Hotel in 1869, the last full-blooded male of his race. Tasmania's premier, Richard Dry, was convinced that anatomists and anthropologists would want a piece of Lanne, as Dr William Crowther, a visiting surgeon at Hobart Hospital, had earlier requested that his skeleton be given to the Royal College of Surgeons in London.

Dry ordered Dr Stokell, Hobart Hospital's resident surgeon, to secure Lanne's body in the hospital morgue before burial, to ensure it was not mistreated. Stokell, however, left the morgue unattended after accepting an invitation to have tea with Mrs Crowther. While his wife kept Stokell occupied, Dr Crowther and his son crept into the morgue and, with a barber's assistance, removed Lanne's skull, replacing it with that of a recently deceased white man. Crowther later studied Lanne's brain, which he believed exhibited physical changes that demonstrated "the improvement that takes place in the lower race when subjected to the effects of education and civilisation".

When Stokell returned, he decided to get in on the act and removed Lanne's hands and feet for future study. Lanne's remaining remains were buried the next day, but Stokell, his scientific appetite whetted, crept into the cemetery at night and dug up Lanne for further anatomical examination.

Crowther, not to be outdone, broke down the morgue door with an axe after Stokell had departed and was outraged to find only a few scraps of Lanne remained (which he souvenired). We know that those scraps did not include Lanne's scrotum, which had been taken by Stokell for use as a tobacco pouch.[30] Lanne's hands and feet were later found in the Royal Society's rooms, and his skull in Edinburgh. The location of his scrotum remains unknown to this day.

The scandal of Lanne's dismemberment led to the Tasmanian parliament passing the *Anatomy Act 1869*, which ruled that the anatomical examination of a corpse could only take place with the consent of the deceased or his or her relatives. Crowther was sacked for the skull switch, but later that year was made a fellow of the Royal College of Surgeons, the first Australian so honoured. A decade later, the man who desecrated the corpse of the last full-blooded male Tasmanian Aborigine was made premier of Tasmania.

Truganini, now Oyster Bay's sole survivor, feared she would suffer a similar fate to Lanne. She told Reverend Atkinson, "I know that when I die the Museum wants my body," begging him to cremate her and scatter her ashes in Bruni's waters.

Atkinson was unfortunately away when "the last Tasmanian Aborigine" died on 8 May 1876.[31] Truganini's body was guarded by a constable "to prevent any mutilation or snatching", before being buried under two feet of concrete in the Cascades Female Factory (to

---

30 WARNING: Having your nutsack filled with tobacco ruins your health.

31 Truganini was not actually the last "full-blooded" Tasmanian Aborigine. Sal, Suke and Betty continued to live with sealers on Kangaroo Island after her death, and the Tasmanian government accepted in 1889 that Fanny Cochrane Smith, the girl born on Flinders Island, was the last full-blooded Tasmanian Aborigine, granting her 300 acres of land and a £50 a year pension. Fanny lived on the Tasmanian mainland until her death in 1905.

deter grave robbers). Two years later, the government gave the Royal Society of Tasmania permission to exhume her body on condition that it was "decently deposited in a secure resting place accessible by special permission to scientific men for scientific purposes". It ended up on public display in the Tasmanian Museum.[32]

"*Aborigines, the last of the race, Tasmania, c.1866,*"
Henry Frith.

Mary Ann   William Lanne   Bessie Clark   Truganini

FIG. 4: "SMILE!"

---

32   Truganini's skeleton was removed from display in 1947 and put in a cupboard. The Royal College of Surgeons, which had somehow made off with skin and hair samples, returned its bits of Truganini in 2002. The rest of her had been cremated in 1976, her ashes scattered off Bruni as she had requested 100 years earlier.

Truganini's death made international headlines, with the extinction of the Tasmanian Aborigines offered as evidence in support of Darwin's Theory of Evolution. As Darwin had predicted just five years earlier, a civilised race of man had exterminated and replaced a savage race.[33]

Except...

---

33   The "extinction" of the Tasmanian Aborigines inspired H.G. Wells to write his 1897 classic *The War of the Worlds*, in which foreign invaders (Martians) attempt to destroy a technologically inferior race (us).

Coda

TODAY'S TASMANIAN ABORIGINAL PEOPLE RESENT being called extinct.

Most of the Palawa are descendants of the Bass Strait sealers and the daughters of Mannalargenna. Others are descendants of Fanny Cochrane and the English convict William Smith.

The descendants of the sealers were taught Aboriginal culture, including muttonbirding, by their foremothers. These Straitsmen, as they were known, were removed from many of their islands after the Tasmanian *Waste Lands Acts* of 1861 and 1870 encouraged European occupation of "empty land" in Bass Strait. Many of the islands were bought by Robert Gardiner, known as Resurrection Bob due to his enthusiasm for digging up Aboriginal bones and selling them to scientists.

In 1881, the Tasmanian government revisited the Flinders Island experiment by establishing the Cape Barren Island Reserve for the "half-caste" descendants of the sealers and Aboriginal women. The reserve was only closed in 1951.

Keith Windschuttle insists that Palawa leaders like Michael Mansell, the descendant of the sealer Edward Mansell and the man who led the campaign for Palawa recognition and land rights in the 1970s, are opportunistic Aboriginals of convenience. He further contends that contemporary Tasmanian Aboriginality is "not a product of any continuous cultural link to ancient people. Instead it was invented in Launceston in the 1970s by modern, urban, tertiary-educated political activists like Michael Mansell."

Conservative commentator Andrew Bolt argues that Aboriginality is skin deep and that when Mansell refers to "white people", "he means those few people even whiter than him". Bolt is the Dulux Colour Atlas of indigenous affairs. The legally qualified Mansell is no darker than PN1E6 (Barrister White), most token Aborigines are barely PN1D8 (Kahlua Milk), and very few handout-seeking bludgers have the proper duskiness of PN1B9 (Terrible Billy).

Bolt is obsessed with handouts. His 2009 *Herald Sun* piece "It's So Hip to Be Black" argued that a number of prominent people of mixed Aboriginal and European descent identified as Aboriginal for political and career reasons (academia, the arts and lefty politics being three areas where it helps to have some skin in the game). And then of course there are the paper Aborigines, who are black for benefits.

When Bolt was successfully sued for his article, with the Federal Court finding that his writing was "reasonably likely to offend, insult, humiliate or intimidate some Aboriginal persons of mixed descent who have a fairer, rather than darker, skin", an ostentation of conservaratti strutted to the dispatch box and slithered atop the Murdoch bully pulpit to water down the definition of racial discrimination and defend Bolt's right to be an opinionated cock.

The test for Aboriginality in Tasmania, as in other parts of Australia, is not one of skin tone or "blood purity", but a combination of descent, self-identification and communal recognition.[1] By this test, the Tasmanian Aborigines are not dead yet.

---

1   Michael Mansell and other Palawa leaders refuse to recognise the Aboriginality of the Lia Pootah, a group claiming to be descended from Aborigines who were never taken to the Bass Strait islands. The chairman of the Tasmanian Aboriginal Land Council, Clyde Mansell, has also denied Tasmanian senator Jacqui Lambie's 2014 claim that she descends from Mannalargenna.

5

The People's Poet

And I suppose you think ideas like peace
and freedom and equality are boring too.

Rick, *The Young Ones*, 1982

THE OFFSPRING OF THE UNFORTUNATE CONVICT

G ENOCIDE WAS THE LAST THING ON BRITISH MINDS
in 1816. They'd just given the old enemy a jolly good thrashing
at Waterloo, but even the most rabid Francophobe would
have drawn the line at exiling the French to waste away on a remote
island.[1]

The War of 1812 had also wrapped up the previous year, with Britain believing it had scored a points victory against the United States
after burning down the White House and Capitol Hill (the Americans
having only managed to torch Toronto's Legislative Assembly).[2] For

---

1   Except, of course, in the case of Napoleon, who was exiled to Saint Helena,
    which is far more remote than Flinders Island. The former emperor was kept
    in substandard accommodation (the 27-room Longwood House) and, like his
    Tasmanian counterparts, complained that his island was damp, windswept
    and unhealthy. He wasted away in 1821, aged only fifty-one (much younger
    than Truganini), before men of science took a plaster cast of his head and the
    authorities ignored his request to be buried in his native land. The Tasmanian
    Aborigines were really treated no worse than Napoleon, so Michael Mansell
    should stop his whingeing.

2   The 1812 War should really have been called the War of 1812–15. Similarly, the
    Seven Years' War and the Hundred Years' War would more accurately be the Nine

the first time in decades, Britain was at peace.

That peace was disturbed when William Charles Wentworth returned to London in December 1816. Wentworth had hurriedly left New South Wales, pleading that the healing airs of London would fortify his ailing constitution. This excuse raised suspicions, partly because London's smog and typhus made it the unhealthiest city on the globe and partly because Wentworth had the appearance of a professional wrestler, albeit one who hadn't changed his unitard for several months.

William, the illegitimate son of a convict woman, had been adopted by his suspected father, D'Arcy Wentworth, upon his mother's death. D'Arcy, one of Sydney's richest men, had more public offices than an Indian railway station – he was colonial surgeon, justice of the peace, magistrate, member of the Governor's Court, commissioner of police and chief toll collector.

The young William had been packed off to a British public school, where he developed an inflated sense of self-worth, a lazy competence, an interest in liberal-conservative politics, a keen grasp of Latin and classical poetry, sociable wit and charm, a fondness for port and gambling, the ability to thumb his nose at authority while pandering to it, and the artfully casual disarray of the well-practised louche, complete with rumpled, ill-fitting suits and foppishly long hair that had never been in the same county as a comb: the prototype Boris Johnson.[3]

After his return to the colony, William won Australia's inaugural public horserace and made the first recorded crossing of the Blue Mountains: hardly the actions of an invalid.

Years' War and the Hundred-and-Sixteen Years' War. The people responsible for naming wars should buy a calendar and stop confusing history students.

3   Like Boris, the most entertaining lord mayor of London since Dick Whittington (but without the cat), William would carve a niche for himself in the worlds of print media (considering truth an optional extra in reportage) and politics (happily crossing political divides for personal gain). Wentworth would also later lead the successful Auxit campaign, enabling the Australian colonies to break away from British rule.

The dishevelled adventurer was in rude health, apart from the odd twinge of port-induced gout. His real reason for leaving New South Wales was fear of prosecution for the scurrilous poem he'd written about the colony's military commander, Lieutenant-Governor George Molle. To conceal his authorship, he'd penned a similar verse attacking his friend Alexander Riley, "as a cloak to cover me". Friendship, throughout Wentworth's life, was both an enjoyable diversion and a disposable commodity.

After arriving in London in 1816, Wentworth, like later generations of Australian backpackers, sponged off family friends and distant relatives. But unlike these less ambitious countrymen, satisfied with pulling pints for three quid an hour or stacking shelves in Tesco, William announced to his kinsman Earl Fitzwilliam:

> My deliberations have entirely confirmed the bias I have always felt
> towards the Bar ... and I calculate upon acquainting myself with all
> the excellence of the British Constitution and hope at some future
> period to advocate successfully the right of my country to a partici-
> pation in its advantages.

Wentworth had left a colony where inhabitants were denied the vote, the right to jury trials, and a free press. These fundamental British rights were considered wrongs in a society where most of the citizens were convicts or emancipists (ex-convicts). Wentworth was passionate about extending these rights to the (white, male, propertied) people of New South Wales.

Wentworth's interest in constitutional reform appealed to Fitzwilliam, a leading Whig parliamentarian.[4] Fitzwilliam had advocated

---

4   *Whig* derives from *whiggamore*, the name for backwoods Scots cattle drivers, and
    was a term of abuse for supporters of the Protestant succession during the reign of
    Charles II, before being adopted by the more constitutionally progressive faction.
    The Whigs believed in the supremacy of parliament over the monarch, free trade,
    the abolition of slavery, taxation by representation and equal rights for Catholics.
    The Tories, the other main political faction in early nineteenth-century Britain,
    took their name from the Irish *tórat* (meaning outlaw or bandit), as the Royalist

voting rights for (white, male, propertied) American colonists and was a leading figure in the campaign for Catholic emancipation.[5] He also owned Wentworth Woodhouse, which was the largest mansion in Britain and sported the longest facade of any private home in Europe, if that sort of thing impresses you. It certainly impressed Wentworth, who spent the next seven years freeloading off Fitzwilliam at every possible opportunity.

Wentworth would regularly turn up on Fitzwilliam's fifty-metre doorstep, give Lady Fitzwilliam a parrot and then hit Fitzwilliam up for cash. Fitzwilliam bankrolled Wentworth's enrolment as a law student and provided several other handouts, which Wentworth used to holiday in Paris and Italy (again for "health reasons").

Wentworth's five-year law course was not demanding and the ambitious young colonial busied himself with other things. He suggested that Earl Bathurst, the secretary of state for war and the colonies, commission him to make an east–west crossing of Australia between exams and, when Bathurst showed no enthusiasm for this proposal, commenced writing a book on the "political state of the colony" of New South Wales.

The book project had been recommended by John Macarthur junior, who'd lent Wentworth his apartment in Paris. Wentworth had also attached himself to John Macarthur senior, despite having earlier mocked him for his pretensions, which Wentworth surmised were

---

Tories were hunted down by Oliver Cromwell during the British Interregnum. The Tories believed in king, country, chasing foxes and twelve-course breakfasts in the conservatory.

5   British law precluded Catholics from holding civil, military, judicial or political office and from graduating from Oxford or Cambridge. The House of Lords blocked the repeal of anti-Catholic laws because a majority of the Protestant lords were convinced Catholics were still plotting to install a papist on the throne, declare Ireland independent and ask for the return of the grand Catholic estates on which many of the Protestant lords were living. The prince regent (later George IV), who ruled Britain from 1811 as his father had again started talking to trees in German, was also staunchly opposed to Catholic emancipation, despite having secretly and illegally married Maria Fitzherbert, a Catholic commoner, in 1785.

"meant to cast a shadow on [his] low extraction". Wentworth wrote to D'Arcy of his intention to marry Macarthur's daughter Elizabeth to create a great Australian dynasty "for the future respectability and grandeur of our family".

The Macarthurs tired of Wentworth's requests for loans and free continental accommodation, which increased when Fitzwilliam turned off the tap after one too many trips to Italy. John senior, a rabid anti-emancipist, told Wentworth in no uncertain terms that his daughter would not be marrying a convict's bastard. Wentworth hated Macarthur thereafter – and he was a good hater.

While Wentworth knew of his mother's low birth, he'd always considered his father a gentleman. He was therefore blindsided when the politician Henry Grey Bennet tabled a pamphlet in the British Parliament that referred to D'Arcy Wentworth as a convicted highwayman. William informed Bennet he would shed his "last drop of blood in the effort" of defending his father's name, but called off the duel when told of D'Arcy's four appearances before the courts. Bennet apologised for using the word "convicted" – D'Arcy had been acquitted each time – but Wentworth's sense of identity was shaken and he redoubled his efforts to bring honour to the family name.

Wentworth's 1819 book was the first to be published by an Australian-born writer. *A Statistical, Historical, and Political Description of the Colony of New South Wales and its Dependent Settlements in Van Diemen's Land, With a Particular Enumeration of the Advantages Which These Colonies Offer for Emigration, and Their Superiority in Many Respects over Those Possessed by the United States of America* is hated by library indexers to this day. It talked up sheep ("No country ... is so well adapted to the growth of fine wool") and talked down Aborigines ("the lowest place in the gradatory scale of the human species"), but its core message was that New South Wales needed free government to supplant America as the migrant's destination of choice.

Wentworth's 466-page magnum opus advocated replacing the colony's military juries with civilian ones and electing a popular assembly, although government nominees might serve in the interim (Wentworth would graciously accept such a nomination). While the governor's tyrannical powers needed to be curbed, Wentworth praised Macquarie for his emancipist policies and condemned Macarthur's exclusive faction for their opposition to granting ex-convicts the same rights as free citizens, accusing the exclusives of wishing "to convert the ignominy of the great body of the people into a hereditary deformity ... and raise an eternal barrier of separation between their offspring and the offspring of the unfortunate convict".

Macarthur senior, who'd by now returned to New South Wales to resume his favourite pastime of ritualistically disembowelling governors, accused Wentworth of plagiarising his views on sheep and claimed that the introduction of representative government or civilian juries "would seal the destruction of every respectable person here".

Macarthur's views were so eighteenth century. He was yesterday's man and Wentworth was the future – or so it seemed until Wentworth met his Peterloo.

THE PEOPLE ARE REVOLTING

Three months after Wentworth called for elected government in New South Wales, 80,000 people gathered at St Peter's Field, Manchester, to demand electoral reform. They objected to the near one million voters of Lancashire having only two elected MPs, the same number as Old Sarum, which had no resident voters, and Dunwich, which had been underwater since 1670.

The English love tradition. What else could compel otherwise sane men to dress up in clogs and bowler hats, tie bells to their knees, wave handkerchiefs in the air and beat each other with sticks in their spare time?[6] It was English nostalgia for the past that had left electoral boundaries untouched for centuries, with 152 of the 406 members of the House of Commons in the early nineteenth century elected by fewer than 100 voters. The small electoral boroughs were rural backwaters, while the labouring masses of the large towns and cities were under-represented – a model that Joh Bjelke-Petersen replicated in Queensland in 1972.[7]

In the days before the secret ballot, small rural "pocket boroughs" were controlled by local lords who terminated the leases of tenant farmers who didn't vote for their chinless sons or chums from the gentlemen's club.[8] This allowed House of Lords aristocrats to influence the composition of the House of Commons and stymie reforms that eroded their power base.

In January 1817, Lord Cochrane tabled petitions in parliament proposing the vote for all men, while outside a mob demanding electoral reform attacked the carriage of the prince regent, with either a bullet or a stone shattering the carriage window.[9]

Parliament had no intention of giving people who were interested

---

6   These elements are common to Morris dancing and Tory sex scandals, both of which are proud English traditions.

7   The peanut farmer turned politician entrenched the power of his rural base by establishing new remote electorates that had a third of the voters of some Brisbane seats.

8   These electorates were known as pocket boroughs because their votes were considered to be "in the pocket" of an individual or family.

9   The idea that men without property or significant income should vote was preposterous. Corsica was the first place in the world to give all men and women the vote, in 1755, but it also gave the world Napoleon and was therefore not a precedent to be followed. (In any event, France abolished universal suffrage when it conquered Corsica in 1769.) Vermont, in 1777, was the first place in the Anglosphere to extend suffrage to non-propertied males (excluding slaves, who were themselves property). Vermont also gave America the first restrictions on slavery, free public education and Bernie Sanders, proof that it is a socialist state. Kentucky, which gave us Colonel Harland Sanders, was the second place in the Anglosphere to grant non-propertied males the vote. Don't eat the Colonel's chicken – it will turn you into a socialist.

in politics the vote and, citing the attack on the prince regent, rushed through sedition laws that banned unauthorised meetings of more than fifty people called "for the purpose ... of deliberating upon any grievance, in church or state". Those who refused to disperse would be subject to the death penalty.[10] The laws also banned political reform bodies like the Spencean Philanthropists, who were believed to have been agitating for revolution.[11] Parliament also suspended the *Habeas Corpus Act*, removing the right of prisoners to challenge the lawfulness of their detention.

In March 1817, disaffected weavers from Manchester set out for London on foot, carrying petitions decrying conditions in the textile industry and demanding the restoration of habeas corpus. The protesters were known as Blanketeers for the symbolic (and warm) blankets they carried. A number were arrested for unlawful assembly before leaving Manchester, despite gathering in groups of only ten – others were taken into custody as vagrants for sleeping outside under their blankets during their march to the capital.

Revolution was catching. In 1818, the schoolboys of Winchester College, armed with axes, cried "Liberty!" as they held the school warden hostage for expelling students who had snuck into town at night, before soldiers put down the rebellion with bayonets. Soon after, the young men of the Royal Military Academy Sandhurst

---

10 Bjelke-Petersen went further than this (except for the death penalty bit, although not through want of desire) by instructing his crooked police commissioner, Terry Lewis, to ban all street marches under his repressive "two's a crowd" policy. In 1978, the ludicrous nature of Joh's restrictions was highlighted by Bundaberg dentist Henry Akers, who was refused permission to walk down a no-through road at 2.45 a.m. on April Fool's Day in the company of his dog, Jaffa, carrying a placard that read, "The majority is not omnipotent. The majority can be wrong and is capable of tyranny."

11 The Spenceans were disciples of Thomas Spence, who advocated the socialisation of land and heretical concepts such as giving all men and women the vote, the introduction of unemployment benefits and the right of infants to be free from abuse and poverty. Spence's attempts to publicise his social reforms were hampered by his insistence that Spencean pamphlets be written in a phonetic script of his own devising.

"put their training to practical use by drawing up in full battle array against the staff".[12]

In March 1819, the citizens of New South Wales got in on the act, with the colony's most knighted citizen, Sir John Jamison, chairing a citizen's assembly that petitioned the prince regent to curb the governor's autocratic powers and introduce jury trials.[13]

The mass gathering at St Peter's Field on 16 August 1819, organised by the liberal *Manchester Observer*, was a turning point in the campaign for political reform. The peaceful demonstrators, carrying banners with slogans such as "Universal Suffrage" and "Vote by Ballot", were set upon by 120 yeoman cavalry, who were described as "younger members of the Tory party in arms". When the crowd responded to the cavalry's sabres with bricks and stones, 600 cavalry and 400 infantry charged, while soldiers with bayonets blocked the main exit. Eleven protesters were killed and over 600 injured in the Peterloo Massacre, named ironically after the British victory at Waterloo four years earlier.

Peterloo was followed by a savage crackdown by the Tory ascendancy. Libel and sedition cases were brought against the protest

---

12 British public schoolboys had a proud history of rebellion, but not over low political
    matters. Winchester boys also mutinied over beer rations in 1710 and fired pistols
    and threw cobblestones at teachers in 1793 over the headmaster's decision to punish
    them all for the misdeeds of a single student. In 1690, the boys of Manchester
    Grammar locked the masters and school servants out of the school (except for
    Cook, who was needed to make breakfast) during a two-week dispute about the
    proposed length of Christmas hols, firing warning shots at anyone who attempted
    to enter the grounds. In 1768, Eton's prefects rebelled because the headmaster would
    no longer allow them to beat junior boys for breaking bounds, while the Great
    Rebellion of 1797 at Rugby resulted in the calling in of the militia and the reading of
    the Riot Act after senior boys blew up the headmaster's room with gunpowder.

13 Sir John was made a knight of the Swedish Order of Gustavus Vasa in 1809 for
    combatting scurvy in the Swedish Navy and appointed a knight bachelor by the
    prince regent in 1813. His achievements pale in comparison to those of Australia's
    most beknighted figure, HRH Prince Philip, who was made a Knight of the Order
    of Australia by Prime Minister Tony Abbott on Australia Day 2015. Prince Philip's
    commitment to building relationships between Britain and other peoples has seen
    him awarded twenty-five other knighthoods, many of which were conferred by
    appreciative wog, dago, spic, dune bunny, fuzzy-wuzzy and nig-nog nations.

organisers and the *Manchester Observer*. The soldiers were exoner-
ated and thanked by the prince regent for their "preservation of the
public peace". Parliament passed the Six Acts, legislation to tighten
sedition laws, regulate the press, restrict access to bail, strengthen
search powers and outlaw weapons-training outside the military.[14]

The Whigs saw these laws as an attack on both the people and
the cherished tradition of a free press. Fitzwilliam protested the
massacre and was dismissed from his government posts.

In the wash-up of Peterloo, the War and Colonial Office was in
no mood to consider the political reform agenda of an upstart colonial
Whig and his convict mates.

THE CHARACTER AND APPEARANCE OF A GENTLEMAN

Wentworth, of course, was undeterred. He continued to advocate
political reform in New South Wales, publishing a second edition of
his book and adding *"and a Word of Advice to Emigrants"* to its earlier
34-word title.[15] The book supported Britain's proposal for a legislative council of government appointees to advise the governor, and
attacked the Macarthurs as hypocrites who opposed progress in order
to feather their own nests.

Wentworth asked his father to lobby his fellow colonists for an
end to "arbitrary government", which D'Arcy ignored as he was arbitrary government's chief beneficiary. Wentworth also asked D'Arcy
for an increased allowance, to be backdated two years, attributing
his total lack of legal clients to his poverty. He wrote, with Whit-
lamesque humility:

---

14 There are uncanny similarities between provisions of the Six Acts and current
    Australian anti-terrorism laws.

15 In Wentworth's day, lawyers charged by the word for their advice, which nurtured
    the growth of Wentworth's natural windbaggery. His *Word of Advice* was actually
    several thousand words.

> I will not suffer myself to be outstripped by any competitor and will
> finally create for myself a reputation which shall reflect a splendour
> on all who are related to me.

In the same letter, he informed D'Arcy that he'd be visiting France for six weeks to see friends. Upon his return, he again complained his income was "utterly inadequate to maintain the character and appearance of a gentleman".

While Wentworth was busy holidaying, the British government, responding to public pressure, started repealing the more offensive provisions of the Six Acts. However, it continued its campaign against radical reformers by infiltrating their organisations, with government spies entrapping the radical leadership by proposing acts of terror and armed insurrection.

In 1820, George Edwards, a government agent who'd been appointed deputy leader of the Spencean Philanthropists, proposed assassinating the entire British Cabinet as it dined at Earl Harrowby's house. The Spenceans thought this was a great idea and planned to establish a "Committee of Public Safety" after the assassination, to continue purging Britain of non-Spenceans. One conspirator, James Ings, who ran a coffee shop when he was not plotting the destruction of the fascist patriarchy, planned to display the heads of cabinet ministers after he'd removed them from their bodies, proving that the nutbags who run ISIS are not even original thinkers. The government arrested the conspirators in their Cato Street headquarters as they prepared to set off for Harrowby's house.

The same year, government agents encouraged poor, angry Scots (i.e. Scots) to strike against high unemployment and food prices, unfair work conditions and the fact that only one in 250 Scots had sufficient declared income or property to vote. The agents encouraged Scottish radical leaders to take up arms for Scottish independence, spreading rumours that an army of kilt-wearing Jacobites and 50,000 French soldiers were hiding in the highlands, waiting to join them.

The rebels marched out, were roughed up by the waiting cavalry and arrested.

The leaders of the Cato Street Conspiracy were hanged and then beheaded. Their heads were mounted on spikes and displayed on May Day, the saint's day dedicated to workers, which the Tory leadership considered delightfully ironic. The leaders of the Scottish Insurrection met a similar fate. However, a number of the lesser conspirators and rebels were transported to Australia, where they joined Luddites, Irish nationalists and other political prisoners. These convicts were natural supporters of reform in the Australian colonies.

But any push for liberal reform Down Under was put on hold by Commissioner Bigge's reports on Macquarie's administration, which were published in 1822–23. Bigge condemned proposals for civilian juries and free government in a land populated by criminals; suggested increased free settlement to improve the moral tone of the colony; proposed that the rights of emancipists be restricted and that British immigrants have greater access to land than the native born; and regurgitated Macarthur's vision of a feudal colonial aristocracy in which power was concentrated in the hands of men who had a lot of money and sheep.

Bigge, to Wentworth's horror, also identified Wentworth as the author of the Molle poem. Wentworth had always publicly denied authorship, despite admitting it to family and close friends. Outraged that others might label his attacks on the hypocrisy of others as hypocritical, Wentworth challenged Bigge to a duel, becoming so unhinged that he had to be placed under police restraint.

Denied the satisfaction of shooting Bigge, Wentworth unloaded on him in the third edition of his book, referring to Bigge's reports as "nauseous trash" and to Bigge as "a public scavenger" and:

> ... a booby commissioner – himself either the unconscious dupe, or
> the corrupt coadjutor of as turbulent and tyrannical a faction, as ever
> any community was yet cursed with ... he has polluted almost every
> page ... with private scandal and vituperation ... he has not scrupled

to promulgate to the world on the faith of mere ex-parte evidence collected with mischievous industry from the very dregs and refuse of the people – from the whores, and rogues, and vagabonds of Sydney.

Wentworth's savaging of Bigge further endeared him to the emancipists (the former whores, and rogues, and vagabonds of Sydney).

William, now over thirty, single and unemployed, was at risk of becoming the Georgian equivalent of the guy who lives in his parents' basement and only ever stirs from his stained waterbed to play *Call of Duty*, surf the net for porn and eat cold curry from a tin. He'd audaciously applied to be the first attorney-general of New South Wales, but had been passed over for the bumbling Saxe Bannister. He was now so hard up that he took a fellowship at Cambridge. Here he entered the Chancellor's Medal poetry competition, which that year had the theme "Australasia". Wentworth's imaginatively titled "Australasia" started:

> *Land of my birth! tho' now, alas! no more*
> *Musing I wander on thy sea-girt shore,*
> *Or climb with eager haste thy barrier cliff,*
> *To catch a glimmer of the distant skiff*

"Australasia" was the first published work by an Australian to use the word *girt*, but was otherwise crap. Wentworth boasted "Australasia" was "the longest prize poem that was ever written at this University" and was disgusted that his masterwork came second to that of Winthrop Mackworth Praed, who'd never been anywhere near Australia.

Praed's verse, however, was more in keeping with the Bigge line that Australia was a vile convict shithole:

> *In exile and misery, lock within*
> *Their dread despair, their unrepented sin, –*
> *And in their madness dare to gaze on heaven,*
> *Sullen and cold, unawed and unforgiven!*

Wentworth modestly dedicated his own "crude effort" to the recalled Macquarie and to women he wanted to sleep with, with his dedication to Ms Bella Taylor reading:

> *And shall my tongue alone be mute?*
> *Shall I be wanting here?*
> *Ah no, dear girl, my author's lute,*
> *Shall speak while I am near.*

Having a bet each way, his dedication to the mysterious "Jane" began:

> *Why Jane, oh why, thou glory of thy kind,*
> *Supreme in loveliness, and grace and mind ...*
> *Relentless charmer, I must love thee still.*

Neither of these relationships progressed and it was back to the basement for William.

But not for long. In 1823, the British Parliament established the New South Wales Supreme Court, permitted jury trials in non-criminal cases before that court where the parties agreed and, most importantly for Wentworth, allowed British barristers to practise in the colony. Wentworth asked Fitzwilliam for a final £250 loan to cover the £80 fare to Sydney. He was joined on the voyage by Robert Wardell, a young barrister and one-time newspaper proprietor.

Wentworth had earlier railed against the dull timidity of the *Sydney Gazette*, the New South Wales government newspaper, writing:

> An independent paper ... which may serve to point out the rising interests of the colonists, and become the organ of their grievances and rights, their wishes and wants – is highly necessary.

Wentworth and Wardell packed a printing press on the *Alfred* as she set sail for Sydney in February 1824. They would hit the colony with all the pure muckraking force of Rupert Murdoch on ice.

WINDRADYNE'S WAR

As the People's Poet was setting sail, trouble was brewing in Wiradjuri country, and Wentworth, ever a lightning rod for discontent, was partially responsible for it. In 1813, he'd crossed the Blue Mountains to the west of Sydney with Gregory Blaxland and William Lawson, opening up the Australian interior for settlement. Two years later, Macquarie established Australia's first inland town, Bathurst, slap-bang in the middle of the Wiradjuri's lands.[16]

Relationships with the Wiradjuri were generally cordial, if a little strained, as most settlers preferred to live closer to the rough comforts of Sydney. That ended when Governor Thomas Brisbane, Macquarie's successor, shot viagra into the veins of rural settlement, following Bigge's recommendation that New South Wales be converted into a giant shearing shed. Brisbane wanted pastoralists, aided by the more responsible convicts, to open up the fertile western plains for grazing.

The Wiradjuri's sacred sites and hunting grounds were suddenly overrun by farmers, felons and their strange white fluffy animal totems. In 1822, the Wiradjuri commenced guerrilla raids on remote stations, spearing sheep, cattle and the occasional unlucky shepherd. Many of the attacks were led by a man barely out of his teens – his people knew him as Windradyne, the settlers as Saturday.[17]

In December 1823, soldiers marched out to bring Windradyne in. The *Sydney Gazette* of 8 January 1824 reported:

---

16   Wiradjuri means "not having" in the Wiradjuri language, which proved remarkably prescient after the British came and took away their lands and children.

17   Settlers commonly named Aborigines after days of the week. This trend was started by Robinson Crusoe, who met a black man one Friday and said, "Right, I'll call you Friday." How Crusoe knew what day of the week it was after spending twenty-four years alone on an island has never been satisfactorily explained.

Advices from Bathurst say, that the natives have been very troublesome in that country. Numbers of cattle have been killed. In
justification of their conduct, the natives urge, that the white
men have driven away all the kangaroos and opossums, and the
black men must now have beef! ... The strength of these men
is amazing. One of the chiefs (named Saturday) of a desperate
tribe, took six men to secure him and they had actually to break
a musket over his body before he yielded, which he did at length
with broken ribs ... Saturday, for his exploits, was sentenced to a
month's imprisonment.

The skirmishes escalated into out-and-out conflict after the Potato
Field Incident, in which a farmer offered potatoes to the recently
released Windradyne and friends. The next day, the Wiradjuri,
believing the potatoes to be growing on their land, returned to dig
up the crop. The enraged farmer shot a number of the potato eaters
and a wave of revenge attacks followed.

William Cox, who'd built the road across the Blue Mountains and
received the first land grant on the western plains, advised a public
gathering that the "best thing that could be done, would be to shoot
all the Blacks and manure the ground with their carcases, which is
all the good they were fit for".

On 14 August 1824, Brisbane declared martial law and the 40th
Regiment joined the settler militia in terminating the Wiradjuri
with extreme prejudice. A reward of 500 acres of Wiradjuri land was
offered to anyone who brought Windradyne in alive.[18] A week after
the declaration of martial law, the word *alive* was removed from the
reward notices.

Wiradjuri men, women and children were shot and poisoned,
with up to a third of their people wiped out during the 1824 conflict.

---

18   This offer was circulated among the Wiradjuri, in the hope they would hand in
     their leader. The Wiradjuri couldn't work out why some white guy was offering
     them their own land.

Windradyne, who'd provided the most sustained resistance to British occupation since Pemulwuy, knew when he was outgunned. He sought to end the conflict when he crossed the mountains to attend the governor's annual feast for the tribes at Parramatta on 28 December 1824. The *Sydney Gazette* reported:

> Saturday wore a straw hat, on which was affixed a label, with the word "PEACE" inserted, besides a little branch representing the olive, which rather increased the interest as regarded him.

Brisbane issued a pardon to Windradyne, who was killed in an intertribal dispute a few years later.[19] Everybody else lived happily ever after. The End.[20]

THE RETURN OF THE PRODIGAL SON

When Wentworth and Wardell arrived in Sydney, they did what any good lawyers would do – they sued the *Alfred*'s captain for the cost of their passage. The pair complained that they'd been forced to eat salted meat, that their cabins were ankle-deep in water and, worst of all, that the captain had sailed before the 600 bottles of beer they'd bought for the voyage cleared customs. They won.

---

19 An obituary for Windradyne in the *Sydney Gazette* concluded with the following lines from the African slave and Roman playwright Terence: *Homo sum, humani nihil a me alicuum puto* ("I am a man, I consider nothing human as alien to me"). The *Gazette* helpfully explained: "This quotation from the Roman dramatist contains a fine sentiment for those persons who think no more of man in a state of nature than they do of a wild animal."

20 Well, that's one version. The other involves lots of Wiradjuri being carted off to reserves, missions, children's homes and the houses of concerned Christians who'd greet them with the familiar words, "The Mr Sheen is under the stairs." Despite these disappointments, the Wiradjuri remain the largest Aboriginal group in New South Wales and the Wiradjuri language has been reintroduced into some schools. Journalist Stan Grant, Labor MP Linda Burney, tennis player Evonne Goolagong, rugby league player David Peachey, cricketer Daniel Christian and writer Anita Heiss are among those who identify as Wiradjuri.

Deprived of alcohol at sea, Wentworth went on a bender after arriving in Sydney and was arrested three times for being drunk and disorderly. He was not one of those quiet drunks who sits in a corner with the French onion dip before passing out on the couch – he was 100 decibels of raw aggression or raucous bonhomie, depending on his mood.

Wentworth and Wardell were admitted as barristers in September 1824 and spent two hours during the admission ceremony making submissions to Chief Justice Francis Forbes on why lowly solicitors should be excluded from the courts and barristers should do all the colony's court work. They lost.[21]

Wentworth had returned to Sydney at a time when the exclusive and emancipist factions were waging war over the future of the colony. John Macarthur, the undisputed leader of the exclusives, was driven through the streets of Sydney in his bespoke carriage, with its emblazoned coat of arms proclaiming him a lord of the new colonial aristocracy. He dismissed the emancipist faction as "renegade Jews, shopkeepers, Americans and a man who had married a convict woman – Tambourine Sal who made a living singing and dancing at country fairs".[22]

---

21 When their campaign finally succeeded in 1834, Wentworth hosted a drunken bash for the colony's nine barristers, with a tub of wine placed in Wardell's vacant chair (Wardell having been shot dead before he could enjoy the fruits of legal exclusivity). The barristers, toasting "Good Fees and plenty of them" and "Take no Briefs without the cash", became so pissed that Wentworth had to ring a giant auctioneer's bell for five minutes to quieten them for his after-dinner speech, which started: "I need not repeat the occasion of our meeting, for the bottles you have emptied cannot have washed that from your memory, though they seem to have impaired your understanding. Look at me, the father of the Australian Bar, yet here I stand, with six bottles under my belt, and none the worse. I feel for your degeneracy, my sons, but trust that practice will soon make you perfect, and trust by punctual attendance at bar dinners, under my tuition, you will emulate the British Barrister in all his habits. Next to wine, my brethren, devotion to the fair sex is the characteristic and pride of the English Barrister – but in this respect you are not wanting – so I have good hopes of you."

22 This was a reference to William Lawson, Wentworth's old exploring buddy, and Lawson's wife, Sarah Leadbeater. Lawson and other wealthy settlers who'd married convicts generally supported the emancipist cause.

Brisbane, although responsible for implementing Bigge's pro-exclusive reforms, was personally inclined to liberalism. He'd taken the job as governor not to pursue an ideological agenda but to study the southern stars. The posting was secured by his teenage friend-ship with the Duke of Wellington, the hero of Waterloo. Brisbane was happy to stay at his observatory at Parramatta, where the skies were clearer, and delegate many of the decisions of government to his colonial secretary, Frederick Goulburn, or the new Legislative Council that had been established to advise him.

Still, Brisbane's egalitarian sympathies shone through. When he proposed that settlers, like convicts, be subject to the census, Macarthur, who'd torn down Brisbane's four predecessors, fumed, "Reptile! Damn him! He had better take care, or he will see more of me than is agreeable to him."

An early observer of Australian farmers' love of government handouts, Brisbane complained, "Not a cow calves in the colony but her owner applies for an additional grant in consequence of the increase in his stock." He began selling Crown land at five shillings per acre. This was anathema to Macarthur, who was used to being granted vast tracts of prime pasture for free.

Brisbane had completely fallen out with the exclusives over their attempts to prosecute his friend Dr Henry Douglass, an emancipist sympathiser. Douglass, the head of Parramatta's hospital and female factory and a magistrate, had been accused of "lifting the petticoats" of his servant, Ann Rumsby, a charge both he and Ann denied. Samuel Marsden, Hannibal Macarthur (John's nephew) and Parramatta's other exclusive magistrates, unable to convict Douglass without Ann's corroboration, convicted Ann of perjury.

Concerned that a powerless servant had been punished for frus-trating the exclusives' designs, Brisbane pardoned Ann and sacked the magistrates for their continued refusal to sit on the bench with an alleged petticoat lifter. Marsden and Hannibal were censured by the War and Colonial Office, and Douglass, still a magistrate, ordered the seizure of Marsden's prized £100 piano for non-payment of a fine. The exclusives had lost their public positions, aura of invincibility and keyboard. They blamed Brisbane.

FREE PRESS AND FREE LOVE

Most of the exclusives also condemned Brisbane's decision "to try the experiment of the full latitude of the freedom of the press". Wentworth and Wardell were the principal beneficiaries of this decision – on 14 October 1824, the two barristers published Australia's first privately owned newspaper, the *Australian*, writing in the editorial, "a free press is the most legitimate and ... powerful weapon that can be employed to ... frustrate the designs of tyranny."

On the same day, Brisbane lifted censorship of the government paper, the *Sydney Gazette*. The *Gazette*, edited by Robert Howe, the son of a shoplifter, promptly laid into the exclusives, writing that Macarthur and his cronies "owed their present eminence in society, not to the dignity of birth, not to liberality of sentiment, but to the petty retailing of three-watered grog". Macarthur, who hated being reminded of his Rum Corps origins, blasted the "unprincipled wretches the editors" and damned Brisbane for not punishing Howe.

Wentworth used the *Australian* to promote emancipist and native-born causes, jury trials for all cases and representative government – and to promote himself as a shining angel of justice for the disenfranchised and the poor (as long as they could pay his fees).

He was also not above using the paper to advance the interests of his clients.[23] When Brisbane commissioned the *Almorah* to import rice during a food shortage, the ship's captain also brought in 350 chests of tea, in breach of the East India Company monopoly. Charles Mitchell, an opportunistic naval officer, argued the ship was an illegal vessel and captured it as a prize, claiming that the rice now belonged

---

23   The thought of the *Australian* pandering to vested interests now seems laughable.

to him, rather than to Sydney's hungry. Brisbane retained Saxe Bannister to represent the government, and Wentworth, who'd never forgiven Bannister for being preferred over him as attorney-general, represented Mitchell.

When Bannister rowed out to the ship with a warrant for the release of the rice, Mitchell ordered warning shots to be fired. Bannister gamely continued, frantically waving the warrant in one hand and a white handkerchief in the other, but retreated when he heard musket balls falling around him.

The *Australian* laughed off this use of arms against the colony's chief legal officer, reporting, "The dull monotony of Sydney ... has been a little broken by a comical incident," and claimed only a few blanks were fired.[24] Wentworth successfully defended Mitchell on the basis that the officer who'd actually fired the shots had sailed for Calcutta and the court couldn't be certain that he hadn't decided to shoot up the attorney-general off his own bat.

On the day the *Australian* first went to print, Chief Justice Forbes determined that jury trials should be available for non-criminal matters in all of the colony's courts. D'Arcy Wentworth, who was responsible for appointing jurors, had been ordered to exclude ex-convicts. William helped Simeon Lord, a wealthy emancipist, sue his father for discrimination. The government conceded that "respectable" ex-cons might sit on juries, a significant step forward for emancipist rights.

Wentworth took the credit for jury reform and other progressive initiatives of Brisbane's administration, with his paper's first-anniversary edition gushing, "the first Authors of The Australian will be referred to as the founders of liberal politics in the Colony."

The self-proclaimed founder's slovenly appearance, disconcerting wall-eye and propensity for vomiting all over himself at any function

---

24 The *Australian* loved belittling Bannister. In a later case, the paper summed up his performance in appearing against the masterful Wentworth: "For six hours did this poor man rant and roar ... resembling an over-driven ox ... then whining pitifully like a lamb."

held after breakfast ensured he'd remained single. But the rumpled Rumpole's luck was about to change.

In May 1825, Wentworth represented Francis Cox, who was suing John Payne for a breach of promise to marry his daughter, Sarah. Payne had sent Sarah a note asking if she had any objection to changing her name to Sarah Payne, and Sarah's employer, Mrs Forster, gave evidence that she had "heard the defendant make love to the young lady". Payne then made love to a Miss Redmond and the recently widowed Mrs Leverton, with Wentworth intoning, "A case of greater treachery never came before a court."

Wardell, who represented Payne, argued Sarah had suffered no financial loss as she was a good sort who would have no trouble finding another bloke. He summed up his case, "Captain Payne was the only pain that could give her pleasure; yet he was not the only suitor that would suit her."[25]

Although Wentworth won the case, Wardell was proven correct. Wentworth, pushing the monogrammed envelope of lawyer–client privilege to its very limits, had knocked Sarah up before the case went to trial. A greater case of hypocrisy never came before a court.

While Wentworth was not prepared to marry Sarah either, she moved into his Petersham Estate and gave birth to Thomasine, named after Thomas Brisbane.

Brisbane had been recalled two months before Thomasine's birth. His willingness to delegate resulted in criticism that he spent his days shooting parrots and his nights playing with telescopes. He'd fallen out with Goulburn over the secretary's insistence that the governor's orders were invalid unless they first passed through his office, and John Macarthur junior had white-anted him at Whitehall. Wellington philosophically acknowledged of his friend, "there are many brave men not fit to be governors of colonies."

---

25   The barristers of Sydney's Wardell Chambers still crack open bottles of Grange to toast their forebear's zinging wit.

Freed from the shackles of office, Brisbane campaigned for colonial jury reform and representative government after his return to London. Wentworth, who'd railed against the exclusives as "the yellow snakes of the Colony" at Brisbane's farewell, would soon discover Brisbane's successor to be the yellowest serpent of them all.

THE EXCLUSIVES' DARLING

Governor Ralph Darling was not given to liberal sentiment or, indeed, sentiment of any kind. Unique in the British Army for having climbed through the ranks after enlisting as a private, Darling was the very model of a modern lieutenant-general. He stood straight, put on freshly creased trousers each morning and sported an upper lip that was stiffer than Nicole Kidman's brow line on Oscar night.[26] As one contemporary observed, Darling "mistook formality for dignity" – even his wife referred to him as "the general".

Eliza Darling, twenty-seven years younger than her husband, made up for the general's lack of sentiment by throwing herself into the arts. She was a tolerable painter and an intolerable poet, as evidenced by this effort:

> What! Shoot little birds, with a great, long, big gun,
> Poor dear little things! And they say, it's all 'fun'.

She was not, however, a patron of the stage, as her husband "ruthlessly and implacably countered all attempts to establish a theatre in Sydney". Darling, who considered actors provocateurs and theatregoers

---

26 Botox is an abbreviation of *botulism toxin*, the most lethal toxin yet discovered (market researchers recommended rebranding for obvious reasons). Botulism toxin was first described five years before Darling arrived in Australia, when the small-town German doctor and romantic poet Justinus Kerner noted the paralytic symptoms of patients who had consumed a dodgy batch of German sausages (botulism derives from *botulus*, Latin for "sausage", and was originally known as "the sausage poison"). The link between English breakfast sausages and the British stiff upper lip is yet to be conclusively established.

anarchists, applied British political protest laws to the performing arts. He outlawed public entertainments not approved by his private secretary and brother-in-law, Lieutenant-Colonel Henry Dumaresq, and instructed Henry to refuse all applications, other than those for music recitals.

The ultra-conservative Darlings were champions of the exclusive cause. And with Brisbane gone, the exclusive faction was again flexing its muscle. John Macarthur and two fellow anti-emancipists were appointed as the first private citizens on an expanded Legislative Council. Macarthur was also an inaugural director of the Bank of Australia, known as the "pure merino bank" for its exclusion of ex-convicts as shareholders.

John Macarthur junior had successfully lobbied the British government to establish the Australian Agricultural Company, which was allocated a million acres for an outlay of £10,000 – 4 per cent of the land's value. Other family members were appointed as managers and recommended the purchase of Macarthur merinos at inflated prices. Chief Justice Forbes described the company's operations as "fraud committed with impunity by the better orders of society".

The Macarthurs ceased their attacks on Wentworth, believing his star would implode under the pressure of his own ego and rebel tendencies. Australia's favourite native son would disappoint them.

THE RAKE'S PROGRESS

Wentworth was worming his way into respectable society, renovating the stately Vaucluse House to accommodate his girlfriend, love child and fine wine collection. The man who'd won Australia's first public horserace helped found the Sydney Turf Club, where he threw drunken parties for gentlemen of influence. He sat on the board of the Bank of New South Wales, where his insistence on lowering interest rates resulted in the bank's holdings falling from £123,000 to £4,739.

While Darling bore the financial pain of the £20,000 government bailout that followed, Wentworth's cheap rates further endeared him to the masses.

Wentworth left the *Australian* in March 1826 to focus on his lucrative legal career. Other newspapers were springing up, including the *Monitor*, published by Edward Smith Hall. The *Monitor* championed the rights of convicts and the poor, consistent with Hall's role as the founder of The Benevolent Society of New South Wales, Australia's first charity. The expanding Sydney media, high on press freedom, spawned a plague of libel cases that kept Wentworth in *Château Lafite* for years.[27]

Wentworth also became the colony's leading criminal defence barrister. In 1827, he argued that the courts had no power to find a soldier guilty of murdering an Aborigine, Jackey Jackey, on the grounds that offences committed by or against Aborigines were not subject to British law. The same year, another Aborigine, also known as Jackey Jackey, elegantly disproved this argument by being sentenced to death for killing a white shepherd.[28]

While Wentworth believed that Aborigines were not civilised enough to give evidence in court, he overturned centuries of British precedent in successfully arguing that convict witnesses should be able to do so. The colony's liberal press applauded him for his humanitarianism.

As Wentworth's professional life flourished, his personal life foundered. D'Arcy died in 1827, sending Wentworth into an alcoholic spiral. His erratic behaviour caused the *Gazette* to speculate that he was "either a little cracked in the upper story ... [or] downright mad".

Wentworth was now on rocky ground with Sarah, who refused to register him as the father of her second child. This was probably

---

27   Some exclusives chose bullets over briefs to settle libel actions. Saxe Bannister and Robert Wardell exchanged fire over an attack on Bannister in the *Australian*. Wardell also traded six shots with Henry Dumaresq over an offending article.

28   *Jackey Jackey* had become a generic name applied to Aborigines whose real names you couldn't be bothered learning.

payback – Wentworth had fathered a child with the abandoned wife of a friend, Jemima Eagar, whom he'd installed in one of his properties. Wentworth had also become entangled with Jane New, the beautiful convict wife of a client.

Jane, who'd married James New after being assigned to him as a servant, had a theft conviction overturned on a technicality. Darling, furious that a convict hussy should make a mockery of the legal system, revoked her assignment and sent her to the female factory.[29] Wentworth, hired by James to return his wife, argued that the governor had no power to cancel a convict's assignment unless it was for the convict's benefit.

The judge refused to rule on Wentworth's novel argument that the governor could only be nice to convicts, but Jane was rescued by the Supreme Court registrar, John Stephen, who'd fallen madly in love and provided her with a false certificate of freedom in the hope she would elope with him to New Zealand. Jane instead holed up at Vaucluse House and later boarded a New Zealand–bound vessel without Stephen, leaving him to face the music for his role in her escape, and her heartbroken husband to face Wentworth's large legal bill.

Wentworth claimed he had no idea the runaway seductress had been living with him, as he'd been ill in bed for the three weeks that she may (or may not) have been (or not been) in his house (or somewhere else entirely). Could anyone seriously suggest he would abuse his trusted position by behaving improperly with a client's female relative?

Sarah, who was altogether too familiar with Wentworth's form on that particular track, sent him to the doghouse. The wandering barrister briefly withdrew from public life to rebuild his relationship, marrying Sarah that year. Australia's rake may have been temporarily quietened, but he would never be tamed.

---

29   *Hussy* is a contraction of housewife. Similarly, *slut* was a term for a kitchen maid or household drudge. Why did words associated with female domestic work take on pejorative meanings? Discuss.

STOP PRESS

Wentworth had been on a collision course with Darling since the Sudds–Thompson affair of 1827. Privates Sudds and Thompson had stolen some cloth in the hope of being drummed out of the army. Darling, who couldn't tolerate the suggestion that convict life was preferable to army service, increased the sentence imposed by the judge. Drawing on the experience of his own Tory initiation, he then stripped the soldiers naked in front of their regiment and clapped them in fourteen-pound spiked iron collars linked to ankle chains, which he'd designed specially for the occasion. The collars, three times heavier than those worn on chain gangs, prevented Sudds and Thompson from straightening their bodies. Sudds died five days later.

The *Australian* savaged Darling as a despot, while the *Monitor* accused him of extra-judicial torture. The governor responded by cracking down on the press. He introduced laws requiring editors to be registered, after Wentworth successfully argued that nobody could prove Wardell was the editor of the *Australian*. Darling tried to drive papers out of business by imposing a four-penny tax on every copy sold. Wentworth then successfully argued that the *Monitor* was "no more a newspaper than the Encyclopaedia Britannica" and that the *Australian* was now a magazine.

Chief Justice Forbes, who'd earlier voiced the opinion that Darling's treatment of Sudds and Thompson was illegal, declared the newspaper tax "an excessive instrument of suppression" and refused to validate it. Darling now had a rogue judiciary on his hands.

Wentworth also successfully defended *Monitor* editor Edward Smith Hall against charges that he'd failed to comply with new laws requiring copies of all papers to be forwarded to the colonial secretary's office for vetting, pointing out that the colonial secretary, Alexander McLeay, hadn't appointed anyone to receive the papers. The embarrassed McLeay later branded Wentworth "an infamous blackguard ... worthy of his birth being the son of an Irish Highwayman by a convict whore".

Hall, who was even more anti-establishment than Wentworth and Wardell, came under sustained attack from the exclusives. Darling removed his right to graze his stock on public land and Archdeacon Scott, Bigge's brother-in-law, locked him out of his rented pew in church. Hall's printer was a convict, so Darling revoked his assignment and sent him to a road gang. When the printer returned to work, Hall was charged with harbouring an escaped felon. Wentworth had Hall's conviction overturned, as the War and Colonial Office had now accepted his earlier argument that the governor should not be able to unilaterally revoke convict assignments.

Hall, later serving a three-year sentence for libel, continued to publish the *Monitor* from his prison cell. If gaol didn't silence him, Darling reasoned, then maybe exile would. Darling passed a law that any editor twice convicted of blasphemous or seditious libel could be deported to Britain.

Darling was poorly served by his lawyers in his battles with the press. Saxe Bannister had returned to Britain after failing to shoot Wardell, and his replacement, Alexander Macduff Baxter, had the legal acumen of a dead wombat.

Baxter, known as Dandy for his lavish parties and expensive suits, was so incompetent Darling reported to the War and Colonial Office that "he had never before had a brief in his life". Unable to cope with the stresses of office, Dandy threatened to sue Darling for libel, stayed permanently drunk and beat his Spanish wife with a poker when she gave birth to twin girls. When the girls were baptised as Catholics, Dandy left his wife and took his young son to Van Diemen's Land, where he'd been offered a judicial post to keep him out of everyone's way.[30]

---

30 Arthur "found him in a high state of neurotic excitement and such a habitual sot that it would have been a violation of all public decency to have suffered him to take his seat on the Bench". Arthur paid Dandy £400 to go back to Britain, where his playboy lifestyle, coupled with a lack of any discernible talent or income, landed him in debtors' prison.

Wentworth, meanwhile, was lighting fires on another front. He'd submitted a 25,000-word indictment to the War and Colonial Office, accusing Darling of murdering Sudds and interfering with his corpse to conceal the crime. Wentworth was playing chicken and was determined that the governor would swerve first.

Darling was now an embarrassment back in Britain, where reform was gathering steam. In January 1828, the secretary of state for war and the colonies, William Huskisson, introduced a bill to "gradually assimilate the administration of justice in New South Wales to that of England".[31] The same year, it was discovered that the electors of East Retford had formed a corporation to sell their votes to the highest bidder, and that Wentworth's kinsman Earl Fitzwilliam had been paying forty guineas per voter to buy the seat for the Whigs. The scandal added impetus to the push for electoral reform, with the Whig prime minister, Earl Grey, passing the *Great Reform Act* of 1832 to modernise electoral boundaries and extend the franchise to one in five adult males (up from one in seven).[32]

While Huskisson's bill was watered down, the 1828 colonial reforms broadened access to jury trials and required Darling and Arthur to abide by a majority vote of their legislative councils, which had been expanded to include more private citizens. While Wentworth was furious these laws did not go further, the slow stream of reform was trickling steadily in his direction.

---

31 William Huskisson also gathered steam, being the first person in history to be killed by a train. Huskisson stepped onto the track during the 15 September 1830 opening of the Liverpool and Manchester Railway, the world's first fully steam-powered railway line. He was attempting to shake the hand of Wellington (then prime minister), who was sitting in a nearby carriage, when John Stephenson's famous *Rocket*, driven by Stephenson himself, came hurtling down the track. Huskisson attempted to clamber through Wellington's carriage door, but the door, with Huskisson attached, swung open over the track just as *Rocket* was passing. Despite Huskisson's death, the day was hailed a resounding success, with Britain leading the world into a new era of transport.

32 Earl Grey, the greatest liberal political reformer of the nineteenth century, is now best known for lending his name to bergamot-infused tea.

Darling's law to banish repeat libel offenders was the last straw for the War and Colonial Office. Britain had worked hard at shipping its radical reformers off to the arse end of the world and didn't take kindly to Darling's "return to sender" policy. The British government disallowed Darling's law and sacked him.

On the day Darling left for England in 1831, the *Monitor* advertised "Mr Wentworth's Fete and Illumination", at which an ox and half a dozen sheep were to be roasted and washed down with Cooper's beer to celebrate Darling's departure. Four thousand revellers turned up at Vaucluse House to party, fight and riot in a distinctly Australian way. Wentworth, shouting and laughing, with a bottle in one hand and a bottle in the other, was carried above the heads of the adoring throng.

The People's Poet was only just getting started. His next stanza would rewrite the history of Australia.

FIG. 5: WILLIAM CHARLES WENTWORTH WAS THE FATHER OF AUSTRALIAN POLITICAL REFORM, PRESS FREEDOM AND CROWD-SURFING.

Postscript for Macarthur

Yet each man kills the thing he loves.

Oscar Wilde, "The Ballad of Reading Gaol", 1898

JOHN MACARTHUR'S INFLUENCE OVER THE COLONY waned in the later years of Darling's rule. When Darling refused to indemnify Legislative Council members for personal libel actions, Macarthur hissed that "he had never yet failed in ruining a man who had become obnoxious to him".

Darling wrote of Macarthur to the War and Colonial Office: "Naturally factious and turbulent, he considers the accomplishment of his plans as secondary to the subjugation of his opponents."

Macarthur, whose "acute melancholy and depression of spirits" left him increasingly confined to bed, would emerge during manic phases to announce grandiose business plans on which he never followed through. He would invent a new irrigation system. He would go to South America to breed asses. He would import thousands of Chinamen to shear his sheep on the cheap.

The Australian Agricultural Company was losing money, and Macarthur, determined that his name would not be attached to business failure, seized control of its operations. His autocratic and erratic management saw the company's share price crash from £100 to £8.

By 1832, Macarthur was investing all his manic energy in home renovation. He knocked down a wall to extend a corridor by a few inches and converted the main bedroom into a library. Elizabeth moved out because every time she looked for the kitchen John had moved it somewhere else. She wrote to John junior, "I cannot but consider that he labours under a partial derangement of mind and views many objects through a distorted medium."

John's depression deepened into paranoid psychosis. He moved into his new library and barred the doors. He shouted and swore. He took an inexplicable dislike to the kindly Mrs Lucas, a long-time family friend and neighbour.

Macarthur, who had always loved his family above all else, drew pistols and swords on his daughters and threw them out of the house for robbing him. He accused the ever-faithful Elizabeth of adultery and attributed a sore on his hand to poison administered by a family member. He further complained that his sons, "under the influence of a similar poison which had completely deranged their intellects, but that ... had not in the slightest degree affected the intellects of [me]", had seized "some remote part of the Colony from which it would be necessary to dislodge them by force of arms".

The following month, James and William Macarthur had their father declared, in the mental health terminology of the day, a complete gibbering nutbag. They took charge of John's business affairs and confined him to his bedroom/library under round-the-clock guard.

The following year, as rumours of John's recovery spread, James and William had him transferred to the remote Macarthur estate at Camden. As the carriage took John away, he shouted that his family had plotted against him and that he was not mad.[1] He died at Camden in 1834, estranged from his wife and children and utterly alone, except for the servants who guarded him and the sheep he had always loved.

---

1   There is a school of thought that Macarthur's sons had him sectioned so they could seize control of his vast estates, an early example of Australian elder abuse. If so, a small part of Macarthur, who had lied and cheated to destroy others and raise himself to greatness, would have been proud of their ruthless entrepreneurial spirit.

6

Batman Begins Melbourne
(and other stories)

I'm Batman.

John Batman, 1835

EXPLORING AUSTRALIA BY PRAM

J OHN OXLEY WAS A COASTAL EXPLORER, EVEN WHEN
trudging through the interior. This was because Oxley believed
that all of Australia was coast.

Oxley's insistence that the continent was filled by a vast inland
sea halted further western settlement. However, his discovery of
Port Macquarie in 1819 and Moreton Bay in 1823 allowed new penal
outposts to be established to Sydney's north. It was hoped that putting a few criminals in what is now the central business district of
Brisbane would deter the French from turning Australia's north-east
coast into a new Riviera.

Oxley was also pessimistic about southern settlement. After a
desultory expedition in 1819, he concluded that the land south of
Sydney was "uninhabitable and useless for all purposes of civilised
men". His companion on this trip was a wiry native-born youth,
Hamilton Hume, who by his early twenties had explored much of
the land between Sydney and Yass and established a station on the
colony's southernmost fringe. He considered himself civilised, his
land habitable and useful, and Oxley a bit of a knob.

In 1824, Hume offered to lead an overland expedition from the settled areas to Australia's south coast. Governor Brisbane was only willing to provide the most basic supplies, but a retired naval officer, Captain William Hovell, offered to help fund the venture on the condition that Hume let him tag along.

The Hume and Hovell expedition was the first in Australia to use bullock carts. It was also the first to use a pram, with a primitive odometer rigged to a wheel to measure distance travelled.

Hume and Hovell were the Odd Couple of Australian exploration. Hume was an experienced bushman who got on well with the party's convict helpers. Hovell, eleven years older and forty years more reserved, pushed the pram and spent his spare time sulking in the tent he shared with Hume.

Hovell, like most sailors, was terrified of water. When confronted with the Murrumbidgee River, Hume wrapped a bullock cart in tarpaulin and told Hovell it was now a boat. Hume mocked Hovell for cowardice, before coaxing him into the makeshift vessel. The duo discovered another river, which Hume named the Hume, insisting that he had named it not after himself, but his father.[1] This time he wrapped some sticks in tarpaulin and, when Hovell refused to climb aboard, shouted, "If you don't do what I tell you, I'll throw you in!"

Hovell often wanted to turn back, but was unlikely to make it alone: once when he split from the main party he was found wandering in the opposite direction to his intended route (this was a worry, as he was the expedition's navigator). After a fight over their proposed course, the couple agreed to separate and cut their tent in half. However, they couldn't decide who would keep the expedition's

---

1   Nobody else would have named a river after Andrew Hume. Although an established landholder by 1824, he'd earlier been charged with rape and stealing wheat. He was described by Governor King as "a worthless character", dismissed from a government post for "indications of dishonesty" and his wife was forced to leave her position as senior mistress of the Female Orphan School due to "unpleasant domestic circumstances".

frying pan, which was broken in the ensuing scuffle. Hovell stormed off but sheepishly rejoined Hume later that night.

The pair reached the coast after ten weeks, but couldn't agree on which coast it was, as the pram had broken. Unable to calculate the distance travelled, Hovell fiddled with his compass, looked at the sun and claimed they were at Western Port. Hume pointed out the lack of any big islands or small penguins and suggested they'd reached Port Phillip. Hovell pulled rank as the navigator and Western Port it was.

The return journey was like Lennon and McCartney after Yoko started cooking breakfast. The explorers only communicated when necessary and eyed each other with suspicion. Each tried to make a break for Sydney while the other wasn't looking, hoping to be the first to advise Brisbane of the great rivers and coastal meadows they'd found.[2]

In 1826, Governor Darling decided to establish a new convict settlement on the coast discovered by Hume and Hovell. Hovell, who accompanied the settlement party, was embarrassed that the sandy scrubland looked nothing like the area he'd visited two years earlier, which we now know to be near Port Phillip's Geelong. The settlement failed after two years.

Had Hovell's pram not broken, Port Phillip would have been settled nine years before John Batman and John Pascoe Fawkner crossed Bass Strait to build new lives for themselves. The faulty pram proved a blessing for these Tasmanian entrepreneurs, but was the wonky-wheeled herald of disaster for Australia's Indigenous people.

---

2   Hume was outraged that the Sydney press wrote about the exploits of Hovell
     and Hume, rather than Hume and Hovell. His anger intensified when Hovell's
     record of the journey claimed Hovell had been the brains behind the two
     adventurous river crossings and downplayed Hume's role. When Hovell was
     invited to Geelong in 1855 as the discoverer of the region, Hume published his
     own account of the expedition, backed up by the party's convicts, characterising
     Hovell as weak, cowardly and incompetent. The pair bitched about each other
     until Hume's death in 1873.

GO WEST

Darling's Western Port settlement, like Moreton Bay and Van Diemen's Land, was established to deter the French from engaging in their traditional pastimes of taking off their clothes and leaving bottles on Australian beaches. Darling now had the east and south covered, but was convinced that it was only a matter of time until patisseries started springing up in the north and the west.

Britain claimed Australia's north coast in 1825, establishing a small settlement at Port Essington, about 150 kilometres north-east of Darwin. The settlement relocated to Melville Island due to insufficient fresh water, but isolation, disease, lack of supplies and a surplus of very angry Melville Islanders resulted in its abandonment after three years.[3]

Darling had more luck in the west, which had been claimed by George Vancouver at King George Sound in 1791.[4] Darling decided to make good Vancouver's claim by sending Major Edmund Lockyer, twenty-three convicts and a few soldiers and public servants to settle the west. Lockyer sailed into the Sound and founded Frederickstown (now Albany) on Christmas Day 1826.[5]

Lockyer was surprised to discover he was not the first European settler in the area – sealers were clubbing their way around the west coast and abducting Noongar women on their days off. Lockyer raided the sealers and sent two to Sydney to face kidnapping charges. He returned the abducted women, establishing good relations with the Noongar, although the peace would not last for long.

The following year, Captain James Stirling went in search of another suitable site to keep the west French-free and set up a trading

---

3   An 1827 attempt to settle the Cobourg Peninsula failed for similar reasons. Port Essington was resettled in 1838 but abandoned in 1848 after being struck by malaria and a cyclone. Civilised man was clearly not meant to live in Australia's hostile north.

4   Vancouver, despite the French name, was one of the good guys. He is now best remembered as a large Canadian city.

5   Merry Christmas, Noongar people!

base with the East Indies. He was greatly taken by the Swan River because just a few cannons positioned on nearby Mount Eliza would be able to blow any passing Frenchmen into whatever special hell God had reserved for them.

Stirling sailed for Britain to lobby for a colony on the banks of the Swan. This would be Australia 3.0, with all the bugs of previous versions (i.e. convicts) removed. Stirling's utopia would be peopled by men of capital who would grow money, shear money and dig up money. Free enterprise and government would work together in ushering in a golden age of wealth and prosperity, where "colourful racing identities" would be able to afford merchant banks, land speculators would be able to afford paintings of flowers by one-eared Dutch madmen, and friendly political leaders would be able to afford large stamp collections.[6]

Britain approved the venture, appointed Stirling lieutenant-governor of Swan River and Frederickstown and agreed that land should be released to settlers in proportion to their investment. A special deal was struck with Western Australia's first land speculator, Thomas Peel. A wealthy lawyer and cousin to Britain's first Conservative prime minister, Peel negotiated a 250,000 acre purchase, which was to be doubled if he brought out 400 tenants by 1 November 1829 and quadrupled on development of the initial purchase.

Captain Charles Fremantle arrived with the first settlers on 2 May 1829 and claimed all of New Holland outside New South Wales for Britain. Stirling returned from Britain a month later and on 18 June founded the Swan River Colony.

The settlement got off to a rocky start when the first three vessels to arrive ran into the rocks blocking the mouth of the Swan. Stirling had chosen to build a trading port on an inaccessible river hundreds of miles from the nearest deep-water harbour.

---

6   Readers unfamiliar with WA Inc should look up Laurie Connell, Alan Bond and Brian Burke.

The settlers lived in leaky tents on a coastal island for over three months, but things were looking up when Perth was founded on 12 August. The new capital was inaugurated when Mrs Helen Dance, the wife of a settler captain, ceremonially chopped down a tree. Mrs Dance's symbolic demonstration of nature's inability to stand in the path of progress is still honoured by today's Western Australian mining companies and marina developers.

The celebrations became more muted when the settlers were unable to find adequate fresh water. Perhaps building the capital on an estuary hadn't been such a great idea. And why had they established their other village, Fremantle, across the river, when the nearest crossing was miles in the opposite direction? And why the hell were they living in the remotest capital on earth, an honour Perth still holds to this day?

The English novelist Anthony Trollope noted the soil of Perth "was ideal – for hour glasses".[7] Unfortunately Perth's sand was not ideal for crops and when corn and wheat were later grown inland, the fields were raided by kangaroos and emus.[8]

---

7   Western Australians are colloquially known as Sandgropers. This name derives from a singularly ugly relative of the grasshopper that lives in Western Australia's excess of sand.

8   The emu problem peaked in 1932, when 20,000 emus invaded the Western Australian wheatbelt. Not only did they destroy crops, but their damage to fences also allowed insurgent rabbits to advance into previously unoccupied Western Australian territory. Sir George Pearce, Australia's minister for defence, responded by sending in soldiers of the Royal Australian Artillery armed with Lewis Automatic Machine Guns. A Fox Movietone cinematographer was embedded with the troops and filmed various heroic engagements, including an assault on an emu position by a truck-mounted gun. Major G.P.W. Meredith, who commanded the Australian forces, noted the ability of the emus to strike, even when severely wounded, earning them a comparison with the fearless Zulu. The Emu War – or the Great Emu War, as it was sometimes known – was won within thirty-nine days. Meredith's report claimed 986 emus were killed by machine-gun fire, with 2,500 more birds likely to have died as a result of their injuries. There were no Australian troop casualties, making the Emu War one of Australia's most successful military campaigns. However, some of the gloss was taken away when it was revealed that Australian troops had desecrated the

Western Australia, as the Swan River Colony was rebranded in 1832, abounded with the usual poisonous animals, but its toxic plants left the rest of Australia (and the settlers' livestock) for dead. Its ninety-eight species of gastrolobium (poison pea) are so deadly to foreign wildlife that gastrolobium pest controls have been banned in forty-two US states. Its rattlepod shrub causes blindness, jaundice, drooling, paralysis and prolapse of the rectum and afflicts horses with the dreaded "walking disease", an ailment that compels them to walk in straight lines, regardless of obstacles. Identifying and then removing hostile flora from grazing runs was a labour-intensive business and there were no convicts around to do the labouring.

The settlers had to contend not only with the world's most poisonous plants and animals, but also with the Noongar, who stopped being friendly as the colonists spread further into their hunting grounds. The warrior Yagan led raids that killed a number of Stirling's people.

In 1833, Yagan's father, Midgegooroo, was executed by firing squad. Yagan was shot by a teenage boy for a £20 reward the same year, his back skinned for a trophy and his smoked head sent to London for display as an "anthropological curiosity".[9]

Between fifteen and thirty Noongar were shot during the 1834 Battle of Pinjarra, with Stirling warning the survivors that women and children would be targeted in retaliation for any further Noongar

---

bodies of enemy combatants, with feathers taken as trophies and to make hats for Australian light horsemen.

9   Yagan's head was stored in a cupboard for over a century, before being buried in an unmarked grave in 1964. It was dug up and handed to a Noongar delegation on 31 August 1997. Ken Colbung, the Noongar man who accepted the skull, suggested that Princess Diana's death earlier that day was payback for English wrongs against Aboriginal people, which took some of the PR gloss off the handover ceremony. Perth's bronze statue of Yagan was repeatedly beheaded after the return of Yagan's remains, with a local chapter of the Lady Di fan club suspected. Yagan's head was finally buried in 2010, after years of Noongar infighting and numerous government reports on reburial options. It would have been simpler for Yagan and everybody else concerned if he'd never been beheaded in the first place.

attacks. Stirling believed that terror was necessary to deter the tribes from uniting "for the extermination of the whites".

News of Western Australia's failings soon filtered back to Britain, and prospective immigrants traded their tickets for passage to New South Wales, Van Diemen's Land or America. Some of the colony's early arrivals joined them.

Thomas Peel must have wished he'd done likewise. Western Australia's first entrepreneur had invested in the wrong start-up. His crew mutinied before setting sail and, with his arrival deadline looming, Peel sued his sailors rather than attempting to resolve the dispute. After Peel finally left Britain, his ship's captain insisted on docking at Cape Town to marry a passenger and then refused to return to sea until after his honeymoon.

Peel and 179 of his immigrants arrived six weeks past the agreed date, only to find that Stirling had given their land to others. Peel demanded the captain return him to England and challenged him to a duel when he refused. He was finally convinced to settle ten kilometres south of Fremantle, where limestone soil, the lack of any harbour, and Aborigines burning down his camp cruelled his farming and trading interests. After the ship carrying the last of his 400 immigrants ran aground off the Western Australian coast, Peel challenged her captain to a duel and was shot in his right hand.

Peel's settlers suffered from scurvy and dysentery, with twenty-nine dying in 1830. The rest drifted off to Perth. Peel sued them for the cost of their passage and they sued him for unpaid wages, embroiling him in lengthy and costly litigation. John Morgan, the colonial storekeeper, wrote to the War and Colonial Office:

> The Proprietor of a million acres of land – one of the founders of what may be hereafter a mighty nation – is now to be seen ... plodding along upon a miserable half-starved pony, and without a shilling in his pocket.

Peel's wife arrived with three children, twenty-two pieces of luggage and a piano in 1834, only to discover that Peel's residence, the grandly named Mandurah House, was a dirt-floored, three-roomed "despicable hut". Peel cleared enough of his debts for his wife and two daughters to return to England in 1839. But the king of the empty sands stayed on. The next great deal lay just around the corner – he could feel it.

THE RIVER GUY

Hamilton Hume was not yet done with exploring. In 1828 he received a knock on the door from Charles Sturt, Governor Darling's devoutly preppy in-law. Sturt had convinced Darling to let him test Oxley's theory that the Macquarie River drained into a vast inland sea. Would Hume like to join him? He could rest assured that there'd be no pram on this trip.

Sturt's appointment enraged Major Thomas Mitchell, who'd replaced the recently deceased John Oxley as surveyor-general. Mitchell told Darling that searching for inland seas was surveyor-general business and that Sturt, who'd never explored anything in his life, was "an amateur traveller". Darling would not budge and Mitchell hated Sturt for the rest of his life.

Sturt and Hume set off down the Macquarie and chucked a right down the Bogan.[10] They then fanged it up the Darling, a river they'd

---

10   The word *bogan* is now associated with flannelette- and ugg-boot-clad outer-suburban throwbacks who sport bleached mullets and tattoos of Peter Brock on their arses (men) or breasts (women and men). Bogans subsist on a diet of Bundy and Coke (men) or Bundy and Diet Coke (women and poofters) and are noted for their interesting teeth. Their favourite colour is Winfield Blue and they hate the arts (except anything written by Barnesy). In 2015, the good folk of the Bogan Shire, on the Bogan River charted by Sturt and Hume, unveiled the Big Bogan, a five-metre statue of an overweight male wearing a singlet, thongs, stubbies and Southern Cross tattoo (bogan summer wear), standing beside a big Esky, and holding a big fishing rod, complete with a big dead fish. They hope this will encourage other bogans to visit them, as building and visiting big things are popular bogan pastimes.

just discovered. The Darling was salty, convincing Sturt that Oxley's sea couldn't be far away.

Hume retired from exploring after returning to Sydney, but Sturt was tasked with following the Lachlan and Murrumbidgee rivers in 1829. If you wanted someone to mindlessly follow a river, Sturt was your man. He soon found another river, which he could follow all the way to the southern coast of Australia – he named it the Murray.[11]

Sturt was elated by the lush grasslands he found near the Murray's mouth, but the high wore off when he realised he would have to row over 900 miles against the current of Australia's biggest river to return to the settled districts. After enduring exhaustion, starvation and an illness that later left him temporarily blind, Sturt staggered into Sydney and told everybody about all the rivers he'd followed. He was dubbed Sturt of the Murray, which is like Scott of the Antarctic or Lawrence of Arabia, only crapper (unless you live in Wodonga).

Darling was surprisingly cool about Sturt's discovery of new southern pasturelands and rivers that might support inland agriculture. He didn't even inform the War and Colonial Office of the expedition until eight months after Sturt's return. New land meant increased pressure for colonial expansion. And that was something Darling no longer wanted.

SQUATTING FOR FUN AND PROFIT

Darling had a land problem. Although Governor Brisbane had introduced land sales, a parallel system of grants remained – a recipe for nepotism and confusion. Even worse, the colony's most powerful men had expanded their holdings to occupy land they claimed had been

---

11   This was actually the Hume. Hovell had taken credit for Hume's southern discoveries and now Hume had lost his river to Sturt. He still has the Hume Highway, best known for the Big Merino (a fifteen-metre-tall concrete sheep), a popular bogan pilgrimage site.

promised to them by previous administrations, even if the land had never been granted to them per se.

Per se was the sort of Latin legal mumbo jumbo used by William Wentworth. Wentworth defended a settler whose occupation was challenged by the government, convincing the jury that the land had been promised by Governor Macquarie and that invalidating the claim would call into question the holdings of three-quarters of the landholders in the colony. This was not so much a legal argument as an appeal to the self-interest of the landholding jury members.

Landholders were meant to pay a nominal government rent for granted land according to an honour system, which meant nobody bothered paying. When Darling cracked down on this, Wentworth, by now one of the largest landholders and tax evaders in the colony, joined with the Macarthurs to challenge this unfair tax. He severed the uneasy alliance when he was given three years to pay the back rent at a reduced rate.

Darling had stopped Mitchell wandering off down rivers so he could focus on surveying the colony's existing holdings, which he hoped would stop people lobbing onto new land and saying, "Governor Hunter once told his secretary, who told a bloke down at the pub, who told my father, who told me that I could put all my sheep here," or "The dog ate my land grant."

Mitchell drew up new boundaries, and settlers were told they would be punished for trespassing if they occupied land outside these "limits of location". The limits were set within a rough 200 kilometre radius of Sydney, and the northern convict settlements were to expand no further than necessary to support their prisoner populations. As far as Darling was concerned, the natives could have the rest of New South Wales.

Expansion beyond a few strategically placed outposts to bolster British territorial claims against the dastardly French would make containing the convicts more difficult. It would require additional police to search all the new places in which criminals might hide. It would require additional troops to keep hostile natives out of those new places. It would demand infrastructure, which was a swearword in Britain after Macquarie wasted its money building marble palaces for pickpockets and prostitutes. Most importantly, it would reduce the government's ability to control the people, most of whom, quite frankly, were not to be trusted.

In 1831, Lord Goderich ended land grants in Australia and required all land to be purchased or leased from the Crown. Making land more expensive encouraged people to squat (i.e. move onto "unoccupied land"[12] [13] they had no right to occupy and then assert that occupation granted them that right). Today we associate squatters with homeless people, poor people, students, anarchists, socialists, gypsies, hippies, artists, dreadlocked ferals who sit in trees owned by forestry companies, those bastards who plant flowers and organic vegetables on nature strips, and other undesirables, but squatting is an ancient British tradition.

British peasants had long cultivated wasteland and grazed their livestock on commons (land open for collective use). In 1649, Gerrard Winstanley gave squatting a political twist when he founded the Diggers (a.k.a True Levellers), a collective that argued the Norman ruling class had robbed the common Englishman of his land, forcing him into poverty and starvation. The Diggers started digging up common land for giant vegetable gardens and inviting people to join their communes. The authorities did not prosecute them for growing vegetables on common land, which was not illegal, but for being Ranters – members of a breakaway Christian cult noted for its liberal sexuality and naked protests. The Diggers had nothing to do with the Ranters, but the public would be more sympathetic to cracking down on pervy nudists than people who fed and housed the poor.

---

12   See Aborigines.

13   I see no Aborigines.

By 1830, thousands of Enclosure Acts had been passed in Britain. The acts required the fencing of land for the benefit of established landowners, shutting down the commons that the rural poor had squatted on for centuries. The Enclosure Acts required poor country folk to go to the city or sell their labour to landowners. The landowners, meanwhile, introduced threshing machines that enabled them to reduce both the number of agricultural workers and their pay. Unemployed farmhands were sent to workhouses to labour for the church or landowners for no wage.

These factors led to the Swing Riots of 1830, in which agricultural labourers, much like their Luddite cousins, created a fictitious revolutionary, Captain Swing. The Swingers would send local worthies threatening letters signed by Swing, demanding increased wages and the destruction of threshing machines. When these demands weren't met, the rioters would assemble to smash agricultural machinery and burn down workhouses. Even the new reformist Whig government felt threatened by the Swing Rioters, so it prosecuted almost 2,000 of them and transported 481 Swingers to Australia.[14]

In 1834, six men from the village of Tolpuddle formed a group to encourage farmhands to strike against lower wages. The Tolpuddle Martyrs, as the six became known, were not tried for forming a union, which had been legal since 1825, but for swearing oaths on skeletons during their meetings (the public would be more sympathetic to cracking down on blasphemous graverobbers than people who campaigned for workers' rights). The Tolpuddle Martyrs also found themselves on a boat to Australia.

The Swing Rioters and Tolpuddle Martyrs arrived just in time to see Australia undergo its own agricultural revolution. In 1834, more

---

14   The Swing Riots led to the introduction of the New Poor Law in 1834, which centralised the workhouse and poor-relief systems under state, rather than church, control. The aim was to incarcerate the unemployed poor in workhouses that were so horrible that they would get off their arses and become rich. The best thing about the New Poor Law was that it gave Charles Dickens something to write about.

and more pastoralists were placing sheep and shepherds outside the limits of location, but settlement was still well contained.

Then John Batman happened.

BATMAN BEGINS MELBOURNE

John Batman had a nose for business, despite no longer having a nose for anything else – nasal syphilis had eaten it away.[15] The Tasmanian bounty hunter turned entrepreneur believed the future was made of wool and he wanted to help knit it.

Tasmania was the economic powerhouse of the British Empire in 1835, with twice the number of sheep of New South Wales and the highest land prices in the southern hemisphere. But Arthur and Batman had a problem. Tasmania was running out of quality land to sell and put sheep on. The lieutenant-governor and vigilante sheep-fancier turned their eyes across Bass Strait.

Batman had applied to settle Western Port in 1827, after his old schoolfriend Hamilton Hume told him of the wonderful pasture he'd discovered. Although knocked back, he continued to hatch plans for sheep and cattle runs on the southern mainland.

In 1833, Arthur suggested to the War and Colonial Office that Van Diemen's Land might annexe southern Australia, writing:

> Nothing would individually afford me greater gratification than being instrumental in aiding in the occupation of that part of the coast by means which might tend to secure the protection and promote the civilization of the Aborigines.[16]

---

15 You can get nasal syphilis from sticking your nose into other people's business. Symptoms other than nose loss include disfiguring lumps and lesions known as gummas, poor balance, constricted pupils, sore legs, seizures, apathy, dementia and nobody wanting to sleep with you.

16 Arthur's statement was the standout winner of the 1833 Irony Awards.

Arthur was reminded that the southern mainland was part of New South Wales and that he should confine his ambitions to his own backyard.

In 1834, eight Launceston settlers unsuccessfully sought Britain's approval to purchase south-coast land. The same year, Edward Henty, a Swan River refugee, built a farm across the strait on Portland Bay, to service the sealers and whalers who scoured Australia's south coast for fur, blubber and Aboriginal girls.

Batman knew he needed to move quickly to settle Port Phillip, as other land vultures were circling and his advanced syphilis meant they'd be picking over his carcass in years rather than decades. But a number of obstacles lay in his way, the first of which was being John Batman.

Batman was a socially suspect pox-ridden landgrabber. George Augustus Robinson said of him: "Batman is a bad and dangerous character. He married a prison woman. He recently lost part of his nose to the bad disease." Batman's neighbour, the artist John Glover, called him "a rogue, thief, cheat, liar, a murderer of blacks and the vilest man I have ever known".

Batman needed partners to give his venture a respectable face – or at least a face with a nose – so he gathered Tasmania's most respectable landgrabbers to form the Port Phillip Association. The association included holders of high public office, surveyors and road builders, a leading banker and an emancipist who was told to keep his involvement quiet, as Port Phillip was to be convict-free. Intriguingly, the association also included Henry Arthur, the lieutenant-governor's nephew.

George Arthur, who was renowned for mixing politics and real estate speculation, may himself have been a silent member. The Donald Trump of Tasmania earned more than three times his government salary from land deals, all while setting colonial land policy.[17] He'd advised his nephew and Batman of his support for their venture, and

---

17   During the Black Line, Arthur, like Trump, had proposed deporting undesirables to southern lands and building a wall to stop them getting back in.

once the legality of the settlement was confirmed he appeared on the books as a significant investor.

Batman's second obstacle was the limits of location. It was likely that Governor Richard Bourke, Darling's successor, would prosecute him for settling New South Wales land outside the approved areas.

The solution?

To say the land was not New South Wales land, but Aboriginal land.

TREATY ... YEAH?

On 6 June 1835, Batman met with eight Wurundjeri elders of the Kulin people and asked them to scribble on two pieces of paper. The pieces of paper said that John Batman and whoever else he wanted could "occupy and possess" about 600,000 acres of Kulin land, for which the Wurundjeri would receive "the Yearly rent or Tribute of one hundred Pair of Blankets, One Hundred Knives, One Hundred Tomahawks, Fifty Suits of Clothing, Fifty looking Glasses, Fifty Pair scissors and Five Tons of Flour", on top of a smaller one-off payment in similar goods. Batman emphasised to the Wurundjeri that "although a white", he was "a countryman of theirs, and would protect them".[18]

The Batman Treaty, as the pieces of paper became known, had been drafted by Joseph Tice Gellibrand, former attorney-general of Van Diemen's Land and a leading member of the Port Phillip Association. Batman believed it would be supported by Arthur, who'd recommended to Britain only a couple of months earlier that the southern tribes be given "presents (the most trifling will satisfy them)" in return for land.

---

18 Critics of the deal point out that the Wurundjeri had no idea they were being asked to sign away their rights to their land, and that the annual tribute was about 0.0007 per cent of the value of the cheapest land in Australia. Others argue that at least Batman acknowledged the land was theirs and offered more than anyone else ever did, and that a limited white presence in return for protection from the sealers and other foreigners with guns and bad attitudes would have appealed to some of the Wurundjeri.

FIG. 6: "I'LL TRADE YOU THESE BAT-MIRRORS AND BAT-BLANKETS FOR ..."

Batman also hoped the treaty would find favour with Britain. Lord Melbourne's administration, the most Evangelical in British history, was happier than laughing gas and clappier than Batman – it was constantly on the lookout for new ways to be nice to natives.[19]

Treaties with indigenous people were central to Evangelical Whig philosophy and there was increasing disquiet in Whitehall about

19 Melbourne was the most liberal of the nineteenth-century Whigs. He was a Romantic Radical in his Cambridge days, drinking, partying and reading poetry with Byron and Shelley. His wife, Lady Caroline "Caro" Ponsonby, embarked on a public affair with Byron, famously characterising him as "mad, bad and dangerous to know". Caro stalked Byron after he ended the affair, slashed her wrists with a wine glass at a public ball after again being spurned by him, started writing poems in his name, became addicted to alcohol and laudanum and wrote the steamy Gothic novel *Glenarvon*, a thinly veiled account of her passion for the poet (who'd married her cousin in the interim). Melbourne supported his wife until her addictions caused her death, all the while caring for their autistic son. While prime minister, Melbourne had a well-publicised affair with the author Caroline Norton and was accused of getting off on spanking aristocratic ladies and whipping "orphan girls taken into his household as objects of charity", none of which dampened his popularity.

the impact of settlement on the Aborigines. Saxe Bannister, the former failed attorney-general, had transformed himself into a leading Evangelical upon his return to London. A founder of the Aborigines Protection Society, Bannister wrote the influential *Humane Policy; or, Justice to the Aborigines of the New Settlements*, which argued colonial rule had "crushed irretrievably many millions of unoffending men" and urged the use of treaties in further colonial endeavours.

Batman even thought that Governor Bourke, who asserted New South Wales' authority over Port Phillip, might be sympathetic to his claim. Bourke was an Evangelical pin-up for his reforms while acting governor of the Cape Colony in southern Africa, where he'd freed indigenous people from forced labour, granted them equality before the law and, most importantly for Batman, recognised their property rights.

Surely all the stars were aligned for a new approach to British–Aboriginal relations?

OF CLAIMS AND COUNTERCLAIMS

Two days after signing the deal of the century, Batman sailed six miles up the Yarra and declared, "This will be the place for a village." He then rushed to Launceston to declare himself the new owner of Port Phillip, stopping briefly to leave an advance party at Indented Head, east of the current city of Geelong.

Batman visited John Pascoe Fawkner's hotel for a celebratory drink upon his return. Flushed with success and a few pints, he declared himself to be "the greatest landowner in the world".

Fawkner listened on, perfectly sober. Despite his hotel business and sly grogging, Fawkner was a teetotaller who abhorred drink and the drunkards who drank it. When shouted by a merry customer, Fawkner would pour himself cold tea from a bottle behind the bar and charge for the finest brandy. Fawkner made a habit of listening to lips loosened by the liquor he sold – information was opportunity and opportunity was money. He was very interested in what Batman had to say.

Fawkner quizzed Batman about the land he'd explored, the treaty and his use of Aboriginal guides, before telling Batman he intended to purchase land to the east of Port Phillip from the natives. This was no skin off Batman's nose – the newly minted land baron welcomed the idea of a civilised neighbour.

Batman left the pub and spruiked his success to the Launceston media, with the *Cornwall Chronicle* announcing the establishment of the new settlement of Batmania. He reported to Arthur, "The Chiefs appeared most fully to comprehend my proposals, and much delighted with the prospect of having me live among them."[20] "The Tasmanian Penn", as he was hailed by his fellow islanders, then set to work organising the biggest squat in Australian history.[21]

As Batman feverishly worked on the logistics of colonising Port Phillip, a pale, mute giant with matted hair shambled into the association's camp at Indented Head and, with increasing urgency, pointed to the tattoos on its arm – a sun, a moon, something that looked like a beaver drawn by a kid with a blunt pencil and serious Ritalin addiction, and the letters *W.B.* When the apparition was offered a slice from a loaf, it stuttered, "b ... b ... bread". William Buckley had come home.

Buckley at first claimed to be a recently shipwrecked soldier, but finally confessed he'd been living among the Wathaurung people to Port Phillip's west for the past thirty-two years. Following his escape, Buckley had taken a spear marking an Aboriginal grave and used it as a walking stick. The Wathaurong recognised the spear and believed Buckley to be its recently deceased owner, risen from the dead. Murrangurk, as Buckley was known to his adopted people,

---

20 A treaty could be invalidated if a party didn't understand its terms. Batman was assiduous in portraying the Wurundjeri as world experts in British property law.

21 William Penn had been the world's largest private landowner after Charles II granted him 125,000 square kilometres of America to form the colony of Pennsylvania for Quakers to quake in. Penn bolstered his claim by entering into a treaty with the local Lenape Indians.

was given a wife after showing them new fishing techniques, had a daughter and eventually became an *arweet*, a respected wise man.

Buckley offered his services as intermediary and translator in an attempt to minimise conflict between the Port Phillip Association and the Kulin. He was offered £50 a year and granted a pardon by Arthur for his 1803 escape.

On 2 September 1835, the association's surveyor, John Wedge, sailed up the Yarra to mark out Batman's new township. To his considerable surprise, he found buildings already there, Fawkner having sent Captain John Lancey to found a settlement on his behalf. According to the later Melbourne journalist Edmund Finn (a.k.a. Garryowen), the founders of Melbourne under Lancey were "five men, a woman, and the woman's cat".[22]

Wedge and Batman were furious. While a few huts wouldn't stop them establishing pastoral runs, they knew the greatest profits lay in enthusiastic speculators buying their land. Fawkner baldly asserted that he'd entered into a separate treaty with the locals and that his claim was just as good as Batman's.

Matters became more complicated when John Aitken, who'd intended to settle to the east of Port Phillip, rocked up with a couple of hundred sheep. Batman wanted to use his alliance with the Wurundjeri to drive out the claim-jumpers, but Wedge noted that arming the Aborigines to attack Britons would likely be frowned upon and result in *all* the settlers being kicked out of Port Phillip. Wedge got his way after threatening to resign from the association if Batman went to war.

Fawkner arrived at the new settlement on 11 October. He'd spent his youth as a shepherd and never wanted to see a sheep again – he wanted to establish a town, not a paddock. Batman arrived with 500 sheep on 9 November. He told Buckley to gather the Kulin and reaffirmed his earlier promise to provide them with supplies, but,

---

22   Pretty much your average Fitzroy share house.

according to the Kulin leader, William Barak, then an eleven-year-old boy, Batman ended his speech with the warning, "If you kill one white man white fellow will shoot you down like a kangaroo."

And so the three parties of squatters and the Kulin hunkered down together, gifting each other glances filled with mistrust.

THE EMPIRE DOESN'T STRIKE BACK

Batman and Fawkner constantly bickered over which one of them had established the settlement. In November 1835, Fawkner's servants dug up an old rusty kettle. This was the very kettle Buckley had discarded during his 1803 escape, as the young Johnny Fawkner farewelled Port Phillip for Van Diemen's Land. Fawkner cleaned and polished the Foundation Kettle and kept it in his study as a symbol of his connection to the first settlement of Port Phillip.

Yet Batman and Fawkner shared a common goal – both wanted to establish a colony of free men independent of Hobart, Sydney and Britain. Fawkner even drafted a constitution for his beloved republic, which provided for "each individual acting as to him may seem just and conducive to his interest, comfort and whim".

Of course, those whose whim was to get drunk were not welcome in Fawktopia, with the constitution providing, "if any man or woman persist in this vice they shall, after properly warned, be expelled to one of the drunken towns of Sydney, Hobart or Launceston." Fawkner's wowserism did not stop him from becoming the settlement's first liquor importer and converting his house into Fawkner's Hotel, the settlement's first pub.

Arthur waited three months to inform Bourke of Port Phillip's settlement, instead writing a letter to Britain requesting that it be placed "temporarily" under his rule. When Bourke was finally notified, he curtly reminded Arthur that Port Phillip was within his territory and issued a proclamation:

> Any bargain or contract made with the Aboriginal natives of New
> Holland for the possession of any land within the limits of the
> Government of New South Wales will be held to be null and void
> as against the rights of the Crown.

All persons in possession of such land, Bourke said, would be dealt
with as intruders.

Bourke's proclamation caused a number of association members
to sell their interests, but Batman, Fawkner and other risk-takers
settled Port Phillip in defiance of the order.

Bourke, while wishing to show the upstart Tasmanians who was
boss, argued for the settlement of Port Phillip behind closed doors.
He urged Lord Glenelg, secretary of state for war and the colonies, to
abandon the limits of location policy, having earlier failed to convince
Sir Robert Peel's Conservative government of this course.[23] Bourke
believed new lands needed to be opened up to guarantee Britain's
wool supply and support the colonial economy, arguing: "Sheep must
wander or they will not thrive, and the Colonists must have sheep or
they will not continue to be wealthy." In any event, Bourke claimed,
he was powerless to prevent settlement outside the limits.

Bourke could have taken steps to enforce his proclamation while
waiting for Glenelg's response, but chose not to. He was one of the
first of a new breed of liberals who believed in private enterprise and
minimal government interference with the market. Squatting was
the embodiment of this liberal ideal.

Like his new masters in the War and Colonial Office, Bourke was
also a devout Evangelical who supported government intervention
where it would protect and Christianise native peoples. He believed

---

23   In 1834, shaken by the great reforms of 1832 and continuing social unrest, Peel
     rebranded the Tories as the Conservative Party. The Conservatives supported
     the minimum change necessary to maintain social cohesion, a policy of "reform
     to survive". Sir Robert Peel is otherwise best known for establishing the modern
     British police force, with British police known as Bobbies and Peelers in his honour.

that the wrong sort of people (runaway convicts, emancipists and the poor) would settle beyond the limits, whatever his instructions, and act with unrestrained violence against the natives. Therefore, he should encourage settlement by the right sort of people (Christian men with money and sheep) to protect the Aborigines from their countrymen. Put simply, Aboriginal lands should be settled to protect the Aborigines from settlement.

A sealer attack on Aborigines at Western Port gave Bourke the excuse to intervene – he declared the southern tribes under his protection and ordered George Stewart, a magistrate, to investigate the killings and report on the Port Phillip settlement. The government had now come to the independent squatter state of Bearbrass, Bareport, Bareheep, Barehurp, Bareburp, or whatever else its settlers chose to call it on any given day (Fawkner having put the kibosh on Batmania).

In July 1836, Bourke passed the *Squatting Act*, as it became known. To obtain a licence to occupy Crown land, squatters needed to obtain a certificate of character and pay a £10 annual licence fee, which ensured only the right sort of people (see above) could squat.

Still, this did not address settlement outside the limits of location or the validity of Batman's Treaty. Batman waited for Glenelg's ruling on whether he was a legal occupant or a trespasser. The answer, received by Bourke on 1 September 1836, was that Batman was both.

Glenelg made it clear that Batman's Treaty, if accepted, "would subvert the foundation of which all proprietary rights in New South Wales at present rest". Acknowledging Aboriginal land-ownership would invalidate *terra nullius*, rendering the entire British colonisation of Australia unlawful.

On the other hand, the limits of location stopped Christian men with money and sheep from protecting and converting the Aborigines, which was just not fair to the natives. Batman seemed like a decent chap who'd settled Port Phillip with the best of intentions. Couldn't the Port Phillip Association receive some sort of compensation for all its hard work, and its members be allowed to stay in Port Phillip, as long as they never mentioned the T-word again? Fawkner and everybody else should be able to stay too – the more the merrier!

And so it was done.

Bourke took over the settlement, gave the association £7,000 in hush money, issued the squatters with licences, renamed the settlement Melbourne and started selling land to the flood of new arrivals. The limits of location were abolished and so began a land grab "as fast as any expansion in the history of European colonisation", with settlers pouring into previously off-limits Aboriginal lands across the eastern half of the continent. More land was occupied between 1835 and 1838, and more people conquered, than in the previous forty-seven years of British settlement.

In 1837, George Langhorne, a missionary sent to convert the Kulin, observed that William Buckley was "always disconnected and dissatisfied, and I believe it would have been a great relief to him had the settlement been abandoned and he left alone with his sable friends".

Buckley had good reason to be despondent. The treaty was in tatters, the supplies to be paid as tribute slowed and then disappeared, and the Kulin were forced off their hunting grounds by sheep and men with guns. In August 1836, Henry Batman, John's brother, led a raid against a group of Aborigines believed to have killed an association member, with at least ten Kulin shot in retaliation before their huts and possessions were put to the torch. In 1837, Joseph Tice Gellibrand of the association went missing, and it was speculated he'd been murdered and eaten by natives.[24] Some of the parties hunting for Gellibrand also hunted the Kulin. An ill-omened wind was blowing for the southern tribes.

---

24 Gellibrand had taken out Australia's first life insurance policy. When his family was paid £2,000 after his disappearance, London insurers were terrified that all their colonial policyholders would be murdered and eaten by natives, with some amending their policies to avoid claims arising from "a collision with an Aboriginal native of New Holland". Nobody was prepared to take on the risk of offering life insurance to the Aborigines.

Buckley left for Hobart in 1837, married a midget and worked in menial odd jobs. In 1852, hard up for cash, Buckley collaborated with John Morgan, a Hobart journalist, in writing *The Life and Adventures of William Buckley*. This authorised biography described Australian Aborigines as "generally treacherous, cowardly, and mere creatures holding the link in the chain of animal life between the man and the monkey", a view completely at odds with Buckley's earlier statements and actions.

Morgan tried to sex up the book by recasting Buckley as a latter-day Gulliver, describing his encounters with the Pallidurgbarrans, a race of potbellied, bronze-coloured cannibals whom Buckley's tribe suffocated with a huge fire.[25] The book's description of a beast "covered with feathers of a dusky grey colour ... about the size of a full grown calf" popularised the myth of the bunyip.

William Buckley died on 2 February 1856 after being thrown out of a carriage. His first Aboriginal wife, Purranmurnin Tallarwurnin, was living in a Victorian Aboriginal mission as late as 1881. By then, so were most of Victoria's other surviving Aborigines.

A NONCE OF INFLUENCE

Edward Gibbon Wakefield, a Quaker cousin of Elizabeth Fry, made

---

25 While there is evidence of cannibal Tasmanian bushrangers and governors, there is none of cannibal Aborigines outside reports of family funeral rituals in a handful of areas. The Aboriginal cannibal myth, which legitimised the "savage native" trope in the British mind, was started by Joseph Banks, who wrote in his 1770 *Endeavour* journal, "I suppose they live entirely upon fish, dogs and enemies." In 1827, John Jamieson was acquitted of the manslaughter of Hole-in-the-book, one of the more obscurely named Aborigines, because he believed Hole-in-the-book had eaten a missing servant, who later reappeared very much alive and undigested. In 1997, Pauline Hanson's *Pauline Hanson - the Truth : On Asian Immigration, the Aboriginal Question, the Gun Debate and the Future of Australia* claimed that Aborigines were cannibals who enjoyed eating babies. At the time of writing, Pauline Hanson leads the fifth-largest political party in the Australian Parliament. Please explain.

his fortune from abducting young girls, aided by his skills as a mesmerist.[26] In 1816, he eloped with Eliza Prattle, a wealthy underage ward of the state. Although he secured a £75,000 fortune from this match, he needed more money to enter the British Parliament.

After Eliza's early death, Wakefield lured fifteen-year-old heiress Ellen Turner, whom he'd never met, from her school by claiming her mother was ill. He then convinced Ellen her wealthy father was on the verge of bankruptcy and the only way to save the family's name and fortune was to marry Wakefield, which she did. Ellen returned to her family soon after, the marriage was annulled by an act of parliament and Wakefield was sentenced to three years' imprisonment for kidnapping, along with his brother William, who'd assisted in the abduction.

While languishing in Newgate prison, Wakefield studied British colonisation and wrote *A Letter from Sydney*, despite never having been anywhere near Australia. The 1829 pamphlet proposed abolishing land grants, with the Crown to sell land and use the proceeds to support the immigration of the industrious poor, thereby reducing the colonies' dependence on convicts. Land prices would put property beyond the reach of the new labouring class for a number of years, ensuring they kept working for landowners rather than striking out on their own. Government should take a step back and the power of the church should be checked by allowing freedom of worship and refusing state aid to religions. Wakefield argued this "systematic colonization" would encourage investment and immigration, and prison colonies would transform into free societies.

Wakefield may have been a nonce, but he was also, in the minds of many, a bloody genius. Systematic colonisation, Wakefield's supporters believed, was the answer to Britain's population problem. The number of Britons was on track to double between 1800 and 1850 and

---

26 Fry was not Wakefield's only famous relative. His mother, Priscilla, conceived of and founded the world's first savings bank and was one of the world's first children's book writers.

leading thinkers, influenced by Thomas Malthus's *An Essay on the Principle of Population*, thought this was a very bad thing.

Malthus's arguments boiled down to:

1. People like breeding;
2. People don't like working;
3. Breeding rates naturally outstrip work rates, which means more people must make do with less;
4. When I say "people" in point 3, I mean poor people;
5. The poor are made to work harder for lower wages, becoming so miserable that they stop breeding;
6. This allows work rates to catch up with breeding rates and everyone is happy for a while, but this only works if there is more land for the poor to work;
7. Shit, we're running out of land;
8. Quick, invade France so we can kill off our excess poor people – this is quicker and kinder than the alternatives of disease and starvation;
9. Or become a monk or a nun, visit the old gypsy woman down the road with the novelty coathanger collection, or wear a bloody condom.[27]

Many parliamentarians saw Britain's rapidly growing population as the cause of social unrest. As points 8 and 9 had limited appeal, they had a closer look at point 7 and realised that the Australian colonies had plenty of land where the excess poor could breed. In 1831, Lord Goderich, influenced by Wakefield, commenced a limited program to assist immigration to Australia.

But the adoption of Wakefield's ideas was piecemeal until the South Australian Land Company came along. It proposed a

---

27 Condoms, before the use of rubber in 1855, were made from treated linen or sheep's intestines, but were too expensive for the poor people who needed to stop breeding. Condoms intended for birth control were marketed as Malthus sheaths.

company-administered Wakefield colony near the mouth of the Murray. The War and Colonial Office, burned by the Western Australian disaster, was having none of it. However, Robert Torrens MP lobbied for the creation of a hybrid colony in accordance with Wakefield's principles – with a British governor responsible for laws and administration, and a Colonization Commission, backed by the private sector, responsible for land sales and immigration.

Britain passed the *South Australia Act* in August 1834. Torrens was appointed chairman of the Colonization Commission, Captain John Hindmarsh was appointed governor, and George Fife Angas, a puritanical Baptist shipping magnate who wanted a place where fellow religious nonconformists could enjoy freedom of worship, formed the South Australia Company to buy land not taken up by other private investors.

Wakefield didn't join the 636 settlers who established the colony of South Australia on 28 December 1836, having accused Torrens of selling land too cheaply to maintain a sufficient labour force. However, he was still honoured as the Father of South Australia.

CITY OF CHURCHES AND GRAVEYARDS

South Australia was the brainchild of a convicted child abductor, and its first Supreme Court judge, Sir John Jeffcott, was tried for murder two years before assuming office.[28] This explains a lot about South Australia ...

South Australia is the Jekyll and Hyde of Australia. In Adelaide, its capital, it's always a sleepy Sunday afternoon in 1958. Magpie and cicada song mingle with cricket commentary on the new Bakelite wireless. Lovable scamps cajole blue-hatted matrons as they set out for evening service, selling ice-cold Passiona at a penny a glass.

---

28 Jeffcott had shot Dr Peter Hennis, a promising young physician, during a duel arising from Hennis's comments about Jeffcott's treatment of a former fiancée.

Crocheted golliwogs and toilet paper dolls, jars of nougat, Holden
hood ornaments, boxes of *National Geographic* and the latest pho-
tographs of Marilyn Monroe (in colour!) are sold at charity jumble
sales. Then you wake chained in a barrel, deep in an underground
bank vault, while members of a suburban sex cult, their naked bodies
smeared with wombat blood, drown you in a mixture of cod liver oil
and sulphuric acid as the phonograph plays Dame Joan Sutherland's
haunting rendition of "*Principessa di morte*" on endless loop.[29]

South Australia's reputation for ritual dismemberment and DIY
burials is all the more surprising as it was planned as a convict-free
colony and, unlike Port Phillip and Western Australia, remained
true to this ideal.

The colony didn't get off to an auspicious start, with its emigration agent, John Brown, lamenting, "The fact is that we have not
either literary, scientific or cultivated men amongst us at all." This
reflected Torrens' narrow vision of a colony "based upon the science
of wealth". Torrens wanted to import an Irish labouring class to
generate wealth for respectable people, with his emigrant's hand-
book promising South Australia "would tame the wild Irishmen
and end their improvidence". Unsurprisingly, wild and improvident
Irishmen responded poorly to this marketing campaign, with South
Australia never enjoying the same levels of Irish immigration as the
other colonies.

Governor Hindmarsh was slow to arrive. His secretary, George
Stevenson, moaned that his shipboard water ration had been reduced
so that:

---

29 Sleepy Adelaide has a reputation as the child abduction and serial killer capital
    of Australia. At least five youths were gruesomely murdered by a group known
    as The Family between 1979 and 1983, and the bodies of eight Adelaide residents
    were found in barrels in a bank vault in Snowtown in 1999. Adelaide is also
    the home of Humphrey B. Bear, a large, mute, trouserless bear, described by
    co-workers as "a funny old fellow". Only Adelaide would give such a figure a job as
    a children's entertainer.

... the Governor's mules, pigs, cow, geese, turkeys and dogs ... may not suffer. Everything is sacrificed to his own selfish purposes. The mainsail has been kept single reefed now for a month, in order that his cow and mules in the long boat may not suffer by the draught of the wind.

Hindmarsh arrived to find that Colonel William Light, the colony's surveyor-general, had chosen to site the South Australian capital several miles up the Torrens River, with its port on the edge of a mangrove swamp. The port, which housed the largest concentration of mosquitoes in South Australia, was only accessible by small vessels. Ships lay grounded in the mire when the tide went out and luggage unloaded onto the mud flats was frequently damaged by the rising tide. Light's completely unsuitable port was dubbed Port Misery, which didn't convey the air of optimism the Colonization Commission had been aiming for.

Hindmarsh suggested it might be a good idea to build the settlement on the coast to support shipping trade and save on calamine lotion, but land selection was a matter for James Hurtle Fisher of the Commission. The site of the settlement was put to a vote, with eligible landholders backing Light – their priority was suitable soil for farming, not access for shipping or foreign trade. So Light laid out his town, naming it Adelaide after the wife of King William IV.[30]

Hindmarsh and Fisher argued over which of them should name Adelaide's streets, with a committee of twelve finally appointed to resolve the deadlock. The disputes over Adelaide's location and street names were typical of South Australia's absurd pushmi-pullyu government. The attempt to share power between Britain and the Colonization Commission was an abject failure. Justice Jeffcott reported:

---

30 William, the younger brother of George IV, was the last of Britain's Hanoverian kings. He had no children with Adelaide and the ten illegitimate kids he had with the Irish actress Dorothea Bland (stage name Mrs Jordan) weren't considered monarch material, so the crown passed to his niece, Victoria, upon his death in 1837.

The population, split in two by discussion, would not unite for their own protection, and the members of the Council spent their time squabbling, while the public interest was left to take care of itself.

Jeffcott must have tortured and murdered an albatross during his voyage to South Australia, as he had terrible luck at sea. The vessel bringing his belongings to the colony was wrecked and, after hearing only a handful of cases, he drowned in a freak whaleboat accident while attempting to board a ship that couldn't dock at Adelaide's useless port. Like many future South Australians, his body was never found.

Light, too, met an unlucky fate. Criticised for his slow survey of the country around Adelaide, he suffered a nervous breakdown and resigned, joined by his junior surveyors. Two years later, his house burned down and he died of tuberculosis. The Curse of Adelaide had struck again.

Rural development stalled as the colony waited for Britain to send it some surveyors who were prepared to do some surveying. As farmland was not being assigned, the settlers lived in Adelaide's mud huts and relied on imported food. Meanwhile, Torrens had abandoned the Wakefield principle of concentrated settlement, promising settlers they could buy land anywhere they wanted, greatly increasing the workload of the non-existent surveyors. Torrens' change of policy also encouraged rampant land speculation and a real estate bubble.

South Australian land was much more expensive than that of New South Wales, and Bourke's decision to allow squatting made the old colony more attractive to many immigrants, particularly the aspirational labourers South Australia wanted to attract.

The one part of the original vision that remained untarnished was the commitment to freedom of religion. Faith flourished in South Australia, as many of its settlers were devout Methodists, Calvinists, Baptists and other miserable, fun-hating bastards who sought to escape Britain's religious prejudices. Each faith erected its own churches and meeting halls, with places of worship the first substantial buildings erected in Adelaide. The town soon became known as the City of Churches. But the thing about having lots of churches is that you also have lots of graveyards ...

ICH BIN EIN AUSLÄNDER

South Australian church building got a fillip when Pastor Augustus Kavel brought 200 German Lutherans to South Australia in 1838.[31]

The Germanic tribes had been enthusiastic emigrants since the Middle Ages, when they migrated to neighbouring states and razed them to the ground. The Germans refer to this as *Völkerwanderung* (folk-wandering or migration), while everybody else calls it invasion.[32]

The German states had enjoyed violent religious differences since 1546, when the Holy Roman Empire was riven by war between the Lutheran princes of the Schmalkaldic League and the Catholic princes loyal to Emperor Charles V. The conflict ended with the signing of the Treaty of Augsburg in 1555, which allowed the states to choose either Lutheranism or Catholicism, and for dissenting citizens to migrate to a place that accepted their religion.

Things got nasty again when Emperor Ferdinand II attempted to enforce Catholicism within the empire. This began the Thirty Years' War of 1618–48, a period of bloodshed and famine during which the German states invaded each other and invited the rest of Europe

---

31   The Lutherans followed the teachings of Martin Luther, whom American readers will be surprised to know was not shot by James Earl Ray in Memphis in 1968. Luther kicked off the Protestant Reformation when he nailed his *Ninety-Five Theses* (a.k.a. *95 Things I Hate About Catholics*) to the door of All Saints Church in Wittenberg on 31 October 1517.

32   The Germans folk-wandered into Poland on 1 September 1939, commencing a six-year period of migration with extreme prejudice.

to join the party.[33] The war ended with the Peace of Westphalia, where the Germanic states agreed each ruler could select Catholicism, Lutheranism or Calvinism as a state religion and that dissenting citizens could practise their own faith.

The Germans briefly stopped invading their neighbours and became enthusiastic and well-respected travellers. George Ludwig, the Prince-Elector of Hanover, travelled to Britain, where he was so well respected (and Protestant) that the British made him their king. Heinrich Zimmermann travelled round the world with Captain Cook and wrote a book called *Round the World with Captain Cook*.[34] Arthur Phillip, the first governor of New South Wales, was the son of a German-language teacher; the First Fleet's Philip Schaffer introduced winemaking to Australia; and Augustus Alt, who laid out the towns of Sydney Cove and Parramatta as the colony's first surveyor-general, knew one end of a sausage from the other.

The Australian Agricultural Company established Australia's first assisted immigration program when it imported four German shepherds (not the dogs) in 1825. In 1835, the company struck a deal with Senator Hudtwalcker, Hamburg's chief of police, to transport Hamburg's convicts to New South Wales after Hudtwalcker assured it that German criminals were "not so dangerous as the English", polite and knew how to just follow orders. Glenelg killed off the plan just before the German transports set sail, as Britain had quite enough of its own criminals to deal with, *danke schön*.

Pastor Kavel's congregation from the village of Klemzig were the first Germans to folk-wander into Australia en masse, having left Prussia because King Frederick William III insisted that Lutherans and

---

33 While the British were completely off the mark in naming the Seven Years' War and the Hundred Years' War, the Germans are a pedantically efficient people. When they committed to the Thirty Years' War, you could rest assured that the war would run for precisely thirty years.

34 German literalism meant readers knew exactly what they were getting after reading a book's title.

Calvinists use a common prayer book and join his new State Union Church. Old Lutherans were driven out of their churches and had their homes confiscated.

Pastor Kavel decided to take his Old Lutheran flock to a country where they could use whatever prayer book they wanted. Kavel considered Russia and the United States, but then heard of South Australia, where George Fife Angas had employed forty German tradesmen. It also helped that Adelaide had a German name.[35]

Angas, a fellow Protestant dissenter, was sympathetic to the plight of the Klemzigians and stumped up the fares for their emigration. In return, the Klemzigians would buy his land for much more than he'd paid for it and repay him at 15 per cent interest per annum.

But Kavel's followers didn't want to integrate into Adelaide society. They marched six kilometres out of town and founded a village that, with typical German creativity, they named Klemzig. Within three months, these subsistence farmers were producing a surplus and delivering twenty-two different kinds of vegetable to Adelaide's hungry settlers. The women took in washing and did much of Klemzig's agricultural work, while the men built fences, raised barns, planted vines, wove cloth and grew ridiculous chin beards.

Captain Dirk Meinertz Hahn brought out another boatload of Old Lutherans later that year. They trudged thirty kilometres into the Adelaide Hills, carrying their goods by wheelbarrow or in carts pulled by teams of sweaty Germans, and established the hamlet of Hahndorf.

The citizens of Klemzig and Hahndorf wrote to their friends back home, telling them how lovely it was to be able to pray and grow vegetables and beards without being trampled by the Prussian cavalry. Their friends came out and wrote letters to their friends, and the trickle of German immigrants became *ein flut*, even after

---

35   Queen Adelaide was born Prinzessin Adelheid Amalie Luise Therese Carolin of Saxe-Coburg Meiningen.

religious persecution in Germany ended with Frederick William's death in 1840. Pastor Gotthard Daniel Fritzsche was notable among the new arrivals, bringing 200 of his followers to establish the village of Lobethal (Valley of Praise) in 1842.

The Germans were model Wakefield labourers. They were sober, industrious and didn't want government handouts – or anything to do with government at all. They paid top dollar for their land and worked it to pay off their debts, believing that labour was God's work and that land speculation was sinful. Like the Amish in America, they eschewed modern innovations, using hand scythes long after modern harvesters were introduced.

German women were sought after as shearers and could be seen pulling ploughs in their settlements' fields. Hahndorf's women would leave their village at midnight, laden with baskets, and complete the fifty-seven-kilometre round trip to Adelaide on foot in a single day, selling their surplus vegetables in the capital's markets. In between these chores, they had lots of healthy German sex, with German women having the highest number of children of any ethnic group in Australia during the nineteenth century.[36]

Most importantly, the Germans knew their place, coming from a feudal society where respect for local landholders was ingrained. German labourers treated their bosses like lords, which class-conscious British farmers and merchants loved. Everybody wanted a German labourer.

Religion was central to the lives of South Australia's German Lutherans. Bible quotes, rather than paintings, hung in every room. Sunday services ran for three hours and spare time was spent reading the Bible, telling religious stories and singing "Mein Gott Ist Wunderbar".

The Lutherans built their churches before they built their homes and those churches multiplied as a result of religious divisions. Biblical

---

36 German women had an average of 5.81 children in Australia, women from the British Isles had 3.46, native-born Australians had 3.3, while the French, despite their reputation as great lovers, had only 1.86 children on average, the lowest of any ethnic group.

literalists are not noted for their flexible thinking, so minor differences in doctrine resulted in schisms within the church.

Pastor Kavel had brought his flock to South Australia for the imminent Apocalypse, as Adelaide is a great place to get ready for the end of the world. His followers in the Barossa Valley, believing the Rapture was upon them, trooped into the bush one night during a storm, as they didn't want to meet the returned Christ in a sinful city (the tiny village of Tanunda). They returned to Tanunda the next morning, very much alive, unsaved, cold and soaking wet.

Pastor Fritzsche's belief that the world wasn't going to end anytime soon led him to establish the Evangelical Church in Australia, while Kavel presided over the United Evangelical Church in Australia. Johann Friedrich Krummnow, "a queer fellow, deformed and gnome-like in appearance", formed his own breakaway cult, which allowed him to indulge his obsessions for exorcising young girls, beating children of both sexes, using his followers' money to build a commune and making them work for him for no wages because he was God's Prophet.

Some of the Germans held on to old pagan practices, with *hexen* (witches) laying curses on an unfriendly neighbour's goats or rubbing herbs onto a husband's chair to ensure his fidelity. Casting spells was outlawed by the various Lutheran churches, but South Australia remained the witchcraft capital of Australia.[37]

The Germans remained the largest non-British immigrant group to Australia during the nineteenth century and comprised about 10 per cent of South Australia's population. Many continued to live in their own towns, speaking German and maintaining German cultural practices – until 1914, when lots of Schmidts changed their name to Smith and traded in *"Guten morgen, freund!"* for an overenthusiastic "G'day, mate!"[38]

---

37 Surprise, surprise ...

38 Lots of citizens of the British Empire tried very hard not to be German after World War I began. Even the British royal family was forced to change its name from Saxe-Coburg and Gotha to Windsor after Gotha aircraft bombed London.

THE FANTASTICAL ADVENTURES OF MRS FRASER

Apart from the Moreton Bay penal settlement, the area we now know as Queensland remained unsettled by Britain at the time Melbourne and Adelaide were established.

The Aborigines of the northern rainforests, who'd fatally speared Moreton Bay's commandant in 1830, were considered both exotic and dangerous. This perception was reinforced by Eliza Fraser, who was marooned on the island that now bears her name after her husband's ship crashed into the Great Barrier Reef in 1836. Eliza gave birth in the longboat that took her to the island, her baby and husband died, and she lived with the Butchulla people for fifty-two days before being rescued by a party from Moreton Bay.

Eliza told increasingly wild stories about her time with the Butchulla after her arrival in Sydney. She'd been kidnapped. She'd been made the slave of bloodthirsty cannibals who couldn't decide whether to eat her or ravish her. She'd been tormented by the cruel gins who were jealous of her sensuous white skin. She'd lost her husband and protector to illness ... no, wait ... to the painted man-eaters who'd turned him into a human shish kebab.

While white men kidnapping and ravishing Aboriginal women on the frontier had become passé, the thought of leering savages making free with a white woman sent the colonists into a frenzy. Newspapers tried to outdo each other in sensationalising Eliza's story, and the more lurid the claims, the more money the public donated to the "reluctant heroine".[39]

Eliza made a small fortune from her story, remarried, sailed back to England, re-embellished her tale for a morbidly titillated

---

39   Innocent white woman meets lustful black man was a powerful trope. Patrick
     White later wrote about Eliza in his novel *A Fringe of Leaves*. Sidney Nolan was
     obsessed with painting her. Peter Sculthorpe composed *Eliza Fraser Sings*. And
     David Williamson wrote the screenplay for *Eliza Fraser*, a bawdy '70s sex-romp
     that makes *Alvin Purple* look like *Citizen Kane*.

British audience, claimed to be a destitute widow and asked for yet more money.

Eliza's story changed the way many Australians and Britons perceived the Aborigines. They were no longer naive natives who could be coaxed into civilisation, but crazed cannibal sex addicts with a taste for white woman's flesh.

Eliza's story also excited the interest of another group.

Missionaries.

THE MISSIONARIES' POSITION

Queensland's first free settlers were a mix of German Old Lutheran, Evangelical Lutheran and Pietist missionaries brought to Australia by the Reverend John Dunmore Lang, Australia's leading Presbyterian minister.[40] Lang funded the mission to convert the natives before the Catholics could turn up with their free wine and biscuits, drawing on the Fraser case to drum up popular support.

Reverends Christopher Eipper and Karl Wilhelm Schmidt, accompanied by ten laymen and eight laywomen, established the Zion Hill mission in 1838. The mission was to be Moravian in style – a self-supporting farm where all goods were collectively owned.[41]

The missionaries tried to engage the Jagara tribes in building houses and planting gardens, but the Jagara thought this sounded too much like hard yakka.[42] This meant the missionaries had to do

---

40   Pietists were Lutherans who believed other Lutherans had too much fun.

41   The Moravians of Bohemia, in today's Czech Republic, founded the world's first Protestant church and led the first Protestant missions. They believed in the brotherhood of all Christians (including Catholics), laypeople preaching the Gospel, agrarian socialism, doing good deeds, thinking good thoughts, singing happy songs and sending out missionaries to encourage everyone to be nice to each other. There should be more Moravians in this world.

42   *Yakka* is the Jagara word for "work" – it is one of only a handful of Aboriginal words (other than place, plant and animal names) to have been incorporated into the Australian lexicon.

their own building and planting, leaving very little time for converting the Jagara.

The Jagara were drawn into the mission by food, but the missionaries were finding the self-sufficiency thing more difficult than they'd anticipated. At times they were forced to push a wheelbarrow to Moreton Bay and beg for supplies, a twenty-four-kilometre round trip. The Jagara knew that when the mission bell rang for morning prayer nobody would be guarding the mission's gardens, and food raids further stretched the missionaries' limited resources.

Teaching Jagara speakers the English Bible in German was also a formidable challenge. Language was a barrier to many missions throughout Australia. One missionary pointed to his chest to ask the local word for "me" and then attempted to craft a rudimentary hymn; for years, Aborigines visiting the mission happily sang "Jesus loves chest hair."

Lancelot Threlkeld, who founded the Lake Macquarie mission in 1825, overcame this difficulty by mastering the Awabakal tongue. With the assistance of Biraban, a tribal leader, he translated St Luke's Gospel into Awabakal. Unfortunately, by the time he finished his work, all of the Awabakal in his mission had perished. Other missionaries made do with pictures (God, Jesus and the angels were white, while the Devil was black). Mime and pidgin were also used.[43]

---

43 In 1930, C.J. Fletcher of Queensland's Yarrabah mission claimed the Ten
    Commandments were beyond the "mental capacities" of mission residents, so
    he gave culturally appropriate lessons on the commandments. He explained his
    teaching methodology thus: "In teaching the First Commandment, I used an
    advertisement for Eno's Fruit Salt, representing an Eastern sitting by the roadside
    and holding a lemon in his hand. After blackening the face in the picture to make it
    more like that of an aborigine, the cutting was shown to the class and introduced as
    the illustration of a medicine man – the lemon was misrepresented as a stone which
    the magician had just pretended to have extracted from the organs of a patient.
    (This, of course, is a common trick of the native witch doctor.) In association
    with this picture was learned by the class, 'Only one God – no more medicine
    man.' ... For the Seventh Commandment a finger was dipped in the dirt and used
    to dramatise, 'No think dirty, no speak dirty, no do dirty'; while the attractive
    properties of another digit smothered in glue were used to illustrate 'No steal'."

When language barriers could be overcome, some Bible stories resonated with Aboriginal people. Creation, virgin birth and resurrection all had Dreamtime parallels. The Aborigines would have also understood the Genesis story of the old white guy chasing people who didn't wear clothes off their land. However, there were no parallels for hell, sin or redemption, and parables about good shepherds bore no resemblance to the Aborigines' experience of being shot by people who looked after sheep.

Reverend Eipper grew disheartened by his proselytising failures and described his spiritual charges as "the living embodiment of *Philippians 3:19* – Whose end is destruction, whose God is their belly, and whose glory is in their shame, who mind earthly things". He regarded the syphilis that infected almost all the Aboriginal children in the area, gifted by the Moreton Bay convicts, as "a judgment upon the Aborigines".

The Zion Hill Mission was disbanded in 1848. While the missionaries failed to bring Christianity to Queensland, they did bring pineapples, with Reverend Handt importing plants from India in 1838 and mission member Johann Gottfried Wagner becoming Australia's first commercial pineapple grower. God moves in mysterious ways.

Or maybe He just likes pineapples.

7

Faith, frauds and
frontier justice

We have taken a vast portion of God's earth, and made it a cesspool
... we have poured down scum upon scum, and dregs upon dregs,
of the offscourings of mankind, and ... are building up with them a
nation of crime, to be, unless something speedily is done, a curse and
a plague, a by-word to all the peoples of the earth. The eye of
God looks down upon a people, such as, since the deluge, has not been.

Father William Ullathorne,
The Catholic Mission in Australasia, **1837**

WILD COLONIAL BOYS

S THE GOLDEN AGE OF BUSHRANGERS DREW TO A
close in Tasmania, the mainland provided exciting new
career opportunities for aspiring banditti. With the spread
of settlement, there were more isolated homesteads to raid, more bush
tracks for ambushes and more people with sheep and money to rob.

Charles Patient led a gang that targeted homesteads on the Cumberland Plains in 1825 and 1826. Patient was a gentle soul who comforted his female victims, "assuring them that not an improper word should be uttered, or the slightest violence offered to their persons by any individual under his command". He stole books from the libraries of houses he raided, politely asking his unwilling hosts if they had anything by Byron or Scott. Patient's gang had pledged not to fight back if cornered by police, but when their hideaway was raided an over enthusiastic constable's shot triggered a firefight. Patient and his men were riddled with bullets, hacked with sabres and then hanged.

John Tennant was more typical of the new breed of bushranger. He wasn't interested in books, he'd never give in to the coppers, and he was Irish.[1] Tennant was assigned to the owner of Canberry, the first property in the Canberra area.[2] He escaped in 1826 and lived on a mountain, descending periodically to steal food and clothing.

Tennant regarded himself as a criminal of circumstance and bushranging as a form of social protest, inscribing his gun with "Death or Liberty", the catchcry of the Irish rebels of the Castle Hill work camp who'd marched on Parramatta in 1804. Like the Castle Hill rebel leaders, Tennant got Death. He was found by the Aboriginal tracker Make-a-Cake,[3] shot in his tent and then hanged.

Patient and Tennant helped build the myth that bushrangers were fundamentally decent young men fighting the twin injustices of poverty and convictism. This myth coalesced around the figure of John "Bold Jack" Donohoe, the golden-haired, sparkling-blue-eyed *enfant terrible* of the bushranging world.

Jack was transported in 1825 for intending to commit a felony, which meant he hadn't actually done anything wrong, only thought about it, and we've all done that, right? And when Jack railed against the heartless tyranny of the state by turning bushranger and robbing bullock drivers on the Windsor Road in 1827, he didn't actually hurt

---

1   Twenty-two of Australia's 100 most prominent bushrangers were born in Ireland, while approximately half of the native-born bushrangers were of Irish stock.

2   Aboriginal placenames like Canberry/Canberra were increasingly adopted as settlement spread. Major Thomas Mitchell, who named the area *Nganbra* on an 1830s survey map, recommended the practice so that lost explorers could ask the locals for directions.

3   This is the sort of upbeat, non-threatening name that other Aborigines should have been given. If Martha Stewart had been responsible for naming Aborigines, Australia might have endured less Aboriginal violence and crime.

the drivers, just threatened them a bit. And everyone agreed he'd been nice to the bullocks. He was also always nice to the women he robbed and never tried any funny business, even though many of them would have wanted him to because Jack was a total studmuffin.

Jack was a top bloke because he stole from the rich and left the poor alone.[4] The story about him tying up two penniless old men and threatening to burn them to death was obviously government propaganda. Or maybe it was just Jack having a laugh. Jack was a funny guy – everybody said so.

Jack was "remarkably clean", his glossy hair was fastidiously maintained and he was a snappy dresser, with the fashionistas of the *Australian* admiring his "black hat, superfine blue cloth coat lined with silk, surtout fashion, plaited shirt (good quality), laced boots rather worn at the toes and snuff-coloured trousers". Jack often targeted people whose wardrobe he wanted, but he apologised to his naked victims afterwards and sometimes even gave them a pair of his old pants.

But the best thing about Jack was that he thumbed his nose at the rich, the coppers and the government. Jack was sentenced to hang for robbing the bullock drivers but disappeared between the court and his cell, even though chained and under guard. When police raided his hideout near Yass, his men were all killed, injured or captured, but Jack escaped. Jack showed his disdain for the justice system by attacking Constables Brown and Hamilton right outside Parramatta Courthouse and locking them in the court. He held up the Flogging Parson, Reverend Marsden, but stopped robbing the nice river guy, Charles Sturt, when he realised who he was, then apologised and returned all his goods.[5]

---

4   It's odd that we admire those who steal from the wealthy as somehow altruistic. After all, not many successful thieves wake up in the morning and think, "Right, the missus wants a new jacuzzi – I'll go and roll a hobo."

5   Jack's charity was outdone by James Wilson, the Philanthropic Bushranger. Wilson, also known as The Little Scotchman, gave Mr Hayes £33 during a robbery and held up Walter Leslie so he could return a watch and horse.

It was Jack's hair-care regime that eventually brought him undone. In 1830, the police found a hut in the bush, its floor covered in human hair. Chief Constable Thorne matched some of the blond locks to a sample he'd retrieved from another of Jack's hideouts and deduced that Jack's gang were using the hut to give each other haircuts.[6]

Knowing Jack was near, the police concentrated their patrols in the area and snuck up on the immaculately coiffured bushranger. Jack shouted, "Come on, you cowardly rascals, we are ready, if there's a dozen of you!" while sensibly hiding behind a tree. But when Jack peered out, John Mucklestone scored an incredible shot from over 100 yards, piercing his neck and shattering his temple.

A pipe maker was permitted into Sydney's morgue to take a cast of Jack's fatal head wound and made a fortune selling pipes with bowls moulded from it. Major Thomas Mitchell also visited the morgue to sketch the portrait of Jack's handsome corpse that now hangs in Sydney's Mitchell Library, adding a quotation from Byron's "Mazeppa":

> No matter; I have bared my brow
> Fair in Death's face – before – and now.

The adoration from one of the government's most senior officers, along with the people's desire to suck tobacco smoke from Jack's shattered skull, is testament to the power of the legend of the noble bushranger.

The legend was strengthened by "Bold Jack Donahue", a folk song that honoured Jack's fight against the state. Governor Darling made it an offence to sing the song in pubs, but this only made it more popular and people got around the ban by singing about Jack Doolan or John Dowling. The song, later known as "The Wild Colonial Boy", became Australia's unofficial anthem and was hugely

---

6   Sir Arthur Conan Doyle is generally credited with conceiving of forensic hair analysis in his Sherlock Holmes novels, the first of which was written in 1887. Thorne was way ahead of his time and hair analysis can be chalked up as another great Aussie innovation – up there with the black box, wi-fi, polymer banknote, Hills Hoist and wine cask.

popular in Ireland for its celebration of a Dublin boy sticking it to the oppressive English.[7]

Jack had been able to evade capture because he was harboured by sympathisers among the rural poor. Darling responded by passing the *Bushranging Act*, which increased the penalty for helping bushrangers and allowed police to search for stolen goods without a warrant.

The act also required people to present identification to police. However, the native born were not routinely issued with identification papers, which meant first-generation Australians were arrested and taken to their birthplaces, where it was hoped someone could confirm who they were. Rural labourers might be marched hundreds of kilometres in chains, released, and then have the same thing happen all over again when they went elsewhere to work. No one was safe from the long arm of the law – the chief justice was once arrested for not carrying ID during his morning stroll.

Emboldened by Jack and enraged by the government's draconian response, more of those who lived on the margins of society turned bushranger. Even Sydney was no longer safe, with the cry of "Bail up!" heard on the city's fringes.[8] Lawrence Kavanagh and Thomas Brown haunted Sydney's Balmain, Rose Bay, Double Bay and Elizabeth Bay, now inner-city harbour suburbs haunted by society matrons and the soy latte set. Wentworth survived an attack outside his Petersham home in 1826, when his assailant's pistol misfired, but Robert Wardell,

---

7   "The Wild Colonial Boy" was repopularised by Rolf Harris in 1980 and, unfathomably, by American soft-rockers Dr Hook in 1984. Jack Donohoe is also the only Australian bushranger to feature in a Bob Dylan song ("Jim Jones"). You know you've made it big as a folk protest figure when Dylan writes about you.

8   *Bail up* first appeared in print in the *Colonist* on 27 February 1839. Meaning "stand still and don't try anything tricky," the term derived from the bail used to immobilise angry South African cows while they were being milked by nervous South African farmers, who would cry "Bail up" immediately before placing a cow's head in the bail. Who said the South Africans have never done anything for Australian culture?

who'd bought the Petersham estate from his friend, was not so lucky – he was gunned down in 1834 while trying to arrest three suspected bushrangers on his ride home.

In 1830, convict bullock driver Ralph Entwistle was skinny-dipping in the Macquarie River when Governor Darling rode past. Thomas Evernden, Bathurst's chief superintendent of police, was determined to impress the governor with his enforcement of the new laws and his persecution of degenerate naturists. Entwistle, lacking waterproof identification papers, was arrested, given fifty lashes and had his pending ticket-of-leave cancelled.

Entwistle thought this unfair and turned bushranger. He gathered a gang of eighty followers by raiding farms and threatening convict farmhands with death if they didn't join his revolution. He wore a white ribbon on his hat and called his private army the Ribbon Men. Clearly deranged, Entwistle worked feverishly on improving his ribbon collection and, during a shootout with Bathurst police, was seen with "a profusion of white streamers about his head". He escaped and was hunted down by more than 200 police, troopers and militia, being cornered a week later in what is today Bathurst's Ribbon Gang Lane. Entwistle was hanged fully clothed.

Bushranging didn't just appeal to nudists, but to other marginalised groups too. Coffee was Aboriginal.[9] Mary Ann Ward, doubly discriminated against, was an Aboriginal woman. Sam Poo was Chinese and had a silly name. Robert Cotterall was visually impaired, with the blue eyeshade he wore to protect his failing vision earning him the sinister moniker of Blue Cap. Johnny Gilbert was a cross-dresser. Captain Moonlite was gay.[10] Mad Dan Morgan was

---

9   The Martha Stewart approach to naming Aborigines may need a rethink, as Coffee was not a cheery domesticated Aborigine with whom you could discuss baking or table decorations, but a hardened criminal. Then again, so is Martha Stewart.

10 The name, straight out of an Andrew Lloyd Webber musical, was a giveaway. Those of you who are only reading this book in the hope of some steamy beard-on-beard action can skip straight to Chapter 13.

mad. And Edward Davis, better known as Teddy the Jewboy, led the Jewboy Gang in terrorising the Hunter Valley between 1839 and 1841, except on Saturdays.

Bushranging allowed poor marginalised dreamers to build themselves a better world, in which they were champions of justice, warriors against tyranny, protectors of the weak and enemies of convention. And they got to shoot people – that was the best bit.

CHILDREN OF GOD

Reverend John Dunmore Lang would have put the high number of Irish bushrangers down to popery, rather than poverty. Lang, who emigrated from Glasgow to New South Wales in 1823 as the colony's first Presbyterian minister, hated Catholics, believing they were conspiring to "rivet the chains of popery on a deluded people in the Australian colonies".[11]

Catholic priests had been barred from entering New South Wales and Van Diemen's Land, other than as convicts. Most convict priests were convicted of encouraging Irish Catholics to stick pikes into their Protestant English masters, rather than the crimes with which they are associated today.[12] But when anti-Catholic restrictions were lifted in 1820, Father John Therry entered the colony. One of his first priorities was to establish Catholic schools.

Lang was also a passionate educator. He opened Australia's first Presbyterian primary school in 1826, his first student being a shy boy with a cleft palate and speech impediment. John Robertson thrived under Lang's guidance and went on to become a five-time premier of New South Wales.

In Britain, schooling was provided by churches and a few private institutions. The Church of England was the only church to have an official presence in New South Wales in the first decades of settlement

---

11   The Scottish Presbyterians were Calvinists in kilts.

12   The Jesuits really need to rethink their maxim, "Give me the child until he is seven ..."

FIG. 7: THE BLACKSMITH FASHIONED CAST-IRON YARMULKES AND SEVEN-SHOOTERS FOR THE JEWBOY GANG.

and it hadn't exactly set the colony alight. While the church half-heartedly provided a few schools, they were funded by the state, a radical departure from British practice.

In 1824, Governor Brisbane reported, "every murder or diabolical crime, which has been committed in the colony since my arrival, has been perpetrated by Roman Catholics." Believing strong moral leadership from the church would reduce Catholic crime, Brisbane funded Therry's Catholic schools. He also partially financed the building of Australia's first Catholic church, given the impoverished state of the colony's predominantly Irish Catholics, although he refused to pay for any over-the-top papist frou-frou.

This Catholic aid outraged Lang. The splenetic Scot complained he was forced to deliver his sermons in a schoolhouse shared with diabolical papists, who assaulted his nostrils with their incense and his ears with their bellringing. Brisbane refused his demands for a government-subsidised church because the Scottish Presbyterians had enough cash hidden in their mattresses to build one themselves. He was also concerned that if he gave money to his poor-crying country-men, then the Jews would demand he build them a synagogue – and his ecumenicalism did not stretch *that* far.

The arrival of Therry and Lang brought the long-dormant religious divisions of the old country simmering to the surface of the colonial cookpot. The Catholics hated the Anglicans for not permitting Catholic education in their schools; the Presbyterians hated the Catholics for receiving government support and for being Catholics; and the Anglicans hated the Catholics and Presbyterians for moving onto their turf. Sectarianism had stormed into the previously secular colony, its battlefield the hearts and minds of children.

Some of the wealthier colonists were prepared to pay for secular education. In 1820, Laurence Halloran founded Dr Halloran's Establishment for Liberal Education, before opening the Sydney Free Public Grammar School five years later. Halloran was a gifted, if morally flawed, educator. An Irish poet of no small talent, he'd been gaoled in 1783 for stabbing a sailor to death and spent two decades posing as an Anglican chaplain under various assumed names. He was transported to New South Wales in 1819 for forging a document in the hope of fraudulently accrediting himself as a curate.

Halloran had earlier been prosecuted for immorality, his favourite pursuit. After having six children with his wife, he eloped with his niece (with whom he had twelve offspring), before bigamously marrying a sixteen-year-old girl in 1823 (four more little Hallorans followed). While headmaster of the grammar school, Halloran published an obscene play, *Count O'Candle*, which described O'Candle's wick-dipping "in the grossest of terms". This, combined with his regular appearances before the courts in libel cases, his son's drinking and swearing while working at the school and Halloran's imprisonment for debt, resulted in the school's closure after a year.[13]

---

13   Australia's private education sector was established by a knife-wielding, clergy-impersonating, libellous, sex-addicted producer of obscene publications and incestuous bigamist bankrupt. Unfortunately, fine educators like Dr Halloran

William Bland considered the experiment an educational success, despite the moral failings of its headmaster. A prominent Sydney doctor, Bland had been transported for killing a fellow naval officer in a duel and was later imprisoned for printing rude poems about Governor Macquarie's penchant for building expensive things and naming them Macquarie. Wentworth, who'd had his own issues with defamatory verse, befriended Bland and supported his establishment of the independent Sydney College in 1835.

Governor Bourke passed the *Churches Act* in 1836, which provided religious equality and state aid for Anglicans, Catholics and Presbyterians. Van Diemen's Land passed similar laws the following year.[14] These reforms were meant to reduce religious tension, but had the opposite effect, as the churches dipped their snouts into the state trough and fought over the rich financial slops on offer.

At the same time, Bourke tried to replace church schools with state schools that would offer separate religious instruction – a previously blocked Brisbane initiative. It was hoped this would cool sectarian divisions and save money on supporting multiple schools in areas that only had the population to justify one.

The Anglicans regarded this as a Catholic plot to infect their children with papism, and the reform failed. When Bourke's successor, Sir

---

would today be barred from teaching under namby-pamby Working With Children Check laws.

14   Britain had repealed most of its surviving anti-Catholic laws in 1829, allowing Catholics to run for parliament and other government office, although they were barred from graduating from Oxford until 1854 and Cambridge until 1856, and from teaching at those universities until 1871. The British Parliament simultaneously passed legislation to raise the property qualifications for voting in Ireland, in an attempt to limit Catholic influence in parliament. The Protestant Orange Order responded to Catholic emancipation by holding regular marches to celebrate the defeat of King James II, a Catholic, by Dutch uber-Protestant William of Orange (William III) at the Battle of the Boyne in 1688, ratcheting up sectarian tension in Ireland. The Orange Order also plotted to install its imperial grand master, Ernest Augustus, Duke of Cumberland, on the throne in place of Queen Victoria because she was a woman and didn't hate Catholics enough, ratcheting up sectarian conflict in Britain. These events increased Protestant–Catholic tension in Australia.

George Gipps, proposed common schooling for Protestant children, with Catholics to be educated separately, the Anglicans regarded this as a Presbyterian plot to infect their children with non-conformism.

The colony's Catholics were initially split on the issue of state schooling. While Bishop Polding was sympathetic, his deputy, Father William Ullathorne, was a staunch opponent. On 25 August 1840, Ullathorne mobilised several thousand Catholic convicts, Irish marching bands and 300 Gaelic girls dressed in virginal white to protest any dismantling of Catholic education. Irish nationalists, who'd barely uttered a "Top o' the morning" since the Castle Hill Rebellion of 1804, hijacked the forum to shout slogans in support of an independent Ireland. Religious differences might be tolerated, but angry Paddies who wanted to play Hide the Pike in the Protestant – well, that was a potato of an entirely different skin.

THE HIGH PRIEST OF NEW MAMMON

William Charles Wentworth was a religious puzzle. The motto on his coat of arms was "In God Is Everything", yet he did not attend church and championed secular education.[15] He welcomed the repeal of anti-Catholic laws and unsuccessfully campaigned for the public funding of a synagogue, arguing, "Hebrews contributed just as much as Christians towards the revenue."

The revenue was Wentworth's God and the wealthy his high priests. One's birth, past and creed were as nothing to Mammon,

---

15   Wentworth played a key role in introducing state education in 1848. He also led the movement to establish the University of Sydney, the first colonial university in the British Empire. Wentworth unsuccessfully tried to bar ministers of religion from sitting on the university's senate. He also introduced laws to bar ministers from political office, in an attempt to banish John Dunmore Lang, then one of his fiercest political rivals, from New South Wales' Legislative Council. These laws were scotched after the attorney-general pointed out that bishops and other men who liked wearing dresses and silly hats were members of the British House of Lords.

whose divine right to rule flowed through the Taxpayer who sat at his right hand.

The central tenet of the Book of Wentworth was that the rich should determine how their money (and everybody else's) should be spent. Accordingly, people with property portfolios and sheep should be given the vote and people without them should not. The poor were not fit to determine the future of the colony, as "ignorance and poverty went together". In the world of Wentworth's faith perfected, the moneychangers would be keepers of the Temple once more.

Wentworth's disdain for the poor did not endear him to his servants. In 1835, Wentworth's butler led a household mutiny, stealing his master's schooner in an attempt to escape to New Zealand. When the servants were recaptured, the butler requested, "Tell Mr Wentworth that if I had not got away ... [I] would have settled him in another way." Poison was found at Vaucluse House and Wentworth was convinced it was meant for him and his family.

Wentworth, shocked by this near-death experience, left the Bar to focus on his family and pastoral interests. He'd already taken a back seat in the reform movement, ceding its leadership to Sir John Jamison, "a pleasant man of a vain, ostentatious ... character" who loved watching his hounds disembowel defenceless native animals.

Wentworth played the coquette at those reform gatherings he still attended. He would wait for the crowd to shout his name and then either assault them with the thundering rhetoric of old or modestly demur, insisting that the baton of reform had passed to more able and ambitious men.

Wentworth's dwindling interest in progressive politics might charitably be attributed to the major battles having already been won. Press freedom had been secured and Governor Gipps dismantled the last military juries early in his rule.

The less charitably inclined viewed the dimming of Wentworth's beacon as evidence of increasing conservatism. William Charles Wentworth still called for change, but only change that would benefit

William Charles Wentworth and the landowners and squatters with
whom he now associated.

The one issue that still stirred Wentworth's combative juices was
Britain's failure to allow the rich white men of the colony to vote rich
white men of the colony onto the governor's Legislative Council.
Instead, the War and Colonial Office appointed its own rich white
men, who squandered Wentworth's hard-earned taxes on chinless
bureaucrats who did absolutely nothing for Wentworth.

Wentworth complained that the colonial botanist was paid £700
a year to grow cabbages in his pathetic Botanical Garden and condemned Archdeacon Scott's £2,000 salary, inquiring, "Gentlemen,
do any of you know the meaning or use of an Archdeacon?" And as
for the government resident of New Zealand, Wentworth roared:

> This gentleman may be sent to New Zealand to strut about in his
> uniform to be stared at by savages – they may make a roast of him
> for all I care – but why should £500 a year of our money be voted
> into his pocket without our consent?

Wentworth had an ally in the press. Horatio Spencer Howe Wills,
publisher of the *Gazette*, established a new weekly journal, the *Currency Lad*. Under the banner "RISE AUSTRALIA", the *Currency
Lad* advanced emancipist and native-born interests and demanded
representative government in New South Wales. Dissatisfied with
the pace of reform, Wills was the first Australian to seriously float
the idea of an independent Australian republic. He wrote:

> Look, Australians, to the high salaried foreigners around you!
> Behold those men lolling in their coaches – rioting in the sweat of
> your brow while you – yes, you, the Sons of the Soil, are doomed
> to eternal toil – the sport and ridicule of pettifogging worldlings.
> A House of Assembly would remedy this grievance ... WE WERE
> NOT MADE FOR SLAVES.

In 1835, Jamison and Wentworth founded the Australian Patriotic Association to lobby the British Parliament for representative government. The membership fee of £5 kept the riffraff out and the association's policy of denying the vote to poor people, blacks and women encouraged a number of the more progressive exclusives to join.

Governors Bourke and Gipps lent their support to the campaign. Gipps even recommended Wentworth's appointment to the Legislative Council, advising the War and Colonial Office, "though in former days he was extremely violent in his opposition to Government, he has now for a long time past ... become moderate in his politics".[16]

However, the secretary of state for war and the colonies directed Gipps to appoint James Macarthur to the council vacancy. James was everything his father was not – quietly spoken, adaptable and a stranger to violent emotion. His boots were polished to perfection, his cummerbund pleasantly pleated and he could tie a cravat for Australia, although he'd obviously prefer to represent Great Britain.

The urbanely understated James saw no reason to rush reform and travelled to London to prosecute the old exclusive cause. James's motto was "Once a convict, always a convict." And who in their right mind would hand the keys of government to the unreformed thieves, fraudsters and ha'penny heavies who were now some of the wealthiest men on the empire's wild southern frontier?

MORE PROS AND LESS CONS

Britain accepted James Macarthur's advice to delay representative government for New South Wales until it had solved the convict

---

16   Think of all the tedious Trots you met at university who now can't join the revolution because the Volvo needs a service and Tarquin is trying out for the school rowing crew.

problem. James proposed two solutions: more immigration and an end to transportation.

John Dunmore Lang was a passionate supporter of both ideas. A non-believer in earthly reformation, Lang despised convicts and ex-convicts alike. Crime was the start of a slippery slope that led to Sabbath picnicking, fancy-dress balls and other mortal sins. The convict stain could only be washed from Australia's moral fabric by increasing the proportion of non-criminals in the colonies. Breeding new non-criminals was too slow, so Lang became the champion of immigration.

Lang had visited Britain in 1830 to perform the traditional Scottish ritual of marrying a cousin and to secure funding for a Presbyterian secondary school. He used some of the money raised to import 140 duty-free Scots into New South Wales. Lang's migrants were hard-working tradesmen, who repaid their passage by building Lang's school, before moving on to other building and public works projects. They were the finest craftsmen the colony had seen and Lang was hailed a hero for Scottifying Sydney.

But the first arrivals under the next immigration scheme, which commenced in 1831, were not so well received. This Wakefield-inspired program targeted single women due to the colonial gender imbalance and whispers of "funny business" between male convicts, particularly down in Tasmania.

Lieutenant-Governor Arthur, who received the bulk of the migrants between 1830 and 1837, despaired at the "sickly and diseased" women foisted upon him, denouncing them as "more depraved than the convicts". His chief police magistrate complained that the new arrivals, "if not actually common prostitutes, were of easy virtue". Lang attacked "the flagrant enormities of the Female Emigration System" (i.e. most of the women were Catholics). Governor Bourke, concerned that "an almost unlimited intercourse existed between the seamen and a great number of the female passengers", temporarily suspended the program in 1836.[17]

Of the 110,000 immigrants to the Australian colonies in the 1830s and 1840s, approximately half were Irish and over 80 per cent of the Irish were Catholic. The *Sydney Herald* referred to them as "Popish serfs" and the "low, depraved and bigoted classes".[18]

In 1837, concerns about being overrun by "ignorant, uncivilised, degraded Catholic paupers" led to the introduction of a bounty scheme, under which the colonies paid employers and migration agents to import skilled mechanics and agricultural workers.

Lang threw himself into importing hordes of ginger, skirt-wearing Presbyterians to counter the papist plague. The Industrial Revolution had taken seventy years to climb over Hadrian's Wall and stagger into the Highlands, but was now in full fling. Scotland's agricultural sector and once vibrant kelp industry declined as coal and iron transformed the economy, with Highland shepherds, crofters and seaweed gatherers forced into poverty.[19] In the late 1830s, Lang encouraged more than 4,000 Highlanders to seek purpler pastures in New South Wales.[20]

Not all of the 1830s migrant labourers were European. John Mackay, a farmer and distillery owner, imported forty-two Indian coolies in 1837, who would work for rations, clothes and a measly £6 a year for five years before receiving a free passage to India at the end of their contracts. Two coolies subsequently ran away and, when recaptured,

---

17 The British Evangelicals wanted a Beyoncé-style immigration scheme – all the single ladies would make Australian men like it and put a ring on it. Instead they delivered Jay Z's "2 Many Hoes".

18 The irony of the bigotry charge appears to have been lost on the *Herald*'s editor.

19 Kelp was once a major Highland export, with burned seaweed used in fertiliser, soap and glass. Agricultural reform and Britain's removal of kelp duties on imported seaweed destroyed the Scottish kelp industry, sending entire communities into deep depression.

20 Scotland's feudal landlords complained that the bounty scheme took the most-skilled Scots, leaving them to support the "poverty-stricken, aged and destitute". They called for "indiscriminate emigration", which was code for the mass export of poor, old, sick people.

claimed they'd been placed on a starvation diet and received no wages. Britain and India placed a ban on Indian immigration in 1838 and the outbreak of the Opium War in 1839 cancelled James Macarthur's order of Chinese takeaway labour.[21]

The 1830s bounty migrants included the young ivory turner and wannabe poet Henry Parkes, whose failure selling knick-knacks made from dead elephants sent him bankrupt. Parkes's "A Poet's Farewell", published before he left Britain in 1839, condemned a society insufficiently concerned with deceased pachyderm products, through whose injustices men like himself were "compelled to seek the means of existence in a foreign wilderness". Parkes existed very nicely in the foreign wilderness, raising himself from a labourer on Sir John Jamison's estate to a political titan who championed the federation of the Australian colonies into an independent Australia.

Fourteen-year-old Scots lass Catherine Helen Spence was another bounty migrant – the South Australian settler would pen the first novel about Australia written by a woman, introduce foster care for vulnerable children and lead the campaigns for proportional representation and women's suffrage in Australia.[22]

Australia would have been a very different place without the bounty migrants.

The quadrupling of free immigration in the 1830s reduced the need for convict labour. This provided an opportunity for Evangelical

---

21   Britain attacked China to enable it to continue being the world's largest drug
      dealer. The British East India Company had been flooding China with the opium
      it grew in India, and China, concerned about its developing stoner culture, banned
      the opium trade and confiscated over 20,000 chests of the drug. Britain sent in
      its gunboats, told the Chinese they had to keep smoking its gear, insisted on free
      access and European settlement rights in five Chinese ports and demanded Hong
      Kong as compensation for the inconvenience of being forced to invade.

22   Those of you interested in learning more about this amazing Australian woman
      will have to buy volume 3 of *The Unauthorised History of Australia*. Or you can
      Google her if you're a tightarse.

politicians, who were looking for a new cause following the abolition of slavery. They latched onto transportation reform.

In 1837, the British House of Commons appointed Sir Robert Molesworth MP to chair an inquiry into transportation. Molesworth, only in his mid-twenties, was something of a firebrand, having been expelled from Cambridge for duelling his tutor. He was also a leading intellectual who edited the magazines of the Philosophical Radicals, the disciples of Jeremy Bentham who applied his utilitarian principles to government, promoting policies they believed provided the greatest happiness to the greatest number of people.[23]

Molesworth heard evidence from James Stephen, the Evangelical head of the War and Colonial Office, who believed transportation had "converted Australia into a den of thieves".[24] He also heard from Father William Ullathorne, who believed transportation had made Australia a cesspool filled with the refuse of mankind.

Molesworth wanted to abandon transportation, but there was an obstacle. Britain didn't have enough gaols – it was still incarcerating prisoners in hulks, rotting ships that had been introduced as a "temporary measure" in 1776. Instead, Molesworth targeted the system of assigning convicts to private masters.

Molesworth's philosophical pin-up Jeremy Bentham had argued that punishment must be proportional to the crime. Molesworth insisted that assignment was arbitrary punishment, as it depended on the temperament of the master, rather than the crimes of the convict. Assignment was, he concluded, a form of slavery.

---

23   Bentham believed happiness could be mathematically determined by calculating the pleasure and pain arising from an action, and subtracting the latter from the former. Bentham's formula did not account for sadomasochism, resulting in little support for utilitarianism among Tories.

24   James Stephen, nephew of the love-struck John Stephen, had worked for the War and Colonial Office since 1813 and headed it from 1836–47. He, more than any other person, shaped British policy with respect to the Australian colonies. He is otherwise most famous for being the grandfather of Adeline Stephen, better known as Virginia Woolf.

In response, Gipps and Lieutenant-Governor Franklin of Van
Diemen's Land wound back assignment, with convicts transferred
to public works, penal institutions and female factories.

The horrified Wentworth convened a public meeting to demand
the continuation of assignment. As a young man he'd written that the
convict character of New South Wales was a barrier to free government, but as one of the largest landowners in the colony he'd grown
to cherish the convicts as a cheap and powerless labour force.

Wentworth now found himself in opposition to the reform movement he'd once championed.

WENTWORTH AND WAKEFIELD DO WELLINGTON

The government was interfering with Wentworth's ability to make
an honest living in New South Wales. It taxed his land, insisted that
he pay to squat, and now it was taking away his criminals!

The other Australian colonies were no better. Wentworth needed
to find a place where he could make money, free from the interference
of petty bureaucrats – a place that sheep would love and that would
love sheep in return – a place called New Zealand.

Reverend Samuel Marsden had shown the way in 1814, when he
made the first New Zealand land purchase, buying 200 acres from
the Māori for twelve axes, which was a pretty good deal. Britain
had never challenged the purchase and, most importantly, had
never asserted possession over the two islands claimed by Captain
Cook in 1769.

Marsden used the land he bought to establish the first permanent
European settlement in New Zealand, the first of his religious missions to the Māori. He gave Jesus to the Māori and, in return, they
gave him lucrative timber, flax and pork trading rights. The Church
Missionary Society subsidised Marsden's private business ventures,
as long as he dropped off a few Bibles and boxes of second-hand

clothes during his trading runs. Sweet as, bro![25]

Landgrabbers started moving in during the early 1830s, purchasing land for a pittance from the nearest handy Māori. Wentworth wanted in on the action and bought 100,000 acres during 1838 and 1839.[26] Edward Gibbon Wakefield had even grander visions – in 1839, he joined forces with Molesworth and established the New Zealand Company to settle the islands.

The missionaries were alarmed by the increase in settlement, as speculators paid for land with guns, which the Māori turned on each other in inter-tribal conflicts known as the Musket Wars. The missionaries begged Britain to impose order.

When Wakefield became aware the War and Colonial Office was considering making New Zealand a British colony, he rushed to the docks and instructed his brother William to set sail before the government confined his company's ship to port. William was ordered to buy up as much of New Zealand as he could before the government moved in. Eight boatloads of Wakefield's settlers followed.

The Marquess of Normanby, secretary of state for war and the colonies, had had enough of Wakefield. South Australia was a mess and now the notorious kidnapper planned to abduct two islands right from under Britain's nose. Normanby incorporated New Zealand into New South Wales and dispatched Captain William Hobson, the first lieutenant-governor of New Zealand, to negotiate a treaty with the Māori, under which they would cede sovereignty to Queen Victoria. Normanby also made it clear that the title to land purchased from the Māori couldn't be guaranteed.

---

25 Marsden never bothered ministering to the Aborigines, as they had no timber, flax or pork to give him.

26 Marsden died just as Wentworth started building his New Zealand property portfolio. Australians remember Marsden as a whip-happy, sexist bigot, while Kiwis venerate him as the "Apostle of New Zealand" and a founding father, eh bro.

On Christmas Eve 1839, Normanby's news reached Sydney and Wentworth discovered his 100,000 acres might be worthless. This was not what he'd wanted from Santa.

Meanwhile, William Wakefield settled Wellington after purchasing millions of acres from Te Rauparaha of the Ngāti Toa for around 250 guns and 70 kegs of ammunition. Te Rauparaha planned to use Wakefield's weapons to exterminate the Ngāti Tahu, who claimed to own some of the land he'd just sold William.

Tūhawaiki and four other Ngāti Tahu chiefs, concerned that Wakefield's guns would turn their people into unwilling guests at the next Ngāti Toa barbecue, fled to Sydney to "claim the protection of the Queen of England". Wentworth, sniffing a chance to make good his losses, agreed to act as their attorney in negotiations with Gipps.

Gipps met the Ngāti Tahu and Wentworth on 14 February 1840 and explained that Wakefield's purchase might not be recognised, as only "land sales approved by Her Majesty would be confirmed". He told the chiefs to come back in two days, by which time he'd have a treaty for them to sign. He also gave Tūhawaiki a Union Jack to welcome him to Team Britain.

The day after the meeting, Wentworth told the chiefs to sign a deed that would give him and Johnny Jones, the captain who'd brought them to Sydney, almost the entire South Island of New Zealand, including land already claimed by the Wakefields.[27] In return, Wentworth would give the chiefs £200, with Tūhawaiki to get a £20 annual pension and the other chiefs a £10 pension. Wentworth, whose land grab of more than 20 million acres dwarfed William Penn's record land deal, had shafted indigenous people in a way that made Batman look like Mother Teresa.

---

27   The deed was so dense with legalese that it was incomprehensible to experienced lawyers, let alone the chiefs. The chiefs signed by inscribing their facial tattoos on the document, the method Marsden had used for the first New Zealand land purchase. Wentworth was a keen student of precedent.

Wentworth then instructed Jones not to let the chiefs sign away their sovereignty until Gipps confirmed the purchase. This was high-stakes blackmail and Gipps was incensed.

Wentworth's plan started to unravel when news filtered through that Hobson and more than 150 chiefs had signed the Treaty of Waitangi on 6 February. More than 400 chiefs, including Tūhawaiki, signed up in the following months. The treaty granted Queen Victoria sovereignty over New Zealand, guaranteed the chiefs exclusive and undisturbed possession of their land and, critically for Wentworth and Wakefield, stated that the Māori could only sell their land to Britain. Gipps then introduced the *New Zealand Land Claims Bill* to strike out earlier land purchases deemed unfair to the Māori. Wentworth's claim was top of the list.

Wentworth appeared before the Legislative Council and argued his purchase was made before the treaty took effect and, in any event, the government should recognise the right of the Māori to dispose of their land as they saw fit and their right to get completely ripped off in the process.

Gipps countered that Wentworth had not acted in the chiefs' best interests when their lawyer and had got them drunk before making them sign a document they didn't understand. He ripped into Wentworth:

> He will never get one acre, one foot, one shilling for the land which he bought ... he is not yet safe from prosecution for conspiracy ... All the jobs that have taken place since the expulsion of the Stuarts ... would not equal this job effected by Mr Wentworth ... who purchased a whole island at the rate of four hundred acres for a penny.[28]

The bill was passed and Wentworth's shrill cries for compensation were dismissed. The Wakefields fared better, accepting Britain's

---

28   This heated debate over the future of New Zealand took place in what is now a photocopying room in the New South Wales Parliament House.

offer of land that reflected their colonisation costs. Gipps removed
Wentworth's name from the list of suitable Legislative Council
members and the almost-emperor of New Zealand withdrew to lick
his wounds and plot Gipps's downfall.[29]

FRONTIER JUSTICE

While Britain made treaties with the inhabitants of New Zealand,
Fiji and New Guinea, no British or Australian government has ever
entered into a treaty with Australia's Indigenous peoples. This fact
would have astounded the Evangelicals who dominated British society
in the early 1830s.

In 1835, Lord Glenelg informed the South Australian Colonization Commission that it would need to *buy* land from the locals. The
commission undertook to protect Aborigines "in the undisturbed
enjoyment to the proprietary right to the soil ... in all bargains and
treaties ... for the cession of lands possessed by them".

In 1837, the House of Commons Select Committee on Aborigines,
which was full of happy-clappers, reported:

> It must be presumed that the native inhabitants of any land have
> an incontrovertible right to their own soil; a plain and sacred right,
> however, which seems not to have been understood. Europeans have
> entered the borders uninvited, and, when there, have not only acted
> as if they were undoubted lords of the soil, but have punished the
> natives as aggressors if they have evinced a disposition to live in their
> own country.

However, the South Australians never paid the Aborigines a penny

---

29 In May 1841, New Zealand was separated from New South Wales and became
    a Crown colony in its own right, but the close historic bond between the two
    colonies means New Zealanders still enjoy rights in Australia unavailable to other
    foreign citizens – especially at Centrelink.

and the committee's words were but a puff of principle. The line drawn in the sand after the Batman Treaty meant the T-word was never mentioned again. Evangelicalism had butted its head against the wall of realpolitik and come off second best.

One reason for this was the belief that dead people don't need treaties. In 1838, James Stephen wrote to Sir George Grey, a fellow God-botherer, "nor do I suppose that it is possible to discover any method by which the impending catastrophe, namely, the elimination of the black race, can be averted".

This fatalism infected Aboriginal policy. Britain would no longer attempt to negotiate with natives, but would, in the words of Daisy Bates, a journalist who spent decades living with outback tribes, "smooth the dying pillow".

The Select Committee on Aborigines recommended a small portion of the proceeds of land sales be set aside to establish reserves and missions, where pillow smoothing could be quietly conducted out of the public eye. It was also hoped poor white men would marry Aboriginal women and breed the Aborigines out of existence.[30]

In South Australia the newly arrived governor, George Gawler, addressed an Aboriginal gathering in 1838:

Black men, we wish to make you happy. But you cannot be happy unless you imitate good white men. Build huts, wear clothes, work and be useful. Above all you cannot be happy unless you love God who made heaven and earth and men and all things.

Love white men. Love other tribes of black men. Do not quarrel together. Tell other tribes to love white men, and to build good huts and wear clothes. Learn to speak English.

---

30 It was believed that Aboriginal women would prefer partnerships with white men, who were self-evidently superior, and would stop having children with Aboriginal men. Children of mixed unions were regarded as European, rather than Aboriginal, although "half-castes" were still routinely discriminated against.

For the Select Committee on Aborigines, there was no stopping white settlement. It reported:

> Whatever may have been the injustice of this encroachment, there
> is no reason to suppose that either justice or humanity would now
> be consulted by receding from it.

Justice and humanity demanded continued settlement, as without settlement the Aborigines would not have "the defence of British law" necessary to protect them from the settlers.

Governor Gipps was instructed to ensure Aboriginal people had the same legal rights as other citizens of the British Empire, but advised London it was desirable to delay such a move to avoid giving "offence to the officers and men of the Mounted Police". In 1838, police commander Major James Nunn celebrated the fiftieth anniversary of Australian settlement by shooting a group of Kamilaroi at Waterloo Creek, now known as Slaughterhouse Creek.[31] At a subsequent inquiry, Lieutenant Cobban, who'd missed part of the action, testified that no more than four Aborigines had been killed, while Sergeant John Lee, who'd participated in the main conflict, estimated between forty and fifty casualties.

While not wanting to make waves with the police, Gipps was disquieted by Nunn's actions and came down hard when the next report of major frontier violence hit his desk.

On 10 June 1838, eleven convict stockmen led by squatter John Fleming took revenge for the spearing of their cattle. They arrived at Myall Creek station in northern New South Wales, where a group of Wirrayaraay people, unconnected with the spearings, were camped. The Wirrayaraay, mostly children, women and old men, were roped together and taken to a nearby gully, where they were shot, hacked, bludgeoned and burned to death.

---

31 Happy Australia Day, Kamilaroi people!

About twenty-eight Wirrayaraay were massacred at Myall Creek, although the dismemberment and burning of their corpses made an exact body count impossible. Gipps ordered an investigation and the stockmen were arrested, although Fleming, a reputable landowner, went free. Gipps insisted that his attorney-general, John Plunkett, try the stockmen for murder.[32]

This was like throwing raw meat onto a bull-ant nest. How could eleven men, who had a right to protect their cows, now be facing the noose for clearing the area of savages who, if not cow-killers themselves, almost certainly knew other savages who were?

The stockmen's lawyers acknowledged their clients had taken the Aborigines to the gully and that the Aborigines had been killed, but demanded that the prosecution specify the names of the deceased to prove that they were indeed dead and not off killing cows somewhere else. The attorney-general pointed out this was tricky, as:

(a) most Aborigines don't have proper names and, if they do, we don't know them; and

(b) the defendants had made it difficult to identify the deceased by mutilating and torching their corpses.

In the end, the prosecution confined its case to:

(a) the murder of a giant Aboriginal man known as Daddy, or of name unknown;

(b) the murder of an Aborigine, name unknown, by a pistol found in the possession of Oates, one of the stockmen;[33] and

---

32 Only one person had been convicted of murdering an Aborigine in fifty years of settlement, so trying eleven men was a big call.

33 The trial is of interest to music historians as well as students of frontier violence. Character evidence in support of Oates was given by a Mr Hall. Hall and Oates would go on to record such classics as "Out of Touch", "Some Things Are Better Left Unsaid" and "I Can't Go for That".

(c) the murder of an Aborigine, name unknown, by a sword seen covered in blood while in the possession of Foley, another stockman.

It took only fifteen minutes for the jury to find the defendants not guilty on all charges, as they accepted the defence's arguments that:

(a) while a giant, burned, headless and limbless torso had been found, it couldn't be proved that it belonged to Daddy or an unnamed Aboriginal man, because it hadn't been proved that it didn't belong to a woman;

(b) no unknown Aboriginal corpse with bullet holes or sword wounds had been produced;

(c) somebody else might have fired Oates's gun, or some other gun, or not; and

(d) Foley might have been minding somebody else's sword.

As the gallery and most of the Sydney press cheered the verdict, Plunkett remanded the defendants in custody to be tried for further murders.

In the second trial, only seven stockmen were charged, due to the disappearance of a key witness. The stockmen were charged with shooting an unknown boy and girl child, as well as an Aboriginal infant named Charley, who'd been cast onto a fire.

The defence argued the stockmen had been acquitted of murdering an unknown Aborigine and could therefore now only be tried for murdering a known Aborigine – and, apart from Charley, whose body hadn't been produced, the other murdered Aborigines were unknown. Plunkett countered that the unknown Aborigines in the second trial were different to the unknown Aborigines in the first trial. The defence asked how Plunkett could know this if the Aborigines in both cases were unknown.[34]

The defence then argued that the corpses of the children were so badly burned that the prosecution couldn't prove whether any corpse belonged to an unknown boy child or girl child, let alone a child named Charley, and the prosecution needed to specify whether a particular corpse was male or female so that a defendant who'd only murdered a child of the opposite gender could properly defend the charge.

Plunkett replied that it was unnecessary to name or identify the sex of a murdered child to establish that the child had been murdered, noting that people could be convicted of cattle theft without proof of the name or sex of the cattle.

This time the jury conceded the defence's arguments were through-the-looking-glass batshit crazy and found the stockmen guilty. The seven were hanged.

The colony was torn in half, with those applauding the verdict condemned by those who opposed it. The *Sydney Morning Herald* opined, "the whole gang of black animals are not worth the money the colonists will have to pay for printing the silly court documents on which we have already wasted too much time."

Wentworth and other large landowners, who regarded the verdict as setting a dangerous precedent that might interfere with their own land-clearing programs, labelled the executions "judicial murder".

THIS MONEY-MAKING PLACE

Australia's most enthusiastic land clearers could be found in Melbourne. The first Melbournians,[35] who were obsessed with real estate

---

34 This legal debate was Rumsfeldian in its absurdity.

35 Melbournians have called themselves Melburnians since 1876, when the upper-class twits of Melbourne Grammar School insisted on Latinising the name, despite the fact that the city's namesake, Lord Melbourne, had never worn a bedsheet, had sex with his horse or done anything else that could have caused him to be mistaken for

in the same way Sydneysiders are today, wanted to grab as much of the best land as they could before someone else did.

Squatting licences were issued to whoever first put sheep in an area and squatters could occupy as much pasture as they could put sheep on. Squatters lent each other sheep when inspectors surveyed their runs so they would look fully stocked. In this way, a territory larger than England was occupied in just five years.

Robert Hoddle's "rectangle in the bush" town plan, with its grid of streets and lanes, reduced disputes over town property. While a critic complained that "the only skill exhibited in the plan of Melbourne is that it involved the use of square and compass", Hoddle's design allowed more orderly surveys than in the haphazardly thrown-together Sydney and Hobart and its grid pattern allowed investors to buy off the plan.[36]

Governor Gipps's government made a fortune selling Melbourne land, as did early speculators such as John Pascoe Fawkner. Fawkner bought the first two plots auctioned by the government and made a 1,000 per cent return when he sold them two years later. Auctioneers provided champagne breakfasts to potential investors on vacant blocks, getting the punters pleasantly merry before separating them from their money. Champagne replaced rum as the Melbournian's tipple of choice, with Gipps reporting in 1842 that "the whole country for miles, almost for hundreds of miles around Melbourne, is strewed to this day with champagne bottles".

---

a Roman. Melbourne Grammar argued, "The dipthong 'ou' is not a Latin dipthong: hence, we argued this way, *Melburnia* would be [the] Latin form of name, and from it comes *Melburnian*." Melbournians embraced this because it's the sort of cultural elitism they secretly love. I will stick with the original (and correct) *Melbournian* in this book.

36 This sometimes produced undesirable results. John McEchnie, Melbourne's first tobacconist, found himself next door to John Blanch's Sporting Emporium, Melbourne's largest gun seller. A smoker from McEchnie's popped in next door and flicked his cigar ash into a barrel of gunpowder, sending both shops, himself, Mr and Mrs Blanch and McEchnie's son up in smoke.

Sylvester Browne, an early landowner, described Melbourne's property speculation as "a goldfield rush without the gold". British investors poured money into Port Phillip real estate and capital flowed into the area. Lady Jane Franklin, when visiting Melbourne in 1839, dismissively referred to it as "this money-making place".

Melbourne, with its quick deals and worship of free enterprise, was the perfect place for Fawkner to flourish. John Batman and his brother Henry, however, did not fare so well.

Syphilis had left John Batman too ill to manage his squatting run. It had eaten away his face, which was now swaddled in bandages, and his wife, Eliza, had left him.[37] His only companion was the faithful manservant who pushed him around town in a bamboo wicker pram, the final Batmobile.[38] Batman died a hideously painful death on 6 May 1839.[39]

Henry Batman died five months later, with Fawkner publishing an obituary in the *Port Phillip Patriot and Melbourne Advertiser*, the newspaper he owned and edited:[40]

Died on Friday last, Henry Batman, formerly Chief Constable of Melbourne – another victim to idleness and the dose. For months

---

37 Batman now looked more like Two-Face after the acid attack or the Joker after he fell into the tank of chemical waste.

38 The manservant's name may have been Alfred, but nobody knows because he was an Aborigine.

39 Batman's will was contested by his children, his wife and William Willoughby, his former clerk, who'd married Eliza. Like the *Jarndyce v. Jarndyce* inheritance case in Dickens's *Bleak House*, the dispute went on for years and fed only the lawyers, whose costs of £2,299 exceeded the £1,131 value of Batman's estate. Batman's seven daughters got nothing, his son drowned at the age of eight, and Eliza changed her name to Sarah, became "of somewhat abandoned character", and was murdered in Geelong in 1852. So ended the fortune and family of the Tasmanian Penn.

40 Fawkner, who'd founded the *Launceston Advertiser* in 1828, established Melbourne's first paper, the *Melbourne Advertiser*, in 1838, before rebranding it as the *Patriot* the following year. Fawkner wrote the first ten editions by hand before purchasing the old printing press David Collins had given to Matthew Power in exchange for his wife in 1803.

past, this man devoted his whole time to gambling and drinking: and
has at last fallen as sacrifice to this shrine of Moloch.

Fawkner, despite condemning drunkenness, fought to maintain his
position as Port Phillip's principal liquor retailer. On one occasion
he returned to Launceston on business and left his hotel in the care
of two servants, who promptly handed it over to George Smith, who
renamed it the Port Phillip Hotel and pocketed the profits. Smith
refused to move out on Fawkner's return, so Fawkner took over the
front parlour by force and threshed his wheat crop there around the
clock, making such a din that Smith vacated the premises after several
sleepless nights. Fawkner was back in business.

The dispute with Smith was typical of the lawless approach to
property in Melbourne's early days. If you could park yourself on several thousand acres of Kulin land, why couldn't you squat in another
man's pub?

Fawkner built a second hotel, targeting the prosperous traders
and wealthy migrants who were swarming into Melbourne. He fitted
it out with fancy furnishings, served rum and water at an exorbitant
shilling a glass, and installed Melbourne's first library in an annexe
to the bar. Fawkner marketed the experience as "Mental and Bodily
refreshment unrivalled in this quarter of the globe", with a sign inviting drinkers to browse "a very choise Siliction of books".

Fawkner's new clientele were very different to the earlier settlers
who drank in his first pub. Although Melbournians like to portray
themselves as the children of free enterprise, with their gilded city
untarnished by convictism, this is a load of old cock.

Melbourne's settlers were, for the first eighteen months, almost
exclusively Tasmanians, many of whom were ex-convicts seeking a
place to reinvent themselves. Tasmanians would outnumber other
Australian arrivals two to one until 1839, with the *Sydney Gazette*
describing them as "a drunken, worthless set, and a complete pest
to the place".

Despite the Port Phillip Association's dream of keeping Melbourne convict-free, thirty criminals arrived from Sydney in 1836 and further boatloads followed. Nor were the mothers of Melbourne all formidable dowagers with stately homes, as their descendants suggest – some were "contraband ladies", Tasmanian convict women smuggled across the strait in beer barrels.

Melbourne underwent a demographic shift in 1839, when John Dunmore Lang's Scottish immigration program kicked into full gear. Niel Black, who arrived from Argyllshire later that year to establish a squatting empire, marvelled that Melbourne was "a Scotch colony – two thirds of the inhabitants are Scotch".[41]

Fawkner sold his hotel interests in 1839 to devote himself to his newspaper, which ran frequent stories on immorality and inebriation. The publican turned temperance campaigner printed the names of convicted drunks and reported on the "incessant depravities" of the wealthy young squatters of the Melbourne Club.

Today the Melbourne Club is noted for its air of staid refinement, Pimm's & lemonade, blue ties and captains of industry whose decaying flesh is the same colour as the marble busts that adorn its reading room, heritage courtyard garden and bootblack's cubicle.[42]

But the Melbourne Club of 1839 was a beast of a different pinstripe. The club's young pastoralists drank vast quantities of brandy, rather than rum or champagne. The club didn't have a licence to serve liquor and didn't need one because its members were filthy rich and simply refused to pay licensing fines. The members partied hard and partied loud, which Fawkner objected to because they'd established

41 Scots loved the idea of not paying for land and rapidly established themselves among Port Phillip's squatting elite. The League and Resistance Fund, a squatter association established in 1845 to oppose district taxes, had at least thirty-three Scots among its fifty-three members, highlighting the dominance of Scots in squatter ranks (or, at least, in tax-evader ranks).

42 Or so I'm told. I've never been able to get past the ancient doorman, who's been keeping the riffraff out since 1922.

their clubhouse in his old hotel, right next door to the *Patriot*'s office. When the moleskin tearaways weren't ignoring Fawkner's noise complaints, they were staggering through Melbourne's streets, smashing windows, removing shop signs, sawing through verandah posts and drag-racing their horses.

Fawkner was rabidly anti-squatter, believing that they'd gained their wealth through "a system of robbery" and were grinding "the bulk of the people to the very dust". His paper attacked the squatters at every opportunity and promoted the rights of townsfolk and traders.

Thomas Strode, the owner of the *Gazette*, the main rival to Fawkner's paper, championed squatter interests. He condemned Fawkner's attacks on the Melbourne Club members' rowdy antics as moralising hypocrisy, writing in his deathbed memoir:

> A certain Boniface in bygone years who now assumes the garb of
> sanctity, supplied his questionable customers who visited the dancing
> shed attached to his hotel with pots of porter, whilst a portion of
> the frail sex present were to be seen in the costume of Eve on her
> entry into Paradise, and who would often become transfixed to the
> spot with a fit of grovelling sensuality.

Strode not only attacked Fawkner as the Father of Melbourne Lap Dancing, but also used his paper to belittle Fawkner's *Patriot* as "an old woman whose low and impudent vulgarity would do no disgrace to the forensic abilities of a Billingsgate fish-hag".

Fawkner responded by calling his rival "a dung-hill cock", got the *Gazette*'s delivery boy so drunk he couldn't deliver the paper and paid its typesetter not to turn up to work, forcing Strode to toil twenty-two hours a day until he could find a replacement.

The one thing Fawkner and Strode could agree on was that Melbourne was much better than Sydney and should secede from the mother colony. Melbourne's population had grown from 200 in 1836 to 20,000 in 1841 and money was flowing into the city. However,

Sydney was using the income from Melbourne land sales to prop up its own ailing infrastructure. Melbourne couldn't get a proper water supply, decent roads or a bridge over the Yarra – all Sydney gave it was a massive gaol, which seemed at odds with Sydney's assurances that Melbourne would not be used as a dumping ground for its convicts.

The Separation Association first met in late 1840 to plot the foundation of a breakaway colony, but its work was temporarily put to one side in late 1841 when Melbourne stopped making money.

8
The New Colossus

Give me your tired, your poor,
Your huddled masses yearning to breathe free,
The wretched refuse of your teeming shore.

Emma Lazarus, "The New Colossus", 1883

THE DEPRESSION WE HAD TO HAVE

AUSTRALIA WAS A MARITIME ECONOMY IN 1830, WITH whale and seal exports worth double that of wool. The colonies accounted for only 8 per cent of the world's wool trade, compared with the German states' 76 per cent.

The Industrial Revolution went gangbusters during the 1830s, with British woollen mills increasing output and slashing prices. There was an insatiable demand for mass-produced soft clothes, with Australian merino fleece finer than English wool and tougher than German *wolle*.

International wool prices peaked in 1836, falling 25 per cent the following year. They continued to decline as Australian supply increased, with squatters covering newly opened land with as many white fluffy things as they could breed. British banks opened branches in the colonies, forcing Australian banks to compete. The banks gave out loans like they were lollies, fuelling land speculation. The colonists, flush with cash, imported new luxuries, and Australia experienced its first bout of sheepflation.

By 1840, the colonies had become the world's largest wool produc-ers and were riding on the sheep's back. But by the end of 1841, they were dangling from the sheep's backside. The Australian economy had dagged out.[1]

Sheep were suddenly as little as one-fifteenth of their former value, but, on the plus side, everybody could enjoy a lamb roast for dinner. They could also smell nice while reviewing their mounting piles of unpaid bills at night, as Wentworth and other sheep lords built death-factories to convert millions of sheep into soap and candles.

The collapse of the wool market meant many squatters couldn't repay their mortgages and went to the wall. The Bank of Australia and other lenders failed, as there were no buyers for the sheep runs they now owned. Governor Gipps made things worse by withdrawing government bank deposits to meet the colony's debts.

Gipps cut government spending by two-thirds in 1842, reporting that insolvency was rife "amongst all classes". Wentworth survived, but had to sacrifice his dream of converting Vaucluse House into a Gothic mansion.[2] John Dunmore Lang's secondary school closed as parents could no longer afford its fees.

Tasmania, the engine room of the Australian economy until the late 1830s, was hardest hit, entering a depression that lasted more than thirty years. Those Tasmanians who could moved to Melbourne, Sydney or Adelaide.

---

1   A dag is a woolly ball of poo that hangs from a sheep's rear (later incorporated into Australian and New Zealand slang to mean an unfashionable and socially awkward person). Dags are deadly as they provide a home and food for blowfly maggots that then eat the sheep's bottom. Farmers protect sheep from dags by removing skin from their rude bits, the Australian equivalent of a Brazilian. Animal liberationists, who have never had their bottoms eaten by blowflies, say this is cruel.

2   Wentworth's renovations were never completed and Vaucluse House still has no front door. While Wentworth erected grand servants' quarters, a two-storey kitchen wing, stable, coach house and boathouse, the unfinished home only had three bedrooms for William, Sarah and their ten children. Wentworth's son Fitzwilliam lived in a hallway and slept behind a wardrobe for privacy.

Things had been looking up for Adelaide. Its citizens were thrilled when Charles Sturt followed the Murray River to their muddy hovels in 1838, bringing them some cows he'd driven all the way from Sydney. The man who'd put rivers on the map would surely do the same for Adelaide, and the South Australians were overjoyed when Sturt agreed to be their surveyor-general and survey all the things Light hadn't.

However, South Australia squandered the proceeds of its land sales. Governor Gawler moved out of Hindmarsh's mud hut into a bespoke government house that cost the colony £10,000. The South Australians, paranoid they'd be invaded by runaway convicts, established a 125-man border force to keep illegal arrivals out, even though they only had funding for twenty-three police. Gawler also privatised Adelaide's port, moving out of the mangrove swamp and paying fees to use Port Adelaide, built by George Angas's South Australia Company. Angas also owned all South Australia's banks, which lent money to buy Angas-owned land, sold by Angas at inflated prices, resulting in a massive property bubble. Meanwhile, Robert Torrens had spent more than half the colony's immigration funds on land surveys and glossy brochures.

South Australia went broke. Gawler, the scapegoat, was replaced in May 1841 by Captain George Grey. Sturt wrote to the War and Colonial Office when he first heard of the appointment, criticising Grey's inexperience and offering himself as governor instead. The War and Colonial Office had a money problem, not a river problem, and Sturt was rebuffed. Grey, who was a vindictive bastard, sacked Sturt. Already deeply in debt, Sturt believed the only way he could stay afloat was to do some more exploring. Sturt wanted to be remembered for something other than rivers – this time he would explore "the entire unknown interior of the continent" and find his inland sea.

Sturt was not Grey's only victim. Grey slashed government jobs and decreed that no more money would be spent on immigration or public works. In 1842, he reported, "In North and South Adelaide out of 1,915 houses, 642 are totally deserted; and out of this latter number 216 are neglected and falling into decay."

Britain, forced to pay off South Australia's debts, had had enough. It ended the Wakefield experiment, abolished Torrens's Colonization Commission and took full control of the colony.

The depression didn't greatly affect Western Australia because imploding finances were business as usual. Edward Gibbon Wakefield had attempted to stimulate the colony's moribund economy by joining the Western Australian Land Company, which established a privately owned and administered town called Australind in 1841.

Australind, a portmanteau of Australia and India, would make Western Australia's fortune by selling horses to the British Indian Army. However, Australind's 440 settlers soon discovered there was not enough water for the horses in summer, the horses got rained on in winter, and the poisonous plants made the horses walk in straight lines before their rectums fell out and they dropped dead. The settlers drifted away, abandoning Australind to the sands.

Port Phillip now had 1.4 million sheep and produced more than half Australia's wool. While some squatters went bankrupt, Charles La Trobe, the superintendent of Port Phillip, kept the wheels of industry turning, although champagne imports slowed to a trickle and one commentator grumbled, "Even the lawyers can scarcely succeed in getting paid".[3] John Pascoe Fawkner was declared insolvent,

---

3   La Trobe had no naval or military background and little experience with
    government when appointed as Britain's man in Melbourne in 1839, which was
    highly unusual for a colonial administrator. The son of a Moravian missionary,
    La Trobe moved to Switzerland, became a world-renowned mountaineer and wrote
    The Alpenstock: Or Sketches of Swiss Scenery and Manners (1829), which contained
    lots of useful information about mountains and cheese. He signed on as the tutor
    of the dashing French count Albert de Pourtalès, touring America with him in
    1832. During that trip, he accompanied Washington Irving, the famous American
    essayist, biographer, and author of *Rip Van Winkle* and *The Legend of Sleepy Hollow*,
    on a surveying expedition deep into Apache and Comanche territory, in what is now
    Oklahoma. He wrote books about hiking in Austria, the United States and Mexico;
    published *The Solace of Song*, a collection of short poems inspired by the Italian
    countryside; and worked on freeing slaves in the West Indies. Irving acknowledged

but not before engaging in the time-honoured Australian tradition of parking his assets in his wife's and father's names.

Port Phillip and Sydney recovered relatively quickly, as exports lifted in 1844. South Australia discovered rich copper deposits and John Ridley's revolutionary mechanical wheat harvester, combined with German agricultural knowhow and labour, lifted the colony out of the doldrums.

Australia, except for backwoods Tasmania and Western Australia, was back on track.

GOD'S POLICEWOMAN

Bounty migration trebled to 20,000 arrivals in 1841. Two-thirds of these migrants were Irish and many were young women, as the colonies were again seeking "single women and widows of good character" for "highly paid" jobs in domestic service.[4]

The flood of immigrants arrived just as the depression struck and there were no highly paid jobs – or, indeed, any jobs at all – for most of the new arrivals. While Gipps suspended assisted immigration in 1842, he still had thousands of migrants on his hands. He assigned some of the men to public works, but had no idea what to do with the women. Prostitution was the only option for many, with the government surgeon declaring the large house that accommodated Melbourne's new female arrivals to be "a Brothel on a large scale".

La Trobe as a Renaissance man in this tribute: "He was a man of a thousand occupations; a botanist, a geologist, a hunter of beetles and butterflies, a musical amateur, a sketcher of no mean pretensions; in short, a complete virtuoso; added to which he was a very indefatigable, if not always a very successful, sportsman."

4   The end of convict assignment resulted in a spike in demand for servants. An untrained domestic could earn twice the wages of an experienced servant in Britain, making Australian domestics the highest paid in the world. Irish female servants were notorious for spending their wages on expensive clothes, with one disciplined for refusing to remove her patent leather pumps while working at the washtub. They dressed better than their employers and refused to tug the forelock, fuelling the perception that they didn't know their place.

Poverty. Unemployment. Innocent Irish sheilas on the game.[5] This sounded like a job for Caroline Chisholm.

Caroline, the sixteenth and youngest child of a wealthy and libidinous Evangelical pig dealer, converted to Catholicism after marrying Captain Archibald Chisholm of the East India Company. The Chisholms left England for Madras, where the wives of Indian officers were expected to practise the pianoforte, embroider elephants onto cushions, listlessly play croquet in the stifling heat, tell cook-wallah what to prepare for dinner (nothing too spicy) and combat boredom and malaria by drinking large quantities of gin and tonic.

But Caroline had no time for time-wasters. With characteristic determination, the tall, flame-haired churchwoman threw herself into establishing a school for soldiers' daughters. Helping women make their way in the world became her life's passion.

The Chisholms travelled to Sydney in 1838, where thirty-year-old Caroline was struck by the number of girls whose dreams of easy money and easier wealthy young farmers had not been fulfilled. One morning, she got talking to a "fallen woman", took her into her home and found her a job that enabled her to stop walking the streets. Chisholm had a new mission.

Chisholm saw female immigration as essential to ending the "monstrous disparity" between the sexes in the colonies and to rescue men "from the demoralizing state of bachelorism". Her utopia was a place of "homes for happy men and virtuous women", where "wives and little children" would serve as "God's police" in enforcing Christian laws among men who would otherwise descend into sin.

---

5   Sheila, an Australian slang word for a woman, derives either from *Sìle*, an Irish
     girl's name, or *Sìle*, Gaelic for an effeminate man or homosexual. The first written
     use of the term appeared in an 1828 edition of the *Monitor*, which reported on
     a Saint Patrick Day street brawl in Sydney: "many a piteous Shela stood wiping
     the gory locks of her Paddy". Sheila is one of a surprisingly small number of Irish
     words to have found its way into the Australian lexicon.

Prostitution was a sizeable spanner in the works of Chisholm's perfect society, with venereal disease a leading cause of death in Australia. Prostitution, Chisholm believed, also harmed future generations, as ladies of the red lamp were commonly single mothers who struggled with work–family balance. The newly arrived women could only build a moral society if vice was nipped in the bud.

Chisholm joined the pimps who met docking immigrant ships, offering young women temporary accommodation while she found them work. She made the same offer, without judgement or moralising, to those who'd already taken up prostitution. Chisholm made the following commitment during Easter Sunday prayers:

> I promised to know neither country nor creed, but to try to serve all justly and impartially. I asked only to be enabled to keep these poor girls from being tempted, by their need, to mortal sin; and resolved that to accomplish this, I would in every way sacrifice my feelings – surrender all comfort ... [and] wholly devote myself to the work I had in hand.

Chisholm and her three young sons stayed in New South Wales when Archibald was recalled to his regiment. At the start of the depression, she met Governor Gipps, who "expressed being pleasantly surprised that she was a young, attractive lady". Chisholm convinced Gipps to allow her to use the old immigration barracks as her Female Immigrants' Home. The barracks were infested with rats, so Chisholm stayed there at night and befriended the rodents by feeding them bread and butter. When she judged the rats sufficiently trusting, she laced the butter with arsenic. Sydney's sinners may have considered her a saint, but to the city's rats she was Lucrezia Borgia with a sandwich.[6]

---

6   When she was not busy scouring the streets for souls to save or murdering rodents, Chisholm found time to become Australia's first published female author, writing *Female Immigration Considered* in 1842.

Gipps directed that any letter bearing Chisholm's signature receive free postage, but she received no further financial support from government, instead relying on public subscriptions and her own funds to shelter up to ninety-six women at a time. As Gipps refused to establish an employment office, Chisholm did it herself.[7] She drew up legal contracts for domestic employment, setting out the work to be performed and basic conditions. These were the first standard work contracts in Australia and her proposed payment – equivalent to a weekly food bill for a family of five – was Australia's first minimum wage.

Chisholm found jobs and homes for more than 11,000 migrants and 3,000 established settlers, mostly women, between 1841 and 1844. She tried to place her "respectable well trained girls" with married couples or moral men interested in marriage. She set up employment agencies in a dozen rural centres and spent 1842 touring the hinterland atop her white horse, Captain, a latter-day Joan of Arc fighting unemployment and bachelorism in the bush.

During her country travels, Chisholm would check on the welfare of the women she'd placed and move them if they were being mistreated. Her relocation of single women to the bush transformed outback life.

Successful Irish immigrants such as William Rutledge also tried to find jobs for their countrymen. Known as Terrible Billy for his explosive temper and foul language, Rutledge replicated the Irish tenant system by allocating his land at Kilmore to Irish farming families. The farmers of Kilmore did what they knew best – grew potatoes – and Rutledge was hailed the Potato King. Rutledge established further Irish tenant communities at Farnham, near Koroit, and Belfast, now known as Port Fairy.[8]

---

7   "Chisholmlink" was Australia's first employment agency that operated for public benefit.

8   Terrible Billy was also famous for issuing his own banknotes and coins. The Rutledge was accepted as legal tender in the colonies until his bankruptcy in 1862.

John Dunmore Lang disliked landowners who imported Catholic labour, but he absolutely loathed Chisholm. The only thing worse than a Roman Catholic was a Protestant who'd turned to the dark side.[9] Lang had visited the United States in 1840, where he was "horrified by the wickedness of Catholic immigrants who both desecrated the Sabbath and formed an undue proportion of convicted criminals". He was convinced the wicked Catholics had similar plans for New South Wales.

In 1841, Lang published a pamphlet titled *The Question of Questions! Or, Is this Colony to be Transformed into a Province of the Popedom?* In it, he argued that private agents shipped out cheap migrants who were "carried over, like so many pigs" from "the strongest holds of popery, bigotry, superstition and immorality, in the British Empire". He asked of New South Wales' Protestant landowners:

> Are they willing that the future Colonists of New South Wales should become a second edition of the worst parts of Ireland? Are they willing that ignorance and superstition, bigotry, and intolerance, accompanied with such a system of morality as has filled this Colony for the last fifty years with Irish Roman Catholic convicts, should ere long occupy the length and breadth of this good land?

Lang, a staunch opponent of bigotry and intolerance, harangued both Chisholm and assisted female immigration in his newspaper, the *Colonial Observer*. The *Australian* got in on the act, objecting to money raised from the sale of land to Protestants being used to import "bigoted Catholics".

Chisholm cared not a jot for her critics and simply got on with the job. Like Rutledge, she believed land was the key that would unlock

---

9   Chisholm was not only a religious turncoat, but also a woman! Lang expected
     women to know their place – at home, caring for their families. Chisholm, despite
     her own incredible workload and the long weeks spent away from home, shared
     the same ideal. She wanted to transform prostitutes into domestic servants and
     domestic servants into homemakers, and viewed the difficulties her mission
     imposed on her own family life as her sacrifice to God.

migrants' potential, but her campaign to lease land to migrants on favourable terms was sabotaged by large landowners who didn't want their sheep displaced by potato-grubbing bog-dwellers. So again, Caroline went it alone, convincing Robert Towns, Wentworth's brother-in-law, to settle 240 migrants at Shellharbour rent-free for six years, in return for their clearing his land. She paid for their training and a school out of her own pocket.

As the depression years passed, Chisholm transferred her attention to reforming Australian colonisation, but, living in Sydney, she'd always be the tail wagging the dog. So, in 1846, God's Policewoman returned to England to teach the old dogs of Whitehall some new tricks.

TOO MANY CHIEFS AND NOT ENOUGH INDIANS

William Charles Wentworth was in the political doghouse after Wellingtongate. He'd failed to preserve convict assignment and, rubbing salt into his wounds, Britain ceased transportation to New South Wales in 1840. All future convicts, and their wonderful cheap labour, would be sent to Tasmania and Norfolk Island.

Wentworth withdrew from public life, using the age-old excuse of wanting to spend more time with his family. He pottered about Vaucluse House and devoted himself to gardening, winning prizes at floral and horticultural shows. The *Australian*, the paper he founded, opined in January 1842, "His day is gone by. His opinion is worth nothing."

James Macarthur had reinvented himself as a populist politician. He argued that the end of transportation opened the way for an elected Legislative Council. The champion of the Tory exclusives had married into a British banking family with Whig sympathies, leading him to propose a united front with emancipists on political reform and to withdraw his opposition to them having the vote.

Britain approved a New South Wales Legislative Council of twenty-four elected and twelve government-appointed members in

1842, with the vote confined to men who owned land worth £200 or rented a house for £20 a year – about a third of the adult males in the colony. Tasmania was too criminal for elected representatives, South Australia was too broke and Western Australia was too pissant, so the democratic experiment was limited to the oldest colony.

A galvanised Wentworth threw down his pruning shears and ran for the seat of Sydney with his old emancipist buddy William Bland, reminding everybody that Britain had simply tinkered with the electoral bill he'd drafted in 1835. He, not Macarthur, was the Father of the Ballot and the Voter's Friend.

An opposing ticket, headed by the unfortunately named barrister William Hustler, attacked Wentworth for his support of coolie immigration. Wentworth did not like coloured folk, having opposed Indian immigration in 1837 because it would lead to "an intermixture of races". However, with the end of convict assignment, the suspension of assisted immigration and the unwillingness of Aborigines to work on properties where they might be shot, he was forced to acknowledge that Indians might be worth exploiting. Wentworth joined the Coolie Association, a group of landowners and squatters united in their commitment to cheap Asian labour.

William Augustine Duncan, editor of the Catholic newspaper the *Australasian Chronicle*, led the charge against Indian immigration, accusing the Coolie Association of advocating "mortgaging the colony to English and foreign Jews to purchase Indian heathens, thugs and Mahomedans".[10] Indians, according to Duncan, were "a feeble and degenerate race" whose "physical and mental inferiority" would make them willing slaves who would take all the crap jobs from Irish Catholics.

Hustler campaigned on the slogan "Vote for Hustler and No Coolies" and convened the largest public meeting in the colony's history to that point at the Hyde Park racecourse. There, Henry

---

10   Scaremongering 101: blame an international Zionist banking conspiracy.

Macdermott, a Sydney councillor, thundered that coolies would make free with our women, while Robert Nichols, the colony's first native-born solicitor, insisted they "would introduce crimes, which among Christians and civilised men, were not even named" (i.e. make free with our men).[11]

The colony's first elections were staged between 15 June and 3 July 1843, with an unsuccessful candidate able to get on a horse and contest the next seat. Sydney was the first to go to the polls, and Captain Maurice O'Connell was the clear early favourite. O'Connell had a born-to-rule pedigree, being the son of Sir Maurice O'Connell, Governor Macquarie's second-in-command, and Sir Maurice's wife, Mary, Governor Bligh's daughter – the very same woman who had offered the only armed resistance to the Rum Rebellion when she assaulted the rebel soldiers with her parasol.[12] However, rumours were spread that O'Connell, whose father was Irish, was "the Catholic candidate" and support for him declined in the last days of the campaign.

On polling day, Wentworth's supporters carried placards that read "Wentworth and Bland / Australia's Hope and Sydney's Pride" and marched under a white banner with a Union Jack in the top-left corner and an eight-pointed red star, the earliest banner to bear any resemblance to the Australian flag.

By midday it was apparent Wentworth and Bland were leading Australia's first poll.[13] A mob of more than 400 O'Connell

---

11   In his book *The White Australia Policy*, Keith Windschuttle contends, "Australia is not, and never has been, the racist country its academic historians have condemned." The opposition to coolie labour, according to Keith, had "a clear legal and economic basis" and was not grounded in racial prejudice. Some of Keith's best friends are coolies.

12   Sir Maurice served as acting governor after Gipps's departure, with Mary once again first lady of Government House, thirty-eight years after her father was deposed.

13   In the days before the secret ballot, voters declared their votes. This was done on a show of hands or voices at a mass meeting. If the result was disputed, then a formal poll was held, with electors attending a polling station to publicly commit to their chosen candidate.

supporters, described by the *Sydney Morning Herald* as "infuriated
Irishmen", armed themselves with fence palings and demolished
one of Wentworth's campaign tents. Wentworth's booth captain,
the whaler John Jones, called out his crew to attack the Irish with
harpoons. Mounted police arrived and read the Riot Act, but the
drunken mob had moved on to trash other polling booths. Polling
was suspended until the next day and riots raged into the evening,
resulting in several injuries and one death. This was democracy
Australian-style.

Wentworth and Bland claimed the two Sydney seats and Wentworth travelled out to Cumberland to speak against James Macarthur's
candidacy. He accused Macarthur of being a flip-flop politician with
no policies beyond being popular, likening him to "a barrel of Tom
Underwood's ale – all froth and no substance". Wentworth's nega-
tive campaigning lost Macarthur the election, with the seat falling
to Wentworth's old exploring buddy William Lawson and Charles
Cowper, a sheep breeder who would go on to serve five times as premier of New South Wales.

John Dunmore Lang was elected as a representative of Port Phillip on a platform of limiting Catholic immigration, seceding from
New South Wales and using colonial taxes for colonial needs rather
than paying for convicts and British officials. Lang, like Wentworth,
claimed the colonies would rebel as the United States had done if they
didn't control their own revenue.

When the new Legislative Council met, all bar Wentworth wore
frock coats and top hats. Wentworth, wearing his heart on his legs,
appeared in squatter's corduroys, which the *Australian* termed "a
contemptible affectation". He boycotted a visit to Government House
to protest Alexander McLeay's nomination as speaker. McLeay had
once labelled Wentworth "the son of an Irish Highwayman by a convict whore". Wentworth now called McLeay "a twice superannuated
octogenarian" and tried to scuttle the official opening of the council
by moving that the governor "ought not be received".

The early days of the council were chaotic. There were no political parties, with the newbie politicians pursuing their own immediate priorities. The colony had a host of inexperienced rulers who couldn't agree on the rules. Three factions emerged. Wentworth led the squatters; Robert Lowe, an albino barrister and Oxford debating champion, led the landowners; and Gipps led those who'd do whatever Britain told them to do.

Lowe was the only person in the chamber capable of going toe-to-toe with Wentworth. Although a Gipps appointee, he sniffed the political wind and forged an alliance of landowners and squatters.

Wentworth established himself as the leader of the opposition to Gipps's government. Gipps had destroyed Wentworth's dream of becoming emperor of New Zealand. Gipps was a relic of British rule, while Wentworth yearned for self-government. And Gipps was trying to rein in the squatters.

Gipps had prohibited further north-west expansion in 1838, but John Robertson, Lang's cleft-palated protégé, led squatter protests that resulted in the decision being overturned. Robertson's famous "I could neither think nor sleep for admiring this new world to me who was fond of sheep" may not have been the Gettysburg Address, but it perfectly captured squatter sentiment.

Wentworth introduced bills to help squatters get through the depression. His laws retrospectively capped interest on loans at 5 per cent, initiated a lottery to pay off the Bank of Australia's debt and allowed squatters to mortgage their sheep.[14]

While the depression thinned squatter ranks, survivors like Wentworth were able to buy sheep stations on the cheap and amass even

---

14   As a large shareholder in the bank, Wentworth was personally liable for some of those debts. Getting gamblers to bail him out was an elegant solution. Using unsecured sheep to secure debt was truly revolutionary, with centuries of British law providing only land could be mortgaged. Britain vetoed sheep mortgages after pointing out that land couldn't be eaten by dingoes, speared by Aborigines, have maggots infect its bottom, or be stuffed into a food sack by a happy rough-sleeping itinerant worker.

greater fortunes. However, the depression decimated the exclusives, who had little experience of adversity, with scions such as Hannibal Macarthur forced into bankruptcy.

The exclusives would never again be a power – money, rather than breeding or criminal antecedents, was now the only god. The depression had realised Wentworth's vision of an Aussiegarchy built on bullion and banknotes.

In 1845, Gipps rebooted assisted immigration by raising additional revenue from squatters. He limited squatters' runs to twenty square miles, charging a licence fee for each much smaller run, and required squatters to purchase part of their runs every eight years at a competitive auction.

Wentworth flipped. He railed against Gipps at every opportunity, renewed his call for coolie labour and advocated extending the vote to anyone who owned 200 cattle or 1,000 sheep.

As part of his long campaign to cut government salaries, Wentworth asked why Gipps received the same pay as the president of the United States. But when encouraged to nominate for the role of speaker in 1846, his first action was to move a motion to double the speaker's salary. His second was to call for a speaker's dinner allowance. Mocked in the council and in the streets, Wentworth withdrew the motions and his nomination. Appalled by his hypocrisy, Lowe, Lang, Cowper and other political allies distanced themselves from him.

The landowner–squatter alliance fractured after Earl Grey junior, secretary of state for war and the colonies, was pressured by the squatter lobby and British wool investors to introduce the *Waste Lands Occupation Act 1846*. The act granted squatters rolling fourteen-year leases and allowed them first right to purchase land on their runs, effectively locking others out of the most profitable sector of the economy. By 1850, squatters controlled land from New South Wales' coastal border with South Australia to what is now southern Queensland.

Robert Lowe, aghast that the 1846 act prevented farmers from purchasing land occupied by squatters, became Wentworth's most determined foe. Even John Robertson, unrivalled in his fondness for sheep, thought the 1846 act unfairly favoured wool-growers over smaller farmers.

Wentworth scraped home in the 1848 elections, as protesters shouted, "No coolies! No cannibals!", with Lowe beating Bland for Sydney's second seat.[15] Wentworth's financial and political interests, which always conveniently dovetailed, were now aligned with those of James Macarthur. Wentworth even promised his old enemy support for a run at the speakership, although the continued lack of a dinner allowance led Macarthur to decline.

Wentworth, the one-time champion of the Australian everyman, now supped with the exclusive devil. He'd lost friends along the way, but had replaced them with shinier ones. His two great remaining ambitions were to establish a government that was independent of Britain and to found an Australian aristocracy – both of which William Charles Wentworth would naturally head.

SORRY SEEMS TO BE THE HARDEST WORD

Earl Grey junior explained the *Waste Lands Occupation Act* to Governor Charles FitzRoy, Gipps's replacement:

---

15 The cannibal reference related to Ben Boyd's importation of 226 indentured Kanaka labourers from the New Hebrides (Vanuatu) and Loyalty Islands (New Caledonia) in 1847. The Kanakas absconded, died and were generally more trouble than they were worth. Those who were still alive or could be found were sent back to their islands after about a year. There were rumours that Boyd had kidnapped the Kanakas, making him Australia's first blackbirder (a polite Australian word for slaver). Boyd's dodgy financing of his businesses sent him broke and, after a short and unsuccessful career on the Californian goldfields, he returned to the Pacific to establish a Papuan Republic. He disappeared up a creek in the Solomon Islands and was never seen again. The Kanakas had had the last laugh – and possibly Boyd for dinner.

Leases granted ... give the grantees only an exclusive right of pastur-
age for their cattle, and of cultivating such Land as they may require
within the large limits thus assigned to them ... these limits ... are not
intended to deprive the Natives of their former right to hunt over
these Districts, or to wander over them in search of subsistence ...
except over land actually cultivated or fenced in for that purpose.[16]

While some squatters coexisted peacefully with Aboriginal people on
their runs and employed Aboriginal workers, many did not. Those who
reached an accommodation with Aboriginal people did so because of
their Evangelical beliefs or desire for peaceful relations. However, this
was a moral or pragmatic position, rather than a legal one, as Grey's
instructions were not put into practice. Squatters regarded their runs
as their land and damn anyone who said otherwise.

Despite Britain's instructions, Aborigines did not have the same
legal rights as British citizens. In 1840, concerned by attacks on stockmen, Gipps outlawed Aborigines possessing firearms, although the
law was later rescinded by the War and Colonial Office. The same
year, South Australia's Governor Gawler ordered the hanging of three
Ngarrindjeri men in front of their people, after some Ngarrindjeri
killed the twenty-six survivors of the *Maria* shipwreck, the largest
recorded Aboriginal massacre of Europeans in Australia's history.
This execution without trial contributed to Gawler's recall.

Gipps, to his credit, argued it was unfair that tribal Aborigines were
not permitted to give evidence in court of settler crimes. Wentworth
successfully led a campaign against Gipps's *Aboriginal Evidence Bill 1844*,
arguing it would be "quite as defensible to receive as evidence in a Court
of Justice the chatterings of the ourang-outang as of this savage race".

Only one European, George Stoker, was convicted of shooting an
Aborigine in the twelve years between the 1838 Myall Creek massacre

---

16   Grey's letter was critical to the High Court's 1996 decision in the *Wik* case that
      pastoral leases didn't give leaseholders exclusive possession of land or extinguish
      native title.

and 1850. He received two months' gaol for grievous bodily harm, even though there was a dead body and a white witness willing to testify against him.

While court records suggest a golden age of racial amity, the Australian atlas tells a different tale, with frontier violence celebrated in the names of Fighting Hills, Murdering Island, Skull Camp, Skeleton Creek and, for the more euphemistically inclined, Mount Dispersion and Convincing Ground.

In the 1840s, Port Phillip saw the worst of the violence. George Augustus Robinson, while chief protector of Aborigines, recorded the policy of Mr Hutton, a squatter: "If a member of a tribe offends, destroy the whole." Niel Black, fresh off the boat from Scotland, was informed it was necessary "to slaughter natives right and left" to secure a run. The Whyte brothers shot between thirty and sixty-nine Aborigines for stealing sheep, which they reported to Superintendent La Trobe, who saw no need for further inquiry.

By the late 1830s, Evangelicalism was on the wane and pragmatism on the rise. The government discouraged reports of attacks against Aborigines in subtle ways. Robinson found it difficult to lodge travel expense claims with La Trobe, which restricted his movements. When missionary George Langhorne complained of an 1838 police raid "converting the Mission into a scene of bloodshed and confusion", the government made him file all future reports through the police magistrate who'd attacked the mission.[17]

Geoffrey Blainey, who coined the phrase "black armband view of history", believes some 400 Aborigines were shot dead on the Port Phillip frontier. Richard Broome, a leading writer on Aboriginal history, estimates about a thousand such deaths. Within thirty years of the Batman Treaty, Victoria's Aboriginal population had declined by 80 per cent.

---

17   Three mission residents were shot for taking potatoes from a field. Tullamarine was imprisoned for his role in the great potato heist, but escaped after burning down Melbourne's first gaol. Australia is the only nation in the world to have named a major international airport after a root vegetable–thieving arsonist.

In South Australia, Reverend Ridgway Newland reported that the general doctrine in rural areas was "kill and exterminate". In 1841, there were 650 Aboriginal people in the area around Adelaide – by 1856 there were 180.

In 1837, the *Perth Gazette and Western Australian Journal* argued "savage nations *must* be exterminated sooner or later". A band of Wardandi people were killed at Wonnerup after a Wardandi elder, Gaywal, speared a local farmer for pulling his beard. However, the small scale of settlement and the harshness of the Western Australian interior protected many Aboriginal people well into the twentieth century, with one group of nine Pintupi having no contact with the European world until 1984.

Moreton Bay's penal settlement closed in 1841 and free settlers arrived in Brisbane the following year. In 1849, rumours spread that Aborigines were massing to attack Brisbane. Troops fired into the "town blacks" at Breakfast Creek, which the local paper reported as an understandable response. And things were only just getting started in Queensland.

Gipps's willingness to try white men for the Myall Creek massacre undoubtedly prevented some atrocities, but it also encouraged innovation in the removal of unwanted black people.

In 1847, Thomas Coutts, the owner of Kangaroo Creek Station in northern New South Wales, offered work to twenty-three Gumbaynggirr people, paying them in tobacco and flour. While the health risks of tobacco are well known, it was the flour, or rather the arsenic in it, that accounted for at least seven Gumbaynggirr. Unfortunately the only people who'd seen Coutts distributing the flour were surviving Gumbaynggirr who, thanks to Wentworth's sinking of the *Aboriginal Evidence Bill*, couldn't testify in court. Coutts walked.

The Coutts case resulted in the reintroduction of the bill, which failed to pass the Legislative Council by just one vote. Wentworth was again in fine form:

Any idea of serving subpoenas on such people was perfectly absurd. What avail to go serve a wild man, called Chicky Chicky or Chocky

Chocky, and thrust a piece of parchment into his fist to require his attendance at the Supreme Court.

Yet the white man's law and guns were not the main causes of Aboriginal death. In Port Phillip, about 20 per cent of deaths were attributed to violence, 20 per cent to natural causes, and 60 per cent to infection. Respiratory disease was the biggest killer, but venereal disease, dietary deficiencies, starvation and the liver-destroying dog-borne hydatid worm played their part.

One-third of Port Phillip's Native Police Corps reportedly died from drunkenness, an increasingly common complaint as alcohol found its way into the remnant Aboriginal communities. Mahroot, an Aboriginal whaler born near Sydney in 1796, described in 1845 how alcohol decimated his people:

> They used to fight about town. Knock about like the deuce in liquor ... At least they went away very fast. It was the only thing that destroyed them.

Of the 400 people in Mahroot's language group when he was a boy, only he and three women remained in 1845. By this time, portraits of the noble savage had all but disappeared, replaced by caricatures of semi-naked figures with leering grins, rum bottles, clay pipes, mangy dogs and trouserless children.

This was the new face of dispossession.

A FUCKWITTERY OF HIPSTERS

Melbourne was the place to be after the depression ended, unless you were an Aborigine or a dog.[18] It was in better shape than the rest of Australia

---

18   The squatters imposed a bounty on dingoes and unregistered dogs, with each tail worth five shillings. As in Van Diemen's Land, police were exploiters of the dog laws. John Ewart's eleven-year-old golden retriever, Nelson, was found dead and tailless at the local police watch house. The Herald mockingly referred to the police crusade against Melbourne's dogs as the Canine War.

and open in its ambition to be the premier Australian settlement.

Melbourne's campaign to secede from New South Wales was not just political and economic, but cultural. While Sydneysiders reinvested their wealth in trade and the soil, Melbournians devoted themselves to the finer things in life – fashion, the arts, coffee, artisan provedores and beards.

Melbourne initially followed British fashion, which dictated that a gentleman be clean-shaven. In 1841, Judge John Willis, a bastion of Victorian conservatism, threatened to have a barrister struck off for smuggling a moustache into his court. Writer Garryowen recorded Dr William Henry Campbell's failure to attract patients to his surgery in the same year:

> He had a black beard and moustache, and was informed that Melbournians distrusted people, especially professionals, with other than closely-shaved faces. Whiskers of moderate dimensions might be tolerated, but as far as any medical practitioners who sported a moustache ... it was simply preposterous.[19]

But these were two of the last attacks on the facially hirsute. Melbourne's moleskin set introduced "the hairy look" as early as 1839, with John Pascoe Fawkner writing that while walking down Queen Street he was:

> seriously startled ... by the hideous appearance of some sort of hairy monster on horseback, what added to the Alarm was, the cadaverous and unearthly cast of that part of the face which was not covered with long, mangy hair. It was dressed as a man, but in a fancy coat and tassel, jacket, trousers, and, wonderful to relate, it wore spectacles.[20]

---

19 After Campbell shaved, he was known as the Handsome Doctor and his business thrived.

20 This is the earliest historical record of an Australian hipster. All hipsters, even those with 20/20 vision, wear spectacles.

Fawkner's contempt for beards was unsurprising, given his hatred of the hooligan squatters who were infecting Melbourne with creeping beardism. A British visitor, Robert Dundas Murray, wrote that the squatters sported "moustaches and beards of Turkish luxuriance" that made them look "more like Italian brigands than clean faced Englishmen". In a letter to his family, he noted that other Melbournians were adopting squatter facial fashion:

> This hairy mania is very contagious ... A stranger in town would think he had found himself in some French or Italian town, from the foreign hairy appearance of the persons he meets.

The lone bearded and bespectacled Melbournian of 1839, with his fancy clothes and retro tassel, had spawned a fuckwittery of hipsters.

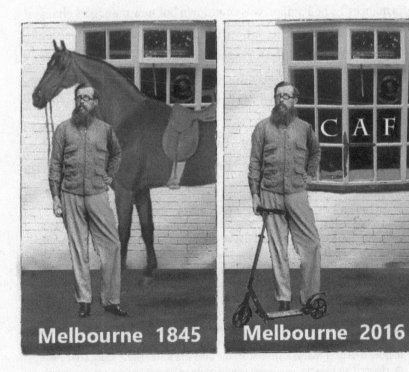

FIG. 8: HISTORY NEVER REPEATS.

Proper hipster beards require careful maintenance. John Lamb opened Melbourne's first barber shop on Little Collins Street in 1838 and Henry Milbourne opened a hairdressing salon in Flinders Lane in 1841, making "Wigs, Fronts, and Ringlets" and cutting and teasing hair in a private room. It had taken only three years for Melbourne's barbers to become hairdressers.

Melbourne's most popular hairdresser was George Cooper, who moonlighted as a baritone for the Victoria Theatre. Melbourne's theatre scene was established in 1839 by Thomas Hodge, a barman who convinced his boss to build the Pavilion Theatre in his beer garden. While Melbourne luvvies adored the performing arts, their government did not; La Trobe refused to issue a permit to stage performances on the grounds that theatres were harmful to community morals.

Hodge obtained a temporary permit for a charity performance and was raided for a ballet exhibition that featured "indecent dancing performances". The Pavilion was shut down but new managers changed its name to the Theatre Royal, which sounded suitably respectable, and reopened it in 1842. Performances were marred by drunken riots and La Trobe again closed the theatre in 1843 after Peter Snodgrass, a Melbourne Club dandy, let off fireworks in a theatre box, seriously injuring a woman.[21]

Melbourne resumed its love affair with the theatre in 1845, when the missionary publican John Thomas Smith opened the Queen's

---

21   Major George Frederick Berkley St John, Melbourne's police magistrate, acquitted Snodgrass on the grounds that the woman was to blame, saying, "I am not surprised that young men should misconduct themselves in such a manner when ... the boxes which should have been reserved for families were filled with women of improper character." Snodgrass had the live fast, die young attitude common to many of the young squatters, having accidentally discharged his pistol into his foot during a duel with fellow squatter William Ryrey in 1840 on the site of present-day Southern Cross railway station. In 1841, Snodgrass challenged fellow Melbourne Club member Redmond Barry to a duel near the current Albert Park railway station. Barry, who would successfully defend Truganini in her murder trial later that year, called off the duel when Snodgrass again accidentally discharged his firearm. Snodgrass would go on to become a long-serving member of the Victorian Parliament.

Theatre in the beer garden of the St John Tavern. Smith, who would go on to be mayor of Melbourne seven times, obtained a permit after promising La Trobe he would only stage works of a "chaste and moral nature". The renowned English comic actor George Coppin performed at the theatre for the next five years, with his chaste and moral performance of *Old Kentucky Nigger* a family favourite.[22]

After a blackface matinee, the 1840s hipster might call in on William Nicholson's grocery and coffee house to try one of his international roasts.[23] Or maybe our hipster would just join the crowd gathered outside Nicholson's grocery to watch Melbourne's first steam-powered coffee roaster and grinder in action.[24] Following Nicholson's success, coffee houses sprang up all over Melbourne.

A hipster hankering for a world food experience might dine at Mrs Carroll's Melbourne Restaurant and Confectioner, or just admire its shelves crammed with the best Indian curry powder, pickled mushrooms, Durham mustard, Labrador salmon, licorice, macaroni, chilli vinegar, crystallised banana and other exotic delicacies.

Melbourne's Renaissance men and women didn't just love fine dining and the arts – they also got off on sport. John Batman's

---

22 The advertising flyer for the play read, "Mr COPPIN will appear as the OLD KENTUCKY NIGGER and screech the celebrated nigger melody JIM BROWN, with his unequalled CYMBAL POT-LID ACCOMPANIMENT ... 'surprising to de white folk and sartin death to all Long Island niggers'." Coppin introduced modern set design to Australian productions, with critics condemning this as "evidence that upholstery was going to triumph over acting". Committed to public entertainments, he later imported Australia's first shipment of ice, staged Australia's first hot air balloon flight, built Melbourne's first Turkish baths and operated an amusement park (later converted into a private lunatic asylum). He became the first grand master of Victoria's Freemasons and a longstanding member of parliament. Coppin, similar to a contemporary comic actor, scandalised society by marrying his stepdaughter. Masons get up to some crazy shit.

23 Nicholson's coffees are not to be confused with International Roast. Nor is any other coffee.

24 Some earnestly bearded Melbourne barista will read this and crowdfund a search for the foundation coffee roaster so he can install it in his ethically sourced cafe and scooter shop.

Mrs Datagalla won the Town Plate at Melbourne's first race meeting in 1838 and the Melbourne Cricket Club was established the same year. Twenty years later, MCC player Thomas Wentworth Wills, the son of Horatio Spencer Howe Wills, would create a game for cricketers to maintain fitness during winter – Australian Rules football, a sport that no Sydneysider could ever hope to understand.[25]

Melbournians would sit and watch sparrows fart if it were competitive, with sport embraced by all ages and sexes. On Boxing Day 1846, the St George & the Dragon Hotel staged wheelbarrow races for boys in blindfolds, goat-races for goats, old-person races for elderly ladies competing for "some articles of female adornment", and "that truly English amusement, Grinning through a Collar".[26]

But those down in Melbourne's mother-colony of Van Diemen's Land had little to grin about.

THE CONVICTS JOHN WEST REJECTS

The establishment of Port Phillip and South Australia, and the decision to pipe Britain's convict overflow into Tasmania, hastened the decline of the once prosperous island. Tasmania received 60 per cent of Australia's free immigrants between 1830 and 1837, but only 3 per cent between 1838 and 1850. Free settlers, when given a choice, didn't want to live next door to highwaymen and handkerchief thieves.

The small number of male convicts transported to Norfolk Island laboured under the benign rule of Captain Alexander Maconochie,

---

25   Some historians say Wills drew inspiration from marngrook, a ball game played by Victorian Aboriginal tribes. Other historians say this is cultural revisionism. I have no intention of buying into this debate.

26   The last is a reference to gurning, a competition as to who has the most hideous face (Melbournians are naturally gifted gurners). Gurning contestants traditionally frame their grotesque faces with a horse collar, which is known as 'gurnin' through a braffin'. It's wonderful that Melbourne, a city famed for its diversity, celebrates the sporting achievements of ugly people. It also honours ugly horses, with Gurner's Lane a popular winner of the Melbourne Cup in 1982.

who had an unusual background for a gaoler. Maconochie had founded
the Royal Geographical Society in 1830 and served as its inaugural
secretary, before becoming the University of London's first professor
of geography in 1833. The academic turnkey, who'd been dismissed
as Lieutenant-Governor Franklin's private secretary for his outspo-
ken views on Tasmanian prisons, subscribed to the heresy that the
primary purpose of imprisonment was to rehabilitate, not punish.
Maconochie reduced corporal punishment on Norfolk Island and
introduced a system under which prisoners could be paroled after
earning a certain number of marks for good behaviour. While the
War and Colonial Office shut down Maconochie's scheme before
he could release anyone and recalled him for being a loony liberal,
he is today honoured as "the Father of Parole" and his approach
underpins modern Western penal systems.

In Tasmania, lifers were sent to Port Arthur, while others were
put through the new probation system. Men were sent to stations
in the bush to labour, pray, endure enforced silence, grow beards
and, to the consternation of the authorities, get it on with each
other. Women were imprisoned on the *Anson* hulk moored in the
Derwent, to separate them from the "old hands" who ruled the
female factories.

John "Red" Kelly was one of almost 10,000 Irish prisoners sent
to Tasmania between 1840 and 1853. Transported for seven years for
misappropriating two pigs, he avoided another conviction for stealing "seven fat cows" by informing on an accomplice. The 21-year-old
arrived in Tasmania in 1842 and his stories of life in the probation
stations hardened the sense of injustice felt by his son Ned, who
referred to the island as "that land of bondage and tyranny" – which
was pretty rich coming from a guy who liked to play dress-ups in a
metal gimp suit.

The probation system was overseen by Sir John Eardley-Wilmot,
who succeeded Sir John Franklin as lieutenant-governor of Van Diemen's Land in 1843. Eardley-Wilmot was a baronet, barrister, MP,

juvenile-prison reformer and, according to Lord Stanley, secretary of state for war and the colonies, a "muddle-brained blockhead". He was formally rebuked by the War and Colonial Office twenty-seven times between March 1844 and February 1846, a record that has never been bettered.

Eardley-Wilmot was the lightning rod for Tasmanians who "complained that the free population was being swamped and that the colony was being turned into a giant gaol". To add insult to injury, the colonists were expected to pay for the upkeep of Britain's convicts, with probation more expensive than assignment.

In 1845, six members of Van Diemen's Land's Legislative Council railed against the probation system by blocking Eardley-Wilmot's financial measures, before resigning and leaving the council without a quorum to govern. Eardley-Wilmot condemned the "radical" action of the Patriotic Six, as they became known, but Whitehall acknowledged they had a point and agreed to bail out the colony by meeting two-thirds of its police and court costs. But it was women, not Tasmanian patriots, who brought Eardley-Wilmot down.

Sir John Franklin had ordered an *Inquiry into Female Convict Prison Discipline* in 1841, which noted the case of two women "detected in the very act of exciting each others passions – on the Lord's Day in the house of God – and at the very time divine service was performing". The superintendent of the Launceston Female Factory reported that sexual relations between prisoners were common and that women who played the man's part ruled the inmates. The Hobart factory's superintendent reported four prisoners for "dancing perfectly naked, and making obscene attitudes towards each other ... in imitation of men and women together", which earned them twelve months' hard labour.[27]

---

27 The term *lesbian* was not adopted until the twentieth century and colonial officials didn't have a term for female homosexuality, instead relying on veiled and occasionally salacious descriptions. Lesbian sex was generally regarded as a moral or health issue, rather than a crime.

In 1843, Eardley-Wilmot wrote to Stanley that some female factory inmates "have their Fancy-women, or lovers, to whom they are attached with quite as much ardour as they would be to the other sex, and practice onanism to the greatest extent".[28]

William Gladstone, Stanley's replacement as secretary of state for war and the colonies, wanted to know what Eardley-Wilmot planned to do about Tasmania's swarming lesbians.[29] The answer was not much, as Eardley-Wilmot was more interested in the colony's straight women.[30]

Tales of Eardley-Wilmot's licentious behaviour were published in the *London Naval and Military Gazette*, the Victorian military man's lad's mag. His reputed raunchy adventures, coupled with his apparent tolerance of sapphic soap dropping, resulted in his recall, with Gladstone informing him that the rumours about his private life meant he'd never work in the colonial service again. Eardley-Wilmot stayed in Tasmania, where he compiled evidence of his moral standing in an attempt to clear his name. He died of apparent nervous exhaustion in February 1847, with the *Colonial Times* accusing Gladstone of his murder.

Gladstone arranged for La Trobe to serve as lieutenant-governor until Eardley-Wilmot's replacement, Sir William Denison, arrived. La Trobe was deeply unpopular in Melbourne at the time for accepting British "exiles" into Port Phillip. As Tasmania was full, Britain decided to reintroduce transportation to the mainland by stealth, encouraged

---

28 Onanism refers to the sin of Onan, who was killed by God for being a bit of a wanker (*Genesis 38:9–10*).

29 Gladstone would go on to become a four-time prime minister of Great Britain. His supporters referred to him as the G.O.M. (Grand Old Man or, according to his rival Benjamin Disraeli, God's Only Mistake). Queen Victoria was not a supporter, complaining, "He always addresses me as if I were a public meeting." Gladstone was also London's equivalent to Caroline Chisholm – from 1840, and while prime minister decades later, he would wander the streets of the capital in search of prostitutes so he could lecture them on changing their degenerate ways.

30 Tasmania had the highest per capita rate of prostitution in the world in the mid-nineteenth century. Most of Tasmania's women were convicts, at least a quarter of whom were believed to be on the game.

by William Wentworth and others who continued to call for the return of convict labour. Britain insisted the exiles were not convicts per se, but well-behaved folk from Pentonville and two other prisons who'd been pardoned on condition they relocate to Port Phillip for five years. Seventeen hundred and thirty-nine Pentonvillains, as they were dubbed by the Melbourne press, arrived in Port Phillip between 1844 and 1849.

Eccentric Melbourne medico Dr James Clutterbuck accused the exiles of having "sunk to the lowest depths of vice and wickedness". Britain, Clutterbuck believed, had a secret program to send all its prison poofs to Australia.

Gladstone believed in hating the sin and loving the sinner, but not in a gay way. He was obsessed by rooting out colonial sodomites and instructed La Trobe to investigate accounts that convicts in probation gangs had:

> ... fallen into habits of life so revolting and depraved as to make it nothing less than the most sacred and imperious duty to adopt, without the loss of a single day ... measures ... to arrest the progress of pollution.

La Trobe launched a secret inquiry into the "prevalence of unnatural crime", with probationers cross-examined as to their sexual preferences, but word of the inquiry soon got out because gays are notorious gossips. La Trobe ordered that convict clothing and bedding be inspected for dried semen and that medical officers scour medical records for signs of queerness. He reported to Britain that "vice of every description is to be met with on every hand, not as isolated spots, but as a pervading stain", and that homosexuality was a "stigma on the colony".

Britain was so alarmed by La Trobe's report that it suspended male transportation to Tasmania for two years, before adopting his recommendation that all male convicts take a long cold shower before travelling to the steamy, man-loving south.

Gayness, rather than slavery, was now the main argument against transportation. In 1847, the *Launceston Examiner* published a poem by "Chrisianos", dedicated to "the freemen of Tasmania":

> *Shall Tasman's Isle so fam'd*
> *So lovely and so fair*
> *From other nations be estrang'd*
> *The name of Sodom bear?*[31]

Lieutenant-Governor Denison continued La Trobe's good work. Probationers were subject to regular bottom checks, side walls were installed in their bunks and lamps were left burning all night in their quarters. Spyholes were drilled into walls and guards wore slippers so they could creep up on unsuspecting sodomites.[32]

Meanwhile, Dr William Irvine, the superintendent of the Ross Female Factory, took an obsessive interest in lesbianism and female masturbation, on the grounds that the former involved the latter and the latter caused heart disease – but most likely because he was a creepy perve. Irvine divided lesbians into two categories – "those who fell for women playing the man's part" and "man-women" who had a masculine appearance and cultivated the "development of a pair of imperfect moustaches". He breathlessly (but scientifically) reported, "in other cases I have learned that artificial substances, mechanically secured to the person, form the substitute for the male organ." All of this was obviously too much for Irvine, as he was caught misappropriating alcohol and drugs set aside for his female patients.

---

31 For readers unfamiliar with gay culture, a bear is a plus-size hairy man who likes leather. Sodom bear is not to be confused with Humphrey B. Bear, who likes wearing no trousers around children, or Paddington Bear, who is partial to a "marmalade sandwich".

32 Gay-obsessed Tasmania was the last place in the British Empire to hang someone for sodomy (1867). It had the highest per capita rate of imprisonment for consenting male sex anywhere in the world for the next century and, in 1997, was the last Australian state to decriminalise male homosexual acts.

In 1847, Earl Grey junior sought Governor FitzRoy's advice on a revamped exile scheme, where convicts would serve time in a British gaol and be released into hard labour before being transported to New South Wales. Wentworth was an enthusiastic supporter of the program and FitzRoy agreed to it, subject to Britain transporting an equal number of free immigrants.

Grey's program, coupled with the recommencement of male transportation to Tasmania, triggered a wave of protests. In 1849, La Trobe succumbed to community pressure and barred the *Hashemy*, an exile ship, from unloading in Melbourne, directing it to sail on to Sydney. In Sydney, up to 8,000 protesters rallied at Circular Quay, forcing the *Hashemy* to continue to Moreton Bay.

La Trobe closed Melbourne's port to the next three exile ships and protests escalated in Sydney, where some of the exiles were dumped. The most powerful orator at the Sydney anti-transportation rallies was Henry Parkes, who'd rebuilt enough of his fortune to resume selling dead elephant products and other fancy goods while moonlighting as a journalist. Parkes attacked Wentworth "as the gentleman who misrepresents the people of Sydney", using anti-convict hysteria as the launch pad for his stellar political career.

In Tasmania, the Congregational minister and newspaperman John West attacked transportation from the pulpit and the press box, forming the Australasian Anti-Transportation League. West designed the league's flag, which sported a Union Jack in the top-left corner on a blue background, beside a yellow Southern Cross – an ensign strikingly similar to today's Australian flag.[33]

The last exile ship arrived in New South Wales in 1850 and Tasmania freed itself from the convict yoke in 1853. However, the convicts John West rejected were accepted by Western Australia.

Western Australia, founded as a convict-free colony, wanted cheap labour to kickstart its economy. It offered to take Britain's criminals,

---

33   Our flag is modelled on the original Australian symbol for "No more boat people".

as long as they were not political prisoners, serious offenders or women. As the rest of Australia withdrew from transportation, Western Australia had its first convict boom,[34] receiving almost 10,000 criminals, including Irish political radicals and Britain's nastiest psychos. But at least it received no women, allowing Western Australia to distinguish itself from the prostitute- and lesbian-infested eastern colonies it so jealously despised.

THE PROTOTYPE JELLABY AND THE POTATO EATERS

Caroline Chisholm had plenty of women for Australia. After returning to London, she convinced Earl Grey junior to support a family reunion program, in which several hundred wives and children of emancipists and bounty migrants were offered free passage to the colonies.

Next Chisholm established a loan society to help families save money and lend them half the cost of their passage, with her husband returning to Sydney to collect repayments from migrants after they found jobs. Her 1847 pamphlet *Comfort for the Poor! Meat Three Times a Day!! Voluntary Information From the People of New South Wales* further encouraged migration to Australia and the use of gratuitous exclamation marks.

Chisholm opened her London home as an Australian information centre, patiently answered tens of thousands of letters, accompanied emigrants to the docks, travelled Britain and the Continent on lecture tours, successfully lobbied for lower colonial postage rates and browbeat the government into passing the *Passenger Act 1852* to establish minimum standards for passenger ships.

The Emigrant's Friend, as Chisholm was affectionately known, collaborated with Charles Dickens, who saw Australia as a land of

---

34   It had its second convict boom in the 1990s, when Western Australian businessmen Alan Bond and Laurie Connell and former premiers Brian Burke and Ray O'Connor were gaoled.

opportunity for Britain's working poor, printing "A Bundle of Emigrants' Letters" in the first edition of Dickens's weekly magazine, *Household Words*.[35] Dickens promoted Chisholm's loan society, but also used her as the basis for *Bleak House*'s Mrs Jellaby, a "telescopic philanthropist" with an all-consuming passion for doing good works at a great distance, while oblivious to her own children.[36]

Chisholm helped thousands of migrants travel to Australia, including many refugees of *an Gorta Mór* (the Great Hunger) or, to those with less poetry in their hearts, the Irish Potato Famine. One of Chisholm's charges was 25-year-old Peter Lalor. Within three years of landing in Melbourne, Peter would lead his own revolution.

Potato blight, a Mexican disease that makes potatoes feel poorly, struck Europe in 1845. The blight affected Ireland most of all because the farms of poor Irish tenants were too small to grow anything other than potatoes, with a third of the population dependant on spuds for sustenance. As the mostly Catholic families starved, the predominantly Protestant landlords, many of whom were living in England, continued to export food from Ireland and kicked tenants off their land for failure to pay their rent. The laissez-faire Whigs in power believed the free market would feed the masses, while Charles Trevelyan, in charge of the government relief effort, believed "the judgement of God sent the calamity to teach the Irish a lesson". Over a million Irish died of starvation and related diseases between 1845 and 1852.

---

35 Dickens also sent two of his sons, nineteen-year-old Alfred and fifteen-year-old Edward, to "seek their fortune" in Australia. Both managed cattle stations and became stock agents. Edward was the member for Wilcannia in the New South Wales Parliament, before becoming a rabbit inspector, drifting into unemployment and dying penniless in the country town of Moree. Alfred stayed in Australia for forty-five years, before lecturing on his father's work in Europe and America and dying of acute indigestion in New York's Astor Hotel in 1912.

36 Mrs Jellaby had no interests beyond arranging for 200 families to grow coffee and educate the natives in Barrieboola-Gha. Chisholm had placed her three sons in the care of a neighbour while working in Australia, and somehow found the time to have a further three children while working around the clock on her emigration schemes.

The famine also resulted in a million more Irish leaving for mainland Britain, the United States, Canada and Australia. In seven years Ireland's population fell by about a quarter, with Ireland still having one and a half million fewer people today than before the famine.

The Irish understandably had a giant chip on their shoulder about the famine, or would have if there'd been enough potatoes left to make one. The 23,000 Irish famine immigrants who came to Australia during the 1840s brought heightened sectarian tension and Irish nationalist sympathies with them.

In 1848–50, during the height of the famine, 4,175 Irish orphan girls were shipped to Australia, which John Dunmore Lang argued was a papist plot to marry them off to Protestants, whom they'd seduce into Catholicism.

The orphans arrived just as anti-Irish sentiment in Australia peaked. Melbourne's *Argus*, then Australia's largest newspaper, mocked them as "useless trollops", "lawless savages", and "coarse useless creatures" with "squat stunted figures, thick waists and clumsy ankles". A January 1850 edition called them:

> ... a set of ignorant creatures whose whole knowledge of household duties barely reaches to distinguishing the inside from the outside of a potato, and whose chief employment hitherto, has consisted of some such intellectual occupation as occasionally trotting across a bog to fetch back a runaway pig.

Anti-Irish sentiment killed off the orphan scheme, even though Australian domestic positions remained unfilled and 104,000 children under the age of fifteen were still in Irish workhouses.

Only South Australia took a different view. Sure, the Irish girls were short, ugly and mostly Catholic, but liberal South Australia welcomed the vertically, fuglyly and religiously diverse. South Australia also needed more women, who were strangely reluctant to go there voluntarily, and foreign, homeless, unprotected teenage girls would fill an important niche in Adelaide society.[37] By 1851, Irish orphans made up half of Adelaide's prostitutes.

The colonies had accepted, if not always welcomed, the tired, the poor, the huddled masses yearning to breathe free. The unique mixture of convicts and free immigrants had made Australia the New Colossus of the south. Only one more ingredient was needed to transform the one-time convict hellhole into a global Titan ...

GOLD!!!

---

37   The niche was about six foot long and two foot deep, with a cast-iron lid and airholes.

9

We've golden soil

Eureka!

Archimedes, c. 250 BC

ALL THAT GLITTERS

IN 1844, REVEREND WILLIAM CLARKE SHOWED GOVERNOR Gipps some specks of gold he'd discovered west of the Blue Mountains. The horrified governor responded, "Put it away, Mr Clarke, or we shall all have our throats cut."

The gold finds of James McBrien in 1823 and Polish scientist-explorers John Lhotsky and Sir Pawel Edmund de Strzelecki in 1834 and 1839 received a similarly hostile response.[1] The government feared that gold, and the hysteria it sparked, would trigger a convict uprising.

However, colonial governments were keen on digging up everything else. The Australian Agricultural Company, granted a monopoly over Newcastle's coal reserves in 1828, made a tidy fortune exporting black gold – it also opened Australia's first railway in 1831, with

---

[1]   Strzelecki is hated by Australian schoolchildren for being the most difficult-to-spell Australian explorer and for naming Australia's highest peak, Mount Kosciuszko, after some equally unspellable Polish freedom fighter. Strzelecki's greatest contribution to Australian culture is *Kath & Kim*'s Sharon Strzelecki, portrayed by Magda Szubanski, who also has an un-Australian name.

full coal carts rolling downhill powering the return of empty carts to the mine.[2]

Coal was discovered in Tasmania in 1833, although it was of poor quality. The island's mine ran at a loss, but was kept open as a place of punishment for the most troublesome convicts. An 1844 inspection found that the workings were infested with fleas and that the convicts had not a single towel or item of cutlery between them. Many worked naked, except for leather halters they donned to pull the mine carts. During Tasmania's sodomania crisis, the government became suspicious of men who lurked in the dark wearing nothing but leather harnesses, and privatised the mine.

In 1848, Augustus Gregory found lead near Western Australia's Murchison River. The Geraldine Mining Company sunk a mine in 1849 and, when it rained, concluded that digging a big hole in the middle of a dry riverbed may not have been such a great idea. Despite this early setback, small lead and copper mines sprang up around the Murchison, but they were no more than a small part of a small economy.[3]

But it was in South Australia that mining really took off, thanks in large part to Johann Menge. Born in the Germany duchy of Hesse in 1788, Menge was a savant who also placed highly on the idiot spectrum. He spoke German, English, Russian, Dutch, French, Latin, Ancient Greek, Hebrew, Arabic, Persian, Mandarin and three Aboriginal

---

2   Anorak-wearers will be interested to note that Australia's first passenger railway was established by Lieutenant-Governor Arthur in 1837 to cross the Tasman Peninsula to Port Arthur. Trains on the seven-kilometre line were not powered by steam or horses, as in Britain, or gravity, as in New South Wales, but by pickpockets and rapists. The carriages were pushed across the peninsula by four convicts, with 4 cp equivalent to about 1 hp.

3   While New South Wales and Victoria were having their gold rushes, Western Australia had a shit rush. Bird poo from the Lacepede and Abrolhos Islands was Western Australia's second-largest export after wool from the 1850s until the 1880s. In 1876, the United States' vice-consul-general in Melbourne, Samuel Perkins Lord, declared the Lacepede Islands American possessions so that a buddy could harvest poo there. Shitgate was a major diplomatic incident, with President Ulysses S. Grant ultimately renouncing America's claim.

FIG. 9: "So, do you come here often?"

tongues. He obsessively collected Bibles in different languages and published Christian mystical works based on Jewish oral tradition. But Menge's greatest passions were rocks and wine.

Menge travelled to South Australia in 1836 as the South Australia Company's mine and quarry agent. Although "the Professor", as he was known, found traces of iron, copper, tin, marble and slate, he was sacked because his tactlessness and anti-social behaviour freaked out his workmates.

This didn't worry Menge, who retired to a cave he'd dug into the bank of Jacob's Creek in the Barossa Valley, diverting the creek to form an island where he grew vegetables and planned to open an oriental languages school. The Hessian hobbit believed the Barossa was ideal for winemaking and declared that it was "the cream, the whole cream and nothing but the cream of South Australia". He encouraged German immigrants to settle there and plant vines.[4] [5]

Menge walked everywhere because he believed motion drove out the evil spirits that caused sickness. His constitutionals, some of which were hundreds of kilometres long, allowed him to look for new minerals and learn about Aboriginal people and languages. While the tribes were busy spearing settlers, they always welcomed Menge.

Menge had no interest in money, another clear sign of his insanity. During his perambulations, he'd say things like, "Your farm appears to be sitting on a huge copper deposit. Why don't you have a bit of a dig?", while anybody else would have stayed shtum and tried to buy the land for themselves.

Still, South Australians didn't need Menge to hit paydirt. Picnickers discovered silver and lead at Glen Osmond in 1838, and the small mine established on the picnic site exported Australia's first metal in 1841.

In 1842, a young boy called Charles Samuel Bagot showed his father an interesting green rock he'd found while picking wildflowers. A neighbour, Francis Dutton, was searching for lost sheep when he

---

4   The Barossa produces some of the world's finest reds. Johann Gramp, a Bavarian viticulturist, bought a property on Jacob's Creek in 1847 and established Orlando Wines, which still produces the Jacob's Creek label. German winemakers have continued to flock to the Barossa, with Wolfgang Blass establishing his vineyard there in 1966.

5   Neither Orlando Wines nor Wolf Blass have sponsored this book, but if they'd like to send me a case, they can get my address and wine preferences from my publisher. A jar of olives and a nice pâté would also be appreciated.

discovered more lovely green rocks. Dutton and Charles Bagot senior quietly bought the land they were leasing and opened the Kapunda Copper Mine in 1844, kickstarting the Australian mining industry.[6]

Thomas Pickett, an aged shepherd, discovered copper at Burra Creek the following year. Burra was bought by two syndicates, known as the Nobs and the Snobs. The Nobs' land produced no ore while the Snobs set up the Burra Burra "Monster Mine", which produced 15 per cent of the world's copper for fifteen years. Pickett received a £20 finder's fee but was refused the "unwarranted expenditure" of shares in Burra. Six years later, he got loaded, fell into the fireplace of his small hut near the mine and burned to death.[7]

Kapunda and Burra Burra dragged South Australia out of insolvency. Francis Dutton was twice elected premier of South Australia and Henry Ayers, the manager of Burra, got the job a record five times. South Australians, for some reason, really admired people who were good at digging deep holes.

The Hanoverian government paid the passage of 1,300 unemployed German miners to make a new life in South Australia, and gnome-like Cornishmen, who'd spent centuries crawling into small holes in southern England, also emigrated en masse.

In 1845, Governor Frederick Robe introduced a bill to collect mining royalties, but withdrew it after landowner representatives on his Legislative Council walked out in protest, leaving his government paralysed.

From Robe to Rudd, Australian politicians have discovered that miners get antsy when taxed. Lieutenant-Governor Sir Charles Hotham of Victoria would learn that lesson the hard way just nine years later at Eureka.

---

6   Next time the mining industry wants to run a feel-good campaign about digging big holes in a food basin, it could do worse than link Australia's mineral riches to an innocent child out picking native flowers.

7   This would not make such a good mining industry campaign.

I HAVE FOUND IT!

New South Wales withdrew its opposition to local goldmining, as James W. Marshall's cry of "Eureka!" at Sutter's Mill, California, echoed around the globe.[8] More than 6,000 Australians sailed for San Francisco in 1849, joining the 300,000 prospectors who swarmed to California after news of Marshall's gold find got out. The New South Wales government responded to the loss of some of its most adventurous and enterprising citizens by offering a reward for the discovery of payable quantities of gold in the colony.

One of the 49ers, as the Californian prospectors were known, was 33-year-old Edward Hargraves. Hargraves had come to Australia as a cabin boy and dived for aphrodisiac sea cucumbers in the Torres Strait.[9] He then farmed less sexy sheep west of Bathurst, opened a pub and worked as a steamship agent. Hargraves' Gen-Y CV told of a restless spirit with an eye for the main chance.

At 1.93 metres tall and 115 kilograms, Hargraves was a brick shithouse of a man with the gift of the gab and a knack for making friends. One such friend was Simpson Davison, a gold-struck sheep farmer he'd met en route to California.

Newly captured from Mexico, California was the Wild West, where the law rode in a holster and government was a four-letter

---

8   Marshall actually said, "Hey boys, by God, I believe I've found a goldmine," after finding nuggets while building a sawmill on the American River on 24 January 1848 – but "Eureka", adopted as California's state motto in 1850, is more poetic. Greek for "I have found it", "Eureka" was the catchcry of Greek egghead and exhibitionist Archimedes upon discovering how to determine the volume of an irregularly shaped object (himself) while having a bath. (Archimedes noted that his body displaced water, the volume of which could be calculated in a regularly shaped bathtub.) Archimedes was so excited by his discovery that he leaped out of the tub and ran naked through the streets, screaming, "Eureka!" The goldmining term "lucky streak" may also derive from this event.

9   Readers interested in knowing how a big black slug can be used as a marital aid may refer to "Is That a Slug in Your Pocket?" at pages 15–16 of *Girt*.

word. Hargraves and Davison lived a hand-to-mouth existence, narrowly avoiding freezing to death by sleeping in flour sacks that had been wet, which meant the flour remnants formed a thick insulating paste. The gold rush involved going hungry, being leered at by toothless, trigger-happy Americans and shivering in a bread bag. This was less glamorous than Hargraves had anticipated and he returned to Sydney in January 1851.

For the next few months, accounts of Hargraves' activities diverge. There is Hargraves' version and there is everyone else's. According to Hargraves, he'd immediately realised that California was just like Bathurst.[10] So, upon returning to Sydney, he resolved to look for gold at Carcoar, near Bathurst, where he knew a landowner, Thomas Icely. However, after a seemingly chance meeting with Icely on the road, he diverted to Guyong's Wellington Inn, which was, amazingly, owned by Susan Lister, the widow of the ship's captain for whom he'd worked as a cabin boy. Taking this apparent coincidence in his stride, Hargraves asked the good widow for a tame blackfellow to serve as a local guide, but, as none were conveniently to hand, had to make do with Mrs Lister's eighteen-year-old son, John. Hargraves borrowed a pick and a cooking plate to use as a gold pan and followed John Lister down Lewis Ponds Creek on 12 February 1851. There, as he later wrote:

> I found myself surrounded by gold; and with tremendous anxiety panted for the moment of trial, where my magician's wand should transform this trackless wilderness into a region of countless wealth.

The outback alchemist found tiny specks of gold in five of his first six pans, recalling, "At that instant I felt myself to be a great man." He said to Lister:

---

10   Today, Bathurst is recognised as the Hollywood of Australia, or at least the bit of Australia between Lithgow and Orange.

This is a memorable day in the history of New South Wales. I shall be a baronet, you will be knighted, and my old horse will be stuffed, put in a glass case, and sent to the British Museum.[11]

Hargraves, Lister and Lister's friend James Tom scoured the country-side for the next six weeks. Lister and Tom made small finds, while Hargraves found nothing. Hargraves showed Lister and Tom's brother William how to make a mining cradle to sluice soil away from heavy gold particles, before telling them he had to travel to Sydney. Oh, and could he have the gold they'd found?

In Sydney, Hargraves asked Colonial Secretary Edward Deas Thomson for the gold reward. Thomson was unimpressed by the minuscule flecks Hargraves produced and told him the reward would depend upon the value of any goldfields that might eventuate. Hargraves rejoined Lister and William Tom, who'd now made significant finds. They begged him not to tell others of the gold.

But more miners equalled more gold equalled more reward money, so Hargraves told every man and his dog of the riches that awaited them in the river gullies west of Bathurst. He may not have been much good at finding gold, but he was a damn fine publicist.

Fortune-seekers flocked to Lewis Ponds Creek and erected a tent town that Hargraves named Ophir, after King Solomon's legendary city of riches. There they found gold – buckets of it. And so Australia's first gold rush was born.

On 19 May 1851, the *Sydney Morning Herald* reported:

A complete mental madness appears to have seized every member of the community, and as a natural consequence there has been a universal rush to the diggings. Any attempt to describe the numberless scenes – grave, gay, and ludicrous – which have arisen out of this state of things, would require the graphic power of Dickens.

---

11   The horse would enjoy the same privileges as Aboriginal people.

Thousands of Sydneysiders hurried to Ophir, while country centres like Goulburn and Maitland became ghost towns. The wealthy carted their goods in wagons and the poor pushed wheelbarrows across the Blue Mountains. Wiradjuri men like Tommy-Come-Last joined the throngs of the hopeful and the desperate.[12]

Major Thomas Mitchell, who set off for Ophir in May to plan its layout, noted a continuous line of men, with a scattering of women and children, stretching the 160 miles from Sydney. Sailors deserted their ships, leaving them stranded in Sydney Harbour. Teachers and police left their posts. Hotels between Sydney and Bathurst lay abandoned. Lady Charlotte Godley despaired that well-bred families were returning to Britain because they could no longer find a decent butler:

> You hear endless stories of ladies who have been used to large establishments, and giving parties now obliged to give up all thoughts of appearance, and open the doors even themselves.

Governor FitzRoy despaired that the rush was "unhinging the minds of all classes". The urban poor saw gold as their chance to get rich.[13] Farmers and businessmen saw it as their chance to get richer. Before leaving town, aspiring miners would visit the few shops that remained open, which were now all selling mining kit, along with their usual goods rebranded for the goldfields.[14] There was clothing modelled

---

12 Major Thomas Mitchell liked naming Aborigines after himself. Two Wiradjuri boys joined Mitchell's 1836 expedition to the rich pasturelands of western Victoria. Mitchell named the first Tommy-Come-First and the second Tommy-Come-Last.

13 Gold has now been replaced by pokies and sports betting.

14 Frying pans were marketed as gold pans; fruit juice was rebranded Ophir Cordial, "a drink for the health and comfort of miners"; and purchasers of "Lyndon's best diamond pointed Miners Shovels" were disappointed that the shovels didn't have hardened diamond points, but were just the same diamond shape they'd been when sold at a fraction of the price for digging up potatoes. It was storekeepers such as James Dalton, who'd been transported to Australia for abducting a wealthy Irish widow, who profited most from the gold rush. Dalton and his sons went from running a simple bark store outside Blackman's Swamp, near Ophir, to operating a

on the Californian look – sombreros, red or blue serge shirts, and trousers held up by colourful sashes rather than belts. And, of course, every miner who wanted to look the part needed a pair of pistols to protect his claim.

On 20 May, Governor FitzRoy announced that Queen Victoria owned all the colony's minerals, and people who wanted to look for any gold she hadn't already pocketed would need to pay thirty shillings a month for the privilege. Men with a shovel and pick in the middle of the goldfields insisted to the new gold commissioner that they weren't mining. Who knew when they might need to dig a hole to collect rain or trap a bunyip? The avoidance of licence fees had begun.

While some struck it lucky at Ophir, there were many failures. Refugees started the long march home from the frigid goldfields as winter set in, with Colonel Godfrey Mundy describing the returning prospectors as:

> Mortified, half starved, and crest fallen fellows ... Some looked so gaunt, savage, ragged, and reckless, that my thoughts turned involuntarily to my pistols as they drew near.

But the rush was spreading. About 400 prospectors descended on the sleepy hamlet of Araluen, south-west of Canberra, in September 1851, although pickings were initially slimmer than Kate Moss after a week on the gear. In October, a Mrs Baxter set up a cradle in nearby Major's Creek and found four ounces of gold. Miners rushed to the site and soon gold was being extracted throughout the Araluen district. Hargraves, who'd been given £500 and a plum government job to search for more gold after the Ophir find, had been in the area the month before and tried to claim credit for the discovery, but nobody was buying it.

Doubts were now being cast on his Ophir "discovery". Simpson Davison, returned to Australia, said Hargraves had never compared

---

vast commercial and agricultural empire out of Orange, as Blackman's Swamp was renamed – their fortune built on selling overpriced picks and shovels.

California to Bathurst. Instead, he'd researched the reports of McBrien, Strzelecki and Clarke, all of whom had found gold in the area. In 1849, William Tipple Smith advised that he'd found gold at Lewis Ponds Creek. Hargraves' tale of ending up at the site after a series of chance encounters was looking decidedly threadbare.

John Lister also disputed Hargraves' account and claimed he'd found gold at Lewis Ponds Creek before Hargraves arrived. He and the Tom brothers insisted they were Hargraves' business partners and that he had taken their gold to Sydney without telling them he was seeking the reward. They also alleged the first payable gold was found *after* Hargraves returned to Sydney and that it was the Toms' father, a Wesleyan preacher, who'd named Ophir.

The Legislative Council recommended a £5,000 reward for Hargraves and £1,000 for Lister and the Toms, but Edward Deas Thomson, who'd publicly backed Hargraves, doubled his reward to £10,000. Clarke, Strzelecki and Lhotsky crawled out of the woodwork to claim they'd discovered payable gold earlier, with the first two receiving a government payout. Sir Roderick Murchison, the president of Britain's Royal Geological Society, who'd never been anywhere near Australia, made a particularly ambitious bid for the reward on the grounds that he'd told some hard-up Cornish miners to look for gold in New South Wales in 1846. That they hadn't done so was an irrelevant detail.

Lister and the Toms spent the next four decades campaigning for recognition as the discoverers of Australian gold. In 1890, the Legislative Council held another inquiry. Sadly, Lister died of influenza on the morning he was to give evidence. The inquiry found:

(a) Lister and the Toms "were undoubtedly the first discoverers of payable gold in Australia";

(b) Hargraves had given up on the search and was over 100 miles away when they discovered the gold; and

(c) Hargraves had taken their gold to claim the reward, which
     made him a lying, thieving bastard.

This was extremely embarrassing, as Hargraves had been received
by Queen Victoria, granted an annual pension for the discovery and
was a deadset Aussie legend. Sir Henry Parkes, in his final term as
premier of New South Wales, didn't know what to do with the report,
so he sat on it.

Hargraves died the following year, leaving an estate worth less than
£375. This was even more embarrassing, given the amount of money
he'd received from the government. One of the first acts of George
Dibbs' new administration was to vote down the inquiry's report.

Some tall poppies are better left uncut.

THE DUKE OF VAUCLUSE

William Charles Wentworth thundered that Edward Hargraves
was a "very shallow and impertinent person" who shouldn't receive a
farthing for the Ophir find. This was another shameful example of
the government spending money on people who didn't own sheep.

Of course, people who did own sheep should be paid for any gold
found under them. Australia's second major gold find was made on
Wentworth's Frederick's Valley estate, just south of Ophir. Wentworth first tried to make prospectors pay him royalties, then sold
the property to the Wentworth Gold Field Company (of which he
was a director). The company then opened Australia's first commercial goldmine.

But gold was a sideshow for Wentworth. His main game was cutting the colony's umbilical cord to Mother Britain so that he might
build a new government in his own image.

In 1848, Britain had transferred responsibility for running Canada
from the governor to ministers appointed by an elected legislative
assembly. This was the first responsible government in the British

Empire outside Britain itself. Wentworth should have been thrilled, as he'd demanded two houses of parliament and responsible government during his spats with Governor Gipps. However, with the pro-squatter FitzRoy in office, Wentworth was no longer so keen on an elected assembly governing the colony.

All in all, 1848, known as the People's Spring, was a big year for democracy. Popular revolutions rocked Europe as protesters demanded an end to feudalism, the creation of independent states and a voice for the people.

Like the Arab Spring of 2011, the People's Spring saw the triumph of adversity over hope, as governments cracked down on dissidents. The Young Ireland movement, which demanded Irish self-government, was outgunned by police at the Battle of Widow McCormack's Cabbage Plot.[15] Karl Marx, who'd co-written *The Communist Manifesto* earlier that year, was expelled from Brussels for using his inheritance to arm Belgian revolutionaries. In Austria, Emperor Ferdinand I, the mentally deficient son of double first cousins, famously asked of the revolutionaries, "*Ja, dürfen's denn des?* (But are they allowed to do that?)", before abdicating in favour of his nephew Franz Josef I, who restored order. Franz Josef's troops combined with French forces to expel Garibaldi's republicans from the Italian states, and with Russian Cossacks to put down the Hungarian Revolution. In Germany, Otto von Bismarck restored aristocratic rule in Berlin after the intellectuals who'd led the uprising couldn't agree on what a German state should look like. And eighteen citizens of Stockholm were shot by the king's troops at a place only the Swedish Chef can pronounce (*Storkyrkobrinken*).

The French, however, knew how to do revolution properly. The French monarchy had been restored after the fall of Napoleon, but

---

15   Irish republicans were famous for their passionately half-arsed uprisings, but being thrashed in a small cabbage field in Tipperary was a new low.

King Louis Philippe I abdicated in the face of the 1848 riots, ushering in the Second Republic.[16] There were also green shoots in Denmark and the Netherlands, where the kings voluntarily surrendered some of their power, and in Switzerland, where the cantons federated under a new Swiss constitution.[17]

Britain, except for the Irish cabbage fiasco, saw peaceful protests. On 10 April 1848, 150,000 Chartists rallied in London to call for the adoption of the 1838 People's Charter, which demanded the vote for all men; the secret ballot; pay for MPs and an end to MP property requirements, so that working men could run for parliament; electorates with equal populations; and annual polls. A petition calling for these reforms, signed by an estimated six million people, was presented to parliament.[18]

The suffragette movement was born in the same year, with the signing of Elizabeth Cady Stanton's Declaration of Rights and Sentiments at Seneca Falls, New York. The declaration called for women to have the same voting, property, education, employment, marriage and divorce rights as men, with the outraged *Oneida Whig* magazine

---

16 Louis Philippe had himself come to the throne after the July Revolution of 1830 deposed Charles X. The French, who were now completely jacques of the monarchy, attempted to assassinate the affable Louis Philippe on seven occasions. The most notable attempt was made by Giuseppe Fieschi, who tried to shoot the king with an ingenious weapon of his own devising – a wooden frame holding twenty-five simultaneously firing guns. The *Machine infernale*, as it became known, only grazed Louis' forehead but killed eighteen bystanders and injured twenty-two more. When the people finally got rid of him in 1848, Louis Philippe caught a public cab to England under the *nom de plume* Mr Smith.

17 The Australian Constitution of 1901, with its allocation of federal and state powers, borrows heavily from the 1848 Swiss Constitution. Its referendum provisions are directly lifted from the Swiss, so the Swiss are responsible for giving us all our constitutional amendments, as well as chocolate, cheese, fondue (chocolate or cheese) and those fucking irritating clocks where the little bird pops out of a chalet window and keeps you awake all night.

18 Some of the signatures may have been fake, as signatories included Queen Victoria and No Cheese. The real Queen Victoria, unnerved by the Chartist protests, took refuge on the Isle of Wight. Nobody knows what happened to No Cheese.

describing the Seneca Falls gathering as "the most shocking and unnatural event ever recorded in the history of womanity".[19]

Wentworth, who regarded all democratic sentiment as shocking and unnatural, was profoundly disturbed by the events of 1848. The man who'd once organised a petition for voting rights for "the entire of the free population" (except women, blacks and foreigners) now "agreed with that ancient and venerable constitution that treated those who had no property as infants, or idiots, unfit to have any voice in the management of the State".

Henry Parkes, in contrast, declared himself a Chartist. He argued that "down-trodden labourers" could no longer be locked out of "a fair share of political power", and successfully lobbied Britain so that men who occupied property worth only £10 a year could vote.

Wentworth was rattled, as he represented the interests of country farmers while holding Australia's most urban electorate. Terrified that the working class would rise against him, he temporarily retracted his calls for self-rule, arguing, "If the feelings that existed now were carried out, Sydney would be like Paris under the government of the people altogether."

In 1850, Britain passed the *Australian Colonies Government Act*, which allowed New South Wales to develop proposals for voting and two houses of parliament.[20] Even Wentworth's critics acknowledged he was Australia's greatest constitutional thinker, so he naturally took the lead on reform.

---

19   Stanton also helped to popularise a new "rational" dress for women. As comfortable shoes were not yet in vogue, she opted for comfortable pants, adopting the billowing garment gathered at the ankle worn by her cousin and fellow suffragette, Libby Miller. Stanton displayed her new pants to fellow Seneca Falls resident Amelia Bloomer, the editor of the *Lily*, the world's first women's newspaper. Bloomer promoted the pants and they became known as bloomers, the garment of choice for the independent woman. Bloomers were eventually superseded by blue stockings.

20   The act also affected the other colonies. South Australia initially had no idea what those effects were, as the ship's captain responsible for delivering the act to Adelaide put it in his laundry bag for safekeeping and promptly forgot where he'd hidden it – but it all came out in the wash.

Wentworth attacked the 1850 act for not allowing the colonies to control their own revenue or public service appointments, earning a ringing endorsement from John Dunmore Lang. But Wentworth now considered Lang a fruit loop in every other respect – a lover of all things American, Lang espoused secession from Britain and the establishment of an Australian republic.[21]

Wentworth savaged Lang for his mad republicanism and support for a vote for all men, spitting, "Wherever the principle of universal suffrage has prevailed, it has been the signal for rapine, massacre and bloodshed." He ridiculed Lang's vision of "a great federation of all the colonies of Australia ... each State to have a separate local government and sending members to Congress to form a great central government", with Legislative Council members hooting and jeering at this ridiculous concept.

With the discovery of gold, Britain agreed the colonies had the resources for self-government and invited them to draft constitutions (except for Western Australia, which was too small, poor and generally backwards).

Wentworth had sniffed the political wind and knew an elected legislative assembly was inevitable. The constitution he drafted provided for one, but protected the squatters' primacy by rejecting electorates based on population for those based "on the great interests of the country" (i.e. sheep).[22] He justified this squattermander on the grounds that sheep owners had more money, and therefore paid more tax, than anyone else.

Wentworth had transcended the tired old line of "No taxation without representation". He now preached "No representation without

---

21 Lang, with Parkes's aid, established the Australian League to promote "the entire freedom of the Australian colonies and their incorporation into one political federation". However, Parkes, like Malcolm Turnbull after him, shelved his support for an Australian republic when he realised there were no votes in going up against a popular queen.

22 Wentworth was a ewetilitarian. Ewetilitarianism seeks to provide the greatest happiness for the owners of the greatest number of sheep.

taxation", and those who paid more tax were entitled to more representation. Sydney's merchants didn't deserve an equal vote as they
"simply engaged in exchanging one commodity for another ... produc-
tive of absolutely nothing". Sydney had "really nothing to represent ...
except a large mass of people ... the most vacillating, ignorant and
misled body of people in the Colony".

Wentworth was clearly not interested in continuing as the Member for Sydney. Instead, he wanted to serve on a reformed Legislative
Council that could veto the assembly's laws. The council would only
be open to former council members, most of whom were squatters,
who would be granted hereditary titles. Only members of this new
squattocracy could serve on future councils.

Wentworth was proposing the colonial nobility once championed
by John Macarthur. The sons of the Sheep-Kings, ensconced in the
rich leathered comfort of a Down Under House of Lords, would rule
for generations.

Henry Parkes, a surprise loser in the recent election, was now owner-
editor of the *Empire*, the newspaper for the aspirational working man.
The *Empire* proposed eligibility tests for Wentworth's "mongrel body",
including being "rich as a lord" and "drunk as a lord". Parkes organised
popular protests, where Dan Deniehy, "the boy orator", came into his own.

Deniehy, the son of a transported Irish vagrant, was a 25-year-old
polymath who championed an Australian republic. He was a solicitor
and literary critic, lectured on French poetry and wrote racy novellas.
He mocked "the Duke of Vaucluse" and his "bunyip aristocracy". James
Macarthur, who supported Wentworth's scheme, was derided as "the
Earl of Camden", his coat of arms a rum keg. Deniehy, who had the
radical spirit, rhetorical power and sheer bitchiness of Wentworth in
his heyday, made the old squatter an object of ridicule.[23]

---

23 Deniehy later entered the New South Wales Parliament as an "extreme liberal",
    but was unable to compromise his principles where pragmatism was demanded.
    Disillusioned with the culture of politics, he hid from his friends and took to drink,
    his alcoholism worsened by the death of his young son. The sensitive wordsmith

Wentworth's proposal died in the dust. The Legislative Council endorsed a constitution that would enable new council members to be appointed for life, but they would carry no ancient title, nor would their sons rule after them.

The constitution needed to be approved by the British Parliament, and New South Wales wanted a man on the ground.[24] Sarah Wentworth had already taken her younger children to England to further their education and William was unelectable after trash-talking his constituents.

William Charles Wentworth had left England as a third-class lawyer, a second-class poet and a first-class sponger. Now he would return as the grand old man of colonial politics to champion the first Australian constitution and defend his political legacy.

INDEPENDENCE DAY

While Wentworth dreamed of New South Wales' independence from Britain, Britain was helping Lang and Fawkner fulfil their dream of independence from New South Wales.[25] The *Australian Colonies Government Act* required New South Wales to cede its rich southern pasturelands to a new colony, Victoria, that would be ruled from Melbourne.

Melbournians discovered their independence by reading a copy of the *Times*, delivered by ship on 11 November 1850. The news was

---

who protected Australia from a parasitic peerage was only thirty-seven years old when he died from "loss of blood and fits induced by habits of intemperance" in 1865.

24   This was a bit rich, as Britain doesn't have a written constitution of its own. Britain claims to have an unwritten constitution, which really just means parliament can do whatever it likes and the courts must say that is OK, after citing ancient laws written on the tanned hides of Saxon peasants or Henry VIII's favourite breakfast napkin.

25   Melbournians, pissed off at being ruled from distant Sydney, had claimed they would be just as well represented from Britain. In an unusual protest vote, they elected Earl Grey junior, secretary of state for war and the colonies, as their representative on the New South Wales Legislative Council. The vacant seat in council meetings was a symbol of Melbourne's political alienation.

contained in a small article on page five, nestled between notice of an amendment to the *Dog Act* and an advertisement for an impotence cure.

Melbournians celebrated with a day off work and enjoyed it so much that they had two more. An impromptu party was held under the sweeping boughs of the Separation Tree and hot air balloons with "SEPARATION" written in two-foot letters were released.[26] Two thousand sticky buns were "distributed to children of all denominations", bonfires and rockets were lit and members of the Melbourne Club got drunker than David Boon on a Qantas flight.

And what would a Melbourne festival be without sport? There were the usual feats of strength and sack races, and Fanny Anstey and Maria Spiggot were declared joint winners of the competition for the most impressive bunion. La Trobe's cocker spaniel, Byron, won a dog show and a pig was greased with lard, painted red and chased through the streets of inner Melbourne, before being taken into custody by two policemen on Brunswick Street, Fitzroy, the following day.[27]

The only person who didn't enjoy the festivities was Mrs La Trobe, who was woken at 6 a.m. by a polka-playing saxhorn band and suffered "one of her neuralgic headaches", incapacitating her for the formal separation parade.[28] And Mayor Augustus Greeves was disappointed that his plan for ten oxen to carry a six-foot-wide meat pie in the parade had come to naught, as he couldn't find a big enough oven.[29]

---

26 The Separation Tree, a magnificent 400-year-old river red gum in Melbourne's Royal Botanic Gardens, is dying after being ringbarked – no doubt by some uncultured bastard from Sydney.

27 By which stage, it had presumably acquired a full shoulder-to-trotter tattoo and some interesting piercings.

28 Sophie La Trobe had a delicate constitution and soon returned to the spas of her native Switzerland, where she died in 1854. Charles La Trobe returned to Switzerland later that year to marry Sophie's sister. In a film history of Australia, Charles La Trobe would be played by Jack Thompson.

29 This is the earliest record of our national fascination with big things. Greeves is today remembered as the Father of Australian Boganism.

Melbourne woke up after the separation party to the mother of all hangovers, in the form of the New South Wales gold rush. The city's economy flatlined and government services faltered as Ophir-bound shearers left sheep unshorn and mild-mannered public servants reinvented themselves as swashbuckling goldfield adventurers.

In June 1851, desperate to stop people leaving, La Trobe offered a £200 reward for finding payable gold within 200 miles of Melbourne.[30] On 1 July, New South Wales got around to passing the laws that formalised Victoria's separation, with La Trobe appointed lieutenant-governor of the new colony.[31]

When Victoria was just four days old, Louis Michel, the owner of Melbourne's Rainbow Hotel, walked through the Gold Discovery Committee's door and announced he'd found gold within twenty miles of the capital. He could not have imagined the tsunami that was about to engulf his city.

---

30 The Van Diemen's Land government, which was spending its ever-diminishing resources on combatting the gay menace, only managed to scrape together a £20 reward.

31 La Trobe was only a lieutenant-governor because Earl Grey junior appointed Charles Augustus FitzRoy governor-general of all the Australian colonies, as he believed a general assembly of the colonies should be established to deal with railway lines, lighthouses, mail and other inter-colonial matters. This early attempt at a limited Australian federation never got off the ground and the other colonies received fully fledged governors upon FitzRoy's recall in 1855. FitzRoy had long requested an extension of his term, but personal tragedy and scandal played a role in its refusal. FitzRoy had driven his coach too fast in the grounds of Parramatta's Government House in 1847, and his wife and aide-de-camp were killed in the ensuing crash. The despairing FitzRoy then behaved like the early lieutenant-governors of Van Diemen's Land, with rumours of his liaisons with young women tarnishing his reputation. John Dunmore Lang, in responding to FitzRoy's farewell speech in the Legislative Council, accused him of a "moral influence" on the colony that had been "deleterious and baneful in the highest degree". While staying at a Berrima inn, FitzRoy had fathered a child with eighteen-year-old Mary Ann Chalker, the innkeeper's barmaid stepdaughter. Mary Ann, rather than doing the decent thing in staying quiet, named her child Charles Augustus FitzRoy, to the delight of the governor's critics. FitzRoy junior was not acknowledged by his father and was adopted by former convict John Fitzsimons. Had FitzRoy behaved in a manner more befitting a governor (i.e. not got caught), his rule might have been extended and federation of the colonies progressed earlier.

10

Under the Southern Cross I stand

Under the Southern Cross I stand
A sprig of wattle in my hand,
A native of my native land,
Australia, you fucking beauty!

Rodney "Iron Gloves" Marsh, Victory song of
the Australian men's cricket team, 1974

THE MAKING OF SMELLBOURNE

L A TROBE DIDN'T PAY OUT ON LOUIS MICHEL'S GOLD find, as he was inundated with claims for the reward. On the day Michel reported his discovery, William Campbell announced he'd found gold on Clunes Station the previous year, but had kept quiet because he didn't want miners digging up his neighbouring farm. The same day, James Esmond showed the *Geelong Advertiser* gold he'd found near Clunes on 28 June.[1]

The *Advertiser*'s story on Esmond's discovery triggered the biggest gold rush in human history. Rich finds at Buninyong, Ballarat,

---

1   It took until 1854 for the Victorian government to decide that Campbell was the first to find gold, Michel was the first to claim a reward for it and Esmond was the first to sell it. They were each given £1,000, but the government recommended Hargraves receive £5,000 (in addition to the New South Wales reward) for being Australia's gold go-to guy and an all-round top bloke.

Bendigo and Mount Alexander later that year sent shockwaves around the world.

Victoria produced one-third of the world's gold between 1851 and 1861, and its population leaped from 77,000 to 540,000.[2] There were more arrivals in the first two years of the rush than there were convicts in the first sixty-five years of British settlement, with Australia's population tripling by 1861. Things were looking up for Melbourne, which twenty-five years earlier had been nothing more than a glint in Batman's eye.

But before the rise, there was a fall. The Victorian goldfields were much closer to Melbourne than Ophir was to Sydney, resulting in an exodus. The American author Mark Twain wrote:

> This roaring avalanche swept out of Melbourne and left it desolate, Sunday-like, paralysed, everything at a stand-still, the ships lying idle at anchor, all signs of life departed, all sounds stilled save the rasping of the cloud-shadows as they scraped across the vacant streets.

South Australia saw a third of its adult males hotfoot it to Victoria. Lord Robert Cecil, a 22-year-old future prime minister of Great Britain who visited Adelaide in 1852, wrote:

> In consequence of the emigration mania, excited by the discovery of the goldfields, the colonial revenue has for the time almost vanished. The customs, which used to produce £3,000 a week, have fallen to zero, land is unsaleable, property on which £1,500 has been spent has sold for £43.[3]

---

2   These are underestimates, as census collectors didn't count people who didn't count – i.e. Aborigines. Section 127 of the Australian Constitution later stated, "In reckoning the numbers of the people of the Commonwealth, or of a State or other part of the Commonwealth, aboriginal natives should not be counted," ensuring that Indigenous Australians continued not to count until the provision's repeal at the 1967 referendum.

3   Cecil is reputedly the source of the phrase *Bob's your uncle*, meaning "everything's worked out nicely with bugger-all effort", for his habit of giving plum government jobs to his nephew, Lord Balfour.

Most Germans stayed put, saving South Australia from total ruin. As one stolid burgher phlegmatically noted, "We make gold with the plough." However, some, such as Johann Menge, *Völkerwanderunged* across the border. The peripatetic mineralogist, accompanied by fifty German South Australians, walked more than 600 kilometres (far even for him) to mine at Castlemaine.

Victoria welcomed the South Australians, but tried to keep the Tasmanians on their side of Bass Strait by introducing immigration restrictions to prevent ex-convicts from entering the colony and stealing its gold. Ships crossing the strait were quarantined, with police burning sulphur below decks to smoke out stowaways. When Britain overturned these laws, Victoria introduced new ones requiring Tasmanians to carry papers to prove they'd never been convicts.

John West led protests against the Tasmania Card, pointing out that John Pascoe Fawkner, a member of Victoria's inaugural Legislative Council and keen supporter of the laws, was a Tasmanian, the son of a convict, and had himself served time. But Victoria's golden cloud had a silver lining for Tasmania. Worried that people would commit crimes to win a free trip to the goldfields, Britain ended transportation to the island in 1853. With transportation over, Lieutenant-Governor William Denison was determined to wash out the island's convict stain. He wrote to the War and Colonial Office, "There is a feeling here that to the name Van Diemen's Land a certain stigma attaches."

In 1856, Britain accepted Denison's advice to rebrand Van Diemen's Land as Tasmania. This did not stop everybody thinking that Tasmanians were degenerate criminals and/or prostitutes, or Tasmanians from developing a giant chip on their shoulder about their convict past.[4]

---

4   Thomas Reibey, the grandson of teenage cross-dressing horse thief and $20 model Mary Reibey, was the colony's first native-born Anglican clergyman, but resigned after attempting to seduce a young married woman due to inherit an estate for which he was the trustee. This didn't stop "the ecclesiastical debauchee", as he became known, from later serving as Tasmania's premier. While Tasmanians didn't care about Reibey rooting around, they were deeply embarrassed by his convict ancestry. In 1956, the Tasmanian government published *A Century of*

In 1853, almost 78,000 gold-hungry immigrants arrived in Victoria, most of whom were young, skilled, middle-class men. There were youths fresh out of British public school, American 49ers, German intellectuals, Irish republicans, French and Italian revolutionaries, Polish merchants, Hungarian Jews and exotic Chinese.

Caroline Chisholm sent out a contingent of Jewish girls who were seeking husbands in the hope that they might one day become mothers-in-law. The growing Jewish population of Melbourne and Ballarat participated fully in commercial life, which they'd been denied in Britain and Europe for centuries. OK, they weren't allowed into the Melbourne Club, but who really wanted to hang out with a bunch of sloshed *schlemiels*?

The incoming miners at first associated mostly with their own kind. Little Irelands, Americas and Adelaides sprang up in the new shanty suburbs of Richmond and Collingwood. There were tensions – the English thought the Americans considered themselves superior in all things and the Americans agreed. The Irish distrusted the English, the English distrusted the French, and everybody distrusted the Jews, most of whom avoided the manly digging of holes to work as hawkers, auctioneers, jewellers, publicans and tobacconists.

Australia allowed newcomers to reinvent themselves. Rag-and-bone men might become couturiers, and London prostitutes country vicar's daughters.[5] Thirty-four-year-old unmarried Irish mother

---

Responsible Government in Tasmania (oxymoron), which described Reibey as the grandson of Mary Reibey, "a colourful personality of early Sydney".

5   The French didn't bother with this sort of thing. The *Mémoires* of Céleste de Chabrillan, the wife of the French consul-general to Victoria, recounted her days as a teenage prostitute, exotic dancer, scantily clad stunt horserider and courtesan. Céleste was a wry wit who acknowledged that her well-publicised past made her "an object of fear and repugnance to certain members of Melbourne society". While in Australia she wrote a further memoir, the aptly named *A Death at the End of the World*, which won praise from Alexander Dumas. She also wrote twelve novels (three of which were set in Australia), twenty-six plays, seven operettas and countless poems and songs. After her husband died in 1858, she lived a long life as a successful artist in France. During the Franco-Prussian War she founded *Les Soeurs de France* to care for the wounded and converted her grand chalet into a

Clara Lodge transformed into twenty-year-old Clara Du Val, the glamorous actress wife of a famous French painter, sadly deceased. Everyone was too polite to ask how she had a son who would soon need to shave.

By August 1854, Melbourne was a teeming metropolis of 110,000 souls, with a further 115,000 on the nearby goldfields. Fast American cutters and new iron-hulled British steamships connected the city to the wider world, while the American Telegraph Line of Coaches, later rebranded as Cobb & Co, could get you to the goldfields in a day. Australia's first steam train left Flinders Street for Port Melbourne in 1854. The year before, Australia's first telegraph line had connected Melbourne to Williamstown, opening up a world of instant communication.[6]

Money from the goldfields built marble and sandstone palaces, while Redmond Barry oversaw construction of the grand Melbourne Library, filling it with classical statues and friezes to rival the great buildings of Europe and ordering copies of all of the works mentioned in Gibbon's *Decline and Fall of the Roman Empire*. World-famous performers, like Lola Montez with her erotically charged Spider Dance, packed out Melbourne's theatres.[7]

---

home for war orphans. She is without a doubt the most interesting French person to have ever visited Australia.

6   For younger readers, the telegraph was the nineteenth century's equivalent to the internet, but with less porn. It's hard to sext in morse code (-.. --- / .. / -- .- .-. / -.-- --- ..- / .... --- .-. -. -.-- --..-- / -... .- --- -.-- ..--..).

7   Lola, real name Maria Gilbert, wore a spider mask while weaving a web across the stage, before becoming the web-trapped prey and, finally, a woman desperately searching for the spider in her petticoats. Lola's fans would throw flowers, money and gold nuggets at her as she performed (the latter could really hurt). She endeared herself to the miners by christening a new shaft by being lowered into its depths on a rope looped about her foot while drinking a glass of the finest French champagne. They were also amused by her publicly horsewhipping Henry Seekamp, editor of the *Ballarat Times*, following a bad review. During her voyage to Australia, Lola attempted to stab a ship's mate for kicking her dog. A Sydney sheriff tried to arrest her for non-payment of bills on a Melboune-bound steamship, but she stripped naked and taunted him to remove her from her cabin in that state (he didn't). The Irish exotic dancer had affairs with Franz Liszt, Alexandre Dumas, Tsar Nicholas I of Russia and King Ludwig I of Bavaria, the

Melbourne couldn't keep up with the human tidal wave surging into it. The 1852 report of the Select Committee on Melbourne's sewerage grimly noted:

> ... in the backyards and enclosures, more astounding accumulations of putrescent substances and rubbish of all kinds, than I ever inspected in the very worst parts of the dirtiest English or Continental towns: or that I should have thought could have occurred in a civilized community. Many of the foundations of the buildings are greatly injured owing to the saturation of the subsoil by liquid excrementious matter.

The city, which didn't start work on a sewerage system until 1891, earned the unflattering sobriquet of Smellbourne. People packed sardine-like into tents, and shacks incubated deadly flus and fevers, with dysentery claiming the life of French consul-general comte de Chabrillan. Typhus, known as putrid fever for its stench of rotting flesh, was spread by lice – the health-conscious minimised the risk of infection by removing their pubic hair.

Those forced to get a Melbournian while assailed by noxious vapours also had to pay five to six times the price of a London house for the Melbourne equivalent. Wages tripled due to labour shortages and inflation was more rampant than Shane Warne on a spinning pitch.

Flush with cash, successful miners spent big, with a witness reporting, "One man put a £5 note between two pieces of bread and butter and ate it like a sandwich." Lord Robert Cecil, who was something of a wowser when it came to the lower classes enjoying themselves, wrote:

---

latter making her Countess Marie von Landsfeld. Lola lived up to her spider reputation: her second husband drowned in Spain; a German doctor with whom she had an affair was found shot dead in the Californian hills, her third husband the chief suspect; and her fourth husband-cum-manager drowned on the return voyage from Australia after falling overboard while drinking champagne with her. The Black Widow's career waned and she died alone in a New York boarding house in 1861, syphilis having ravaged her body and mind. She was forty-two.

Melbourne thronged with ephemeral plutocrats, generally illiterate, who were hurrying to exchange their gold nuggets for velvet gowns for their wives and unlimited whiskey for themselves, and who made the streets and hotels clamorous with drunken revels which now and again culminated in crimes of audacious violence.

All of the drunken revellers waving gold about proved irresistible to those who lived on the wrong side of the law.

THE BAD BOYS ARE BACK

The bushrangers had gone into hibernation during the 1840s, but gold roused them from their slumbers. Some left their lonely bush tracks to hold up banks, overflowing with bullion and banknotes.[8] Others turned pirate, with twenty desperadoes bailing up the lightly guarded *Nelson* in Melbourne Harbour. They divided up £30,000 worth of bullion on St Kilda Beach, making headlines around the globe.

Bushrangers such as Frank McCallum stuck to what they knew best – leaping out from behind trees on deserted roads, shouting and waving guns about. McCallum, whose bushranger alter ego was Captain Melville, bailed up two miners on Christmas Eve and stole £40 in cash and gold. In keeping with the spirit of the season, he returned £3 to his victims so that they might enjoy Christmas.

Captain Melville did not enjoy Christmas. Like the Christ Child, he'd received a gift of gold, although the men who'd given it to him were clearly not wise. He too had been turned away from the inn, but the Geelong brothel he slept in was better than a manger.[9] And the blessed Melville received a visitation in the morning, although

---

8   In 1854, over £13,000 was stolen from a Ballarat vault. One of the robbers returned to deposit his share, unaware that banks recorded the serial numbers of banknotes. People hadn't yet got the hang of the whole bank-robbing business.

9   The watering hole where Melville enjoyed a few drinks before being turfed out at Christmas Eve closing was named Christy's Inn, consistent with the yuletide vibe.

he would have preferred shepherds to the police who'd followed a reward-seeking prostitute, rather than the traditional star, to arrest him. Judge Redmond Barry, determined to send a message to aspiring gold thieves, sentenced Melville to thirty-two years' hard labour.

Melville, imprisoned on a hulk, was granted three days off a week to translate the Bible into a local Aboriginal language. Instead, he used the time to plan his escape. Melville seized a cutter with nine fellow gaolbirds, including Harry Power, who'd shot and wounded two troopers when they tried to arrest him for horse theft. As the authorities closed in, one of Melville's accomplices murdered a police hostage. Melville and Power were acquitted of escaping, as they'd been sent to the hulk contrary to the terms of their imprisonment. They were also acquitted of being part of a joint enterprise to murder the policeman, with their barrister successfully arguing that as they were not escapees, they were not part of a joint enterprise to escape and were therefore innocent bystanders when the murder took place.

Melville and Power were returned to prison. Melville hanged himself with a scarf after failing to convince a visiting priest to take off all his clothes and let Melville escape in them. Power's escape attempt would be less dramatic, but far more effective – and it would leave an indelible mark on the whiteboard of Australian history.

A DAY ON THE DIGGINGS

Lord Robert Cecil was concerned about being bailed up when travelling by coach to the Victorian goldfields. One would have thought he'd be grateful to have arrived at his destination unmolested, but Cecil took Pommy whingeing to a whole new level. He complained of the "infamous roads", "fagged horses", "characteristic Australian unpunctuality" and his carriage companion, a "coarse, hideous, dirty looking American armed with two pistols in his belt who wore … a pair of ear rings".

Cecil's American friend was a typical miner. English travel writer William Howitt described miners as "wild Backwoods-looking fellows", continuing, "Almost every man had a gun, or pistols in his belt, and a huge dog, half hound half mastiff, led by a chain."

A traveller would be unlikely to sight an Aborigine on the coach ride from Melbourne, with merchant Robert Caldwell observing, "the wild animals and native inhabitants seem to have almost melted away". The miners continued the work the squatters had begun, driving the Wathaurong further into the hills and swamps, although a few of the first people guided prospectors or sold baskets and possum-skin cloaks on the diggings.

Approaching a gold town, the traveller would pass through a lifeless moonscape, pocked with gaping craters from which mud-bespattered miners would periodically emerge to dump their tailings, like ants cleaning out their nests after a storm.

On arriving in town, our traveller would be confronted by a sea of tents. Some of the more established residents built huts in the style of their homelands: the Americans built log cabins, the Germans fashioned neat little houses with pointy roofs, while Irish shacks, according to Howitt, were "more remarkable for their defiance of symmetry than any others".

If arriving between Monday and Saturday, our visitor would find giant hounds guarding empty tents, the miners having left for the diggings. Work down the shafts was tough and many miners were rewarded with nothing but rock and clay. Raffaello Carboni, an Italian revolutionary turned Ballarat gold-hunter, referred to the diggings as "a Nugety Eldorado for the few, a ruinous field of hard labour for many, a profound ditch of Perdition for Body and Soul to all".

But if arriving on a Sunday, our visitor would be swept up by the carnival atmosphere as miners and their families, decked out in their Sunday best, poured out of church to shop, gossip, eat and drink.

Miners bought their food from local stores or mess tents, as most didn't have land of their own on which to grow vegetables or raise chickens. La Trobe had tried to help miners become more self-sufficient by selling them land near the diggings, but squatters and speculators bought it up.

Miners' lack of land barred them from voting. This irked them, as British Chartists, American republicans, Irish nationalists and refugees from the 1848 People's Spring had flocked to the goldfields, carrying their democratic aspirations alongside their picks and shovels.

In the closely packed tent towns, young adventurers, who dressed alike for labour down pit, mixed freely and social barriers dissolved. Englishman John Capper rejoiced, "The equality system here would stun even a Yankee. We have all grades and classes ... The outward garb forms no mark of distinction – we are all mates."[10] "Diggers", the name miners adopted for themselves, had an egalitarian vibe and may have been borrowed from Britain's vegetable-loving communal squatters, the Diggers (True Levellers).[11]

The goldfields called to independent-minded women. Some dug with the men, while others worked as domestics or opened stores – sisters Martha Clendinning and Sarah Holmes, selling baby clothes and breast pumps during the 1854–55 Ballarat baby boom, made more money than most miners.

Jane Fryer, a 22-year-old Chartist making a new life in Ballarat, "refused to wear a wedding-ring, on the grounds that it symbolised servitude to her spouse". She devoted her life to political reform, co-founding the Australian Secular Society, campaigning for women's suffrage and the eight-hour workday, and, in her eighties, addressing rallies opposing World War I conscription. Ballarat's Fanny Smith demanded the right for women to be elected to local council, while

---

10   *Mate*, a convict contraction of *shipmate*, was a friend or associate in Australian goldfields-speak, in contrast to the Californian gold rush *partner* – the Australian term was comradely, the American commercial.

11   The matey term *digger*, taken up by Australian and New Zealand soldiers in World War I, is now only used by old men who buy their first middy of Tooheys Old at nine in the morning and spend the rest of the day talking about greyhounds.

Anastasia Hayes, one of those thought to have sewn the Eureka flag, took on the Catholic Church over equal wages.

Women were in great demand, with diggers rushing to meet ships in the hope of securing a wife or tent-mate. However, many of the incoming women were determined to remain single and earn their own wages, a position that confounded respectable society. Visiting Viennese violinist Miska Hauser marvelled:

> Emancipated wenches in unbecoming riding habits, and with smoking cigars in their mouths, appear on horseback, and crazy gentlemen ... career madly after them and laugh delightedly if a flirtatious equestrienne in a spicy mood aims a mock smack at them with her riding crop.

An 1857 song from the *Colonial Songster* summed up the independent spirit of these new female immigrants:

> *The gals that come out to Australia to roam*
> *Have much higher notions than when they're at home.*

Yet women were not always safe on the diggings, "the wife-bashing capital of the world", where a woman's black eye was known as a "Hobart Town coat of arms".[12]

La Trobe appointed police, soldiers and gold commissioners to keep order on the goldfields. These lawmen lived in camps outside town, their disintegrating tents and moth-eaten uniforms evidence of a shoestring budget. They had no interest in protecting women or anyone else, crime-fighting being a distraction from collecting fees for the hated gold licence or extorting miners found in breach of the numerous goldfields regulations limiting gambling, drinking, swearing and generally having a good time.

---

12   Crime and violence? Blame a Tasmanian. The French referred to domestic violence as "the English disease" – the Englishman is the Frenchman's Tasmanian.

A licence was needed to mine or trade on the diggings, irrespective of gold found or income earned. This was a poll tax, pure and simple, but most of those who paid it had no right to step into a polling booth. American miners reminded their fellow diggers that taxation without representation had triggered the American Revolution. Shouldn't every Australian enjoy the same rights as Americans, and be free to talk loudly about things they knew nothing about, condescend to foreigners and own a bigger armoury than New Zealand?

What's worse, the miners were denied the inalienable Australian right to get on the piss, as La Trobe banned the sale of alcohol in an attempt to maintain order and stop drunk diggers falling down mineshafts.[13] This was a bridge too far.

Sly grog tents, mostly operated by women, sprang up, selling watered-down spirits spiked with tobacco juice for an extra kick. The police burned down the canvas speak-easies or took bribes to ignore them, further hardening anti-police sentiment.

In 1853, Bendigo miners wore red ribbons and paid only a third of the gold licence fee in an act of civil disobedience. They gathered more than 23,000 signatures for a petition against the licence, and 12,000 miners marched through the streets in protest.

William Dexter designed a flag for the miners to rally around, but his jumbled pick, shovel, mining cradle, bundle of sticks and kangaroo and emu creation was something that Pro Hart and Ken Done would have dreamed up after a night on magic mushrooms – just looking at it made the miners nauseous. Dexter also urged the protesters to demand "women having the vote as well as men", which was cloud-cuckoo-land stuff.[14]

---

13   In the days before OH&S consultants would come to your office, raise your desk by a fraction of an inch and make you sit on a ridiculous rubber ball, there was little interest in workplace safety. Miners were not required to cover their mineshafts. The only requirement was to tie a red rag near the shaft entrance, which made no difference whatsoever at night.

14   William Dexter's wife, Caroline, was "London's apostle of Bloomerism". Caroline, who tirelessly promoted the wearing of big puffy underpants in Britain, was a

Bendigonians, who are mild-mannered by nature, still celebrate the Red Ribbon Agitation. As far as the people of Ballarat were concerned, the Bendigonians could keep their wussy agitation, with its little ribbons, funny flags and polite petitions. Ballarat would stage a capital-R Rebellion.

CHILDREN OF THE REVOLUTION

Ballarat had transformed from an isolated sheep station into a thriving town in three short years. Of the 32,000 people living there in late 1854, 9,000 were Catholics, most of whom were Irish. The Irish pitched their tents on Eureka Flat.

Henry Seekamp, editor of the *Ballarat Times*, had hooked up with Clara Du Val, who'd run away from the theatre to join the paper. The *Times* was unabashedly pro-miner and anti-government, with Ellen Young penning poems about the oppressed digger, and George Lang, John Dunmore Lang's Chartist son, writing about the need to redistribute power and wealth.[15]

Things were looking up for the miners in June 1854. Pubs were permitted on the goldfields for the first time and James Bentley's Eureka Hotel was soon the centre of town life. Patrons could enjoy a mint julep in its San Francisco–style saloon, discuss the latest find over a game of billiards or score a strike in the pub's ninety-foot bowling alley (with en suite bar). The £30,000 pleasure palace even had two toilets!

confidante of the trouser-wearing, cigar-chomping French female novelist George Sand. Caroline came to Australia in 1854, divorced William, published Australia's first "Ladies Almanack", and founded the Institute of Hygiene, which railed against close-fitting corsets and promoted the wearing of well-ventilated divided skirts.

15 George Lang, manager of the Bank of New South Wales in Ballarat, was particularly keen on redistributing wealth to himself. He was caught embezzling £9,000 from the bank and sentenced to five years' hard labour. Refusing to admit his son's guilt, John Dunmore Lang accused the judge of bias and the bank's investigator of "a degree of low-bred brutal malignity worthy only of an incarnate daemon". He was gaoled for six months for criminal libel.

La Trobe left Victoria that month to marry his sister-in-law and it was hoped his successor, Lieutenant-Governor Sir Charles Hotham, would see reason and abolish the hated gold licence.

Hotham was welcomed as a hero on his tour of the goldfields. Bendigo erected triumphal arches, flew flags and let loose its oompah band as Hotham's carriage was pulled into town by a team of sweaty miners. Ballarat proudly showed him recent gold finds and plied him with mint juleps, while Lady Jane Hotham tramped gaily through the mud and entertained the miners with her earthy humour. Hotham promised to unlock farmland for the diggers and made sympathetic noises about the licence.

But the new lieutenant-governor soon showed his true colours. Determined to curb spending, he served local beer, rather than French champagne, at a vice-regal ball. The beer, brewed with Smellbourne water, made his guests violently ill. "The Small Beer Governor", as he became known, had shown he was tight on the shout – and there's nothing more un-Australian than that.

Showing Hotham shiny nuggets and miners drinking fancy cocktails over a game of bowls had been a tactical mistake. Not only could miners afford the licence fee, Hotham reasoned, they could afford to pay more. He ordered the gold commissioners to increase licence inspections.

James Johnston, Ballarat's assistant gold commissioner, led the "digger hunts", as these inspections were known. Diggers without licences would be arrested if lucky, and be arrested, assaulted and have their tent burned down if not. Johnston, the most hated man on the diggings, was the Dick Dastardly of Ballarat. He was also the nephew of George Johnston, who'd put down Australia's first rebellion at Castle Hill in 1804 and led the Rum Rebellion against Governor Bligh in 1808. If you wanted to stage a rebellion in Australia, then you needed to invite a Johnston.

Johnston was holding up to five digger hunts a week by October 1854 and anti-government sentiment was at an all-time high. On 6 October, James Scobie, a young Scots miner, broke into the Eureka Hotel after closing and called Catherine Bentley a whore after she refused him a drink. Scobie was pursued by bar staff and beaten to death that night.

Four days later, Johannes Gregorious, the disabled Armenian servant of Ballarat's Catholic priest, was pulled up during a digger hunt. Gregorious found it difficult to explain he was exempt from the licence, partly because of his halting English and partly because he was having seven colours of shit beaten out of him. After the policeman let up, his horse had a go, trampling the unfortunate Armenian. Johnston then charged Gregorious with assaulting a police officer and fined him £10. At the same time, the authorities found the Bentleys had no case to answer for Scobie's death.

Ballarat exploded. A wealthy businessman with friends in high places was to walk free after murdering a miner, and a humble servant of the church had been beaten and fitted up by the police.

On 17 October, 5,000 protesters pelted the Eureka Hotel with stones. Gold Commissioner Robert Rede pleaded for calm, but the mob was not to be denied. The uninsured Eureka was stormed, looted and burned to the ground.

Fearing further riots, the government charged the Bentleys and two bar staff with Scobie's murder. Three men were charged with arson for razing the Eureka.

More than 4,000 angry miners, convinced that the Eureka Three had been cast as unwilling stars of a government show trial, held a protest meeting the next day. At the rally, Welsh Chartist John Basson Humffray proposed the establishment of a Digger's Rights Society to defend the right of every digger to burn down someone else's hotel.

The *Ballarat Times* complained, "We are worse off than Russian serfs or American slaves" and called for the expulsion of government officials from the goldfields. Sarah Hanmer, the proprietress and leading lady of Ballarat's Adelphi Theatre, staged a benefit concert for the Eureka Three, while the police and troopers hunkered down and waited for reinforcements to arrive.

On 11 November, 10,000 miners gathered at Bakery Hill to form the Ballarat Reform League, which was largely bankrolled by Sarah Hanmer and operated out of her theatre. The league's charter – drafted by Humffray, Chartist lecturer George Black, Irishman Timothy Hayes, Scot Thomas Kennedy and German republican Frederick Vern – called for the abolition of the licence, the relaxation of regulations on the goldfields, the opening up of farmland for miners and the adoption of the 1838 People's Charter. This, Seekamp trumpeted, was "the draft prospectus of Australian Independence".

The miners had a cause and nobody loved a cause more than Caroline Chisholm. The gold rush had put her out of business, as the colonies no longer needed her immigrants. She'd left London for Port Phillip, and the Victorian government, overjoyed that she'd chosen Melbourne over Sydney, gave her £5,000. Chisholm, who was near bankrupt, used the money to open a small shop – and to campaign against the government's treatment of the miners.

Chisholm embarked on a study tour of the diggings. She recommended that shelter sheds be built between Melbourne and the goldfields to offer protection against bushrangers and provide weary travellers with "good pudding". She criticised the gold licence as unjust and called on the government to release land to the diggers. At a speech in Melbourne on 17 November, she warned, "If something is not done to remove the difficulties under which these men are placed, the consequences will be terribly felt."

Judge Redmond Barry heard the Scobie case the morning after Chisholm's speech and sentenced Mr Bentley and his bar staff to three years' hard labour for manslaughter. On the same day, he sentenced the Eureka Three to between three and six months' gaol.

Humffray, Black and Kennedy met Hotham to present their charter and demand the release of the Eureka Three. Hotham did what any politician will do to buy time – he agreed to an inquiry. The delegation said the lieutenant-governor's establishment of the

Goldfields Commission to consider their grievances did not go far enough. Hotham ordered another 150 troops to Ballarat.

Hotham, however, did not favour a military response. He reported to the Colonial Office that troops wouldn't be able to march more than four abreast without falling down mineshafts and that the diggers would simply disappear into their tunnels, like Victorian Viet Cong. He believed that love, not war, was the answer and that encouraging more women to move to the goldfields would soothe the miners' fury. But things spiralled out of control before he could put his hippy plan into action.

On 28 November, Ballarat's American miners celebrated Thanksgiving by drinking bourbon and doing something horrible to a turkey. They also drunkenly declared that Ballarat should become an independent republic. That night, miners attacked the troop reinforcements marching into town, shooting a little drummer boy.[16]

The next morning, 15,000 people met at Bakery Hill to burn their licences. A giant blue flag emblazoned with the Southern Cross suspended upon a white cross was hoisted atop an eighty-foot pole by Canadian digger Henry Ross. Raffaello Carboni recounted:

> I called on all my fellow-diggers, irrespective of nationality, religion, and colour, to salute the "Southern Cross" as the refuge of all the oppressed from all the countries on earth.[17]

The authorities considered the miners' replacement of the Union Jack with the Eureka flag an act of treason. On 30 November, James Johnston responded with the largest digger hunt yet, knowing that the miners had consigned their licences to the flames. When eight miners were arrested, troopers were pulled from their horses and police stoned.

16 Pa rum pum pum pum.

17 This unifying symbol of national, religious and racial tolerance is now tattooed onto people called Wazza and Ferret who want Asians to take their halal muck with them on the boat back to Asiastan.

Police fired warning shots and Commissioner Rede read the Riot Act, ordering the crowd to disperse. The arrested miners were taken to the lockup. The diggers downed tools and gathered around the Eureka flag. A young Irish miner, Peter Lalor, took to the stage and said one word:

LIBERTY!

A short speech was a good speech, as far as the diggers were concerned. The more militant among them elected Lalor their leader, splitting from Humffray, who advocated nonviolent protest and negotiation. Peter Lalor was the son of Patrick Lalor, an Irish MP and Home Rule campaigner, and brother of James Fintan Lalor, a leader of the Young Ireland movement, although Peter had steered clear of republican politics in the old country.

A cadre of would-be revolutionaries gathered around him. Black, Kennedy, Hayes, Vern, Carboni and Ross were joined by Irishmen Patrick Howard, Patrick Curtain and John Manning, and Edward Thonen, a Prussian Jewish lemonade seller. James McGill took charge of 200 mounted Americans who called themselves the Independent Californian Rangers, brandished revolvers and Mexican knives and said "Yee-hah!" a lot.

Lalor commandeered firearms and instructed Ballarat's blacksmiths to forge pikes. This was when warning bells should have started to ring for his followers. The pike, essentially a long pointy metal stick, was the Irish revolutionary's weapon of choice, despite everyone else having switched to guns and cannons centuries earlier. Irish republicans loved charging British musket lines with their trusty pikes (although not for long). The pike was the enduring symbol of Irish heroic failure.[18]

---

18   The Battle of the Eureka Stockade was one of the world's last epic pike fails. However, it was the English, rather than the Irish, who were responsible for history's last pike disaster. In 1941, Prime Minister Winston Churchill was concerned that many of Britain's Home Guard were unarmed. He sent a memo to the War Office, replete with his usual dry wit, that "every man must have a weapon of some sort, be it only a mace or a pike". The War Office took him at his word and manufactured a quarter of a million pikes to defend Britain's beaches

The bells should have rung louder when Lalor decided to build a stockade on Eureka Flat, rather than on higher ground. The Eureka Stockade, like Ballarat's Irish shacks, was remarkable for its defiance of symmetry, the traditional circular defensive structure eschewed for a drunken parallelogram of planks, barrels, carts and bits of rope, straight from the set of a school production of *Les Mis*. The stockade, only three foot high in parts, may have held off a leprechaun attack, but was good for bugger-all else.

It was time to pull out the earplugs when Lalor chose "Vinegar Hill" as the password to enter the stockade. The first Battle of Vinegar Hill had resulted in the annihilation of Irish republican forces, ending the Irish Rebellion of 1798, while the second battle of that name saw George Johnston's ninety-three troops defeat 300 predominantly Irish revolutionaries at Castle Hill. If you wanted a name associated with Irish military defeat at the hands of British forces, you couldn't do better than Vinegar Hill.

Lalor's choice of Irish nationalist symbols alienated the non-Irish and non-Catholic. He tried to rekindle their enthusiasm by returning the stockade's flag to Bakery Hill, saluting it and pledging, "We swear by the Southern Cross to stand truly by each other, and fight to defend our rights and liberties."

On the evening of Saturday 2 December, most of the stockade's defenders drifted back to their tents, secure in the knowledge that the troops wouldn't attack on the Sabbath. They were wrong. Australia's own Bloody Sunday started at 3 a.m., when 282 troopers and police under the command of Captain John Thomas stormed the stockade. Most of the 150 remaining defenders were asleep, although American barber Robert Burnett is credited with firing the first shot in the Battle of the Eureka Stockade.

---

against the Nazis' new light machine guns. Lord Croft, the under-secretary of state for war, defended the pike as "a most effective and silent weapon", earning him a lifetime of ridicule (except in Ireland).

The rebels were completely outgunned, particularly as some of their firearms were props from Sarah Hanmer's theatre. They surrendered within twenty minutes.

But the police continued shooting, ignoring Thomas's order to stand down. The wounded were bayoneted and, according to one witness, a woman "was mercilessly butchered by a mounted trooper while pleading for the life of her husband". Tents were set alight, with John Sheehan's wife and children burned alive. Ballarat's Eureka Memorial honours twenty-two digger and six soldier casualties, but ignores the women and children killed.

The Eureka flag was taken down by Constable John King, with the victors trampling it and taking scraps for trophies. Peter Lalor, his left arm shattered by the troopers' fire, escaped in the confusion. Frederick Vern and James McGill fled Ballarat dressed as women. One hundred and fourteen prisoners, including those with serious injuries, were crammed into a tiny wooden cell and the captured leaders charged with treason.[19]

As the smoke was still clearing, Henry Seekamp set his press with the words, "This foul and bloody murder calls to High Heaven for vengeance, terrible and immediate." He was arrested for sedition before the paper went to print, but Clara du Val published his words in the *Ballarat Times* later that morning.

Clara took over the running of the paper, her New Year's Day editorial perfectly capturing the spirit that moved the rebels of Eureka:

> What is this country else but Australia? Is it any more England than it is Ireland or Scotland, France or America, Italy or Germany? Is the population, wealth, intelligence, enterprise and learning wholly and solely English? No, the population of Australia is not

---

19 In his book *The Irish in Australia*, historian Patrick O'Farrell argues the Eureka uprising was typical of Irish rebellions – it was "just as incompetent, just as doomed, just as confused as to objectives and ideology – and just as much a mixture of the glorious, the farcical, and the stupid".

English, but Australian ... The latest immigrant is the youngest
Australian.

And who could argue with that?

THE PEOPLE PREVAIL

Hotham put Australians in the same basket as the Tooth Fairy and the
Easter Bunny. There were only two types of people on the goldfields:
Britons and foreigners. Britons, by definition, were loyal to the queen.
Therefore the rebels must have been led by a foreigner. Hotham's
money was on the German guy in the dress, so a £500 reward was
offered for the capture of Frederick Vern.

A £200 bounty was placed on Lalor's head. The rebel leader,
recovering from the amputation of his left arm, was being sheltered
in Geelong by Alicia Dunn, his schoolmistress fiancée.[20] If captured,
he'd be tried for high treason, like thirteen of his followers – and the
penalty for high treason was death.

Hotham chose the first defendant for his post-Eureka trials carefully. John Joseph was an American, so the jury would naturally
assume him to be a gun-toting, redneck republican. As an added
bonus, Joseph was black, so the jury would naturally assume him to
be guilty. Hotham was flabbergasted when Joseph was acquitted and
carried in triumph through the streets of Melbourne by 10,000 miners.

The acquittals continued. Raffaello Carboni was found not guilty,
despite eight witnesses testifying he'd attacked them with a pike. The
last six defendants were tried together before Redmond Barry on 27
March 1855. All walked free.[21]

---

20 Lalor had more left arms than a Hindu god, with several doctors later claiming
    credit for the amputation.

21 The Eureka rebels were defended by the dashing Irish barrister Richard Ireland.
    Ireland regarded practice of the law as a necessary inconvenience to finance his
    true passions – drinking and adultery. The *Australian Dictionary of Biography*
    portrays Ireland as a nineteenth-century Cleaver Greene: "Ireland was neither

It was now clear that Melbournians supported the miners and condemned the actions of the government. Henry Seekamp, the only person associated with the rebellion to serve time, was released after Clara Du Val presented a petition for his freedom signed by 30,000 Victorians.[22]

The Goldfields Commission reported on the same day that the last of the rebels were acquitted. It found the treatment of the miners "repugnant to British experience and derogatory to the manly feeling of independence" and recommended replacing the gold licence with an export duty, so miners would be taxed only for gold they sold. In return for paying for a miner's right, they ought to be allowed to dig, vote and occupy vacant land. Popularly elected magistrates should resolve disputes on the diggings and government officials should abandon their apartheid camps to live in the community.

The government, defeated, accepted these recommendations. It even funded Caroline Chisholm's shelter sheds, which became known as Chisholm Shakedowns. Raffaello Carboni was chosen as a mining magistrate and John Humffray and Peter Lalor, now out of hiding, were elected as Ballarat's representatives on the Legislative Council. The two now sat in the government chamber with the increasingly uncomfortable Hotham.

Karl Marx, almost wetting himself with excitement, wrote that Eureka was "the symptom of a general revolutionary movement in Victoria". The socialist revolution would begin in Melbourne, where the proletariat would rise up like the froth on a Brunswick Street cappuccino to smash the small wine bars and beard-grooming salons of the Collins Street bourgeoisie.

---

industrious nor learned and resorted to alcohol for his best performances, but few juries could resist his shrewd mixture of eloquence, wit and vituperation."

22 Seekamp and Du Val later separated, with the newspaperman demonstrating the same capacity for reinvention as his former partner. He moved to Brisbane, where he offered French lessons as Monsieur Henri Seekamp, a professor of Paris's *Institute Chatelaine*. Henry Seekamp died of "natural causes accelerated by intemperance" in 1864, aged just thirty-five.

WENTWORTH AND THE WORKING MAN

William Charles Wentworth had moved from London to Brussels so that he wouldn't have to travel far to holiday in Paris. He regularly popped over the border to shoot pheasants in the grounds of a rented château and twice visited Rome to sit for the renowned sculptor Pietro Tenerani, whom he'd commissioned to make a life-sized statue of William Charles Wentworth.[23]

Wentworth crossed the English Channel to lobby MPs to support his New South Wales constitution, which was passed in July 1855. Victoria and Tasmania were given self-government later that year, with South Australia following in 1856. Western Australia, however, would have to wait until 1890 to run its own affairs.

Stuart Donaldson was New South Wales' inaugural prime minister, as premiers were then known. He lasted only three months in the job, as the absence of political parties resulted in unstable government.[24]

Still, Wentworth was hailed as the father of Australian representative government, an achievement acknowledged by Henry Parkes, who proposed that a portrait of his rival hang in the Legislative Assembly. Wentworth's crusty visage, with crossed eyes and port-flushed nose, still gazes down upon the lesser figures who govern New South Wales today.

But it was Victoria, reeling from the heady fumes of Eureka, that transformed Australian and world politics. Mark Twain wrote of Eureka and the democratic reforms that flowed from it:

---

23 Tenerani had recently made a statue of Simón Bolívar, who'd liberated much of Latin America from Spanish colonial rule. Wentworth saw himself as an Australian Bolívar, who would bring self-government to the Australian people – although he would do so while enjoying pheasant pâté and a cheeky little Beaujolais, rather than slogging through the Venezuelan jungle.

24 Donaldson is best remembered for participating in the last-known Australian duel in 1851, after criticising Sir Major Thomas Mitchell's management of the surveying budget. Mitchell put a bullet through Donaldson's hat and the two men loathed each other thereafter.

I think it may be called the finest thing in Australasian history. It was a revolution – small in size; but great politically; it was a strike for liberty, a struggle for principle, a stand against injustice and oppression ... It is another instance of a victory won by a lost battle.

In 1855, Victoria removed property qualifications for the lower house, allowing working-class men to seek election to the legislature, and provided for an elected, rather than appointed, upper house. The other colonies gradually followed.

William Nicholson, the proto-hipster who served Melbourne its first cup of steam-powered coffee, now served on Victoria's Legislative Council, where he successfully lobbied for the secret ballot. In 1856, Victoria was the first place in the world to allow the voter to choose from a list of candidates in the privacy of a cosy little booth. London's *Times* labelled this anonymity in voting a "vile system", yet the Australian ballot, as it is now known, was adopted by Britain in 1872 and American states from 1888. It is now used around the globe.[25]

South Australia's democratic reforms of the 1850s owe much to a group of fifty working men who met in an Adelaide pub to design an ideal system of government. After a couple of shandies, they decided that all men over the age of twenty-one should have the vote. In 1856, South Australia became the first colony to embrace universal manhood suffrage, sixty-two years before Britain – although all men did not achieve the vote in Australia until 1965.[26]

---

25 Tasmania and South Australia also like to claim credit for the modern secret ballot. In early Victorian elections, officials wrote the voter's electoral number on their ballot, making their vote theoretically traceable. Tasmania, in its 1856 election, dispensed with this. In 1858, South Australia abandoned the Victorian practice of crossing out the names of non-preferred candidates, instead requiring voters to put a cross in a printed square beside their chosen candidate, the method commonly used today.

26 While Indigenous men could vote in most colonial elections, they were not encouraged to do so. But then Queensland, in 1885, and Western Australia, in 1893, banned them from voting, as did the Australian government in 1902, when it excluded "any Aboriginal native of Australia, Asia, Africa, or the islands of the Pacific, except New Zealand" from the federal vote, unless they'd enrolled

While it is commonly believed New Zealand led the world in granting women the vote in 1893, Victoria extended the vote to all "persons" who paid municipal rates in 1863. This was, of course, an embarrassing accident. When it was pointed out that some women paid rates and those women were "persons", surprised politicians were forced to accept women voting in the 1864 Victorian election. Victoria, a laughing-stock around the globe, moved swiftly to add the word "male" before "persons" after the new parliament convened. Nevertheless, women's suffrage was rolled out across Australia between 1894 and 1908, with Australia a world leader in promoting (non-Indigenous) women's voting rights.

The extension of the vote to working-class men meant politicians had to consider working-class interests. The shortage of labour during the gold rush also increased the bargaining power of workers. And the Holy Grail for workers was the eight-hour workday.

The eight-hour workday was proposed by Welsh socialist Robert Owen in 1817. Owen came up with the catchy slogan, "Eight hours labour, eight hours recreation, eight hours rest". But it was in Australia that the eight-hour movement really took off, leading Karl Marx to enthuse once more that Australia would become the world's model socialist state.

In 1855, New South Wales stonemasons went on strike and won an eight-hour workday, although their wages were reduced. In 1856, Melbourne's stonemasons downed tools and marched on Parliament House. The Victorian government agreed that workers employed on public works should enjoy an eight-hour day with no loss of pay.

On 12 May that year, representatives of nineteen trades marched through the streets of Melbourne to celebrate, with a brewery float handing out free beer and the tobacconists hurling carcinogens into

---

before 1901. Australian Aboriginal and Torres Strait Islander people were not all able to vote until 1965, when Queensland, the last bastion of White Australia, opened its polling booths, if not all its pubs and public swimming pools, to Indigenous Australians.

the crowd. The eight-hour workday was adopted in every Australian workplace by the 1920s. Today, every Australian state and territory celebrates workers getting time off work by giving them more time off work, honouring the stonemasons' fair dinkum victory with a public holiday.[27]

Peter Lalor, elected to Victoria's first Legislative Assembly, enjoyed a distinguished political career, serving as postmaster-general, commissioner of trade and customs and speaker of the assembly. But the son of an Irish republican family who'd espoused Chartist ideals before Eureka condemned Chartism and republicanism after being elected to parliament. Lalor voted against giving unpropertied men the vote and, as the later owner of a profitable goldmine, cracked down on miners who protested a wage cut by introducing Chinese scab labour.

The loss of his left arm had made Lalor swing to the right.

THEY ALL LOOK THE SAME

One group of diggers was excluded from this new egalitarian Australia.

The Chinese.

Ahuto, the earliest-recorded Chinese settler, shipped out in 1803 to work as a carpenter. Mak Sai Ying arrived in 1818, married an English woman and ran Parramatta's Lion Hotel. They were welcomed into the community, as were Queng and Tchiou, who worked on John Dunmore Lang's estate from 1827.

Anti-Chinese sentiment in the British Empire grew during the 1839–42 Opium War, with the 1842 *Encyclopaedia Britannica* informing its readers:

27 *Fair dinkum* means "genuine" or "honest" in Australian slang and the term *dinky-di*, meaning "truly Australian", springs from it. It does not derive from the Cantonese *din kum* (real gold) or the Mandarin *ding kam* (top gold), as suggested by those who believe the term was introduced by Chinese gold-diggers. *Dinkum* was originally a Lincolnshire dialect term for "work" – so fair dinkum meant fair work and probably had its origins in mid-nineteenth century Australian industrial disputes.

> A Chinaman is cold, cunning and distrustful; always ready to take
> advantage of those he has to deal with; is extremely covetous and
> deceitful, quarrelsome, vindictive, but timid and dastardly.

This was at odds with the early Australian experience, which was:
"A Chinaman is hard working, polite and will do all the shit jobs for
about 40 per cent of the cost of a European worker."

In 1848, squatters arranged for 120 Chinese workers to be shipped
to Sydney, as restrictions had been imposed on Kanaka and Indian
coolie labourers. Robert Towns, Wentworth's brother-in-law, imported
a further 2,500 Chinese labourers over the next five years.[28]

When the first Chinese labourers disembarked in Geelong, the
Argus praised their good nature and orderly behaviour. The *Corio
Chronicle*, reporting on the same event, described "the cut-throat
and barbarian" Chinese, "like so many wild beasts", fighting "in an
infuriated state of drunkenness". Australia's demonisation of the
Chinese had begun.

While the occasional Chinaman had been a novelty, larger groups
triggered a hostile response. The Chinese were *different* – they were
typically less than 150 centimetres tall; the fronts of their heads
were shaved, with a ponytail at the back; they wore soft slippers or
sandals, loose tops, baggy breeches and conical straw hats; and they
carried their goods in baskets slung from a bamboo pole carried over
their shoulders.

Thomas Smeaton, a bank manager who observed the unloading
of a Chinese passenger ship, wrote, "the passengers were alike and
undistinguishable. All Chinese, all men, all with mooney faces, all
with pig-tails."

Many Australians never knew which Chinese person they were
speaking to – and the inscrutable responses they received to questions

---

28 Towns was an enthusiastic exploiter of foreign labour. He later employed cheap
     Kanaka workers in establishing cotton farming in Queensland. The Queensland
     town of Townsville is named after him.

or commands were frankly unsettling. Couldn't the Chinese show some emotion, or swear, or get drunk like normal people?[29]

Still, most of the Chinese disappeared onto squatters' runs to do things with sheep and were rarely seen in the towns. While they were out of sight, they were out of mind. But things changed in 1851, when Louey Ah Mouy, a builder's labourer working in Melbourne, wrote to his brother about the discovery of gold. The letter sparked a rush of Chinese to Australia, which emigration agents marketed as "New Gold Mountain" (California being the first Gold Mountain). More than 100,000 Chinese people, most from coastal Canton, arrived between 1852 and 1900. They were the third-largest Australian immigrant group in the nineteenth century, after the British and Germans.

The new arrivals were, almost without exception, men.[30] Most had no desire to settle in Australia – they would mine for two or three years, often to work off debts in China, and then return to their families. A few, however, settled permanently and married local women, usually refugees from Ireland who, following Orphangate, were also targets of discrimination.[31]

---

29   The inability of Australians to identify individual Chinese people is a recurrent theme in Australian history. Police on the goldfields later had blank summons forms to serve on arrested Chinamen, justifying these illegal arrests on the basis that they couldn't understand Chinese names. Chinese criminals, the police complained, would slip away while police were trying to establish their identity and stand next to their nearest countryman, preventing police from ever finding them again "in consequence of their peculiar similarity of personal appearance".

30   Victoria recorded 25,424 Chinese men in the colony in 1857, but only three Chinese women. The 1861 New South Wales census recorded 38,337 Chinese men and eleven Chinese women.

31   The Chinese arrived at a time when the British Empire was obsessed by miscegenation (breeding between the races). The prevailing view was that Asians having sexual relations with Europeans would, in the words of James Stephen, "debase by their intermixture the noble European race". In 1866, Dr Langdon Down wrote *Observations on an Ethnic Classification of Idiots*, in which he claimed Caucasian "idiots" commonly displayed the characteristics of other races. He was particularly interested in a group of children he believed displayed Mongolian characteristics. These children were referred to as Mongoloids, but are now

By 1855, hundreds of Chinese lived in a tent village outside Melbourne, with similar enclaves on the goldfields. Communities were run by clan groups or triads that resolved disputes, administered punishments, ensured the sick and poor were cared for, and found immigrants employment. Triads like Sheathed Sword also smuggled goods and operated illegal gambling and opium dens.[32]

The gold rush turned anti-Chinese sentiment up to 11. The Bendigo press wrote of the "disgusting practices, fearful immorality and unknown vices" of the new goldfield arrivals. Less discreet critics were more specific.

Sexual immorality was top of the list. Australia had been invaded by an army of short, slight men with long hair and feminine slippers. The Chinese were clearly a race of sodomites who'd come here to corrupt the flower of Australian youth.[33]

In 1855, the *Argus*, which had earlier championed Chinese immigration, reported, "A large number of Chinese had arrived in the colony, many of whom had disgusting and filthy pictures, which they exposed to sell." The Chinese were now foreign gay pornographers.

Others told tales of Chinese "dens of infamy and immorality", where "abandoned European women" succumbed to opium and other "vices which would never enter the head of a European". Who were these foreign gay pornographers who plied our women with party drugs so they could have their wicked way with them in a foreign gay way?

Frederick Standish, who became Victoria's chief commissioner of police in 1858, claimed Chinese men had "a penchant for the young",

---

diagnosed with Down syndrome, named after the good doctor. Sadly, others used Down's work to claim that Europeans with Asian ancestry were more likely to "racially degrade" into "idiots", while Down believed that the races shared a common humanity.

32 Sheathed Sword was later incorporated into the Victorian Freemasons. I told you Masons get up to some crazy shit.

33 Tasmanians were thrilled by this characterisation, as there was now a group of people in Australia considered gayer than them.

while the *Ballarat Star* called for laws to prevent "a wholesale system of debauching, by Chinese, of girls of tender years".[34]

The Chinese were not only foreign gay drug-dealing pederast pornographers who wanted our women, but also notorious carriers of disease. When a European child contracted smallpox in Melbourne, the city's Chinese were ordered to have vaccinations.

Victorian MP Richard Vale announced that the yellow skin of Chinese people was the result of leprosy, to which they were otherwise immune. In the resulting hysteria, people believed they could catch leprosy from Chinese clothing, furniture or vegetables. The Member for Ballarat West, C.E. Jones, expressed concern that rabbits would burrow under Chinese cots, catch leprosy, be trapped by small boys and put in pies, thereby infecting entire families.[35]

The Chinese stole and gambled. They killed children. They ate puppies and rats. They crippled their daughters by binding their feet. They burned money in funny temples. They muddied water-holes on the diggings. They worked on the Sabbath. They were the vanguard of a Russian invasion of Melbourne. A century later, they

---

34 You had to be worried if Standish thought you were a deviant. Today, Standish would be diagnosed as a gambling and sex addict. In his youth, "no backer of horses was better known or more liked upon English racecourses", with gambling debts forcing him to sell his estate and leave for Australia. He sold sly grog on the goldfields, before being made Bendigo's assistant goldfields commissioner and then the colony's first Chinese protector. Standish's appointment as chief commissioner of police allowed him to indulge in libertine pursuits without fear of arrest – he once hosted a dinner where the room was decorated with naked women, "the whiteness of their forms contrasting with the black velvet of the chairs" on which they were artistically arranged. A habitué of high-end gentlemen's clubs, he served as royal pimp during the 1867 Melbourne visit of Prince Alfred, Queen Victoria's second son, infamously taking him to the uptown brothel run by Sarah "Mother" Fraser. It was rumoured that, after the prince left town, Mother Fraser put up a "By Royal Appointment" sign beside her red light, and Standish had to persuade her to take it down. Oh, and Standish was the provincial grand master of the Victorian Freemasons. Masons get up to some *really* crazy shit.

35 This was similar to the 1980s AIDS crisis, when it was commonly believed AIDS could be contracted from sitting on a public toilet seat, having a homosexual borrow your office coffee mug, or watching a Cher music video.

would have been standing on the grassy knoll, poisoning country people with fluoride and keeping Elvis in a cage to harvest his bile for use as an aphrodisiac.

The real reason many miners disliked the Chinese was that they were bloody good at finding gold. Louey Ah Mouy made a fortune digging near Yea. He opened Chinese-worked mines across Victoria and Malaysia and became a prominent merchant, banker and leader of Melbourne's Chinese community.

A claim normally worked by two diggers might attract ten Chinese miners, who would comb every square millimetre. The Chinese would purchase a claim from diggers who were convinced there was no gold to be found, fiddle around with its feng shui and turn up in town the next day with bags full of nuggets.

The Goldfields Commission voiced early fears of the Yellow Peril:

> The question of the influx of such large numbers of a pagan and inferior race is a very serious one ... and comprises an unpleasant possibility of the future, that a comparative handful of colonists may be buried in a countless throng of Chinamen.

Hotham responded with the White Victoria Policy – tough on Chinamen, tough on the causes of Chinamen. It was one of his last acts before dying of a chill contracted while opening Melbourne's first gasworks. His *Chinese Immigration Act* required ships' captains to declare any Chinese passengers at customs and pay £10 for each one unloaded in Victoria. Captains would also be limited to one Chinaman per ten tons of ship.

Frederick Standish, as Bendigo's Chinese protector, was charged with keeping Chinese diggers in their own camps and protecting them on the diggings. Chinese diggers were forced to cover Standish's costs, but the government received few complaints about this protection racket (probably because it charged Chinese £2 to make a complaint).

FIG. 10: "I'M SORRY, SIR, BUT YOU HAVE EXCEEDED
YOUR DUTY-FREE ALLOWANCE BY HALF A CHINAMAN."

The *Chinese Immigration Act* was remarkably effective in stopping
Chinese entering Victorian ports, but the Chinese were cunning ...
They simply disembarked at Robe, just over the South Australian
border. More than 20,000 landed in the tiny town in 1857, before
embarking on the twenty-five-day Long March to Victoria's goldfields.

John Pascoe Fawkner had had enough. There were more of the
scruteless little blighters than ever. In mid-1857, he formed a parliamentary committee to:

> ... control the flood of Chinese immigration ... and effectually pre-
> vent the gold-fields of Australia from becoming the property of the
> Emperor of China and of the Mongolian and Tartar hordes of Asia.

Victoria then discovered that if the dog whistle is blown for long
enough, the hounds stop barking and start biting.

ROLL UP, ROLL UP, ROLL UP!

In May 1857, forty diggers at Buckland River in the Victorian Alps burned Chinese tents and property and seriously assaulted two Chinese miners. In June, the diggers of Ararat beat Chinese miners with timber poles.

On 4 July 1857, Buckland diggers met to discuss the Chinese problem. The solution was an all-out attack on the Chinese camp. Seven hundred and fifty tents and thirty stores were razed, the Chinese temple pulled down and more than a thousand Chinese pursued for seven miles. Several drowned as they were forced across the Buckland River.

The coroner ruled that the drowned Chinese had been "labouring under debility consequent upon disease". They were not victims of the mob, but of one of the many plagues that all Chinamen carried.[36]

Fawkner blamed the Chinese for being chased into a river and drowned. "No Chinaman should be allowed to work upon, or travel through, or reside upon, the goldfields at all," he thundered.

Fawkner's committee finalised the *Chinese Residence Act* shortly after Buckland. The Chinese would have to pay £1 every two months for the right to live in the colony. Most diggers, who'd railed against a poll tax three years earlier, thought this was a great idea, although Lalor, to his credit, voted against it.

The act also provided that a Chinaman who couldn't produce a residence licence had no right to sue miners who stole or destroyed his property. And so the first item miners stole from the Chinese were their licences. They then stole their gold and their mines. Chinese gold

---

36 Chinese witnesses were at a disadvantage in coronial and other court hearings. They were not permitted to swear traditional oaths, as they were considered heathens. Some would swear on a dying rooster, with court clerks charged with beheading the unfortunate birds in the witness dock. Others would break a plate and swear they hoped their soul would similarly shatter if they were not telling the truth. After a long trial, the courthouse looked like a reception centre the morning after a Greek wedding. Lawyers would mock Chinese witnesses for these oaths and encourage magistrates and juries to ignore their testimony as untrustworthy.

worth £70,000 was stolen at Ararat and all remaining Chinese claims in Buckland were jumped, with at least five Chinese killed.

The 1857 act resulted in a Chinese exodus from Victoria, while the establishment of a new border protection force to stop Chinese crossing the Murray, combined with South Australia restricting Chinese immigration, stemmed the flow of new arrivals.[37]

Other Chinese stuck it out, petitioning parliament, the press and the emperor of China. The protests were generally peaceful, but when unlicensed Chinese were arrested at White Hills in 1859, militants charged the police, banging gongs and letting off fireworks. The police responded with rifle fire and took the arrested Chinese to Bendigo's gaol. Hundreds of Chinese declared they too had no licences and demanded to be arrested, following the police back to the lockup.

That year, more than 6,000 Chinese were arrested for not having a licence, with 2,000 imprisoned. The civil disobedience campaign ended when 13,000 Chinese, about half of those in Victoria, finally paid the tax. This had been a longer and more widespread resistance than in the lead-up to Eureka, but nobody bothered to erect a monument, design a flag or get a tattoo in honour of the Chinese.

In 1860, gold was discovered at Lambing Flat (today the New South Wales town of Young). By year's end there were 2,000 Chinese and 12,000 Europeans on the Flat's Burrangong diggings. The European miners formed the Miners' Protection League to demand that miners be protected from the Chinese.

Riots against Lambing Flat's Chinese soon followed. New South Wales premier Charles "Slippery Charlie" Cowper visited to urge calm. He called the Chinese "pests and nuisances" in a speech to the diggers, but asked that the law be obeyed. Several hundred troops were bought in, but many went home in May, as the riots were less frequent (and it was bloody freezing).

---

37   The government only strengthened the Murray border to prevent illegal riverine arrivals from drowning. OK, probably not ... but it's a damned good excuse.

On 30 June 1861, 2,000 diggers led by a brass band marched on the Chinese camp, carrying clubs, pick handles and festive flags. One flag sported the Southern Cross superimposed over a St Andrew's Cross, framed by the words "Roll up – no Chinese!"[38]

The Chinese miners were driven from the diggings. A *Sydney Morning Herald* journalist reported:

> I noticed one man who returned with eight pigtails attached to a flag, glorifying in the work that had been done. I also saw one tail, with part of the scalp the size of a man's hand attached, that had literally been cut from some unfortunate creature.

Captain Henry Zouch of the Mounted Police came up from Yass and arrested three diggers for leading the riot. A thousand miners marched on the police station that evening. At least one miner and four police horses were shot dead in the confrontation. The next day the three riot leaders were bailed and Zouch ordered all public officials to leave the town. That night the courthouse and police station were burned down.

Following Lambing Flat, Premier Cowper introduced Chinese immigration restrictions similar to those in Victoria, denied Chinese the right to apply for citizenship and brought in laws allowing the government to close goldfields to any foreigners it didn't like.

Anti-Chinese laws were repealed as tensions simmered down, but there were new outbreaks of hostility in the 1870s, when 20,000 Chinese joined the Queensland gold rush. Rising unemployment saw a concerted anti-Chinese campaign in the 1880s and 1890s, with the newly formed Labor movement complaining Chinese workers were stealing the jobs of hardworking Australians.

Barriers to immigration were gradually reintroduced, culminating in the new federal Australian government's 1901 *Immigration*

---

38   Lambing Flat was the first-known use of the Southern Cross as an anti-immigrant symbol.

Restriction Act. The act didn't bar Chinese and other Asians from entering Australia, but their linguistic skills could be tested in any European language chosen by an immigration officer. Later, the test could be in any language (or, more accurately, any language not known by the Asian).[39] The 1901 act was the backbone of the White Australia Policy, the last vestiges of which were dismantled in 1973.

That's really not so long ago ...

---

39   You try answering a question about Don Bradman's batting average in Swahili.

II
Across Australia by bath

P.S. I think to live about four or five days.
My spirits are excellent.

William Wills, last words in a letter
to his father, 27 June 1861

THE HIDEOUS BLANK

AUSTRALIA, IN THE SECOND HALF OF THE NINETEENTH century, was more urban than Britain, the United States or Canada. More than half of all Australians lived in towns, most of which were on or near the coast.

Yet Australians saw themselves as outback pioneers. They romanticised bush life, with its tea and damper and jolly jumbucks shoved into tuckerbags. Bushrangers and stockmen became folk heroes. And so did explorers.

Explorers were variously motivated by fame, the desire for solitude, the discovery of novel plants and animals (most of which turned out to be highly poisonous), or the need for new places to put their sheep. But all explorers were also motivated by something far more mystical – the desire to know the unknown. And nowhere was more unknown than Australia's vast interior, described by the *Argus* in 1842 as "a hideous blank".

South Australians were more interested in exploring the interior than anyone else. New South Wales and Victoria had plenty of fertile land, Western Australia was content with all its sand and bird poo, and Queensland had not yet been invented. South Australia's settlers, however, felt hemmed in by Victoria to the east and the sands to the north and west. Without more agricultural land, South Australia would remain a fifth-rate hick province.

Edward Eyre helped his friend Charles Sturt overland cattle from Sydney to Adelaide in 1838, having brought his own livestock to the town a few months earlier. The 23-year-old drover used the profits to fund exploration of the country north-west of Adelaide. Eyre discovered a lot of "sandy desert interspersed with scrub" and a giant salt lake, which he named Lake Torrens. He wrote of the dusty lakebed:

> The whole was barren and arid-looking in the extreme, and as I gazed on the dismal scene before me I felt assured, I had approached the vast and dreary desert of the interior, or, it might be, was verging on the confines of some inland water, whose sterile and desolate shores seem to forbid the traveller's approach.[1]

Eyre then explored the peninsula to the city's west that now bears his name. He glumly recounted that in more than 600 miles of "hitherto unexplored country, we never crossed a single creek, river, or chain of ponds, nor did we meet with permanent water anywhere, with the exception of three solitary springs on the coast".

In 1840, South Australian pastoralists wanted to overland stock to Western Australia. Eyre got the job, but, convinced nothing good lay to the west, persuaded his backers to look north. Governor George Gawler agreed and tasked Eyre with "the discovery of the interior of Australia".

Eyre skirted Lake Torrens and discovered the salt flats of Lake Eyre, which at 9,500 square kilometres is Australia's largest lake (when it has water in it). Travelling east, he climbed a stony hillock

---

1   Eyre was the Morrissey of Australian exploration.

and looked down on two more salt pans. Believing Adelaide was encircled by endless salty desert, Eyre wrote, "cheerless and hopeless indeed was the prospect before us ... This closed all my dreams as to the expedition." In trademark sunny style, he named the hillock Mount Hopeless.

But the exploring bug had Eyre bit. Dismissing all but three Aboriginal guides and his constant exploring companion, John Baxter, Eyre embarked on the 2,500 kilometre trek to Albany on Western Australia's south coast, swearing "either to accomplish the object I had in view, or perish in the attempt".

Eyre's innate pessimism was vindicated on this trip, as two of the guides murdered Baxter and made off with most of the expedition's firearms and supplies.[2] Australia's greatest writer of cheap Gothic melodrama intoned:

> At the dead hour of night, in the wildest and most inhospitable wastes of Australia, with the fierce wind raging in unison with the scene of violence before me, I was left, with a single native, whose fidelity I could not rely upon, and who for aught I knew might be in league with the other two, who perhaps were even now, lurking about with the view of taking away my life.

Wylie, the remaining guide, remained loyal. The two men continued along the Great Australian Bight and stumbled into Albany on 7 July 1841. They'd just made the first land crossing between the eastern and western colonies. Eyre received worldwide fame and the Royal

---

2   Aboriginal guides, with their bushcraft and diplomatic skills, are the first thing Australian explorers should pack before venturing into the outback. However, it's important to have guides who are willing members of the expedition and don't want to murder you. David Carnegie, a Western Australian explorer, didn't understand this principle. Whenever Carnegie got thirsty, he captured the nearest Aborigine at gunpoint, tied him to a tree until he was dehydrated, released him and then followed him to water. Sometimes he'd force-feed his victim salt beef to speed things along. Carnegie got what was coming to him while oppressing the natives of Nigeria, dying after being shot in the thigh with a poisoned arrow.

Geographical Society of London's highest honour. Wylie received £2, a medal from the Agricultural Society of Perth and a weekly ration of flour and meat.[3]

Exploring the interior was a deadly business. Lurking natives at least offered a quick death. Lack of water did not. William Coulthard, who ran dry while searching for grazing country north of Adelaide, slit his horse's throat to drink its blood. The last drops drained, he stripped naked, neatly folded his clothes, hung his pocket watch from the branch of a nearby bush and lay down to die. His body was discovered three months later, as were his last words, scratched onto the surface of his empty canteen:

> I never reached water ... my Tung is stkig to my mouth – and I
> see what I have rote I know as this is the last time I may have of
> expressing feeling. Blind? altho feeling excu – for want of water –
> my ey dasels – my tong burn – I can see no way – God Help – I
> can't get up

Aborigines and thirst were almost as dangerous as camels. John Ainsworth Horrocks purchased Australia's only camel, Harry, for his 1846 expedition to Lake Torrens.[4] Harry, the first camel used in Australian exploration, savaged the expedition's goats and bit Horrocks' cook, "inflicting two wounds of great length above his temples". One morning, the vicious beast attacked Horrocks while he was attempting to unload his shotgun. The shotgun successfully

---

3   Eyre stopped exploring, became an Aboriginal protector and wrote the insightful
    *Account of the Manners and Customs of the Aborigines and the State of their Relations
    with Europeans.* However, as governor of Jamaica, Eyre responded ferociously
    to a "Negro riot" in 1865. His declaration of martial law ended with 608 deaths,
    600 floggings and 1,000 dwellings being burned down, with the shocked British
    establishment remembering him thereafter as "the monster of Jamaica".

4   A camel with one hump, like Harry, is known as a dromedary. A camel with two
    humps is known as a Bactrian camel. All camels are known as complete bastards.
    They spit, bite, kick and emit a horrible gurgling, burping moan whenever they
    don't want to do something, which is all the time.

unloaded into Horrocks' head, blowing off three of his fingers along the way. Horrocks, who died from his wounds, holds the dubious distinction of being the only explorer to have been shot by his camel.[5]

Charles Sturt was the first European to penetrate deep into the interior. In August 1844, he entered the desert with fifteen men, eleven horses, thirty-two bullocks, 200 sheep, seven carts and a boat.[6] Boats are great for exploring rivers, but are as useful as screen-doors on submarines when it comes to deserts.

Sturt appointed John McDouall Stuart as the expedition's draughtsman. Stuart, rejected by the British Army as too short and skinny to kill people, had the appearance of a novelty garden ornament that had been liberally coated in Perkins Paste and rolled across a busy barber shop's floor.

"Little Stuart", as he was affectionately known by Sturt, had fled Glasgow for Adelaide after seeing his fiancée embracing his best friend, her cousin. Devastated, he shunned society for the solitary life of a bush surveyor. Stuart was so uncomfortable in his Adelaide home that, on the rare occasions he returned to the capital, he chose to sleep in his garden. Or perhaps he just couldn't find his keys, as he hit the whisky bottle harder than Norman Mailer in a Dylan Thomas drink-off.

Sturt's party spent six months sheltering in a narrow gorge, waiting for rain. The desert heat spoiled Sturt's supplies, burned the skin from his dog's feet, exploded his thermometer and caused the lead to fall out of his pencil.[7]

---

5 Camels 1. Explorers 0.

6 Camels are figuratively referred to as ships of the desert. Sturt was a literalist.

7 Not a euphemism. Explorers used lead pencils, as ink was heavy and prone to spillage. Explorers could get lead poisoning from lead pencils, even though pencil lead was made from graphite, not lead. Nineteenth-century pencils were commonly coated in lead-based paint, a hazard to anxious explorers who chewed or sucked their pencils. Exploring is a very dangerous business.

Sturt discovered a desert full of sharp stones (Sturt's Stony Desert) and another full of sand (the Simpson Desert). He failed to discover an inland sea, finally conceding that it didn't exist and that the boat had been overkill. Sturt wrote (after finding a new pencil), "The stillness of death reigned around us. No living creature was to be heard; nothing visible inhabited that dreary desert but the ant."

Scurvy carried off Sturt's deputy, and Stuart was promoted to the role. Sturt wanted to strike out for the centre of the continent with Stuart, but the expedition's doctor convinced him he could not survive the several-hundred-mile round trip. And so Sturt turned for home, his boat left as tribute for the victorious sands.[8]

Sturt, who'd been away for seventeen months, had been given up for dead. The people of Adelaide were amazed when he returned strapped to his horse, near blind, his legs black from scurvy. The man with a boat for every occasion had proved he could do deserts as well as rivers. With Governor Grey gone, the versatile explorer was appointed treasurer, and then colonial secretary, of South Australia.

There were two enduring legacies of Sturt's expedition. His discovery of Cooper's Creek on South Australia's border with Queensland provided a beachhead for further expeditions.[9] And John McDouall Stuart, tempered in the fire of the unforgiving interior, would become Australia's greatest inland explorer.

---

8   Knowing when to throw in the towel is an important explorer survival trait. Ernest Shackleton, after heading for home only ninety-seven miles out from the South Pole in 1909, said to his wife, "A live donkey is better than a dead lion, isn't it?" Shackleton, who was something of a philosopher, also wrote, "the line between death and success in exploration is a fine one".

9   Cooper's Creek is now known as Cooper Creek. Australia has followed America in removing apostrophes from placenames (e.g. King's Cross became Kings Cross). Sometimes the possessive 's' is also removed, as in the case of Cooper Creek. Grammar Nazis continue to campaign for the reintroduction of apostrophes into placenames because they have nothing better to do with their time.

MAJOR MITCHELL'S MISSES

Major Thomas Mitchell was consumed by jealousy. Why was Charles Sturt the go-to guy when it came to rivers? That role, and the glory that went with it, should rightly have been his. So Mitchell dedicated his life to disproving Sturt's claim that all of eastern Australia's inland rivers flowed south. He, Thomas Mitchell, would find a river that flowed north!

In 1831, runaway convict George Clarke claimed that a large river flowed north-west from central New South Wales to the sea. Mitchell rushed off to investigate the claim, losing two of his party to lurking natives. There was no northern river.

In 1835, Mitchell decided to follow the Darling River to its junction with the Murray. Perhaps an arm of the river would veer north. This time Mitchell lost the expedition's botanist, Richard Cunningham.[10] Cunningham had wandered off from the main party to find flowers but instead found the pointy end of a spear.[11] There was no northern river.

In December 1845, Mitchell, with the young surveyor Edmund Kennedy his second-in-command, set out from Boree Station in New South Wales to Port Essington on Australia's north coast. He found lots of new rivers, including one that flowed north. Suck on that, Sturt!

Mitchell named the river the Victoria (now the Barcoo) and wrote:

> There I found then, at last, the realization of my long cherished hopes, an interior river falling to the N. W ... the scene was so extensive as to leave no room for doubt as to the course of the river, which, thus and there revealed to me alone, seemed like a reward direct from Heaven for perseverance, and as a compensation for the many sacrifices I had made, in order to solve the question as to the interior rivers of Tropical Australia.

---

10   Richard Cunningham is the only Australian explorer to have lent his name to a *Happy Days* character.

11   Where's the Fonz when you need him?

Mitchell returned to Sydney without reaching Australia's north coast and rushed to London to publish a vindication of his northern river thesis. Edmund Kennedy decided to follow the Victoria to the Gulf of Carpentaria to confirm his mentor's theory. Unfortunately, the Victoria made a sharp dogleg to the south-west, where it drained into Cooper's Creek and, ultimately, Lake Eyre. Kennedy had shattered Mitchell's dream.[12]

Kennedy, according to his father, possessed an "almost mad ambition to distinguish himself". In 1848, he decided that distinction lay in the impenetrable rainforests of the Cape York Peninsula. Kennedy sailed to Rockingham Bay, today halfway between Townsville and Cairns, intending to walk around the cape.

Kennedy set out with a party of thirteen, which proved an unlucky number. After nine weeks, he'd travelled only forty miles inland and twelve miles north. After six months of struggling through swamps, tropical jungle and jagged mountains, he left eight men on the coast to await rescue. When one of his reduced party accidentally shot himself, Kennedy ordered two more men to wait with him. Kennedy would push on to meet the expedition's supply ship at Port Albany, on Cape York's northern tip, accompanied only by his trusty Aboriginal guide, Jackey Jackey.[13]

Kennedy made it to within twenty miles of Port Albany before being speared to death on the Escape River, a poor choice of name as far as he was concerned. Jackey Jackey cradled Kennedy as he died, buried his body in a shallow grave and made it to the supply ship, the

---

12 Mitchell would have been fine if he'd had broadcaster Alan Jones in his corner. When it comes to water, Jones refuses to be deterred by petty irrelevances like geography, direction and common sense. In 2002, he proposed drought-proofing Australia by making the Clarence, Burdekin, Daly, Pioneer and Ord rivers flow inland, rather than towards the sea as they currently do. King Cnut, according to popular legend, once instructed the incoming tide to halt. Alan Jones is an Aussie Cnut.

13 Yep, another one. His real name was Galmahra.

first man known to have walked the length of Cape York.[14] Only two of the men Kennedy left behind survived.

While Kennedy is the winner of the Most Explorers Killed in an Australian Expedition Award, with a body count of ten, Ludwig Leichhardt boasted a 100 per cent kill rate on his 1848 expedition.

Leichhardt was a zoologist, botanist, geologist, anatomist, linguist and philosopher. He was also, according to those who accompanied him on his early expeditions, "jealous", "selfish", "suspicious", "reticent", "careless", "slovenly", "wholly unfitted for leadership" and "very lax in his religious opinion".

The Prussian polymath considered inland Australia to be the last great frontier for the advancement of the natural sciences, declaring, "the interior, the heart of this dark continent is my goal, and I shall never relinquish the quest for it until I get there." He spent his first two years in the colonies going on long walks, collecting rocks and plants and sketching poisonous mushrooms.[15]

Leichhardt's six-man party set out from Moreton Bay in October 1844 and walked the 3,000 miles to Port Essington in a little over fourteen months.[16] John Gilbert, the expedition's ornithologist, collected an unknown number of birds and one very sharp spear on the journey.[17] He was the expedition's only casualty.

---

14   People remember Jackey Jackey for the support he gave to Kennedy, not for this great feat. Jackey Jackey was awarded a silver breastplate, which he never wore, and a £50 bank account, which he never accessed. In 1854, his "fondness for ardent spirits" saw him enter the spirit world – he fell into a campfire while drunk and burned to death. Jackey Jackey's services to colonial exploration saw him portrayed as "a subservient Aborigine", with the term *Jackey Jackey* later becoming the Australian equivalent of Uncle Tom.

15   You can see his work in "Decades of Fungi", in the *London Journal of Botany* (1844), if you are interested in Germans who draw mushrooms.

16   For those struggling to grasp the scale of Leichhardt's achievement, that's three times as far as The Proclaimers were prepared to walk.

17   The most dangerous position in any exploration party was expedition naturalist. Naturalists had a tendency to wander off into the bush, muttering about an exciting new genus, and never be seen again (at least without spear holes). Naturalists were to explorers what drummers were to Spinal Tap.

Leichhardt, who'd been away for so long that everybody thought he was dead, was hailed "Prince of Explorers" upon his return to Sydney and feted by the Royal Geographical Society of London and France's *Société de Géographie*. Mitchell was furious when he returned from his own failed north coast expedition.

Leichhardt invested his prize money in staging an expedition from the Darling Downs, just west of Brisbane, to Perth. After malaria spoiled his 1846 attempt, Leichhardt and six companions left McPherson's Station on 3 April 1848. They were never seen again.

Mitchell shed no tears for his missing rival. When Augustus Gregory sought his advice on mounting a search for the German explorer, Mitchell responded "in a most discourteous manner". With Leichhardt gone and Sturt retired, he, Major Thomas Mitchell, would be recognised as Australia's greatest explorer.[18]

ICH BIN EIN POINDEXTER

Leichhardt was not the only German intellectual living (and, in his case, dying) in mid-nineteenth-century Australia. German universities produced the world's leading scientists, and Australia, a largely unexplored continent, was an egghead's El Dorado.

Intellectuals, rather than serfs or oppressed workers, led the 1848 uprisings in Germany. After the aristocrats regained control, German nerds fled for the United States, Britain and Australia. The

---

18   Mitchell's star declined after his attempt to shoot Stuart Donaldson, the man who would soon be New South Wales' first premier, although the War and Colonial Office thwarted the government's attempt to dismiss him as surveyor-general. Mitchell, bored and aggrieved, spent little time surveying, instead dedicating himself to the invention of a propeller based on the boomerang and the translation of medieval Portuguese poetry. He is also believed to have written *To Bourke's Statue this Appropriate Effusion of Unprofitable Brass is Unceremoniously Dedicated, by Ichneumon, Anxious to Instruct his Grandmothers in the Inductive Science of Sucking Eggs*, a satirical pamphlet that attacked senior government figures. When he died in 1855, Australia lost a Renaissance man who knew about everything except Australian rivers.

Prinzessin Luise brought a number of German 48ers, as the refugees of the People's Spring were known, to Adelaide, including Dr Moritz Richard Schomburgk, the Prussian government botanist who headed the Adelaide Botanic Gardens; Martin Basedow and Carl Mücke, who developed the South Australian school system; and the composer Carl Linger, who established Adelaide's first philharmonic orchestra and composed "The Song of Australia".[19]

Some German scientists fit the blond-haired, blue-eyed, conduct-experiments-on-unwilling-subjects-in-an-underground-lair stereotype. Amalia Dietrich sailed for Brisbane in 1861 to collect specimens for a Hamburg museum. In her nine years in Queensland, Amalia collected more birds than any other person in history, put together the first significant collection of Australian spiders and was the first person to pickle a taipan, a snake that contains enough venom to kill 12,000 guinea pigs.[20] While staying with the Archer family at Rockhampton, Dietrich reportedly asked one of the family's employees to shoot an Aborigine so that she could have a native's skin mounted for her collection. The horrified Mr Archer expelled "the Angel of Black Death", but a tanned Aboriginal skin later appeared in Hamburg's Zoological Museum.

Many German men of learning settled in Melbourne, including Georg von Neumayer, Victoria's chief astronomer and meteorologist;

---

19 A German came very close to composing Australia's national anthem. "The Song of Australia", with lyrics by Mrs C.J. Carelton of Adelaide, was one of four songs Australians were invited to vote on as the national anthem in a 1977 plebiscite, the others being "Advance Australia Fair" (the eventual winner, which includes the excellent word *girt*), "Waltzing Matilda" (a song about a thieving hobo who commits suicide) and "God Save the Queen" (not the Sex Pistols' version). "The Song of Australia" received the lowest national vote, but won the South Australian poll, as it was the unofficial anthem in that state. "The Song of Australia" is a disturbingly South Australian song, containing lyrics like "grassy knoll", "witching harmonies", "worshippers at Mammon's shrine", "deep in the dark unfathom'd mine" and "no shackled slave can breathe the air".

20 The identity of the sick bastard who made this calculation is unknown, but, adjusting for body weight, it is estimated that a single taipan can kill 183.88 German scientists, demonstrating the hazardous nature of Dietrich's work.

Ferdinand von Mueller, the man who named the macadamia nut; and
Wilhelm Blandowski, a vindictive ichthyologist who named ugly
fish after his rivals, giving them unflattering descriptions such as "a
fish easily recognised by its low forehead, big belly and sharp spine".

These men were all members of the Philosophical Institute of
Victoria, a club for scientists and other eccentrics that produced
academic papers such as "The Acclimatisation of the Llama". In 1857,
the institute decided that Victoria should mount an expedition to
cross Australia from east to west, explore the centre of Australia and
search for signs of Leichhardt. The philosophers sprung into inaction,
establishing a thirty-two-man committee to think about exploring.

Now, if you want to know whether the centre of Australia could be
said to exist before being observed by a rational mind, you might refer
the matter to a committee stacked with German philosophers – but
if you want to speedily assemble a well-organised expedition to the
centre of Australia, you'd go with a different governance model.[21]

The institute's Exploration Committee couldn't organise a piss-up
in a brewery or, indeed, in their own building – the philosophers were
forced to stand on the footpath for one meeting when their rooms
had been booked for a violin rehearsal. At that meeting, Dr John
Macadam, the man for whom the macadamia nut was named, asked
the obvious question: "How could Victoria hope to cross the entire
continent when it had no explorers and no one with any experience
to lead the party?"

The Exploration Committee also had no money, but businessman
Ambrose Kyte offered to contribute £1,000 if the public chipped
in £2,000.[22] The Victorian government refused to cough up any

---

21　Hegel would argue that the centre of Australia would only be discovered when
　　enough people were ready to discover it. Nietzsche would argue that the centre of
　　Australia would be discovered by the person who wanted to discover it the most.
　　And Schopenhauer, if he could be arsed, would argue that discovering the centre
　　of Australia was pointless.

22　Mr Kyte was not noted for his generosity. He once set his arm in plaster before
　　signing a contract so he could later dispute the signature if the deal proved

cash, but it did offer some camels it had sent George Landells to India to purchase for Melbourne's zoo. The committee, ignoring the cautionary tale of John Horrocks, thought this was a great idea. It then raised an impressive £25 from four of its own members before lapsing into inactivity.

After much deliberation, the Exploration Committee decided that an east–west crossing of Australia would be deucedly tricky and that south to north was more their thing. And Leichhardt could stay lost. Which he did.[23]

THE RACE FROM THE BOTTOM

The Victorian expedition was planned during a period of intense competition among Australia's eastern colonies. Each had just been given self-government and was determined to make its mark on the world.

Earl Grey junior's limited federation had come to nought. When the idea was floated, New South Wales insisted its "superior wealth and population" should be recognised in any inter-colonial body. When republican MP Charles Gavan Duffy led the Victorian campaign for federation in 1857, New South Wales rejected the idea because Victoria's then-superior wealth and population should *not* be recognised in any inter-colonial body.

---

unfavourable. Mr Kyte was only interested in benefitting the community if also being for the benefit of Mr Kyte. He supported the Exploration Committee because he believed it would gain him a knighthood.

23   This is surprising, as playing "Where's Wiggy?" was a popular explorer pastime. At least nine expeditions set out to look for Leichhardt. The first search expedition, in 1852, was led by the winner of the Most Ridiculous Name for an Australian Explorer Award, Hovenden Hely. It is not surprising that Hely, who'd done some exploring with Leichhardt, failed to find his former boss, as Leichhardt had accused him of "indolence", "disloyalty" and "disgusting behaviour". Although artefacts of Leichhardt's expedition have been found, we still have no idea of the route he took or whether he died in Queensland, Northern Territory or Western Australia. Ludwig Leichhardt is the *Mary Celeste* of Australian explorers.

Barriers sprang up between the colonies. In 1853, Francis Cadell and William Randell started running steamships up the Murray River, giving South Australia control over trade in inland New South Wales and Victoria.[24] Those colonies erected customs houses on the river to protect their people from cheap South Australian imports, and Victoria built loss-making railways to the Murray to destroy its neighbour's trade advantage.

New South Wales, which generally favoured free trade, later worked to reduce these barriers. However, Victoria, where costs were higher due to the gold boom, moved to protect its manufacturers by taxing goods from other colonies. It was disputes about trade that delayed Australian federation until 1901.

Nothing shows the lack of cooperation better than the colonies' adoption of railway tracks of different widths. Mark Twain, when forced to change trains at the Victoria–New South Wales border, wrote, "Think of the paralysis of intellect that gave that idea birth."[25]

In 1858, while the Philosophical Institute of Victoria contemplated the metaphysics of exploration, Adelaide joined the analogue revolution by completing a telegraph connection to Melbourne. Sydney joined the new communications network later that year. This was a godsend for South Australia, as most Europeans stopped at Adelaide before sailing on to the more interesting parts of Australia. Adelaide received international news before anyone else, and with the new

---

24 Cadell later gained notoriety for kidnapping Aboriginal people, imprisoning them in a camp fifty-six kilometres off the Western Australian coast and making them dive for pearls for no payment. He was forced to leave Western Australia after news of his revival of slavery got out. Cadell was later murdered by his cook, whom he'd not paid for five years.

25 The requirement to unload freight and passengers at colonial (and later state) borders created huge inefficiencies. Common track widths were not adopted between all Australian capitals until 1995, when an uninterrupted rail line was built between Melbourne and Adelaide. States still have different track widths for some less popular lines.

telegraph it was able to sell it or exploit trade-sensitive information before it reached the other colonies.

Western Australia was lobbying for an underwater telegraph cable to connect it to either Ceylon (Sri Lanka) or the East Indies (Indonesia), which would allow near-instant communication with Europe. Sydney and Brisbane wanted a line between the East Indies and northern Queensland. Both of these options would destroy South Australia's information advantage.

John McDouall Stuart had been doing some exploring between drinks. Breaking with explorer tradition, Stuart travelled light, taking only a few companions, horses and basic supplies. He moved faster than any Australian explorer, except on the Sabbath. God might move in mysterious ways on a Sunday, but Stuart wouldn't – his faith made him stay put, even in the harshest conditions.

During 1858 and 1859 Stuart pushed north of Lake Torrens, finding new sheep country and, most importantly, water. The realisation that Australia might have something other than sand in its blank bits encouraged South Australia to dream big – it could continue to control the flow of information into the colony if it could build a telegraph line across the continent and then on to Java in the East Indies.

In July 1859, the South Australian government offered a £2,000 reward for the "first person who shall succeed in crossing through the country lately discovered by Mr Stuart, to either the north or north-western shores of the Australian continent". South Australia was crowdsourcing the new route for its telegraph line.

In response, Victoria's government now decided to invest in a "glorious race across the continent".[26] The Philosophical Institute was also upping its game. Queen Victoria, impressed by how much

---

26 Victoria was the only mainland Australian colony that didn't border unclaimed territory. The expedition offered Victoria the opportunity to forge a land route to northern Australia and claim all the good bits. This would open up more land for Victoria's squatters and allow the development of a northern port to support Victorian trade with Asia. Victoria would rule the south and the north. Winning South Australia's £2,000 would be a bonus.

Victorian scientists knew about fish, llamas and macadamia nuts, approved the institute rebranding itself as the Royal Society of Victoria. Two months later, in January 1860, William Nicholson, the barista balloteer who'd become premier of Victoria, gave the Royal Society £6,000 for its expedition.

But the Victorians would have to be quick. John McDouall Stuart and two companions had set out to cross the continent on 2 March 1860, and the Victorians still had no planned route, camels or explorers.

MEET THE TEAM

The logical choice to lead the Victorian expedition was the experienced desert explorer Peter Egerton Warburton, but Warburton was rejected because he didn't like camels and Victorians didn't like South Australians. Victorian pride demanded a Victorian explorer, so the Royal Society advertised for one in the local papers.

Nothing much happened until 16 June, when George Landells appeared with twenty-four camels and four Afghan cameleers.[27] Landells, dressed like a *Lawrence of Arabia* extra, led the exotic beasts through Melbourne's crowded streets. One of the camels, true to form, galloped into the excited onlookers, "to the terror and confusion

---

27   If there's one thing more dangerous than camels, it's Afghans. The first rule of warfare is don't invade Afghanistan. The fiercely independent Afghan tribes, who have frustrated the United States for more than a decade, had earlier expelled invading Soviets, Greeks, Persians, Mongols, Mughals and Sikhs. But it was Britain that suffered the greatest defeat at the hands of the Afghans when, in 1842, General Sir William Elphinstone agreed to retreat from Kabul to India following an effective guerilla insurgency. Elphinstone also agreed to hand the Afghans all of his gunpowder and most of his guns and cannons. The Afghans started shooting Elphinstone's column with its own guns as soon as they left the city. When William Brydon, one of the 4,500 troops and 12,000 civilians who'd left Kabul, struggled into the British camp at Jalalabad on a dying pony, he was asked what had happened to the army. He replied, "I am the army." The only British soldier to get out of Afghanistan alive had lost part of his skull to a sword, but survived because a magazine he was carrying in his hat deflected the blow. The moral of this story is reading can save your life.

of certain elderly ladies who stood gazing with astonishment at the novel importation".[28]

On 20 June, the Exploration Committee appointed 39-year-old Irishman Robert O'Hara Burke to lead the expedition. Burke had no exploration, surveying or scientific experience, although, as pointed out in his job application (which he got a friend to write), he spoke and wrote French, Italian and German – essential skills for any self-respecting Australian explorer.

Burke was handsome, charismatic and popular. Standing well over six foot, he had piercing blue eyes and a magnificent black beard straight off the cover of *Barista Monthly*. Born to a wealthy family, he'd fought Italian revolutionaries in 1848 as an officer in the Austrian army, but was cashiered after going AWOL – he claimed to have left his troops to receive treatment for constipation, but it is more likely he was fleeing gambling debts.

Burke returned to Ireland and joined the police, before travelling to Victoria in search of gold. After failing on the diggings, he became chief of police in the northern Victorian town of Beechworth, where he led the investigation into the Buckland River riots. His investigation concluded there were too many Chinese people.

The genial Irishman was a haphazard dresser who was forced to borrow items of police uniform from his men whenever dignitaries were in town. He regarded clothing as optional and enjoyed sitting in his outdoor bathtub wearing nothing but a helmet. After a bath, Burke would engage in vigorous exercise, striding through the forest or attacking a tree with an axe. A neighbour speculated he was "a trifle insane".

If he was not insane, he was certainly disorganised. A visitor to his home would find notes on scraps of paper tacked to his walls, with a sign reading, "You are requested not to read anything on these walls, I cannot keep any record in a systematic manner, so I jot things down like this."

---

28 Camels 2. Explorers and Little Old Ladies 0.

Organisation is an essential explorer skill, as is having some idea where you are and where you're going. Falconer Larkworthy, the local bank manager, observed that when Burke was returning from Yackandandah to Beechworth:

> ... he lost his way, although the track was well beaten and frequented, and did not arrive at his destination for many hours after he was due. He was in no sense a bushman.

A potent mix of love, envy and ambition led Burke to apply to lead the expedition. Burke's younger brother had the honour of being the first British officer killed in the Crimean War.[29] Jealous of his sibling's success, Burke returned to Britain to enlist, only to discover that the war had ended while he was in the middle of the Atlantic. He returned to Victoria, desperate to be a hero – and he was willing to die for it. He swore to a friend, "I will cross Australia or perish in the attempt."[30]

Burke had also fallen in love with a sixteen-year-old actress, Julia Matthews. He attended her show every night she was in town and, after her final performance, asked her to marry him. Julia's mother was not amused. She was even less so when Burke trailed her daughter around Victoria, having advised his superiors he was pursuing a gang of horse thieves who, entirely coincidentally, coordinated their thefts with Ms

---

29 The British forces were led by Lord Raglan, who'd distinguished himself at the Battle of Waterloo by demanding the return of his amputated arm so he could retrieve a ring his wife had given him. This display of British pluck assured his progress through the ranks. Raglan was famed for his muddled orders, partly because he referred to every enemy as "the French". As the French were British allies in the Crimean War, his commands to attack French positions inevitably caused confusion. Raglan's unclear orders at the Battle of Balaclava resulted in Lord Cardigan's light brigade charging a distant Russian artillery placement head-on and being blown to bits. Raglan was ridiculed and died three years later from the unusual combination of dysentery and depression (i.e. a shitty mood). Cardigan became a hero and had the daggy knitted jumper he wore named after him. The British also named their daggy knitted face-protecting caps after the battle. No other battle has done so much for British knitting.

30 He was wrong. He'd do both.

Matthew's touring schedule. Crossing the continent, Burke believed, would raise him in the eyes of his love and future mother-in-law.

So why did the Exploration Committee give the job to an inexperienced, disorganised, directionally challenged kiddy-stalker with a death wish? Burke came from a good family, he was "accustomed to command", he could speak to the committee members in German and he'd befriended Sir William Stawell, chief justice of the Supreme Court and president of the Exploration Committee, over drinks at the Melbourne Club. The *Age* condemned Burke's appointment as "a piece of cliqueism".

Landells was appointed Burke's deputy. Experienced in haggling with the camel traders of Peshawar, Landells negotiated a salary 20 per cent higher than Burke's and was assured he'd have the final say on all camel-related matters. Landells selected his crack camel team – the four Afghans, John Drakeford and John King, a shy and consumptive Irish soldier he'd brought back from India to translate for the cameleers.

The committee next appointed William Wills, who was tasked with surveying and stopping Burke from wandering off in the wrong direction. Wills was an Englishman of "slow and hesitating speech", the legacy of a childhood fever. He was dutiful, methodical, stoic, committed to science and, unusual for the age, an atheist. He also boasted some exploring experience, having once navigated London's Hampton Court Maze in less than ten minutes.

Fifty-two-year-old Dr Ludwig Becker, who'd spent much of the 1850s painting miniature portraits in Tasmania, was appointed as the expedition's artist, naturalist, geographer and bearded German.[31] The German contingent was boosted by beardless Dr Hermann Beckler, the expedition's botanical observer.

---

31 Becker, who provided the cover illustration for William Buckley's biography, was something of an eccentric. Lieutenant-Governor Denison's wife said, "He is a most amusing person, talks English badly but very energetically ... very oddish-looking besides, with a large red beard." Becker had a pet bat, and was an enthusiastic bird impersonator, magician and ventriloquist. These skills were ideally suited for crossing the continent.

The Exploration Committee then made a fatal error – they let Burke select the rest of the party. Burke, going for the recruitment land-speed record, interviewed 300 men in three hours. He ignored proven explorers and appointed people he, or members of the Exploration Committee, knew. Six Irishmen, four Englishmen, four Afghans, three Germans, an American and a Barbadian were chosen for the expedition. Not a single native-born Australian was appointed. And while most explorers sensibly employed an Aborigine or three to scout, gather bush tucker and discourage their countrymen from spearing the expedition naturalist, Burke was having none of it. Australia would be crossed by the white man, or not at all.

A COMEDY OF ERRORS

Burke, who wanted to be able to enjoy a nice hot outdoor bath after traversing Australia, suggested that his team be shipped to the north coast to camel-trek back to Melbourne. He proposed starting the expedition at Blunder Bay. The press had a field day and Stawell made it clear Burke would be walking north to the Gulf of Carpentaria – and then he could damn well walk back.

Francis Cadell offered the expedition team a free boat ride up the Murray to Menindee, the farthest-flung outpost of white settlement in western New South Wales. This would dispense with the need for wagons and save the horses and camels for the desert. Burke refused. He didn't want to share credit for the expedition's success.

On 20 August 1860, 15,000 people gathered in Melbourne's Royal Park to farewell Burke's team. One of the camels broke free and chased a policeman across the park.[32] A woman was thrown from her horse

---

32   Six of the camels were completely untrained, having been purchased at the last
     minute from George Coppin's amusement park.

and broke her leg in the ensuing confusion.[33] The crowd regarded all this as jolly good theatre.

Burke was just getting started. For Act II, he sacked one of his party, in front of the biggest gathering Melbourne had ever seen, for being "a little too hilarious through excess of beer", having the previous day dismissed two of the team for drunkenness and incompetence. As a brass band struck up a jaunty exploring tune, Burke delivered his encore with the collapse of one of the expedition's overloaded wagons.

Burke, who had twenty tonnes of luggage, had overpacked. The expedition's manifest suggests Burke wanted to open an outback kink store – why else would he have packed an enema syringe, six kangaroo thongs, four dozen assorted nipples, a grooved silver probe and 150 pounds of sperm candles? He also packed twelve dandruff brushes, forty-five yards of gossamer (for fly veils), two pounds of beads and fifty-four looking glasses (for natives) and a stationery cabinet, oak table, waterbed and Chinese gong. And, of course, a bathtub.

The expedition's sixty gallons of rum was off limits to the explorers, but it was open bar for anything with a hump. Landells had seen Indian sepoys loading their camels up with booze before battle and believed rum to be a cameloid performance-enhancing drug and ward against scurvy.[34]

Landells refused to load up the camels with anything but rum, arguing that they needed to be kept fresh for the desert. The pampered animals were also issued raincoats, with a hole cut out for the hump, and airbags (not for camel crashes, but to help them float over rivers).

The crowd hung around while the wagon was repaired. They had waited for three years, so they could manage another three hours.

---

33 Camels 4. Explorers, Little Old Ladies, Coppers and Equestriennes 0.

34 History is sadly silent as to how much Berocca Burke packed to get the camels moving each morning.

FIG. 11: "WHERE WOULD YOU LIKE THIS, MR BURKE?"

Burke finally got moving at four in the afternoon, but two other wagons broke down almost immediately. At the end of a hard day's exploring, the party had covered the four long miles to Essendon. As the party set camp, Burke galloped back to Melbourne to propose to Julia Matthews, whom he'd just made the sole beneficiary of his will. The young actress refused, but accepted Burke's entreaties to reconsider upon his return. Julia gave the lovesick explorer a lock of her hair, which he kept in a pouch around his neck until the day he died.

The expedition moved with all the speed of a sloth on valium, with the heavily laden wagons and camels bogged down in the rich mud of Victoria and the shifting dunes of western New South Wales. And Burke's personnel problems continued. The fact that three of the cameleers were Moslems and the other Hindu had been overlooked by the expedition suppliers, who'd packed a wagon full of dead pig and dead cow. Samla, the Hindu, resigned two days out of Melbourne as he refused to eat anything other than sheep he'd ritually slaughtered.

Burke stayed in hotels and farmhouses during the early weeks of the trip, while the rest of the party slept in the open. This alienated his men. Burke sacked six in the first month of the journey and hired replacements, including a French chef and Charlie Gray, a 52-year-old Scots sailor turned stablehand.

Burke decided to lighten the expedition's load by jettisoning its sugar and lime juice, which meant the camels could no longer enjoy daiquiris and mojitos. Things soon got worse for the beasts, with Burke insisting they actually carry something.

Things were even worse for the men, who were now ordered to carry all their personal belongings, with a weight limit of thirty pounds imposed. The German naturalists were hardest hit, as they had to leave behind all their little glass bottles and other scientific thingies. Burke ordered them to cease looking at plants, drawing useless pictures of dissected Australian wildlife and poking snakes with sticks – they would damn well work like the rest of the team. Burke had an ulterior motive – he wanted to force Becker's resignation, as Burke's exploits would seem less heroic if a doddering Kraut miniature-painter made it to the Gulf. Landells resigned after Burke insisted on ditching the camels' rum, but relented after Burke begged him to stay.

On 14 October, the unhappy party arrived at Menindee. They'd travelled 750 kilometres in eight weeks. The mail coach did the Melbourne to Menindee run in one.

In Menindee, Burke fired Landells. Landells called Burke insane and Burke challenged him to a duel. Landells refused, saying he'd come to fight the desert, not his commanding officer. Beckler resigned in protest at Landells' treatment. Burke now had only half of his original men.

Burke was able to catch up with recent events while in Menindee. The Melbourne papers were full of stories about his slow pace and divisive leadership. But there was also welcome news. Stuart had returned to Adelaide, his body riddled with scurvy and the glare of the desert sun having burned the sight from one eye.

Stuart had found the centre of Australia and planted a Union Jack there.[35] He wrote that he:

> ... gave three hearty cheers for the flag, the emblem of civil and religious liberty ... may it be a sign to the natives that the dawn of liberty, civilization and Christianity is about to break upon them.

The natives obviously read the sign differently, as they attempted to burn his camp and kill him with boomerangs about three-quarters of the way to the north coast. Stuart retreated in defeat.

The exultant Victorians put the boot in, with the Exploration Committee spreading rumours that Stuart had murdered Aborigines and drunk the alcohol in the expedition's scientific instruments. Victorian conspiracy theorists even suggested that Stuart's setting foot on Australia's centre had been faked, with the sozzled Scot hiding in a pub the whole time. The Melbourne Lands Department provocatively asked the South Australian government for "any authentic information you may possess as to Mr Stuart's recent journey".

Burke was running out of time and money and, disobeying orders, split the party. Using the airbags to float the indignant camels across the Darling River near Menindee, he took seven men with him on the 600 kilometre journey to Cooper's Creek. Wills was his new deputy and John King was placed in charge of the camels, even though he'd

---

35   There is still debate as to where the centre of Australia actually is, although everybody agrees that Tasmania should be ignored in determining it. One method involves placing a model of Australia on the head of a pin until it balances. A second involves dangling a model from a string until it balances. A third involves fitting the largest possible circle within Australia's borders, with its centre considered that of the continent. A fourth involves drawing a box touching Australia's northern, eastern, southern and westernmost points, with the centre situated where its diagonals intersect. A fifth involves accepting a cairn built by the Division of National Mapping in 1965, as this involves much less effort than the other methods. The truth is, the location of Australia's centre remains unknown, but all of the above methods place it well over 100 kilometres from Stuart's flag.

had no experience with the bad-tempered beasts before the expedition. Only one cameleer, Dost Mahomet, remained.

Burke marched sixteen hours a day, convinced that Stuart would have another crack at the crossing. He was correct. Furious at Victoria's attacks on its small, furry explorer, South Australia funded Stuart to undertake a larger expedition, this time providing him with an armed escort to deal with any pesky boomerang-throwing arsonists he might encounter.

Burke had left a team at Menindee, having convinced Hermann Beckler to stay with them until Melbourne sent a replacement German. Burke was briefly accompanied by William Wright, a Menindee station manager, whom he appointed as an officer of the expedition. This was another of Burke's inspired personnel choices – he had never met the barely literate and fully incompetent Wright before. Wright was instructed to return to Menindee, sack Ludwig Becker for being old and irritating and bring those left at Menindee, along with fresh supplies, to Cooper's Creek.

Just before reaching Cooper's Creek, Burke crossed the imaginary line that separated New South Wales from the new colony of Queensland.

BEAUTIFUL ONE DAY, QUEENSLAND THE NEXT

Britain had contemplated a northern Australian state as early as 1842, but it was the professional secessionist John Dunmore Lang who outfitted Brisbane's blushing debutants for the Queensland independence ball.

The man who'd settled Queensland with creationist pineapple fanciers in 1838 lured 550 Scottish Protestant dissenters to Brisbane in 1849 with the promise of free land, despite having no authority to make such an offer. After the New South Wales government refused to honour his commitment, Lang's "armed-to-the-teeth" immigrants, desperate to own land without having to pay for it, forced the local

Indigenous people out of York's Hollow and built a new community there. They named it Fortitude Valley.[36]

In 1852, Brisbane's citizens authorised Lang to travel to Britain to lobby for separation from New South Wales. Upon his return, Lang was elected as Moreton Bay's representative on the New South Wales Legislative Council, a pulpit from which he preached partition.

The colony of Queensland was founded on 6 June 1859.[37] The pastoralists who dominated its parliament gave Queensland police the sort of "move on" powers that Joh Bjelke-Petersen would later have them use against hippies, university students, anti-Apartheid campaigners, people who wanted to stop his friends from transforming turtle breeding grounds into high-rise developments, and other communists.

Queensland's early police had two main advantages over their successors. First, the targets of their powers were members of Queensland's most politically powerless group – Aboriginal and Torres Strait Islander people. Second, they were not confined to moving people on into paddy wagons. Instead, they were tacitly encouraged to move them on into the spirit world.

Most of those tasked with moving on Aboriginal people were themselves Aboriginal. The Native Police were the brainchild of the genial geographer and prison reformer Alexander Maconochie, who in 1838 mused, "To form Aboriginal people into a police force might be a more attractive discipline than any regimen offered by missionaries." Maconochie, who saw policing as an opportunity for Aboriginal advancement, would have been horrified by the strange fruit that would hang from the tree he planted.

New South Wales, impressed with Port Phillip's earlier Kulin police

---

36   The small community of violent ginger happy-clappers is now the "adult entertainment" capital of Queensland.

37   Queensland, like Victoria, was named in honour of Queen Victoria. The capital of South Australia is named after another British queen, while the capitals of New South Wales, Victoria and Tasmania are named after British lords. No wonder Australia is still a monarchy.

experiment, established the Native Police Force in 1848. Aboriginal police units, each commanded by a white officer, were tasked with patrolling the northern frontier. Enlisting was attractive to some young men who, in their own societies, lacked the status of their elders. They received guns, horses, fancy uniforms, rations and even a small wage – trappings generally reserved for the white man. Aboriginal people could be used to attack other Aboriginal people because Aboriginal people are a Western construct. Hundreds of Aboriginal tribes, with different languages and customs, lived in Australia. A person from one tribe would consider the member of another as a Briton would consider a Frenchman or a Russian.

Inter-tribal conflict was part of the rich tapestry of traditional life and the Native Police, who were recruited from lands far from where they were deployed, were the perfect tool to exploit this. The conflict increased after the Native Police and their white commanding officers were placed under Queensland control in 1859.

There were perhaps 200,000 Indigenous people in the newest colony, far outnumbering settlers, and they fought back as pastoralists moved onto their lands. In 1857, Jiman warriors attacked William Fraser's Hornet Bank Station in retaliation for the shooting of twelve Jiman, and for Fraser's earlier gift of a Christmas pudding, lovingly baked with candied fruit, brandy and strychnine.[38] The Jiman raped the station women, castrated the Fraser children's tutor and then murdered everyone they could find, accounting for eight members of the Fraser family and four employees.

By March 1858, up to 300 Jiman had been killed by squatters and police in revenge attacks, with William Fraser, who'd been away on business at the time of the massacre, shooting Aborigines wherever he found them. Fraser allegedly shot two Jiman acquitted of the massacre as they left Rockhampton courthouse, a jockey at the Taroom racetrack and a woman in the main street of Toowoomba whom he

---

38   Merry Christmas, Jiman people!

believed was wearing his murdered wife's dress. For his zeal, he was appointed an officer of the Native Police. Fraser is believed to have summarily executed over a hundred Aborigines, making him the greatest mass murderer in Australian history.

In 1861, Horatio Spencer Howe Wills, the father of Australian republicanism, and his son Thomas Wentworth Wills, the father of Australian Rules football, settled with their workers and 10,000 sheep at Cullin-la-ringo Station on central Queensland's Nogoa River. Nineteen men, women and children, including Horatio, were clubbed to death soon after arriving there, the second-largest massacre of white settlers by Aborigines in Australian history. Thomas and five others, who hid or were absent during the attack, were the only survivors.

The *Rockhampton Bulletin* reported:

> ... police overtook a tribe of the natives who committed the massacre at Nogoa; that they drove them into a place from which escape was impossible; that they shot down sixty or seventy, and ceased firing only when the ammunition was expended.

The Native Police, when controlled by New South Wales, operated primarily as a protective force. Under Queensland rule, they were used offensively to "disperse" Aborigines from areas selected for settlement. "Dispersal" was Orwellian doublespeak for "nothing but firing at them", in the words of a contemporary Queensland police officer.

Queensland's Native Police were not really police, but paramilitary death squads of the kind normally associated with South American dictatorships and failed African states. They operated in remote areas, mounting dawn attacks on Aboriginal camps, their horses and recently invented repeating rifles providing them with an overwhelming tactical advantage.

Queensland's first premier, Robert Herbert, explained the ultimate aim of dispersal:

> Every method of dealing with these very dangerous savages has been

tried, and I believe no more satisfactory system can be devised than that under which the people of Queensland endeavour to deal with a difficulty which it is feared can never terminate except with the gradual disappearance of the unimprovable race.

John Douglas, premier from 1877 to 1879, said the Native Police "did nothing else but shoot them [Aborigines] down whenever they could get at them. That was the sole function of the native police."

Up to 1,500 settlers were killed by Indigenous people on the Queensland frontier, according to historian Henry Reynolds. Historian Ray Evans estimates about 24,000 Indigenous deaths at the hands of the Queensland Native Police between 1859 and 1897, with the settlers accounting for thousands more. In contrast, there were 521 Australian casualties in the Vietnam War and 339 in the Korean War.[39]

Queensland's Aboriginal policy was economic, rather than ideological. Aborigines were a spoke in the wheel of the white man's progress. They killed his cows, burned his crops and raided his mines. The *Queenslander*, the colony's leading news and literary journal, perfectly summed up the policy's rationale:

> The desire for progressive advancement and substantial prosperity is, after all, stronger than sentimental dislike to the extinction of a savage and useless race.

THE FINE LINE BETWEEN DEATH AND SUCCESS

Burke arrived at Cooper's Creek only twenty-three days after leaving Menindee, having picked up the pace after dumping the German scientists. He settled in to wait for Wright and the supplies.

---

39   Henry Reynolds has called for conflict on the frontier to be recognised as a war, with its dead to be honoured at the Australian War Memorial. Horrified Australian leaders of all political persuasions have responded to this proposal in a manner reminiscent of Basil Fawlty.

Wills and another team member scouted for waterholes to the north. There was no water to be found and their three camels took the opportunity to run away.[40] Wills and his companion barely survived the three-day trek back to camp, crawling in with only half a litre of water between them.

A plague of native rats descended on the explorers' camp, eating their supplies, bedding and boot leather. The explorers moved down the Cooper and camped by a billabong under the shade of a coolabah tree. As every student of popular Australian culture knows, this inevitably ends in tragedy.

Wright had not shown up after almost a month and Burke was getting toey. He decided to make a run north with Wills, John King and Charlie Gray. Burke's remaining German, William Brahé, and the others were ordered to wait for three months at the depot camp under the coolabah. Wills quietly took Brahé aside and asked him to hang around for an extra month.

Burke's party encountered a large group of Yandruwandha people on the day they left for the Gulf of Carpentaria. Wills wrote:

> A large tribe of blacks came pestering us to go to their camp and have a dance, which we declined. They were very troublesome, and nothing but the threat to shoot them will keep them away.

Wills' unfriendly approach to wannabe dance partners would ultimately cost him his life.

The march north was easier than anticipated and on 9 February 1861, after enduring 3,245 kilometres of treacherous bogs, barren ridges and scorching dunes, Burke and Wills found themselves in a mangrove swamp. Being from the British Isles, they considered this a beach and decided they'd crossed the continent.

---

40 Two of the camels were discovered near Adelaide, more than 1,000 kilometres to the south, the following year. Desperate for a drink after the loss of their rum, they'd probably followed Stuart's whisky fumes back to their source.

It had taken Burke's party fifty-five days to almost reach the north coast from the Cooper depot and they only had twenty-seven days' worth of food left. Then it started raining. The baked sands of the outback became a sucking quagmire, as evidenced by Wills' names for the party's rest stops on the return journey: Muddy Camp, Humid Camp and Mosquito Camp.

The camels could take no more. One of them, Golah Sing, was left to wander the wilds of Australia without even a tot of rum. The fate of three of the remaining five camels provides evidence of the explorers' growing desperation – they were shot and eaten, as was Billy, the party's only horse.

The explorers' dwindling rations were supplemented by rose moss, which makes an excellent garnish for dead camel, and a giant python that left Burke and Gray doubled up with dysentery. Gray, whose heavy frame demanded more calories, was finding the going particularly tough.

One morning, Wills stumbled across Gray hiding behind a tree, stuffing his face with the party's nearly exhausted flour rations. Being a crawly dobber, Wills insisted Gray confess to Burke. It's hard to beat the shit out of someone who's already suffering from dysentery, but Burke gave it a bloody good go.

Gray rapidly declined and one night announced he would not live to see morning. He was proved correct. The three survivors stopped for the day and dug a grave for him with their bare hands. Gray's beating and burial slowed the party down – time which was to prove crucial.

On 21 April 1861, five days after Gray's death, the weary and starving explorers staggered into the depot. They'd been gone four months and five days. Burke found the still-warm ashes of a fire and the word "DIG" carved into the coolabah. He dug up a box of provisions and a note from Brahé that advised he'd left for Menindee just nine hours earlier. The explorers were too exhausted to follow.

Wills, who was either the sunniest of optimists or descending into madness, wrote, "A note left in the plant by Brahé communicates the pleasing information that they have started today for the Darling." The madness option seems most likely, with King recounting, "I may add that our disappointment at finding the Depot abandoned seemed to excite a feeling of merriment in the mind of Mr Wills."

After five days' rest, Burke decided to set out for Eyre's prophetically named Mount Hopeless, despite the protests of Wills and King that they should follow Brahé. The party decided to leave behind their journals and a note as to their plans. In a moment of brilliance, Burke decided these should be buried and the ground raked to look undisturbed. This would prevent any passing literary Aborigines from stealing their writings.

Meanwhile, Brahé had bumped into William Wright. Wright had waited more than three months before following Burke to Cooper's Creek, having refused to leave Menindee until the Exploration Committee ratified his appointment and give him funds for additional horses and supplies.

Wright's party had made painful progress, lacking a navigator and sufficient water but amply provided with swarms of wild rats and hostile Aborigines. Ludwig Becker, who'd decided to accompany Wright despite being sacked, and two other members of Wright's team died from their privations.

Wright, who really wanted to see the place he'd killed three men to reach, asked Brahé to take him to the depot. The two men reached it on 8 May, noted the camp was undisturbed, had a spot of lunch, and left. Burke's Aboriginal-proofing of the depot was also rescuer-proof.

Meanwhile, Landa and Rajah, the last of Burke's camels, had been shot after Landa got bogged and Rajah refused to move. The party could no longer cross the sands to Mount Hopeless. After garnishing the camels with unpleasant-tasting desert plants, Burke, Wills and King got down to the serious business of starving.

Friendly Aborigines briefly adopted the explorers and fed them fish, nardoo – gruel made from ground fern spores – and some dried leaves that impressed Wills with their "highly intoxicating effect".

But Wills found it unpleasant to "hang about Coopers Creek, living like the blacks" and the explorers decided to return to their own camp, make nardoo, and trap birds and rats for survival.

Wills went back to the depot on 30 May to deposit more of his writings, unaware that Wright and Brahé had recently been there. During Wills' time away, King recounted that Burke did not wish to accept fish from the Aborigines as "he was afraid of being too friendly lest they should always be at our camp". When Aborigines came to the camp offering fish, Burke knocked it out of their hands and fired over their heads. After the inconsiderate natives had been scared away, Burke cooked the fish in a high wind near his highly flammable shelter. The shelter and all of the party's remaining supplies, save two guns, were destroyed in the resulting inferno.

After Wills returned, the party decided they probably should have stayed with the Aborigines after all. But their good neighbours had not become good friends, as they didn't appreciate being shot at. There was nothing for the explorers to do but listlessly gather and pound nardoo.

The problem with nardoo is that, while filling, it has almost no nutritional value. Parts of the fern, when not properly washed, also destroy vitamin B1, causing degenerative brain damage. And so Burke, Wills and King starved on full stomachs and increasingly empty brains.[41]

Wills soon became too weak to move and Burke and King set out to find the Aborigines again, leaving Wills with plenty of nardoo to starve on. Wills asked Burke to give his watch and a letter to his father, his last journal entry reading:

My pulse is at forty-eight, and very weak, and my legs and arms are nearly skin and bone. I can only look out, like Mr Micawber, "for

41   It is likely that the trio suffered from beriberi, a disease caused by insufficient levels of vitamin B1. *Beriberi* means "I cannot, I cannot" in Sri Lanka's Sinhalese language, consistent with the apathy that is one of the disease's principal symptoms.

something to turn up"; but starvation on nardoo is by no means very unpleasant, but for the weakness one feels, and the utter inability to move oneself, for as far as appetite is concerned, it gives me the greatest satisfaction.

Wills' last letter to his father contains a postscript brimming with stiff upper lip:

P.S. I think to live about four or five days. My spirits are excellent.

Burke made only a few miles before he collapsed. He wrote a letter to his sister, in which he apologised for "having foolishly made over what I left behind to a young lady with whom I have only a slight acquaintance" and then disinherited Julia Matthews. His last coherent words to King were:

I hope you will remain with me here till I am quite dead – it is a comfort to know that someone is by; but, when I am dying, it is my wish that you should place the pistol in my right hand, and that you leave me unburied as I lie.

And so died the most incompetent explorer the world has ever known.

EXPLORERMANIA

Brahé and Wright returned to civilisation and reported that Burke and Wills had "done a Leichhardt". Wills' father and Julia Matthews, unaware of her deathbed disinheritance, demanded a rescue expedition. The press leaped on the idea and reported various outlandish plans, including giving the rescue party one end of a several-hundred-mile-long hose, with the other end attached to a giant water tank to be constructed on the banks of the Darling.[42]

---

42 Today, this proposal would be championed by Alan Jones.

ABC

The Exploration Committee sent Alfred Howitt to find the missing explorers. South Australia, not to be outdone, funded a separate team. Queensland, interested in annexing territory to its west, sent out two parties. Stuart, who'd made a second run for the north coast, returned to report his failure in September 1861. Despite being near blind from the desert sun, he offered to return to the wilderness to search for his competitor.

On 15 September 1861, Howitt's party found a scarecrow wearing a few rags and part of a hat. John King, who'd hooked up with the Yandruwandha, tearfully explained that his companions were dead. The dingo-gnawed corpses of Burke and Wills were buried and their journals and letters dug up so that the tale of their ineptitude could be shared with the world.

Word of Burke and Wills' deaths reached Melbourne on 2 November 1861. This was the news that stopped the race that stops the nation – the city was convulsed with mourning and had little interest in the inaugural Melbourne Cup, organised by Frederick Standish for the following Thursday.

Still, not all was doom and gloom. Victoria had won the much more important race across Australia! This point was generally conceded, although South Australians, who are sore losers, insisted that finding some brackish water twelve miles from the coast didn't count. South Australia sent Stuart off again to do the job properly.

Explorermania continued to build as King slowly made his way back to Melbourne. The sole survivor of the continental crossing, crippled by post-traumatic stress disorder, regularly burst into tears. When he stayed at inns, he was locked in his bedroom to protect him from "the many women who offered to look after him". As he was reluctantly paraded through country towns, hysterical onlookers cut clumps of his hair for souvenirs, leaving him with a surprised and mangy look. When his train arrived at Melbourne, thousands of admirers broke through the police guard and stormed the carriages. King was utterly terrified. He declined George Coppin's offer of

352

£1,000 to star in a panorama of the expedition, explaining, "I am totally unable to endure excitement, much less to appear before crowded audiences."[43]

A commission of inquiry into the expedition laid most of the blame for its failures at the feet of Wright, while lauding Burke for his daring and gallantry. Then someone asked why Burke and Wills' corpses had been left in the desert, so Howitt trudged back to retrieve them. When Burke and Wills were decanted into glass-topped coffins upon Howitt's return, Royal Society members souvenired teeth and hair. More than 100,000 Melbournians viewed the explorers' remains over the following fifteen days, with distinguished visitors allowed to fondle the bones. Bits of Burke and Wills were passed around as conversation pieces at Melbourne dinner parties for many years.

On 21 January 1863, Victoria declared a public holiday and held its first state funeral, with the remaining remains of Burke and Wills paraded through the streets to the strains of 60,000 cheering Victorians. The explorers were buried together in Melbourne General Cemetery. They lie there to this day.

THE *WASH-UP*

Stuart chose the day of Burke and Wills' funeral to return to Adelaide, which Victorians considered a base attempt to steal their explorers' limelight. Stuart had been kicked in the head by his horse, had his hand trampled, vomited blood and mucus, suffered the agonies of scurvy, lost most of his remaining vision and been dragged for several hundred kilometres on a stretcher rigged between two mounts. But he'd made it to the north coast and back and, as in all his expeditions, hadn't lost a single man. His expedition had cost only £2,500, in

---

43 King suffered from post-traumatic stress disorder until his death from consumption in 1873. He is believed to have left a daughter with the Yandruwandha, who was known as Yellow Alice.

contrast to the £57,840 expended on Burke and Wills. South Australia awarded Stuart the £2,000 prize but, concerned he'd drink it, only let him access the interest.

Britain knocked back Victoria's request to annexe Australia's north coast, instead extending Queensland's border to its current western boundary and incorporating the current Northern Territory into South Australia. Queensland's squatters started moving their stock in and the Aborigines out.[44]

On 22 August 1872, South Australia completed the Overland Telegraph Line from Adelaide to Palmerston (now Darwin). The explorer Alfred Giles, who helped build the line, recounted, "on that day South Australia touched a key and spoke to the British Empire – she had harnessed the world".

The Australian colonies could now communicate with Europe and America in a matter of hours, rather than months. They could negotiate wheat prices in advance, rather than turning up with a boatload of grain and haggling with merchants who knew they needed to make a sale. Australia had joined the global economy.[45]

Two things made this possible: camels and Afghans. Australia imported Afghan cameleers and their bad-tempered beasts to build Australia's telegraph, railway and overland transport networks. The camels were turned loose after they were replaced by trains and trucks in the early twentieth century and their 750,000 living descendants are the largest wild camel population in the world.

---

44 In 1875, the *Northern Territory Times* opined, "We are invading their country ... They look upon us as enemies and we must do the same by them when they molest us ... Shoot those you cannot get at and hang those that you do catch on the nearest tree as an example to the rest; and let not the authorities be too curious and ask too many questions of those who may be sent to perform the service."

45 Seventeen years later, Western Australia was connected to the Overland Telegraph, the line largely following Eyre's route. The South Australian section of the line was made of steel poles and copper wire. The Western Australian section was made of wooden poles, which were vulnerable to fire, termites and decay, and steel wire, which snapped under extremes of temperature. Australia has modelled its National Broadband Network on the Western Australia telegraph line.

The Afghans erected mosques in their segregated outback communities known as Ghan towns. They were shunned by many Australians, particularly after the Second Anglo–Afghan War of 1878–81, which resulted in the usual murder of British dignitaries, heavy British casualties and the evacuation of Kabul.

Today's Australian government would have reservations about handing over responsibility for critical infrastructure to persons of Middle Eastern appearance with a fondness for blowing up Westerners, but Burke and Wills lived – and died – in a more innocent age.

12

A widow's son outlawed

I am a Widow's Son, outlawed and my orders must be obeyed.

Ned Kelly, closing words of the Jerilderie letter, 1879

THIS VERY IRISH STORY

JOHN KELLY, KNOWN AS RED FOR HIS SHOCK OF GINGER hair, left Tasmania for Port Phillip after being pardoned in 1848.[1] Being Irish, he loved a fight, so he settled in Donnybrook. And being Irish, he loved a drink even more, so he moved to Beveridge.[2]

Red, like many fun-loving Irish folk, saw the glass as half full. Then he drank it. The livestock thief turned rural labourer was well known to the publicans of every community in which he settled.

In 1850, thirty-year-old Red met dairy farmer James Quinn, who'd emigrated from Ireland nine years earlier. He also met James's daughter, Ellen, an eighteen-year-old firebrand with a tongue that could strip ironbark at a hundred yards. Ellen was soon pregnant and

---

1   John, had he lived longer, would have been known as Bluey, rather than Red. *Bluey* originally referred to a drover's swag, which was traditionally covered in a blue blanket. By 1906, it was being used as a name for a redhead, in line with the Australian working-class habit of using a word to convey a contrary meaning. This habit has recently been revived by young people who say "sick" in appreciation of the skateboard or video game that they are using to annoy you.

2   Most Irish, like Tasmanians, didn't worry about spelling.

Red, being a good Catholic, married her. Ellen, being a good Catholic, bore him eight children over the next fifteen years.

Red and Ellen's third child, Edward, known to all as Ned, was "born at the time of the Eureka Stockade", according to his family. His parents were not keen on filing paperwork with the government (which was not to be trusted), so all we know is that Ned entered this world sometime between December 1854 and June 1855.

Red had made a little money on the goldfields and entered into business with the Quinns. The Quinns, like Red, were animal liberationists who were passionately committed to freeing other people's horses and cattle. Jimmy Quinn, Ned's uncle, was charged with possessing stolen livestock when Ned was one year old. Ned was five when Jimmy was charged with horse theft and assault. Jack Quinn, another uncle, went before a magistrate for cattle stealing and armed robbery. Ellen's brother-in-law, Jack Lloyd, was charged with assault, drunk and disorderly conduct and larceny.

Ned had his first court appearance at eight years of age, providing an alibi for Uncle Jimmy, whose obsessive interest in other people's cows had again brought him before the courts. The magistrate did not believe young Ned, and Jimmy was sentenced to three years' hard labour.

Five of Red's siblings joined him in Victoria, with brother James soon in trouble for cattle theft. The Kellys, Quinns and Lloyds were a close-knit family of petty crims. They got drunk, they swore and they fought, but family get-togethers were good fun – and there was always a lot of meat.

The gentlemen of the Melbourne Club would have regarded the family as "typical Irish". In 1861, the Irish made up 15 per cent of the Australian population, but 30 per cent of prison inmates. They were placed on poor relief at almost twice the general rate. Job ads would commonly end with "No Irish need apply".

The 1860s saw a new wave of Irish migrants break on Australia's shores, with the Civil War deterring migration to America. Bishop Quinn of Brisbane arranged for boatloads of Irish Catholics to settle in pineapple country, with Protestant critics dubbing the northern colony Quinnsland.[3]

The Irish newcomers also settled in Victoria, which was still reeling from the failed assimilation of the Potato Famine orphans, many of whom had forged successful careers in the exciting prostitution and vagrancy industries. Anti-Irish sentiment, already high, frothed over like a poorly poured Guinness.

Prejudice against the Irish helped fuel Australians' contempt for the police. By 1874, 82 per cent of Victoria's police were Paddies.[4] Protestants made up about half the Irish police, but dominated senior ranks. Protestant police, many of whom had served in the brutal anti-nationalist Royal Irish Constabulary, were generally hated by their Catholic countrymen, but not as much as Irish Catholic police, who were seen as traitors to their faith, class and a free Ireland.[5]

At the same time, Irishmen dominated Victorian politics and the law. John O'Shanassy, three times premier in the 1850s, was an Irish Catholic, as was federation campaigner Charles Gavan Duffy. Chief Justice William Stawell was an Irish Anglican, as were Justice Redmond Barry, Justice Robert Molesworth and Richard Ireland, who'd entered parliament after representing the Eureka rebels.

---

3   An ardent Irish nationalist, the bishop later changed his name to O'Quinn because Quinn just wasn't Irish enough.

4   The term *paddy wagon*, meaning a police van, derives from the high proportion of Irish people arrested (the British view), the high proportion of Irish people doing the arresting (the American view), or the high proportion of Irish people arrested by the high proportion of Irish people doing the arresting (the Australian view).

5   Ned Kelly, in his rambling Jerilderie letter, called Victoria's police "a parcel of big ugly fat-necked wombat headed big bellied magpie legged narrow hipped splaw-footed sons of Irish Bailiffs or english landlords". An Irish policeman, according to Kelly, was "a disgrace to his country and ancestors and religion as they were all catholics before the Saxons ... a Policeman who for a lazy loafing cowardly billet left the ash corner deserted the Shamrock, the emblem of true wit and beauty to serve under a flag and nation that has destroyed massacred and murdered their forefathers by the greatest of torture as rolling them down hill in spiked Barrels pulling their toes and finger nails and on the wheel and every torture imaginable".

The Irish establishment were still derided for their origins, as shown by the Molesworth Affair (or more accurately, the Molesworth Affairs, as the case centred on the extra-marital activities of Mrs Justice Molesworth). In 1861, Mrs Molesworth sued her husband for divorce on the grounds of cruelty. Molesworth counterclaimed, accusing his wife of adultery with Richard Ireland and an unknown man, to whom she'd fallen pregnant.

Molesworth admitted to spying on his wife through a keyhole, beating her in the street and having sex with her twice after accusing her of adultery (including once in the parlour, which was considered most scandalous). When he suspected his wife of having an affair with Ireland, he inspected her dress for stains, "which were not found wanting".[6] This resulted in Molesworth being mocked as the "Inspector of Linen for Ireland".

Molesworth being (a) a man and (b) a judge was cleared of cruelty, despite being a crazy wife-beating stalker. Ireland being (a) a man and (b) a politician was cleared of adultery. The unfortunate Mrs Molesworth was found to have slept with an unknown man and to have therefore been at fault in the divorce. She became an unsupported single mother, which was not a lot of fun in Victorian Victoria.

Still, Molesworth and Ireland were ridiculed in the press, which loved a bit of Paddy-bashing. The *Argus* reported:

> There is something in the case ... that is quite un-English, and with an odour about it such as only one nationality in the world could furnish ... where can we read anything to match this very Irish story?

The *Age* sermonised, "Some latitude, even in morals, must always be permitted to the inhabitants of that happy land where people and pigs huddle promiscuously."

---

6   If Monica Lewinsky had studied *Molesworth v. Molesworth*, she would have saved
     herself a lot of trouble.

Fear of Fenians, militant Irish nationalists operating out of Ireland and America, grew during the 1860s. The Fenians, formed in 1858 by survivors of the 1848 uprising, started the proud Irish republican tradition of blowing shit up.

Prince Alfred's visit to Australia in 1867–68, the first by a member of the British Royal family, fanned anti-Irish and anti-Catholic sentiment. Melbourne's Orangemen welcomed Alfred by erecting a giant mural that celebrated the Catholic defeat at the Battle of the Boyne. Catholics stoned the Melbourne Protestant Hall in retaliation. The Orangemen responded with gunfire, shooting dead an eleven-year-old boy.

Prince Alfred retired to Sydney after his Melbourne brothel crawl with Commissioner Standish. While enjoying a picnic on Sydney Harbour's Clontarf Beach, the prince was shot in the back by the barking-mad Henry James O'Farrell, who initially claimed he'd been ordered to assassinate the prince by Melbourne Fenians.[7] O'Farrell was hanged despite Alfred's recommendation for clemency.[8]

John Dunmore Lang regarded the assassination attempt as "a priestly plot", while Henry Parkes was convinced Irish terrorists wanted to blow *him* up. New South Wales rushed through the *Treason Felony Act 1868*, making it an offence to speak or write disrespectfully of the queen or "factiously avow a determination to refuse to join in any loyal toast or demonstration in honour of Her Majesty".[9]

---

7   O'Farrell's equally mad brother Peter attempted to shoot Catholic Archbishop Goold of Melbourne in 1882.

8   The attempted assassination of Prince Alfred did wonders for the Australian health system. Alfred was nursed by Lucy Osburn, who'd arrived a week earlier with five other Florence Nightingale–trained women to teach nursing. While Osburn was vilified by male doctors for invading their turf, the popularity she gained from looking after the prince helped her develop Australia's first nursing system. A public fund was also established to build a hospital as a memorial to the prince's recovery. Sydney's Royal Prince Alfred Hospital is now a world leader in healthcare.

9   Australian rugby lock, author, historian and chair of the Australian Republican Movement Peter FitzSimons would have been gaoled under these laws. He would also have been savagely beaten in prison for wearing that ridiculous red bandana.

The same year, sixty-two members of the Irish Republican Brotherhood were transported to Western Australia, with the citizens
of Perth fearing an Irish terrorist prison breakout. These political
prisoners were the last of the 162,000 convicts sent to Australia.

In 1870, the Irish poet, barrister and journalist Gerald Supple
shot Victorian politician George Paton Smith in the elbow for his
anti-Irish rhetoric, and killed an innocent bystander (another proud
Irish republican tradition). Supple declared he was not insane, but
"undertaking a public duty in attacking the slander and vilification
rife in the colony".

New South Wales premier Henry Parkes, who dismissed the Irish
as "jabbering baboons", said in 1872:

> I protest against Irishmen coming here and bringing their national
> grievances to disturb this land of ours ... Until Irishmen learn to be
> Australian colonists ... they must not be surprised if people regard
> their presence as something not very desirable.

In this fevered climate, when even the most powerful Irishmen were
mocked, what chance had poor country Irish like the Kellys?

A VOTE, A RIFLE AND A FARM

Land was the greatest problem for the poor country Irish. Many
immigrants, including Irish serfs who'd worked the estates of the
English invaders, wanted their own land and to be beholden to no
master. However, the squatters occupied Australia's richest country.[10]

---

10 Irish squatters were as rare as Irish Mensa members. Samuel Pratt Winter was a
    notable exception. Winter wanted to create a utopian feudal Ireland in Victoria
    and Irish labourers flocked to work his runs "because he had a very tall hat", a
    sign of distinction, and he paid well. The confirmed bachelor bred Pyrenean
    sheepdogs, collected paintings and antique books and wrote a touching poem
    about the swing gate he invented to separate rams from ewes. Whenever he
    visited the Melbourne Club, he was accompanied by two giant sheepdogs and an
    Aboriginal boy in full footman's livery. In his will, he asked to be buried under an

Victorian Lands Minister Charles Gavan Duffy was determined to shatter the status quo. In 1850, back in Ireland, Duffy had formed the Tenant Right League to unify Catholic and Protestant farmers to campaign for improved access to land. He was elected to the British House of Commons on this platform, but migrated to Victoria in disgust after sectarian divisions fractured the league. Gavan Duffy was elected to Victoria's first Legislative Assembly, where he pursued his passion for land redistribution.

Moses Wilson Gray had sailed with Duffy to Victoria, where he worked as a barrister and a journalist. At Duffy's urging, he led the public campaign to "unlock the lands". Gray's dream was that every man should have "a vote, a rifle and a farm".

John Robertson led the charge in New South Wales.[11] The one-time squatter spokesman believed his former allies' grip on the land was preventing agricultural development and keeping rural families like the Kellys in poverty. He resigned as premier to devote his energies to opening up the colony to farming. Robertson received a boost when Caroline Chisholm rejoined the fray, delivering a series of lectures on the need to open up farmland to migrant families.

In the early 1860s, Robertson and Duffy passed laws allowing farmers to "select" small blocks of land, with South Australia soon following suit.[12] When squatting leases expired, selectors could select

---

unmarked cairn with the Aborigines on his property. This was such a shocking request that it was ignored.

11   Robertson turned up to parliament in his dusty farm clothes. His "peculiar voice", a legacy of his cleft palate, "gave authority to a comprehensive repertoire of profanity". He was a straight shooter with "an enviable capacity to take and hold his liquor". The five-time premier of New South Wales drank a pint of rum each morning, explaining, "none of the men who have left footprints in this country have been cold water men."

12   South Australia had introduced its own great land reform in 1858. Premier Robert Torrens, son of the colony's founder, was upset that 75 per cent of South Australian land holdings were open to challenge because title deeds proving ownership were regularly lost, hidden in laundry bags, eaten by sheep, rendered illegible by spilled cabernet sauvignon, etc. With the assistance of Ulrich Hübbe, a Hamburg lawyer, he introduced a government register that could be relied on to establish

land that had been used by the squatters. The selectors had to pay the government rent and improve the land by cultivating, fencing or building on it before purchase.

The squatters did not take this well. They bought as much of the best land as they could, including through dummy selectors who transferred the land to them. They campaigned for well-watered Crown land to be kept public for stock routes and continued to graze there. The squatter-dominated Victorian and New South Wales Legislative Councils obstructed selection at every opportunity.

Selectors often occupied marginal farmland with poor access to water. They'd wake in the morning to find their fences mysteriously knocked down and squatters' livestock contentedly munching on their crops. It took until the 1870s for the kinks in selection law to be worked through and selectors to make a real go of it, with German, Italian, Swiss and Chinese settlers proving the most adaptable to smaller-scale farming.

Many poor rural families, Ned's included, hated the squatters, who they believed were denying them land to maintain their economic, political and social power and supply of cheap labour. Stealing their horses and cattle seemed a fair way of redistributing wealth.

Rural rustlers like the Quinns and the Kellys inspired the Victorian government to introduce stock protection laws in 1862. People had to notify police before killing a cow and keep the cow's branded hide to prove it had been theirs to kill. Of course, this law was never enforced against squatters.

The Kellys were struggling. Red had sold his small farm at a loss when Ned was two years old and the clan had moved into a two-room wooden shack with an open drain running down the middle of a dirt floor. Red's drinking increased as his family spiralled further into poverty.

Ellen wanted a better future for her kids and Ned was sent to

---

ownership. Torrens title, which incorporated elements of Hamburg property law, is now used in many countries.

the local Catholic school at the age of eight, along with two of his sisters. Ned was a competent, if uninterested, student who excelled at running, jumping and throwing things at nuns. In 1864, the family moved north in an attempt to break free of the criminal influence of James Kelly and the Quinn boys.

Life was even tougher in the tiny hamlet of Avenel, where the 1865 drought cruelled Red's attempt at dairy farming. Red abandoned milk for moonshine, setting up a still and selling the small amounts of paint stripper he didn't drink. That year, a neighbour's calf wandered onto Red's property. Red, needing to feed his family, killed it.

Red, for obvious reasons, hadn't sought police permission to kill the calf, but he inexplicably complied with the requirement to keep its hide. When the police searched his hovel, they found a skin branded with his neighbour's mark. Red was acquitted of cattle theft (to everyone's surprise), but found guilty of illegally possessing a cowskin. Unable to pay the fine, he was gaoled for six months. Ten-year-old Ned was now the man of the house. He left school for good.

The Kellys and their criminally minded kin regularly featured in the court section of local newspapers, but in 1865, Ned made the news for all the right reasons. He'd rescued seven-year-old Dick Shelton from drowning in a swollen creek, earning a green sash with a golden fringe from Dick's appreciative parents. Ned was a hero – and he loved it.

In April 1865, the head of Mad Dan Morgan was carried triumphantly through Avenel, on its way to be fondled by anatomists at the University of Melbourne. The following month, news of the deaths of Brave Ben Hall and Happy Jack Gilbert reached the village. Ned, like many other boys, soaked up stories of bushrangers like a lamington.[13] He would go on to emulate the heroes of his youth. And surpass them.

---

13   For foreign readers, a lamington is an Australian sponge. The delicious dessert, smothered in chocolate and desiccated coconut, was named in honour of Charles Wallace Alexander Napier Cochrane-Baillie, 2nd Baron Lamington and eighth governor of Queensland. Lamington reportedly detested lamingtons, referring to them as "those bloody poofy woolly biscuits". He is otherwise famous for stopping to a shoot a koala on his way to opening one of Queensland's first national parks.

BRAVE BEN, HAPPY JACK AND MAD DAN

After the Eureka Rebellion, police who'd been harassing miners were redeployed to harass bushrangers. Bushranging declined in Victoria, but picked up in New South Wales, where there was more bush and fewer police.

In 1862, the government established the New South Wales Police Force, bringing locally administered units under a central command. Many experienced native-born officers were dismissed or transferred to new districts in the hope this would remove them from corrupting local influences. Senior native-born police were replaced by English and Irish officers who were unfamiliar with the bush.

Sir Frederick Pottinger was one of the beneficiaries of this restructure. He was put in command of the Western District, the epicentre of bushranging in the colony. Pottinger was a black-sheep baronet who'd been sent to Australia for losing his inheritance on the race-track. He'd concealed his background and worked as a trooper on the Goulburn to Gundagai gold escort for years before his title was discovered by John McLerie, the inspector-general of police. McLerie was mystified as to how a chap of such good breeding could be slumming it with the plebs, so he promoted Pottinger through the ranks.

Bushrangers such as Frank Gardiner, the leader of the colony's largest bandit gang, exploited the confusion arising from the police reforms. Gardiner, known as The Darkie for his swarthy skin, was wanted for breaking parole, highway robbery and shooting and wounding a police officer. He was at the top of Pottinger's wanted list.

In June 1862, Gardiner's gang blocked the road near Eugowra and ambushed a heavily guarded gold coach. They came out guns blazing, shooting one trooper in the testicles and making off with £14,000. Pottinger captured two of Gardiner's men, but was ambushed by the bushrangers, who rescued their companions and the banknotes they were carrying. Pottinger and eight police then tried to apprehend

Gardiner while he was visiting his mistress, Kitty Brown. Pottinger's gun misfired and Gardiner escaped.[14]

Pottinger was a laughing-stock for having Australia's largest-ever hold-up take place on his watch, losing two prisoners in another hold-up and failing to capture Gardiner despite having him surrounded.

In reprisal, Pottinger held Kitty's fifteen-year-old brother for six months without trial in a freezing cell, before the boy succumbed to pneumonia. He also arrested local farmer Ben Hall, Kitty Brown's brother-in-law, for involvement in the Eugowra robbery. Pottinger had earlier arrested Hall for holding up a cart with Gardiner and had been furious when he was acquitted. The frustrated policeman was again forced to release Hall, who'd always denied any involvement with Gardiner, for want of evidence. Pottinger did not take defeat well – he was charged with assaulting a critic and threatened to whip politician Joseph Jehoshaphat Harpur for denouncing his handling of the Eugowra affair.[15]

Ben Hall was having problems of his own. His wife had left him for an ex-copper, taking his young son with her, and mounting legal bills forced him to quit his farm. Then the vengeful Pottinger burned down his home.

Hall blamed the police for ruining his life. Declaring that he "may as well have the game as the blame", he turned bushranger, hooking up with Johnny Gilbert, a youthful Canadian who'd run with Gardiner. Hall was one of the new breed of bushrangers. He wasn't a desperate convict or foreign digger down on his luck. He was a native-born Australian who felt that British immigrants controlled the land and government, locking out those raised in the new country.

---

14 Police had limited access to firearms and those they did have were all too often faulty. They were completely outgunned by any half-decent bushranging outfit. The police force only employed men over thirty years of age, while bushrangers were generally younger and fitter. Bushrangers also had better mounts, often stolen racehorses.

15 Harpur very sensibly asked people to call him J.J.

The police had not only brought his world crashing down – they were the embodiment of the unjust state.

Johnny Gilbert, known as Happy Jack for his cheery disposition, shared Hall's hatred of the police.[16] The Gilbert-Hall gang committed crimes designed to cause maximum embarrassment to Pottinger and his cronies. They struck Bathurst while the police galloped off into the bush to look for them. They held up entire towns, with the people of Canowindra kept captive in the local pub for three days. Gilbert and Hall paid for everybody's food and drinks, passed around cigars and allowed their hostages to leave for an hour each day to attend to their business. They stole only £3 and a revolver during their stay.

The *Bathurst Times* understood the gang desired fame as much as money, writing:

> Every new success is a source of pleasure, and they are stimulated to a
> novelty of action from a desire to create a history ... Every word they
> say, and everything they do, is recorded, and they aspire to a name.

Gilbert and Hall were young punks. They spat in the eye of authority and then urinated on its doorstep. Their fuck-you attitude, flash clothing and long hair (a native-born affectation) made them pin-up boys for a generation of disaffected youth. A miserable old person, who had nothing better to do than write outraged letters to the newspaper about the sorry state of young people today, complained to the *Sydney Morning Herald*:

> I am satisfied that there are hundreds of lads in that neighbour-
> hood under twenty, that would give one of their eyes to have the
> same notoriety as Gilbert or Gardiner. They never work, never have
> worked, and they are, without exception, the flashest lot I ever saw.

---

16   The wanted notice for Gilbert described him as having "laughing eyes". They don't
     do wanted notices like they used to.

Something must be done by the Government, or things will become worse and worse, and what will be the end of it no one can tell.

According to the *Yass Courier*, bushranging was the start of a slippery slope that ended in cross-dressing:

> Mr Yuill states that about 10 minutes before he was stuck up he met striding along the road a tall ungainly looking woman, and from what afterwards occurred firmly believes it to have been no woman at all, but Gilbert disguised as one; if so it is not the first time Gilbert has adopted female apparel, for I am credibly informed that when he stuck up Hammond's store in Junee, one of the servant girls there was making some remarks about his long and well oiled hair, and he laughingly observed, "I'm obliged to wear it long, for I've sometimes to dress in women's clothes, and I intend to escape out of the country in petticoats." It is well known that he attended the Young races, mounted on horseback, disguised in a lady's riding habit, hat, and feather. His smooth good-looking face much assists him in this respect.[17]

Gilbert and Hall's popularity meant locals gave them food, shelter and tip-offs. The gang committed robberies on an undreamed-of scale, once holding up sixty travellers in a day. Hall is believed to have committed more than 600 robberies without shooting anyone. His companions, though, were not so reticent, with Gilbert and another gang member killing police.

Pottinger, an excellent horseman, rode in the Wowingragong races and was sacked for enjoying a day at the track instead of slogging through the bush in search of Gilbert and Hall. Aggrieved, he set off to Sydney to seek reinstatement. Unfortunately, while stepping aboard a moving coach, the gun that had failed to fire in

---

17 This did Gilbert's tough-guy image no harm. Aussie blokes love frocking up or squeezing into a tutu. Just look at *The Footy Show*.

his confrontation with Gardiner discharged into his abdomen. The bushrangers' patsy was fittingly buried on a hill overlooking Royal Randwick Racecourse.

Gilbert and Hall's crime wave forced business and government to take new precautions. Banknotes were torn in half, with the pieces transported separately, and money orders and non-negotiable cheques were used. Those who harboured bushrangers faced fifteen years' gaol and declared outlaws could be shot without warning if they didn't surrender by a specified date. The date for Gilbert and Hall's surrender was set for 10 May 1865.

The gang was now under serious pressure. They'd lost a good deal of popular support by robbing their sympathisers, children and the poor; firing on their victims without warning; and letting their horses graze on smallholders' crops. Landowners took the law into their own hands and shot dead two of the gang. Other members surrendered or drifted away. Frank Gardiner had been tracked down to Queensland, where he was running a small store with Kitty – his thirty-two-year prison sentence made it clear that the bushrangers were not invincible.

Gilbert and Hall were betrayed by friends who couldn't resist the £1,000 reward for their death or capture. On 5 May 1865, seven policemen and an Aboriginal tracker crept up on Hall and shot him at least sixteen times. This was an illegal execution, as the outlaw declaration had not yet taken effect. Gilbert was shot dead eight days later.

Dan Morgan was the only bushranger of the era who rivalled Gilbert and Hall in notoriety. Although he committed comparatively few crimes, he made up for this through sheer bloody-minded brutality. Dan was not known as Slightly Odd Dan Morgan or Mildly Disturbed Dan Morgan, but as Mad Dan Morgan.[18]

---

18   Dan Morgan was born John Fuller and also known as John Smith, Down-the-River Jack, Billy the Native, Sydney Native and Dan the Breaker, suggestive of a multiple personality disorder. Dennis Hopper, Hollywood's most unhinged actor,

Mad Dan, whose reign of terror lasted from 1863 to 1865, had hypnotic eyes, a hooked nose, long dark ringlets and a formidable black beard: an Australian Rasputin. He rarely operated in company and shot one of his few partners, German Bill, during a gunfight with police so they would focus on his wounded mate while he escaped.

Mad Dan shot dead police and their informants. He held a woman's legs in a fire while interrogating her as to the location of her money. He tied a squatter to a fence and attempted to burn him to death. He would stampede coach horses after a hold-up, indifferent to the fate of the driver and passengers inside.

Mad Dan delighted in humiliating squatters, forcing them to wait on their servants while he held up their stations. During one station raid, Dan got drunk and accidentally fired his pistol. Thinking he was under attack, Dan went more apeshit than Bubbles at a Neverland enema party, shooting and seriously wounding a hostage and the station manager. Dan, who was known for his rapid mood swings, solicitously treated the wounded hostage's leg and allowed another man to fetch a doctor. Then, thinking better of it, he chased the man down and shot him in the back, returned him to the station and tenderly nursed him until he died.

Dan worked mainly in southern New South Wales, but crossed the border with the intention of "taking the flashness out of the Victorian police". On 8 April 1865, he held up Peechelba Station where, in a moment of kindness, he allowed a nursemaid to leave the room to tend to an infant. Instead, she notified the station's co-owner, who galloped off to fetch the police.

Mad Dan left the station the next morning, was surrounded by police and shot in the back by a station employee. His head was removed and, according to the *Kilmore Free Press*, "tossed around the room like a football" before being transported past Ned Kelly's home

---

was chosen to play Mad Dog Morgan in the highly unreliable 1976 biopic of the bushranger's life.

to Melbourne. There is some debate as to whether police souvenired his scalped chin or his scrotum for use as a tobacco pouch.

The deaths of Mad Dan, Brave Ben and Happy Jack marked the beginning of the end of the Golden Age of Bushranging in New South Wales. The Clarke brothers, Braidwood's answer to the Krays, enjoyed a short and violent spree, and Captain Thunderbolt and his half-Aboriginal wife, Mary Ann Ward, gave bushranging one last hurrah until Thunderbolt was shot, beaten and drowned in 1870. Then it was all over.

New South Wales, which craved respect as a civilised and modern dominion of the British Empire, was embarrassed by the brutal bearded relics of the frontier era. It would be better for all if they'd quietly faded away.

In 1874, Governor Sir Hercules Robinson pardoned Frank Gardiner on condition that he spend the remainder of his sentence in exile. Gardiner sailed for San Francisco, where he opened a saloon. Henry Parkes moved a motion to censure Robinson for exceeding his authority, but parliament backed in the governor by one vote and the defeated Parkes ministry was forced out of office.

The vanquished bushrangers had managed to do what they failed to achieve in their prime – bring down the government.

THE CARDS ARE STACKED

Back in Victoria, Red Kelly was arrested for drunk and disorderly conduct two months after his release from prison. The demon drink claimed his life the following year. Ellen, a single mother of seven children, found life tough. She was fined for abusive language and for assaulting one of Red's sisters.

In 1867, Ellen and her children moved to tiny Greta with two of her sisters. A week after they left Avenel, the *Police Gazette* put out an alert for twelve-year-old Edward Kelly. Ned was wanted for horse theft, his five-year-old brother, Dan, suspected of the same crime.

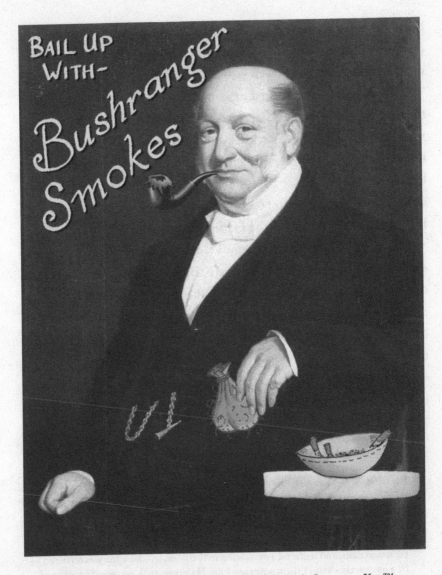

FIG. 12: THE BUSHRANGER SMOKES GENTLEMAN'S SMOKING KIT™
INCLUDES A WILD COLONIAL BOY ENTRY-WOUND PIPE™ AND
MAD DAN BACCY SAC™. BUY NOW AND RECEIVE A COMPLIMENTARY
JEWBOY ASHTRAY™. BACCY NOT INCLUDED.

Red's brother James, fresh out of prison, visited the derelict hotel where the three sisters and their seventeen children were living. He drunkenly propositioned Ellen, who bludgeoned him with a gin bottle. James considered this a waste of good gin and burned down the hotel. Sir Redmond Barry sentenced him to death for attempted murder, commuted to fifteen years' hard labour.

Ellen, working as a washerwoman and seamstress, scrimped together a deposit for an 88-acre selection at Eleven Mile Creek, four miles out of Greta. Her shack served as a one-star hotel and sly grog house for passing travellers. Ellen had a daughter with a partner who left her shortly before the baby died of dysentery. She married 23-year-old Californian horse thief George King at the age of forty-two and had two more children before George abandoned her.

Ellen was charged with furious riding (the nineteenth-century equivalent of a speeding ticket), stealing a saddle, the illegal sale of alcohol, drunk and disorderly conduct, using obscene language and assault during her first eight years in Greta. But whatever criticisms might be levelled at her, Ellen loved her children and they loved her.

Harry Power, who'd broken out of gaol with Captain Melville, escaped again in 1869 after hiding in a hole in the gaol wall.[19] He

---

19 Power was a novice escape artist compared with Western Australia's Joseph Bolitho Johns (better known as Moondyne Joe), the Harry Houdini of the bushranging fraternity. Joe escaped Toodyay Gaol within hours of being imprisoned, galloping off on the horse he'd been gaoled for stealing. After his recapture, Joe escaped from a work party and was placed in leg-irons. This did not stop him from escaping again. Next time he was caught, Joe was chained to the bars of his cell by his neck while an "escape-proof" room was built to hold him. His new accommodation was lined with heavy jarrah sleepers, secured by over a thousand nails, and featured a metal ring in the floor, to which Joe was tethered by a one-metre chain. Prison governor John Hampton told Joe that if he escaped again, then he deserved his freedom. With his health failing from his special confinement, Joe was allowed to exercise by breaking rocks in the prison yard, under the watch of a warder. Nobody thought to clear the increasingly large pile of rocks that Joe produced. The warder thought he had Joe in his sights, only to discover the escapologist had dressed his pick with a jacket and cap and squeezed through the hole in the prison wall he'd been surreptitiously working on behind his pile of rocks. Hampton decided that Joe didn't deserve his freedom after all and offered £20 of his own money to any man who brought Joe back that day, dead or alive. Joe was recaptured two years later when a police wine-tasting group found him in the cellar of Houghton Winery, which he'd broken into for a drink. Joe was returned to prison, but later released by the new prison governor, who felt obliged

headed for north-east Victoria, where his prison buddy Jack Lloyd, Ned's uncle, was living. Power took Ned under his wing and the pair embarked on a horse-jacking spree before the runaway moved on to New South Wales.

That year, fourteen-year-old Ned was charged with assaulting and robbing the onomatopoeically named Ah Fook. The Chinaman claimed Ned told him, "I'm a bushranger; give up your money, or I'll beat you to death." The local police were furious when Ned was acquitted.

Power returned in 1870 and taught Ned how to rob people while pointing a gun at them. The duo held up Robert McBean, the squatter who'd occupied the Kellys' land before it was selected, liberating him of an expensive watch and saddle. McBean was a close friend of Commissioner Frederick Standish, who upped the reward for Power's capture to £500 and sent his favourite pet, Superintendent Francis Hare, to bring in the bushranger.[20] The *Benalla Ensign* prophetically wrote:

> The effect of [Power's] example has already been to draw one young fellow into the open vortex of crime, and unless his career is speedily cut short, young Kelly will blossom into a declared enemy of society.

Ned, outed as Power's accomplice, had fallen out with his mentor. Hare and Superintendent Charles Nicolson, who'd pulled rank to

---

to honour Hampton's earlier statement. Moondyne Joe finally escaped the world on 13 August 1900.

20 Superintendent John Sadleir, who would later join Standish and Hare in the hunt for the Kelly Gang, wrote of Standish's infatuation for Hare: "I have spoken of evil friendships, but his devotion to Frank Hare was of another kind – it was like the love of Jonathan for David. It was almost pathetic to see, during the months Captain Standish spent at Benalla ... how restless and uneasy he became were Hare out of his company. I have seen Standish on the top rail of a fence watching anxiously for Hare's return from a short ride of a mile or two. He said to me he was in constant fear lest some accident should befall him." For those of you interested in what was going on between Jonathan and David, David said unto Jonathan, "very pleasant hast thou been unto me: thy love to me was wonderful, passing the love of women" (2 *Samuel* 1:26). The Bible can get quite racy.

take over the Power case, arrested the boy when he returned to his mother, but strangely presented no evidence against him when the case went to court. Power, captured by Hare and Nicolson in his bush camp, put the word out that Ned's soft treatment was reward for leading the police to him, although it was Ned's uncle and Power's mate, Jack Lloyd, who pocketed the reward money.

Ned had miraculously escaped a conviction for his youthful indiscretions. But the luck of the Irish was about to desert him. Mr and Mrs McCormick accused Ned of stealing their horse when they found him using it to pull another man's cart out of – in Ned's words – "ground ... that rotten it would bog a duck". Resenting the accusation, Ned sent the childless Mrs McCormick a parcel containing a pair of freshly castrated calf's testicles, with a note that she should give them to her husband so he could "tie them to his own cock [so] he might shag her better the next time". The parcel was delivered to Mr McCormick, who didn't see the funny side. The McCormicks set out to find the young practical joker.

Ned, in the Jerilderie letter, explained what happened next:

> Mrs McCormack struck my horse in the flank with a bullocks shin
> it jumped forward and my fist came in collision with McCormacks
> nose and caused him to lose his equillibrium and fall prostrate.[21]

The court did not believe this improbable tale and Ned spent six months in gaol for assault and indecent behaviour (the testicle thing).

After his release, Ned took a stolen mare into town and Constable Hall tried to arrest him. Ned repeatedly threw Hall to the ground and later admitted, "I straddled him and rooted both spurs into his thighs. He roared like a big calf attacked by dogs."

Ned was acquitted of theft after pointing out that the mare had been stolen while he was behind bars. However, the court, which had

---

21   This is up there with "I was having a shower and fell onto that shampoo bottle you
       can see on the X-ray."

seen far too much of Ned recently, sentenced him to three years' hard labour for receiving a stolen horse.

THE DECK IS DEALT

Ned was released from prison in 1874, a strapping six-footer covered with slabs of muscle hardened from hauling rocks. His youthful face sported the first wisps of the beard he'd lovingly tend until the day he died.

The world had changed while Ned was inside. Gleaming new rail tracks brought goods from Melbourne to Glenrowan, an hour's walk from Ned's home. That home was missing a few familiar faces. His brother Jim was serving five years for cattle theft and his sister Annie had died in childbirth while her husband was in gaol. Annie had had an affair with Constable Ernest Flood, a married man who cut off all contact with her after she told him she was pregnant. Flood later arrested Ellen for receiving a stolen saddle and, Ned believed, stole all but one of Ned's thirty horses while he was in prison. A copper had shamed (and in his mind, killed) his beloved sister, persecuted his grieving mother and taken his most prized possessions. Ned's contempt for the police hardened into hatred.

Ned also had to see a man about a horse. Isaiah "Wild" Wright, who'd stolen the mare Ned went down for, had not spoken up in Ned's defence after he was charged. Ned walked into a pub and challenged Wild, the district's most feared bar-room brawler, to a fight. The publican asked the men to take it outside and provided them with the long underpants, silk shorts and singlets that he kept on hand for such occasions. The crowd of drinkers moved outside to watch Ned and Wild beat the bejesus out of each other for twenty rounds, at which time Wild conceded defeat, the only time he'd ever been beaten. The two men bonded over a post-fight beer because that's what Aussie blokes do.

Ned, a natural leader, got a job as the overseer of a local sawmill, but the mill wound down when the railway line to Beechworth was finished. Ned reverted to what he knew best.

When squatters demanded that Ned pay them to release Kelly horses that had strayed onto their property, he simply stole them back. Then he kept on stealing, setting up a sophisticated horse rebirthing racket – a horse's brand would be altered with iodine, the horse would be sold at a distant stockyard using an assumed name, one of Ned's mates would buy the horse and obtain documents of a legal sale, and the horse would be resold to an unsuspecting punter before the iodine wore off.

Ned and Wild Wright gathered a group of young men who rode horses, stole horses and got drunk with their horses. The Greta Mob, as they were known, grew their hair long, Ben Hall–style, donned brightly coloured sashes instead of belts, and strutted around town in high-heeled spurred boots. Damn, they looked hot!

Aaron Sherritt was the flashest of the mob. He wore tight pants, tailored shirts and two-inch heels that added to his already impressive six-foot frame. Sherritt, who was well liked despite being a Protestant, introduced his best friend, Joe Byrne, to Ned. Byrne was quiet, thoughtful and well educated, spoke Cantonese and enjoyed opium while philosophising about the meaning of life. He also had prison cred, having served time for possessing stolen meat. Ned and Joe bonded instantly. Ned's young brother Dan hung around the mob, as did teenage jockey Steve Hart.

Ned got along with one policeman, Constable Alexander Fitzpatrick, an Irishman who knew about drinking and horses. Ned, who could hold more liquor than a Dan Murphy's, got completely legless during a drinking session with Fitzpatrick and believed the copper had slipped him a roofie. Fitzpatrick threw Ned in the cells for drunk and disorderly conduct.

The next morning, the heavily hungover Ned refused to be handcuffed en route to court. Four police tried to hold him down and he was having the better part of the resulting brawl until he was dacked. Constable Lonigan then engaged in the "cruel, cowardly and disgusting act" of twisting his testicles until he sang like a Bee Gee. Ned reportedly squeaked, "Well, Lonigan, I never shot a man yet; but if I do, so help me God, you'll be the first."

The "black-balled" Kelly was lucky to receive only a small fine from a clearly sympathetic court, but his luck turned for the worse in 1878 when police found two prize horses he'd rebirthed. The German farmers who'd bought them provided a description of the seller that resulted in warrants for Ned and Dan's arrest. Everybody agrees Constable Fitzpatrick then went to the Kellys' hut to arrest Dan. What happened after that is disputed.

Fitzpatrick claimed he waited with Ellen and three of her children until Dan returned home; that Ellen refused to let Dan leave with him; that Ned entered and shot him in the wrist; that Ellen beat him over the head with a shovel; that he surrendered when Dan, Ned's brother-in-law Bill Skillion and a friend of the Kellys, William Williamson, trained guns on him; and that Ned apologised and let him go on condition that he not report the incident.

Ellen and Dan's version was they were at home; that Ned wasn't; that Fitzpatrick had threatened to blow Ellen's brains out when she told him he couldn't take Dan without her seeing a warrant; that Dan knocked away Fitzpatrick's revolver and grabbed him in a bear hug; and that Fitzpatrick was released without further incident.

Ned claimed to have been 200 or 400 miles away (depending on when he told the story) and that Skillion and Williamson had not been at the hut either. He insisted that Fitzpatrick demanded that young Kate Kelly "submit her virtue" with a gun at her head and that Dan had sent Fitzpatrick packing without injury. Kate reportedly later admitted she'd been alone in the shack with Fitzpatrick and that Ned entered and shot the policeman, who was behaving improperly towards her.

Ellen, Skillion and Williamson were charged with aiding and abetting the attempted murder of Fitzpatrick. Sir Redmond Barry had seen the Kellys in his court before – they were the sort of lowlife thieving hicks who gave honest Irishmen like himself a bad name. Skillion and Williamson went down for six years, while Ellen, a baby at her breast, was sent to Melbourne's Pentridge Prison for three years. Many in the district were outraged by the sentence, all based on the word of a notoriously dodgy copper. Fitzpatrick was transferred for his own safety.

Their faces plastered on wanted notices and a £100 reward on their heads, Ned and Dan hid out in the Wombat Ranges.[22] They were joined by Joe Byrne and Steve Hart.

Ned believed that the police planned to hunt him down and kill him, the bush telegraph having relayed Senior Constable Strachan's boast, "If I come across Ned Kelly, I'll shoot him like a dog." He converted an old mining hut in the ranges into a fort with two-foot-thick walls, murder holes and an armoured door. Ned had a thing for armour.

Two police patrols were sent into the Wombat Ranges to hunt the Kelly brothers. Sergeant Kennedy, Constables Scanlan and McIntyre and the ball-busting Constable Lonigan, all proud Irishmen, were in one patrol. They set camp at Stringybark Creek.

The police woke on the morning of 26 October 1878. The air was crisp, the sun was shining and the parrots were singing. Kennedy and Scanlan left to scout the area. Lonigan and McIntyre stayed at camp, although McIntyre briefly ventured out to shoot the parrots.[23] Ned, whose hut was just a mile away, heard the shots and went to investigate.

---

22 For foreign readers, a wombat is an intellectually challenged metre-long hamster with a pouch. The wombat was first described in 1798 by John Wilson, the dreadlocked, marsupial-clad paedophile "wild man" who also first described the koala, the wombat's closest living relative, and was declared Australia's first outlaw. Wilson named the animal *Whom-batt*, which means "big stupid hamster" in the Dharug language. The wombat is noted for its heavily armoured backside, which intriguingly produces cube-shaped poos. Like most Australian animals, the wombat is dangerous, particularly if its burrow is threatened. It is able to accelerate from its habitual trundle to a forty-kilometre-per-hour charge and can bowl people over, rake them with its powerful burrowing claws, kick like a donkey and bite through heavy boots. Fatso the wombat starred in the popular Australian soap *A Country Practice*, while Fatso the Fat-Arsed Wombat is the unofficial mascot of the Australian Olympic team. Bogans can find the Big Wombat at Scotdesco Aboriginal Community in South Australia.

23 The parrots escaped. No parrots were harmed during the writing of this book.

Ned and his friends had only two guns between them. If their hut was discovered, they'd be toast. And Ned had had enough of running. He decided to raid the police camp and seize their guns before reinforcements came.

The gang rushed the police camp, with Ned shouting, "Bail up! Hold up your hands!" McIntyre dropped his weapon (the fork he was stirring his tea with), but Lonigan drew his gun and sought cover behind a log. When Lonigan peered out to fire, Ned shot him through the right eye, delivering on the threat he'd made after Lonigan manhandled him.

Ned seized an unusually large arsenal of police weapons (he left the fork) and took note of the heavy leather straps fitted to a police packhorse – straps purpose-made to carry corpses. Ned was further convinced that the police patrol was a death squad.

Ned reassured McIntyre that he did not want further bloodshed, as they waited for Kennedy and Scanlan to return. Ned asked McIntyre to make him some tea, but displayed a little Mad Dan Morgan paranoia when he received it, inquiring, "Is there any poison about here?" McIntyre pointed out that he was unlikely to be carrying poison on the off-chance that some bushrangers would pop in for a cuppa.

As Kennedy and Scanlan approached, McIntyre called on them to surrender as they were surrounded. Kennedy, thinking this was a joke, playfully reached for his gun. Ned fired a warning shot and the police reached for their guns for real. Ned shot Scanlan, who was finished off by Byrne. Kennedy took cover behind a tree and opened fire. McIntyre took the opportunity to escape on Kennedy's horse and spent the evening hiding in a wombat burrow.[24]

Kennedy, outmanned and outgunned, ran into the scrub. Ned followed, shooting the fleeing policeman in the armpit. When Kennedy

---

24 McIntyre was criticised for deserting his fellow officers and mocked for cowardice for the rest of his life. He later wrote, "I left home every morning with full assurance that I would hear something about a wombat hole before I returned at night."

raised his hands in surrender, Ned shot to kill, later claiming he'd believed Kennedy was raising his gun. The mortally wounded officer wrote a note and asked Ned to deliver it to his wife. Ned apologised, said he needed to leave, and shot Kennedy through the heart at point-blank range, writing, "he could not live or I would have let him go". In Ned's mind, this was a mercy killing.

Ned knew he was in trouble. Posting calf testicles was one thing, but three dead coppers was a whole different ball game. Ned later defended his actions at Stringybark Creek:

> This cannot be called wilful murder for I was compelled to shoot them in my own defence or lie down like a cur and die ... I could not be more sorry for them with the exception of Lonigan, I did not begrudge him what bit of lead he got as he was the flashest and meanest man that I had any account against.

Ned could hold a grudge.

Community sympathy for Ned and Dan evaporated when McIntyre, fresh out of his wombat hole, painted them as cold-blooded cop killers. Superintendent Charles Nicolson, who'd hunted Ned as a boy when he ran with Power, was placed in charge of a massive kill-or-capture operation.

On 30 October 1878, Premier Graham Berry issued a £2,000 reward for Ned, Dan and their two unidentified companions. He also rushed the *Felons Apprehension Act* through parliament. Modelled on the New South Wales law that had targeted Ben Hall and Johnny Gilbert, the act allowed members of the Kelly Gang, as the four fugitives were known, to be shot on sight.

Ned was now a widow's son, outlawed.

13

Such is life

Such is life.

Ned Kelly, reputed last words,
11 November 1880

KELLY COUNTRY

NED AND THE GANG RODE FOR THEIR LIVES AFTER Stringybark, making for Aaron Sherritt's hut in the remote Woolshed Valley. Their friend led them to a cave and stood guard while they slept. The area would soon have more police than a discount doughnut shop and Ned decided to cross the Murray River and hide out in New South Wales.

Ned believed that the world in general, and the police in particular, had dealt him a dud hand. Even the weather was against him, with a storm preventing him crossing the swollen Murray. The gang narrowly avoided a police patrol by hiding in a pond, with only their noses breaking the water. Defeated, they returned to Sherritt, who advised them of the reward on their heads and their new celebrity outlaw status.

The police hunt was poorly coordinated. Standish refused to journey north until after the Melbourne Cup. Superintendent John Sadleir, commander of Benalla's police, urged Superintendent Nicolson to send men to the Murray, but Nicolson refused, adamant that the gang would stay in Victoria. And every time the craven

Superintendent Brooke E. Smith of Wangaratta found the gang's
trail, he insisted his men head back into town.

Members of parliament formed a conga line to put the boot into
the police. Why had Victoria's finest failed to find a pair of hick Irish
thugs and their hoodlum accomplices? What was Standish doing?

Standish enjoyed one piece of luck. After receiving reports that
the Kellys had been at Sherritt's, he asked their flash mate to turn
police informant. Sherritt agreed, on the proviso that Standish save
the life of his friend, Joe Byrne. Standish now knew the identity of
another gang member.

Ned knew the country around Greta and the gang hid out in its
most inaccessible reaches. But inactivity began to chafe and Ned was
desperate to obtain money to fund the campaign for Ellen's release.
The solution? Rob a bank.

On 9 December 1878, Kelly bailed up Faithfull's Creek Station
near the sleepy town of Euroa, locking its residents in a storehouse. Ned was polite, almost apologetic, and explained that he'd
been forced to turn bushranger by the police who'd persecuted
his family.

The next morning, Ned gave silver coins to the imprisoned station children, left Joe to guard the storehouse and headed into Euroa
with Dan and Steve. Ned knocked on the door of the National Bank,
claiming that he urgently needed to cash a cheque. When the door
opened, he bailed up the balding and bespectacled bank manager,
Robert Scott, while Steve entered the adjoining banker's house. Scott
refused to open the strongroom and Ned threatened to enter his house
to fetch his wife and kids. Scott replied, "Kelly, if you go in there, I'll
strike you, whatever the consequences may be."

Ned admired Scott's pluck and devotion to family, but admired
the bank's money even more. The tense situation was resolved by Mrs
Scott, who appeared and handed Ned the strongroom key. Ned stole
more than £2,200 in gold, silver and cash. He also took the bank's
deeds and mortgages. Without these documents, the bank would

find it difficult to pursue selectors and other marginal farmers for mortgage default.[1]

Ned demanded that the Scotts get in their buggy and accompany him to Faithfull's Creek, but acceded to Mrs Scott's request that she be allowed to dress first. Mrs Scott came out in her finest clothing and happily ushered her family into the buggy. This was the most exciting thing that had ever happened to her or Euroa and she was determined to enjoy it.

The Scotts joined the thirty-seven prisoners in the storehouse. Ned ordered steak and whisky for everyone and gave Mrs Fitzgerald, the senior woman of the station, a large bag of coins for the inconvenience caused. The gang departed, but not before Ned treated everyone to a display of trick riding.

The police were pilloried. Not only had they failed to capture Kelly, they'd let him rob a bank! Standish was apoplectic and recalled Nicolson to Melbourne. He was forced to take charge of the hunt himself and leave the comfort of his Melbourne Club bachelor pad for Benalla.[2] The only good news was that Hare would be joining him – and the Scotts' maid had identified Steve Hart as the fourth member of Kelly's gang.

Donald Cameron, the member for West Bourke, had been the strongest critic of the Keystone Cops campaign against the Kellys. He soon received a twenty-two-page letter from Ned, penned by the more literate Joe, explaining the outlaw's version of the events leading up to Euroa.

---

1   Ned, one of Australia's first anti-bank activists, would later explain, "banks, as a rule, are crushing the life's blood out of the poor struggling man."

2   Standish lived at the Melbourne Club and ran the Victorian Police Force out of its gentleman's bar. He spent his free hours reading libertine literature and being assaulted for insulting fellow club members. Captain Robert Machell whipped Standish at his breakfast table for accusing him of "trembling while shooting pigeons" and calling him "a damned offensive beast". Colonel Craigie Halkett beat and almost threw Standish out of a Melbourne Club window for calling him Jumbo.

In the Euroa letter, as it became known, Ned acknowledged a life of stock theft, for which he blamed the squatters and their allies who prevented folk like him from making an honest life on the land. He claimed that the police, in particular Constable Fitzpatrick, had persecuted and fitted up his family and friends. He'd only shot the officers at Stringybark Creek after they'd drawn guns on him and his mates, who were blameless in the whole affair. The police, "worse than cold blooded murderers or hangmen", had come after him with an arsenal and body bags. He had only ever acted in self-defence.

Newspapers published Ned's claims, despite Standish's attempts to gag them. The *Herald* wrote:

> The writer does not ask for mercy for himself, and admits that he knows he is outside the pale of mercy. He, however, asks that the grievous wrongs inflicted on his sisters may be righted, and that justice may be done to his mother ... Altogether, the document is a remarkable one, and exhibits both ability and manliness in its construction and tone.

The people of Faithfull's Creek and Euroa were interviewed and praised the gang as decent, polite, and kind to children. Robert Scott, despite having his bank robbed and his family held at gunpoint, gave his assailant a glowing testimonial:

> Ned Kelly is a good looking man ... a splendid specimen of the human kind, tall active, rather handsome ...

Standish read the papers with disbelief. He was no longer hunting a cold-blooded cop-killer, but Ian Thorpe crossed with Jesus Christ.

The papers competed to name the pocket of Victoria where the outlaws, with the aid of a supportive population, had evaded capture and made the authorities look like fools. "Kellyfornia" was briefly in vogue, before everyone settled on the *Herald*'s "Kelly Country".

Yet the media, in its frenzy to give the Kelly story a new populist angle, had ignored the darker tone of parts of the Euroa letter. Ned had written:

> I wish to give timely warning that if my people do not get justice and those innocent released from prison and the Police wear their uniform I shall be force to seek revenge of everything of the human race for the future. I will not take innocent life if justice is given but ... if the Public do not see justice done I will seek revenge for the name and character which has been given to me and my relations while god gives me strength to pull a trigger. The witnesses which can prove Fitzpatrick's falsehood can be found by advertising and if this is not done immediately horrible disasters shall follow. Fitzpatrick shall be the cause of greater slaughter to the rising generation than St. Patrick was to the snakes and frogs in Ireland.

These were not the words of a martyr, but of a terrorist.

BAND ON THE RUN

The Kelly Gang had melted into the mist. Standish demanded the arrest of suspected Kelly supporters, despite there being insufficient evidence to lay charges. Respectable farmers and men who'd done nothing more than marry into the extended Kelly clan were arrested. Some, including Wild Wright, spent over 100 days imprisoned without charge.

The public rightly regarded this as unlawful collective punishment. Community outrage against the government grew and support for the Kellys increased, particularly when it was revealed Ned was funding the defence of those arrested.

Standish's other strategy was to cultivate Sherritt as an informant, with Hare assigned as his handler. Hare forged a powerful bromance with the Greta Mob's most eligible bachelor. He described Sherritt as "a splendid man, tall, strong, hardy", later gushing, "If he walked down Collins Street, everyone else would have stared at him – his walk, his appearance, and everything else was remarkable."

Ned, meanwhile, had decided to rob another bank. Things were too hot in Victoria, so he opted to strike Jerilderie, sixty miles inside New South Wales. His plan was simple. Ned would stake out the town while masquerading as a police officer sent to protect the town from Ned.[3] In order to do this, he would have to take Jerilderie's real police officers hostage.

On the night of 9 February 1879, Ned knocked on the door of Jerilderie police station and begged Constable George Devine and Probationary Constable Henry Richards to break up a fight. The police, rushing out, were surprised to see Australia's most wanted man pointing a gun at their heads. They were locked in a cell with the town drunk, while Constable Devine's wife, Mary, opened the station's armoury and cooked the gang dinner.

The next morning, Mary insisted that the townsfolk would realise something was amiss if she did not prepare the altar for Sunday service. Dan, dressed in police uniform, accompanied Mary to church, while Ned and Joe worked on another letter. Ned read Mary some of the more stirring passages about his bravery and commitment to Victoria's oppressed. Disappointed by her blank-faced response, he set off to rob the bank after threatening to burn down her house if she raised the alarm.

The Kelly brothers, dressed as police, bailed up the Royal Mail Hotel, next door to the bank. Curious townsfolk were taken hostage, imprisoned in the hotel and invited to order drinks, with Ned picking up the tab. Ned was channelling his childhood hero Ben Hall.

After much searching, Ned found the bank manager, John Tarleton, enjoying a bath. Tarleton, when asked to open the vault, replied, "Soon as I have done my bath I will come in." Ned politely waited for Tarleton to towel off, before robbing him of more than £2,000.

---

3   Ned Kelly was the most meta of Australia's bushrangers.

Continuing his campaign against the banks, he burned Tarleton's ledgers and deeds.

During the bail-up of Jerilderie, Ned arranged for his letter to be delivered to Samuel Gill, the local newspaper editor. He also took the time to talk to the fourteen-year-old son of the town's Jewish storekeeper, who later recounted, "A Sunday school superintendent couldn't have given me better advice as to human conduct." That boy would become General Sir John Monash, Australia's most accomplished military commander. Monash later recounted the two greatest moments of his life were cracking the Hindenburg Line in 1918 and "when I had a yarn with Kelly".

Before leaving, Ned took the opportunity to assure his drunken hostages that he was a gentle soul who'd been forced to rob them by the lying police. Then he went all Dan Morgan and threatened to execute his police hostages, but relented after Richards said shooting him unarmed would be the act of a coward.

Ned, riding out of town on a fine stolen horse, was accosted by Reverend Gribble, who told him his mount was a little girl's treasured pet. Ned, chastened, returned the horse. His grand exit slightly dented, Ned rode out of town with his three amigos, shouting, "Hurrah for the good old times of Morgan and Ben Hall!"

Ned may have succeeded in robbing the bank, but he'd failed to get his message out to the wider Australian public, as the authorities forbade Gill from publishing the Jerilderie letter. The thirty-nine-page manifesto detailed grievances against the police dating back to Ned's childhood. It also played to Ned's Robin Hood image, demanding that money be redistributed to Greta's poor. "All those that have reason to fear me," he wrote, "had better sell out and give £10 out of every hundred to the widow and orphan fund." And the letter carried more than a whiff of megalomania, with the king of Kelly Country ordering his foes to leave Victoria or face consequences "worse than rust in wheat in Victoria or the drought of a dry season to the grasshoppers of N.S.Wales".

Premier Sir Henry Parkes, furious that his territory had been invaded, offered £4,000 for the death or capture of the Kelly Gang.[4] Victoria, not to be outdone, matched it. The reward now stood at 200 times a labourer's annual wage.

The press reported that Ned was going to declare Kelly Country an independent republic and called for Standish to accept Queensland's offer of Native Police trackers, commanded by Sub-Inspector Stanhope O'Connor, to hunt down Kelly. The government invited O'Connor and his men to Victoria, despite Standish wanting no assistance from "the ornamental Queensland sub-inspector" and his "niggers".

The Wombat Ranges were much colder than tropical Queensland and Corporal Sambo died of pneumonia within days of arriving.[5] Still, "the little black devils", as Ned knew them, forced the gang to withdraw to the most inaccessible country. Ned and his friends slept little, alert for the near-silent footfalls of the trackers.

ILL MET BY MOONLITE

The Kelly Gang were not the only bushrangers of proud Irish stock roaming north-east Victoria in the summer of '79. Captain Moonlite and his ragtag band of youthful misfits were trudging through Kelly Country, on their way to a better life in New South Wales.

While every self-respecting bushranger had a beard, Moonlite had a BEARD. An echidna weaned on Ashley & Martin's secret formula had been Araldited to his chin, while a wild protuberance of bristles that would shame the Lorax capered gaily atop his lip. If the eye could escape this profusion of manly hairiness, it would espy

---

4   Parkes, once an impoverished English child labourer, was knighted by Queen Victoria in 1877, a living testament to the transformational powers of the Australian colonies.

5   Queensland had taken the naming of Aborigines to a whole new level.

a Clark Kent coiffure framing a handsome face dominated by a blue steel stare that bespoke a quiet insanity.[6]

Moonlite's countenance, like his life, was marked by contradictions. It showed the world an untamed man of action, a jaded philosopher, a generous friend, a selfish scammer, a devoted lover and a capricious crazy bastard. This was Captain Moonlite, Australia's most infamous LGBTI bushranger.

Moonlite started life in mid-1840s Ireland as Andrew George Scott, the son of a well-to-do magistrate farmer. The young Scott was "dark, handsome, active and full of high spirits".

In 1862, Scott travelled with his family to New Zealand, where he worked as a schoolteacher and engineer, before enrolling as an officer in the New Zealand Wars to fight Māori who objected to Britain's confiscation of land they'd refused to sell to Queen Victoria. His men, for reasons unknown, nicknamed him Captain Moonlight.

Scott participated in the siege of Orakau, where he was shot in both legs, leaving him with a permanent limp. Disturbed by the slaughter of fleeing women after the siege, Scott refused to return to service and was court-martialled for malingering.

His military career over, Scott travelled to Victoria in 1868 and became an Anglican lay preacher at Bacchus Marsh. There he befriended Robert Crook – the first of several impressionable young men he would take under his wing. The popular churchman gave Crook an alibi when he was charged with cattle theft, claiming he'd slept over at Crook's place.[7] While Crook was acquitted, Scott's reputation was tarnished by a girl from his Sunday school class testifying she'd seen him and Crook hanging around the crime scene. The bishop quietly moved Scott to the isolated mining outpost of Mount Egerton.[8]

---

6   If this image is not sufficiently clear, you can look at the front cover of this book.

7   Scott testified, "I had slept at Mr Crook's in the same room before," finding it necessary to add, "There are two beds there."

8   Australian churches have been historically reluctant to sack unsavoury officials. It's much better for everyone if they're quietly allowed to transfer to a new parish.

Scott continued his preaching and befriended Mount Egerton's schoolteacher, James Simpson, and the seventeen-year-old Danish bank manager, Ludwig Julius Wilhelm Bruun.

A black-caped and masked figure entered Mount Egerton's bank on 8 May 1869, according to Bruun, and forced him to hand over more than £1,000 in cash and gold. The considerate bank robber then dictated a note:

> I hereby certify that L.W. Bruun has done everything within his power to withstand our intrusion, and the taking away of the money, which was done with firearms.

The note was signed:

Scott, Bruun and Simpson most likely staged the robbery together, but fell out, as Bruun told the police he recognised Scott as the man behind the mask. The preacher protested his innocence, while Bruun was tried and acquitted.

Scott left for Fiji, where he signed a contract to buy Vomo Island, now one of Fiji's most luxurious resorts. He also entered into a partnership to establish a cotton farm with Allan Hughan, whom he'd met on the boat to Fiji. Returning to Sydney to buy cotton seed, Scott racked up a massive hotel bill in New Caledonia, which he skipped town without paying.

In Sydney, Scott sold gold from the Mount Egerton robbery. While this could have set him up for life, he used the proceeds to stay in a

---

9   It was suggested the name was deliberately misspelled to encourage police to look for a semi-literate robber, although the tone of the note suggested it was written by a man of education.

fancy waterfront hotel, splurge on fine clothes and boutique firearms, and hire a groom. He completed the ensemble of a Sydney gentleman by buying a 16.8 metre yacht. Meanwhile, he completely ignored the cotton farm venture.

Hughan grudgingly paid off Scott's overseas debts and chastised him for neglecting the partnership, which appeared to be more than financial. Hughan wrote, "my heart's little treasure, my innocent darling, I would rather see you than anyone on earth", before somewhat bizarrely sending the love of his wife and children.

Scott started passing dodgy cheques in 1870, one of which was used to buy a second yacht. He was charged with fraud and the jury didn't buy his defence that the cheques had been issued under his name by Count Geldern, a German nobleman so elusive nobody else had ever heard of him. Scott was sentenced to twelve months' imprisonment.

Scott escaped gaol by feigning madness – his hysterical claims of being drugged and his refusal to eat anything other than potatoes resulted in his transfer to the comfortably padded and much less secure Parramatta Lunatic Asylum.[10] His attempts to escape by throwing a sand-filled pillow attached to a rope over the asylum wall and inciting the lunatics to charge the guards were sadly thwarted and he was returned to prison.

Scott was extradited for the Mount Egerton robbery upon his release, after a detective hired by Bruun informed the police of his gold sale. He was remanded in the escape-proof Ballarat prison to

---

10 During his stay at the asylum, Scott fell in with Henry Louis Bertrand, the "Mad Dentist of Wynyard Square", a Franco-Jewish cross-dresser who had "a deplorable taste for frivolous French fiction". Bertrand had had an affair with a dental patient, Mrs Kinder, shot Mr Kinder in the head and, when Kinder showed signs of recovery, poisoned him with belladonna. Mrs Kinder then moved into the Bertrands' bedroom, commencing a ménage à trois that thrilled the Sydney press. Mrs Kinder was acquitted of her husband's murder and worked as a barmaid in New Zealand; Mrs Bertrand was freed on the grounds she was a victim of her husband's mesmerism; and Bertrand, who'd taken to speaking in tongues and chewing the carpet, was packed off to the asylum, where he took up playing the organ and bone carving, neither of which are euphemisms.

await trial, but dug a tunnel to an adjoining cell, combined forces with
his neighbour to break the lock to his door, bound and gagged the
warder, released five other prisoners, armed himself and his accomplices with knives and forks from the prison kitchen and scaled the
prison wall with a rope made from blankets.

The story of the charismatic preacher turned masked bank bandit
turned cutlery-wielding escapee, captured the public imagination. By
the time Scott was recaptured and tried before Sir Redmond Barry,
he was a celebrity. Barry, who'd defended Aborigines and presided
over the trial of the Eureka rebels, was not interested in popularity –
he told Scott he could enjoy his new-found fame in Pentridge Prison
for the next ten years.

While in Pentridge, Scott was punished for twenty-one mostly
minor infractions, including "letting water out of the bath" and "having coffee". He also formed a close bond with James Nesbitt, a petty
criminal from Carlton thirteen years his junior. Nesbitt, who was
once disciplined for "taking tea in to prisoner Scott", idolised the
worldly older man. The feeling was mutual.

After Scott was granted early release in 1879, he and Nesbitt
shared a room in a rundown Fitzroy boarding house. With Nesbitt by
his side, Scott gave public lectures on prison reform, but could never
escape the Moonlite tag. The press linked him to every sensational
crime and wrote fantastic tales of his planned depredations, while
the police regularly hauled him in for questioning and warned off
prospective employers.

Scott and Nesbitt, unable to make ends meet from soapbox ora-
tory, gathered together three other broken youths from the slums
of inner Melbourne and set out for Sydney. Scott, who'd distanced
himself from the Moonlite name, now adopted it.

With his charisma and beard from central casting, Moonlite was
mistaken for Ned Kelly while marching through northern Victoria.
He exploited this to obtain weapons and supplies from those who
idolised, or were scared shitless of, Ned.

Southern New South Wales was gripped by drought and the five foot-weary companions, joined by an eighteen-year-old unemployed pianist, found little work. They were forced to sell their clothes for bread, which they supplemented with tea and koala meat.[11] Moonlite's band were ordered off Wantabadgery Station, between Wagga Wagga and Gundagai, where they had again been refused employment.[12]

The reluctant outlaw later wrote, "Misery and hunger produced despair, and in one wild hour we proved how much the wretched dare."

Moonlite snapped. Embracing the bushranger persona he had so long denied, he bailed up Wantabadgery and took its residents hostage. Moonlite aped Ned Kelly, with a dash of Mad Dan Morgan thrown in for good measure. He rounded up folk from the surrounding countryside and kidnapped children from the nearby Australian Arms Hotel so their parents would join his hostage party. He held his thirty-five prisoners in Wantabadgery's dining room, where he demanded lavish meals and after-dinner drinks for them and his men. He threatened to hang the station manager, but was talked down by the female prisoners. He took a shine to a young filly, but it shied when he tried to mount it. Enraged, he threatened to shoot the horse if it didn't stand still – it didn't and he shot it in the head.

Meanwhile, two men who'd heard of the hostage-taking rode the forty-two kilometres to Wagga Wagga to inform police. Moonlite and his men were still eating and drinking when four police arrived on the scene.

---

11   Do not try to eat a koala. These notoriously bad-tempered animals have razor-sharp claws and incontinent bladders, both of which they can deploy against would-be gourmands with devastating effect. Koalas also carry chlamydia and taste like old horse braised in cough syrup. Charles Darwin, who would eat almost anything, steered well clear of the koala. You've got to be really desperate to chow down on Blinky Bill.

12   Scott blamed the lack of work on Wantabadgery's employment of Ah Goon, a "Chinaman contractor who had come to the station to take the work we were refused as Chinamen can live on so little". The end of the gold rush had done little to dampen anti-Chinese sentiment.

Moonlite drove off the police with his pistol, capturing their horses. He left the hostages at Wantabadgery and found some new ones, a group of men assisting the police. He lined up his prisoners and appointed himself prosecutor and judge in an impromptu trial, with his own men on the mock jury finding the prisoners not guilty. Moonlite let out his frustrations by shooting another horse in the head. He then ordered the men to kneel and kicked them all, before retiring to a nearby dairy farm to enjoy a milk and brandy.

This would prove a fatal cocktail, as the police, bolstered by reinforcements from Gundagai, approached the farm as Moonlite and his men were leaving. Several hundred curious spectators had followed the police and watched the ensuing gunfight from a nearby hill.

Gus Wreneckie, Moonlite's youngest companion, was shot in the side and died crying for Moonlite to save him. Senior Constable Edward Webb-Bowen was hit in the spine and expired six days later. The battle raged on, but Moonlite surrendered when he saw James Nesbitt take a bullet to the head.

According to a witness, as Nesbitt lay dying Moonlite "wept over him like a child, laid his head upon his breast and kissed him passionately". Moonlite later wrote from his cell, "when he died in my arms life lost its interest and death its sting." And in another, "when I think of my dearest Jim, I am nearly driven mad."

During his Sydney trial for the murder of Webb-Bowen, Moonlite sought mercy for his three surviving companions, citing their impressionable youth. Only one would accompany him to the gallows.

Although Moonlite was regularly visited on death row by Mrs Mary Ames, who claimed to have been his fiancée in Bacchus Marsh, his condemned cell letters focused almost entirely on Nesbitt and his desire "to fill the grave of him I fondly love".[13]

---

13   Mrs Ames may have been Captain Moonlite's other beard – a beard, in gay slang, is a companion of the opposite gender used to conceal one's sexual orientation.

Moonlite denied his role in the Mount Egerton robbery until the day he died. In his deathwatch manifesto, written on the eve of his execution, he claimed Bruun had given him the gold three months after the robbery to entrap him. He also wrote:

> Nesbitt and I were united by <u>every tie</u> which could bind human friendship. We were one in <u>hopes</u>, one in <u>heart</u> and <u>soul</u> and this unity lasted until he died in my arms.[14]

Moonlite wore a ring of Nesbitt's hair to the Darlinghurst Gaol gallows on 20 January 1880. His request to be buried with his soulmate was refused, his body dumped in an unmarked grave in Sydney's Rookwood Cemetery.

But Moonlite's love could not be denied. His remains were exhumed in 1995 and laid to rest beside Nesbitt's Gundagai grave. Australia's most romantic bushranger was home at last.

THE MAN IN THE IRON MASK

The Kelly Gang had been quiet for almost a year, but they had not been idle. They'd stolen wheel guards from ploughs and melted them down to make cast-iron armour, having earlier experimented with chainmail and rubber.[15] Each gang member's armour was made to fit. Ned's suit, weighing an incredible forty-four kilograms, sported shoulder plates in addition to the breast and back plates, helmet and groin-to-knees skirt worn by his companions. Joe had modified his helmet, with a nose guard bisecting the eye slit making him look like a badass koala.

---

14 Premier Parkes ordered that the 400 pages of Moonlite's prison letters not be sent, lest they excite public sympathy. They were kept by Parkes in a sealed cabinet in his office and remained undiscovered for over a century.

15 The gang would not have been out of place at a BDSM club. Iron was a wise choice, as the Latex Outlaw just doesn't have the same ring to it.

Standish was distancing himself from the failures of the Kelly chase, which had now dragged on for more than eighteen months. He pointedly read a novel during a briefing from Sadleir. Superintendent Nicolson, who'd replaced Hare after Hare suffered a riding accident, was blamed for everything. Standish's golden boy, now recovered, was restored as commander of the operation.

Hare dismissed the Native Police trackers, arguing that the Kellys would be more likely to resurface if they were off the scene. He ordered his men to stake out the Byrne and Hart properties and the home of Ned's sister Maggie Skillion, as Sherritt was adamant the gang would visit their relatives. The police assigned to monitor the Byrne homestead slept in Sherritt's hut during the day.

On 26 May 1880, Joe and Dan forced Sherritt's German neighbour, Anton Wick, to knock on Sherritt's door. When Sherritt stepped outside, Joe shot him through the jugular and finished him off with a shot to the heart, saying, "You will not blow now what you do with us anymore."[16]

Sherritt's pregnant wife fled into the bedroom, where the four police staying in the house had taken cover. Joe and Dan made some half-hearted attempts to burn the hut and then rode for Glenrowan. They hadn't really intended to kill everyone, as they wanted witnesses to rush to the nearest police station to report their crime. The brazen murder of the police's top informant would result in a police train being sent from Benalla to nearby Wangaratta – which is exactly what Ned Kelly wanted.

Joe and Dan met Ned and Steve near Glenrowan. Ned was leading four packhorses loaded with their armour, a keg of blasting

---

16   Joe Byrne's mother had previously discovered that Sherritt was a police informer and alerted the gang. Some think Sherritt never gave the police any real intelligence on the Kelly Gang, but was feeding them disinformation, all while earning a tidy seven shillings a day from his handler. If so, he never passed on this strategy to Joe, who regarded the seven shillings as thirty pieces of silver.

powder, Chinese rockets and enough weapons to start World War III. The Kelly Gang made for the railway line on the Wangaratta side of Glenrowan station. The plan was to tear up the train tracks near a steep gully. Benalla's police would either die when the train crashed into the gully or when the gang members picked them off as they crawled out of the wreckage. After committing this blatant terrorist act, the Jerilderie Jihadist would be free to rob the bank at Benalla.

Try as they might, the gang couldn't lift the tracks. Ned woke nearby quarry workers and the stationmaster at gunpoint, but they were unable to break the line. Two railworkers were dragged from their beds and, after delaying for as long as possible, finally removed a section of track. Ned was relieved – the train was bound to arrive any minute.

Ned kept some of the hostages he'd woken at the stationmaster's home, but most were taken to Ann Jones' Glenrowan Inn. The inn rapidly filled with other Glenrowan residents who'd encountered the gang while going about their Sunday business. Appearing to be flirting with Ned, it is likely Ann Jones was in on the plan.

There was still no train by mid-afternoon. After a few brandies, Dan tried to relieve the tension by asking one of the hostages, Thomas Curnow, to dance with him. Ned agreed to the young schoolteacher's request to return home to fetch his dancing shoes, but changed his mind after it was pointed out Curnow would pass the local police station. Curnow expressed surprise that anyone would think he'd raise the alarm.

As the afternoon leaked away, a party atmosphere lit up the Glenrowan Inn. Dan and Curnow led the dancing. Ned delivered a rousing rendition of "The Wild Colonial Boy". A hop, skip and jump competition was held, with Ned upset by his second placing. Ned, Dan and Joe staged a riding show, while Steve guarded the stationmaster's house. Ned put an unlimited tab on the bar and the locals made the most of it. And still there was no train.

The train had not appeared because the police at Sherritt's hut were too scared to leave their bedroom until the morning after Sherritt's execution. Then, fearing an ambush, they delayed raising the alarm.[17]

Hare was alerted to Sherritt's murder mid-afternoon and telegrammed Standish for permission to deploy the train. When Standish, who'd been enjoying a long lunch, finally got the message, he decided to send a train from Melbourne and asked Stanhope O'Connor, who'd not yet left, if he and his black trackers would join it. O'Connor wanted his new wife to accompany him and insisted that a first-class carriage be found for her comfort. The train, joined by Mrs O'Connor and four journalists, left late that evening. Hare's men would join it at Benalla, with a second engine used to pilot the train in case trees had been felled onto the track.

The party was now in full swing at the Glenrowan Inn. Ned, Dan and Joe sang and danced with their forty hostages. Ann Jones, wearing her finest red dress, was pouring drinks like there was no tomorrow – and for some of the revellers there wouldn't be.

Thomas Curnow, who'd gained Ned's trust during the day, was allowed to take his family home for the night. Upon hearing an approaching train just before 3 a.m., Curnow rushed out with a candle and a red llama scarf to signal the driver. Hare ordered that the train stop at Glenrowan Station.

Ned knew that Curnow had ratted him out, but decided to make a stand rather than return to life on the run. The gang armoured up.

Hare charged the inn in darkness. With the first shot of the siege of Glenrowan, Ned shattered the superintendent's wrist. Hare briefly withdrew to bandage his hand and returned to the front line, only to faint from blood loss. Sadleir was left to command the assault on the inn.

Ned, a grey coat over his armour, marched on the police, who'd now taken cover. The armour had its drawbacks. It was not only exhausting to walk about in, but the eye slit also seriously impeded

---

17   The police were later sacked for "disobedience of orders and gross cowardice".

vision. The helmet prevented sighting down the barrel of a rifle and the shoulder plates meant that a pistol could only be raised while standing side-on to a target. The Iron Outlaw, who felt invulnerable in the thick metal plate, soon discovered his Achilles heel – or rather, Achilles leg, as the armour stopped just above the knees. A stray bullet hit Ned's left foot. Another pierced his left arm. He limped back into the inn as Joe took a bullet to the calf.[18]

Hostages were dropping as the police rained fire upon the inn. Ann Jones' daughter Jane suffered a head wound, while her thirteen-year-old son Jack was shot in the hip. Martin Cherry, another hostage, was hit in the groin. A hostage hopefully waving a white handkerchief in the inn's front window ducked as bullets flew around him. The gang were happy to let the hostages go, but warned that the inn might prove a safer refuge. Ann Jones led women and children towards the police lines, but the Reardon family, who were slow to leave, were fired on. Three of the Reardons made it to safety, the rest running back inside.

During the chaos, the gang fired their Chinese rockets, either to light up the police positions or call friends to their aid. No help came. Ned walked out into the night to find his horse, Music, but couldn't mount her in his armour. And somewhere along the way, his right thumb had been shot off. He lapsed into unconsciousness.

Sergeant Arthur Steele of Wangaratta arrived with five troopers at 5 a.m. Sporting an impressive handlebar moustache and tweed pork-pie hat, Steele looked like an enthusiastic birdwatcher – but he had a warrior's heart. As Mrs Reardon again tried to escape with her family, crying out that she was a woman, Steele fired wildly, narrowly missing her infant. The bloodlust rising, Steele triumphantly shouted, "I've shot Mother Jones in the tits!" As Mrs Reardon and her baby

---

18   Only a person of proud Irish stock could design armour that limits movement, vision and the ability to use a weapon, while leaving its wearer's lower body completely exposed.

reached the police lines, Steele shot young Michael Reardon through the shoulder as he retreated into the inn.

Ned woke up and staggered back into the inn. Joe stood up to have a drink at the bar and was shot in the groin, bleeding out within seconds. Just before 7 a.m., Ned again marched out against the police, calling to Steve and Dan, "Come out, boys, and we will lick the lot of them!" The boys stayed inside.

As the sky lightened, the police were confronted by a terrible apparition walking implacably towards them, mist swirling around its nightmare form. Bullets that would kill an elephant barely slowed it. It kept on coming, a tinwork Terminator. One trooper cried out that it was a bunyip and could not be killed. Another screamed that it was the Devil. Thomas Carrington, a journalist for the *Australian Sketcher*, wrote:

> It looked for all the world like the ghost of Hamlet's father with no head, only a very long thick neck ... It was the most extraordinary sight I ever saw or read of in my life, and I felt fairly spellbound with wonder, and I could not stir or speak.

Injured and weighed down by its armour, the demon could not properly aim its weapon. Sergeant Steele, noting that its legs were unprotected, fired two shotgun blasts at its knees. The beast collapsed, saying, "That is enough, I am done."

The demon's helmet was removed, revealing the tired and bewildered face of Ned Kelly. Steele wanted to put a bullet through Ned's head, but Constable Hugh Bracken warned, "I'll shoot anyone who shoots him." Constable James Dwyer took the opportunity to boot the prone bushranger in the balls, in memory of his best mate, Constable Lonigan, only to discover that kicking someone wearing a cast-iron cod protector is not a great idea.

Dan and Steve emerged with guns blazing, but the police were now targeting their legs. Dan took a bullet to the calf and the pair returned to the inn. Ned refused to ask them to surrender, saying they were cowards for not coming when he'd called.

As Ned was tended by doctors who'd rushed up for the siege, he murmured, "It was as good as Waterloo, wasn't it? As good as Waterloo ..." When they stripped the bullet-riddled Ned from his armour and clothes, they found his last layer of defence – an old green sash with a golden fringe.

WAITING FOR THE LAST DANCE

Steve and Dan were urged to give up, but the pair knew they'd be surrendering to the hangman. They told the last of the hostages to leave, except for the injured Martin Cherry, shaking their hands and wishing them luck. The siege would continue. Sadleir, leaving nothing to chance, ordered a cannon from Melbourne.

Pressmen telegraphed updates to the capital, with newspapers putting out special editions throughout the day – the first example of near-live reporting in Australia. Standish set out to join the siege, with one of the many journalists accompanying him noting with disbelief, "all he talked about throughout the journey was whist".

As the afternoon dragged on, the police inquired about bringing up the new electric lights from the Melbourne Cricket Ground.[19] A crowd of more than 1,000 had gathered to watch the spectacle.

Dan and Steve had stopped firing but the police hung back, before deciding to re-enact the razing of the Eureka Hotel by burning the inn to the ground, even though Cherry was still inside.

Father Gibney, who'd just given the last rites to Ned, ignored orders to stay back. Entering the blazing building, he found Dan and Steve lying peacefully on makeshift pillows in a bedroom. The bodies had

---

19 The Victorian cricket team is now known as the Bushrangers, its logo a helmeted Ned Kelly wielding a cricket bat. Only Australians would choose a bank-robbing cop-killer as a positive role model for their sporting youth.

no signs of serious injury, leading to speculation that they'd taken poison. Unable to rescue their bodies from the flames, Gibney dragged out Joe's corpse and the fatally wounded Cherry. All that remained of the Glenrowan Inn by the end of the day was its welcome sign.

Young Jack Jones died that night as Ned, near death, was transported to Benalla and locked in a cell adjoining the one holding Joe Byrne's corpse. The next morning, Ned was put on a train to Melbourne Gaol.

Sadleir assembled the police who'd participated in the siege to extend the government's congratulations. But what's this? There were black faces in the ranks ... Sadleir refused to start the ceremony until the Native Police had left.[20]

The public was demanding more news of the siege, so the press decided to manufacture an "action" photo. Ned was en route to Melbourne, Dan and Steve were toast, but Joe's corpse, only mildly singed, had potential. And so Joe Byrne, limbs contorted with rigor mortis, was strung up against the door of Benalla police station in a grotesque caricature of life. Australia's first press photograph, taken by J.W. Lindt, shows another photographer, Arthur Burman, capturing a still of the macabre marionette, as gentlemen and children look on with interest.

Joe's family was refused access to his body, which was interred in an unmarked grave at Benalla cemetery late at night. Sadleir had released Dan's and Steve's charred corpses to their families, but Standish instructed that he retrieve them for an inquest. The Harts and Kellys were prepared to go to war to prevent Dan and Steve suffering Joe's fate. Sadleir decided Standish be damned and obtained a magistrate's order to dispense with an inquest.[21] Dan and Steve were

---

20 The Native Police officers were each granted a £50 reward, less than the white participants in the siege. The Native Police rewards were given to the Queensland and Victorian governments to apply at their discretion. The governments discreetly decided to keep the money. In 1994, two descendants of the Native Police trackers sued Victoria and Queensland for $84 million. They failed.

21 The royal commission established to inquire into the "Kelly outbreak" found Standish had exercised poor judgement and insufficient zeal in his handling of

FIG. 13: WEEKEND AT BYRNEY'S.

buried together in Greta cemetery, with a local farmer ploughing the area to prevent the authorities from finding their last resting place.[22]

Ellen Kelly, in Melbourne Gaol, had already heard of Dan's death. She was allowed to visit Ned, but the government barred visits from other family members and friends, afraid that Ned would encourage them to avenge him.

Sir Redmond Barry approved the government's application to have Ned's trial moved from Beechworth to Melbourne. There were too many Kelly sympathisers in Beechworth to find a jury that would produce the desired result. The jury took only thirty minutes to find Ned guilty, as Ned's incompetent barrister advanced no evidence that

---

the case. Standish had by this stage resigned. He died of cirrhosis of the liver at the Melbourne Club in 1883. The royal commission recommended that Hare and Nicolson retire and that Sadleir and Steele be demoted.

22   The burning of the bodies beyond recognition, coupled with the lack of an inquest, has led conspiracy theorists to believe Dan and Steve survived Glenrowan. People were still claiming to be Dan and Steve until the middle of the twentieth century.

he'd acted in self-defence at Stringybark Creek. Barry sentenced Ned to death, ending with the words, "May the Lord have mercy on your soul." Ned replied, "I will go a little further than that, and say I will see you there when I go."[23]

On 5 November, 6,000 people attended a rally calling for the government to commute the death sentence, with the *Argus* reporting, "The larrikin class was strongly represented."[24] Alexander Hamilton, the chairman of the Society for the Abolition of Capital Punishment, gave a passionate speech in defence of Ned's life.[25] Ned's sisters organised a petition for clemency, which they claimed had 32,434 signatures.

But the pleas fell on deaf ears. Bushrangers were incompatible with modern Melbourne. The city's first telephone exchange had opened three months earlier and the Melbourne International Exhibition, the first world fair held in the southern hemisphere, was in full swing. Melbourne was flooded with international visitors and did not want to project the image of a frontier town assailed by wild-bearded bushmen in medieval armour.

On 10 November, the day before he was sentenced to hang, Ned requested to have a photograph taken for his family to remember him by. His mother and siblings were allowed to visit him, with Ellen's last words to him being, "Mind you die like a Kelly, son." Ellen would be working in the prison laundry the next morning, where she could hear the clank of the gallows trapdoor.

---

23 Barry, reportedly shaken by this retort, joined Ned in death three weeks later.

24 Today's larrikin is a likeable knockabout stirrer, but the nineteenth-century larrikin was a young hoodlum. The term was commonly applied to rough urban Irish youths.

25 Hamilton, Melbourne's leading phrenologist, received a mould of Ned's head after the execution. He wrote, "There is not one head in a thousand of the criminal type so small in caution as his, and there are few heads amongst the worst that would risk so much for the love of power as is evinced by the head of Kelly from his enormous self-esteem." The irony of pleading for a man's life before fondling his skull and damning his character was lost on Hamilton.

On the morning of 11 November 1880, the governor of Melbourne Gaol informed his most famous prisoner that the execution would be carried out at 10 a.m. Ned was led to the gallows by Robert Rede, the government's man on the ground during the Eureka Rebellion, now sheriff of Melbourne. Ned's elbows were bound behind him with a leather strap. A nightcap was placed on his head. The noose was tightened. His last words, according to Melbourne's *Herald*, were "Such is life".[26]

CLOSING TIME

As the second hand of the prison clock crept towards the mark of ten, the Golden Age of the Australian Frontier drew to a close.

The timeless land had succumbed to progress's inexorable creep, its people scattered, transformed, cast to the winds of change. The wallaby track lay beneath a rutted road, gouged by the wheels of coaches that sped ever further into the lands of the First Australians. Highways of steel criss-crossed country, soaring above rivers, cleaving mountains, bearing steam-breathing bunyips. The telegraph, the white man's message stick, carried his word to the world – and the world answered.

The sealers and whalers, vanguard of the new order, had withdrawn to the most isolated outcrops or sailed over the horizon in search of fresh prey. The last of the convicts, grey-bearded and bent, waited for their sentences to end, in this world or the next. And soon, in a span measured in broken heartbeats, the bushranger, the king of the borderlands, the scourge of the woods, the thorn in the side of authority, would be no more.

The petty thieves and wigged and powdered men who'd yearned to return to Britain had made way for hardy farmers, intrepid explorers, adventurous pioneers, men of coin and ambition, women of passion and vision: nation-builders all.

---

26 According to other reports, Ned's last words were, "Ah, well, I suppose it has come to this," or the inspirational "What a nice little garden."

And sheep. Always the fucking sheep.

Many of those who'd built this new Australia were as dust, their names, their deeds, half-remembered or forgotten.

George Arthur, deeply troubled by the decline of the Tasmanian Aborigines on his watch, became an advocate of British treaties with indigenous peoples, his advice influential in settling the Treaty of Waitangi with the New Zealand Māori in 1840. He was made a baronet, appointed lieutenant-governor of Upper Canada and then governor of Bombay, elevated into Queen Victoria's Privy Council and promoted to the rank of lieutenant-general. He died in 1854, his career one of distinction – unless you were a convict, street turtle or Tasmanian Aborigine.

Tasmania, Australia's economic engine room in Arthur's day, was now just a pink smudge at the bottom of the atlas. There was a little mining and logging, a few sheep, and the apples were nice, but that was about it. The one thing Tasmania produced in abundance was revisionism, with family histories liberally daubed with Wite-Out to conceal the convict stain. And in the islands of Bass Strait, the children of Mannalargenna's daughters just wanted to be left alone – and for people to stop saying they were extinct.

Thomas Peel, Western Australia's first entrepreneur, spent thirty-seven years thinking about what could have been, the sand of his vast, useless empire running through his fingers. The impoverished landlord of nothing died in 1865, having never raised the money to escape Australia's smallest and most backward colony.

Karl Marx wrote *Das Kapital* two years after Peel's death, citing Western Australian settlement as evidence of the failure of capitalism. Although transportation had ended, Western Australia was required to maintain the convict system until all sentences were completed.[27] John Casey, an Irish republican convict, said of the colony:

---

27 Australia's last six serving convicts were pardoned by Prime Minister Alfred Deakin in 1906. Samuel Speed, the last Australian convict, died in 1939.

> The population of Western Australia may be divided into two classes – those actually in prison, and those who more richly deserve to be there ... More real depravity, more shocking wickedness, more undisguised vice and immorality is to be witnessed at midday in the most public thoroughfares of Perth, with its population of 1,500, than in any other city of fifty times its population.

Western Australia would have to wait until the gold rushes of the 1880s and 1890s to turn things around.

Johann Menge, the oddball mineralogist who unlocked South Australia's underground riches, died six months after arriving on the goldfields and was buried at the foot of a fascinating quartz feature. John McDouall Stuart, the pygmy furball who extended South Australia's territory to the continent's northern coast and helped wire Australia to the world, discovered that you have to disappear or die to be considered a successful explorer. Embittered by lack of recognition, he returned to Britain, where he was described as a "hairy, purblind, silent man in an apparent chronic state of obfuscation". He died in 1866 of "ramolissement and cerebral effusion" (a soft leaky brain), probably the result of his all-whisky diet.

These two great men, and the industrious German farmers who tended the expanding South Australian wheatbelt, gave South Australia the resources it needed to stay strange. South Australia was a bastion of democracy, religious and ethnic tolerance, labour rights and good old-fashioned decency. It was all very Stepford Wives and occasionally people went missing, but South Australia was a nice place to live.[28]

Thomas Wentworth Wills stayed on at Queensland's Cullin-la-ringo Station, determined that the natives would not drive him off the land his father had paid for in blood. He slept only three hours a night, a rifle always at hand, and self-medicated with alcohol. Wills would

28 And die horribly.

periodically leave the property to captain the Victorian or Queensland cricket team and left for good when his mother dismissed him as station manager due to his drinking. He captained the Melbourne and Geelong Australian Rules football teams and, despite his father's grisly death, trained and captained Australia's first Aboriginal cricket team, which undertook the maiden tour of England by an Australian sporting group. But Wills' demons eventually got the better of him, with the scars of Cullin-la-ringo and the bottle leading him to stab himself three times through the heart with a pair of scissors just months before Kelly's own date with Saint Peter.

Queensland briefly mourned the loss of its adopted son and then got on with business. The youngest colony had Australia's fastest rates of economic growth and Aboriginal decline. Yet amid the carnage there was accommodation. Indigenous people became the backbone of the Queensland pastoral industry, working as stockmen, station hands and domestics. OK, they weren't always paid, and when they were, the money was likely to be sitting in a trust account they couldn't access, but you can't have everything.

Caroline Chisholm had opened the New South Wales man shed to women, taken love to the outback, found jobs for the unemployed, laid the foundations for a minimum wage, improved safety and access to puddings on the goldfields and turbo-charged the land-reform bandwagon. However, illness and selfless philanthropy had left her near penniless, forcing her to work as an English-as-a-second-language teacher and cake decorator. The Mother of Australia returned to Britain and spent the last six years of her life bedridden, her death in 1877 unreported by the press of the country for which she had done so much.[29]

William Charles Wentworth stayed in Britain after delivering self-government for his people. Tragedy struck when his daughter, Sarah,

---

29 Caroline Chisholm is commemorated in the Church of England's Calendar of Saints, even though she's a Catholic. The Catholic Church, which is a bit slower in giving women the top jobs, has received proposals to canonise Chisholm. Caroline may one day join Mary MacKillop as a dinky-di saint.

dropped dead while continuing the great Wentworth tradition of holidaying in Europe, and his son, William, died after being driven mad from the chemicals in the new batteries he was developing. Wentworth briefly returned to Sydney in 1861 and, in return for the presidency of the Legislative Council and a £1,200 salary, campaigned for land reform and an elected Legislative Council – a complete backflip on his long-held positions. The arch-conservative's electoral reform bill was so liberal that it was opposed by the liberal government.

Wentworth returned to England, where he died in 1872 at the age of eighty-one. The final wish of the man who'd first envisaged an independent Australia was to be buried inside a rock that could be seen from the main window of Vaucluse House. Henry Parkes arranged New South Wales' first state funeral, with 70,000 mourners lining the route to the cathedral. The 400 native born who marched in front of Wentworth's coffin were outraged at being joined by six "barefoot and bedraggled" Aborigines, whose unwelcome presence, the *Sydney Morning Herald* reported, "publicly disputed" their claim to be "Native Australians".

Wentworth and Chisholm had helped transform a prison state into a modern democracy with some of the most liberal electoral, labour and press laws in the world. People from around the globe were now choosing to live in New South Wales – if they couldn't get into Victoria.

The two Johns who'd fought for an independent Victoria, Fawkner and Lang, were cold in the ground by the time Kelly mounted the gallows. The increasingly doddery Fawkner attended Legislative Council sessions in a velvet smoking cap, occasionally stirring to mutter something about squatters or the Chinese. After his death in 1868, Mrs Fawkner found a disgusting old kettle in his desk drawer. She threw it out.

Lang, who'd championed education, immigration, the establishment of new Australian colonies, republicanism and sinking the boot into Catholics, was regularly sued for libel.[30] A year before his demise in 1878, Lang visited Catholic Archbishop John Bede Polding on his deathbed. The two ancient clerics, sworn enemies for four decades, were alone together for forty-five minutes. When driven home, the uncharacteristically silent clergyman had tears in his eyes. Perhaps there was hope for rapprochement between Australian Protestants and Catholics.

Fawkner and Lang (and, in fairness, gold) had given Victorians the highest standard of living in the world. "Marvellous Melbourne" was Australia's largest and most dynamic city and the second-largest in the British Empire after London. It would soon become the first capital of an independent Australia.

And in a quiet little corner of Victoria, on the Coranderrk Aboriginal reserve, something interesting was happening. The Indigenous people from the many tribes who had been herded there were making a real go of it, under the leadership of William Barak, who'd witnessed the signing of the Batman Treaty as an eleven-year-old boy.

The Victorian Central Board for the Protection of Aborigines had insisted that the people of Coranderrk abandon their work as successful graziers to grow hops for beer-hungry Melbourne. When this too was successful, the board took the profits and sought to close the reserve so that white farmers could take over its operation. But Barak and his people rebelled, having been moved off two previous sites by land-hungry squatters. They petitioned the government and Queen Victoria to remain on the land and run their own affairs. They succeeded on the first count and failed on the second – but it was a start.

---

30 In one case, Lang publicly condemned "a divorced husband with three Scottish names" for marrying "his adulterous concubine", suggesting that the marriage should have been performed "by the lessee of the parish bull, or the jockey who let out stallions for hire". While walking down the street, he was knocked down and thrashed with a whip, his assailant leaving a card embossed with the name Malcolm Melville Macdonald.

Aboriginal and Torres Strait Islander people had, in less than a century, lost much of the land they'd occupied for tens of millennia to the brash colonists of New South Wales, Tasmania, Western Australia, South Australia, Victoria and Queensland. While the First Australians revered continuity, the colonists worshipped change. They would change the world, the continent on which they lived, and themselves. They would no longer be a bubble-and-squeak citizenry of six different British colonies, but a single people: Australians. They were just waiting for Henry Parkes to light the fuse of Federation.

But neither Parkes nor any of the other nation-builders commanded the affection of the Australian public like the poor, thieving, magnificently bearded cop-killing terrorist with a penchant for fetish-wear who patiently waited for the prison clock to chime his last. Australians love the plucky underdog, the brave but doomed hero who transcends his limitations, the voice that cries out against injustice, the stubborn bastard who refuses to bow to the state, the tough guy who loves his mum.

The clock struck ten. The trapdoor opened. A drop, a crack. A mother cried.

Such is life.

Acknowledgements

THIS BOOK HAS BEEN A LABOUR OF LOVE AND I DEDICATE
it to the country I love, a fantastic land populated by fantastic
people of all cultures and creeds. Australia's strength lies in
its diversity and egalitarian ethos; in providing a society where race,
class, gender, sexuality and faith are not insurmountable barriers to the
fulfilment of potential. Sure, there is disadvantage and discrimination,
but Australia's playing field is more level than most.

There is a myth, commonly peddled and all too willingly accepted,
that Australia has always been a tolerant and welcoming place.
Australia has a racist past by any standard. Racism infected Australian immigration legislation between 1855 and 1973 and there is
more than a hint of dog whistle in our current "border protection"
policies. And Australia's treatment of Indigenous people, both
collectively and individually, over the last 228 years is a stain that
must be confronted.

It is important that we acknowledge the uncomfortable parts of
our history, for there is truth in the aphorism, "Those who cannot
remember the past are condemned to repeat it." Donald Horne, in *The
Lucky Country*, lambasted Australia's leaders for their lack of curiosity

about the past, which he believed was mirrored in their approach to present and future challenges. Horne may have been a cantankerous old fart, but he lacked nothing in observation.

This book, like all good histories (and many mediocre and bad ones), is unabashedly political. Those who contend that the historian can shed politics and values to forge a "pure" history are liars, Keith Windschuttle, or both.

True Girt is first and foremost a history, although I attempt to use humour to both engage and inform. The line between comedy and tragedy is a fine one, and sometimes it's not there at all. I found writing parts of the book, particularly some sections dealing with Indigenous people, both difficult and distressing. Yet there is always light in the darkness and humour can be a candle for truth.

Australians have a reputation for taking the piss, often at their own expense. They also have a proud tradition of satire. Satire should discomfort as well as amuse, as the verities it unearths are frequently unpleasant. I have succeeded with this book if I've made people laugh and squirm at the same time, or laugh and then feel bad about laughing. I spend a lot of my life doing that.

One of my favourite pieces of research for *True Girt* was reading Edmund Finn's piss-taking masterwork *The Chronicles of Early Melbourne, 1835 to 1852*, written under the pen name Garryowen. I have shamelessly borrowed some of his stories of early Melbourne life and a little of his literary style.

Henry Lawson, Banjo Paterson, Mark Twain, C.J. Dennis, Barry Humphries, Paul Hogan, Bill Bryson and TISM, the band more terrorists prefer, have all used humour (sometimes gentle, often caustic or barbed) to comment on Australia and Australian identity. I seek to ride on the shoulders of those giants (except for Bryson, who is quite short).

And so, from the political to the personal. My wife, Alison, is an extremely talented writer who offers sage writerly advice. She is compassionate and a wonderful people person, two qualities I greatly admire. She has put up with a lot over the two years it has taken me to write *True Girt*. She has offered me support when my obsessive nature has left me self-absorbed and poorly groomed. I have been the same with many people I care deeply about. My resolution is to be a better person next time I write a book. I hope I can stick to it.

My children, Arabella and Dalton, are my universe. I am blessed to have them in my life and to be a part of theirs. I would also like to thank my cat, Mafi, for her complete indifference to the stresses of writing – it's very grounding.

Thanks to Ad Long for again stepping up as my illustrator and sharing wine, beer and trivia answers at the Woolpack Hotel. And a big wrap for Peter Long (no relation) for coming up with another great book cover. Chris Feik, my editor, is a saint. He has shown remarkable restraint, particularly when the imp of the perverse rode me to include the previously verboten reference to Michael Jackson's chimpanzee. Jo Rosenberg has displayed remarkable sangfroid in not rising to the bait of my mothers-in-law joke and all of the diligence and sheer bloody-minded pedantry one could want in a copyeditor. Thanks also to Morry, Caitlin, Sophy, Anna, Christina and all of the other friendly folk at Black Inc. who have helped me over the last several years and didn't blink an eye when I took a break from *True Girt* to write *The Nose Pixies*, a children's picture book that has nothing to do with Australian history.

Thanks to James Boyce for reviewing my writings on Tasmania and the foundation of Melbourne. His *Van Diemen's Land* and *1835: The Founding of Melbourne & the Conquest of Australia* are two of the finest histories you will ever read. And a big thank you to Graeme Simsion and Nick Earls, two of Australia's greatest observational comic writers, for taking the time to review *True Girt*.

I would also like to acknowledge some of the other historians whose works have informed and inspired this book. Nicholas Clements' *The Black War: Fear, Sex and Resistance in Tasmania* was of great assistance in penning the opening chapters. And if you have children, or just love beautifully crafted books, pick up Simon Barnard's *A–Z of Convicts in Van Diemen's Land*.

Clare Wright's *The Forgotten Rebels of Eureka* is nothing short of remarkable. Robyn Annear's *Bearbrass: Imagining Early Melbourne* is not a traditional history and is all the better for it. Henry Reynolds' *The Other Side of the Frontier* and *Forgotten War*, Richard Broome's *Aboriginal Australians: A History Since 1788* and Bain Attwood's *Possession: Batman's Treaty and the Matter of History* should be read by every Australian who wants a deeper understanding of colonisation's impact on the First Australians. Andrew Tink's *William Charles Wentworth: Australia's Greatest Native Son* is historical biography as it should be and Patrick O'Farrell's *The Irish in Australia: 1788 to the Present* is the gift that keeps on giving.

For those of you interested in hapless explorers, pick up Sarah Murgatroyd's *The Dig Tree: The Story of Burke and Wills* or Ivan Rudolph's *Eyre: The Forgotten Explorer*. Bushranger fetishists may enjoy Evan McHugh's *Bushrangers: Australia's Greatest Self-Made Heroes* and Paul Terry's *In Search of Captain Moonlite: The Strange Life and Death of the Notorious Bushranger*. Ned Kelly fans, who will no doubt pull me up for compressing parts of the Kelly story, can't go past Ian Jones's *Ned Kelly: A Short Life*. Peter FitzSimons' *Ned Kelly: The Story of Australia's Most Notorious Legend* is also a classic Aussie yarn.

For those who like their history with soy sauce or sausage, I recommend Kathryn Cronin's *Colonial Casualties: Chinese in Early Victoria* and Ian Harmstorf and Michael Cigler's *The Germans in Australia*.

The National Library of Australia's Trove database of newspapers and journals is an invaluable resource, not just for historians and genealogists, but for anyone with an interest in Australian society and culture. Many of the newspaper quotes in *True Girt* came from, or were checked against, Trove. Rumours continue that funding cuts to the National Library place Trove's future in doubt. Any minister who allows this to happen should be forced to wear moccasins filled with bull ants before being eaten by an escaped Tasmanian prisoner. Project Gutenberg is also an excellent online repository of primary sources.

Thanks to Dom Knight for co-hosting *Rum, Rebels & Ratbags*, my Australian history podcast that borrows heavily from *Girt*, and thanks to ABC Radio for commissioning it. I hope we do another series.

Kudos to the State Library of New South Wales for providing a great research space and ever-helpful staff. And a big thumbs-up to the Sydney Writers' Room, where I did the actual writing bit. If you want a quiet space to write with fellow creative people, then the Sydney Writers' Room is the place for you.

This book would not have been written without the support of Australian booksellers, who hand-sold *Girt* like there was no tomorrow. Receiving the 2014 Indie Award for Non-fiction from independent booksellers has given me confidence in my writing and the encouragement necessary to have another crack.

And last of all, to those of you read *Girt* and said nice things – this has heartened me immeasurably. I wrote the sort of book that I would like and I'm glad others did too. I hope you also enjoy this offering.

David Hunt, in study with cat, August 2016

Index